British Economic and Social History 1700 – 1982

Fifth edition

C P Hill

formerly Senior Lecturer in Education, University of Exeter

Hodder & Stoughton

A MEMBER OF THE HODDER HEADLINE GROUP

British Library Cataloguing in Publication Data
Hill, C. P. (Charles Peter)
  British economic and social history, 1700–1982.
  —5th ed.
1. Great Britain—Social conditions
I. Title   II. Hill, C. P. (Charles Peter)
  British economic and social history, 1700–1982.
  941.07   HN385
  ISBN 0 7131 7382 3

First published 1957
Impression number 18   17   16   15   14   13   12   11   10
Year   1999 1998 1997 1996 1995

Printed in Great Britain for Hodder & Stoughton Educational, a
division of Hodder Headline Plc, 338 Euston Road, London NW1 3BH
by Redwood Books, Trowbridge, Wiltshire.

Preface to the Fifth Edition

In this fifth edition I have made a relatively small number of alterations. Most are minor, scattered throughout the book. They involve the correction of errors (mercifully few: my thanks go to those who have pointed them out); an occasional shift of emphasis in the light of recent research; the extension of population statistics, mainly in Chapter 1, to cover 1981; and the inclusion here and there of fresh detail. But one change is substantial. I have re-shaped and largely re-written the final Chapter 29, to bring it up to 1982. I do not like 'instant history' very much: our perspective for very recent years is inadequate. Yet what has happened to Britain's economic fortunes since the mid-1970s is far too significant a change to be omitted or (even worse) to be blandly overlooked by continuing to close the book at 1975. What is included here is obviously a tentative assessment, from the stand-point of 1984.

As on previous occasions I have drawn heavily on the learning and advice of others. I am particularly deeply indebted to Dr. Richard Wilson and to Mrs. Pauline Collier, each of whom has gone to great trouble to provide detailed and most helpful suggestions of change. I must thank also my old friends Mr. Peter Harris for his generosity in reading the proofs, and Mr. S. R. James and Mr. C. W. C. Edge for their thoughtful advice, even where I have not felt able to act upon it. None of these must be blamed for the faults that remain in the book. I have thought it justified, in the interests of space, not to reprint the prefaces from the previous editions. But certainly this in no way means that I have ceased to value the help given me by those thanked therein; the continuing success of the book owes much to their wisdom and their determination to keep its author up-to-date, and I remain heavily in their debt.

C. P. HILL
Exeter, March 1984

Contents

Maps

Tables

Acknowledgments

The Publisher's thanks are due to the following for permission to reproduce the photographs, portraits, prints and drawings in this book:

Associated Press (Plymouth, bombed)
Barnaby's Picture Library (Severn Bridge)
British Airways (Comet 4 and Concorde)
British Leyland (Morris Eight Assembly)
British Rail (Swindon Station)
Evening Standard and the Trustees of the David Low Estate (two Low cartoons)
Fox Photos Ltd (Camberwell March and Jodrell Bank)
London Transport Executive (Early London bus)
Mansell Collection (Cover photograph of Iron Work for Casting and A Boreing Mill, River Severn, Shropshire)
Massey-Ferguson Ltd (Combine Harvester)
Mobil Photo Library (North Sea oil rig)
National Film Archive (Interior of Granada Cinema, Tooting)
National Portrait Gallery (James Watt and George Stephenson)
Editor of *Punch* (Dinner Party)
Radio Times Hulton Picture Library (Seven Dials, Broseley smelting-house, Thomas Telford, Ben Tillett, London elementary school, Police arresting suspect, traffic jam at Mansion House, General Strike bus under escort, Fullotone and rationing)
Science Museum (Sir Henry Bessemer and Coalbrookdale)
Suffragette Museum (Suffragette)
Josiah Wedgwood & Sons Ltd (Teaset)
Wellcome Museum (Lister carbolic spray)
Roy Westlake (Plymouth, rebuilt)
Wilberforce Museum, Hull (two illustrations of the slave trade)

1 Population, 1700–1981

In 1707, the year of the Act of Union between England and Scotland, there were probably about 7,000,000 people living in Great Britain. By 1981, the year when the most recent official count, the Census, was taken, there were some 54,000,000. In two hundred and seventy five years the population had risen by over 670 per cent. This remarkable increase is the most notable single fact of British history during those years, and the purpose of this chapter is to consider some questions about it. When did so great an increase first show itself? Why did it happen? Did it continue at the same pace once it had begun? Was it uniform over the whole country, or did some areas grow in population more quickly than others? What were its main consequences for agriculture and industry, trade and welfare?

Clear and certain answers to these questions are not easy to find, particularly for the 18th and early 19th centuries. This is mainly because of a lack of accurate statistics. The first official Census was not taken until 1801. Thereafter it was taken at ten-year intervals (except in 1941, during the Second World War), yet not until 1841 was either the method of counting or the series of questions asked adequate to provide historians with sufficient reliable information. Not until 1837 in England and Wales and 1855 in Scotland did births, marriages and deaths have to be reported to official registrars, and not until 1874 could anyone be legally punished for failing to report them. Therefore at least for the first hundred years covered by this book investigators have to rely on a variety of random and incomplete sources, like the registers of baptisms in parish churches, lists of those paying certain taxes, and the bills of mortality recording deaths in certain towns.

1. THE POPULATION REVOLUTION OF THE 18TH CENTURY

Towards the end of the 17th century many people, including scientists, business men and tax collectors, were becoming interested in what they called 'political arithmetic'—figures about the population, trade, revenue and defence of the country. In 1695 Gregory King, at one time an official of the Treasury, suggested as the total number of inhabitants of England and Wales the figure of 5,500,520. King's figure was well-informed guesswork, founded mainly on information given to the collectors of the hearth tax. About 1707 'a plausible guess by an intelligent but unknown Scotsman' suggested just over 1,000,000 as the total for Scotland.[1] It has been estimated that about 1700 some 675,000 people lived in

[1] T. C. Smout: *A History of the Scottish People, 1560–1830*, p. 258.

London, which was many times bigger than any other city; it is improbable that either Bristol or Norwich, its nearest English rivals, had as many as 30,000 inhabitants, while Edinburgh, the largest Scottish city, had only a few more than that. In 1700 and long after, both in England and in Scotland, the great majority of people lived not in towns but in the countryside, and were spread thinly over the land. Moreover, in England most of them lived in the southern half of the country; much of the north, including the later industrial areas, was quite empty.

During the first half of the 18th century the population of England seems to have grown very slowly, that of Scotland rather faster.[1] The

Table I   *Population of Great Britain, 1700–1981* (in thousands)

(Note. The figures for 1700 and 1750 rest on intelligent contemporary guesswork; while those for the first four official censuses, 1801 to 1831 inclusive, were far from perfect.)

	England and Wales	Scotland	Total
1700	? 5500	? 1000+	? 6500+
1750	? 6400	? 1265	? 7665
1801	8893	1608	10501
1811	10164	1806	11970
1831	13897	2364	16261
1851	17928	2889	20817
1871	22712	3360	26072
1901	32528	4472	37000
1911	36070	4761	40831
1931	39952	4843	44795
1981	49155	5131	54286

plague no longer took its toll: the last serious outbreak had been that of 1665.[2] But smallpox and other epidemic diseases killed their thousands, especially among the young, while bad harvests, food shortages and occasional local famines brought illness and death in their train. Yet even before 1750, although the *growth* of population was slow, there were changes in its *distribution* which pointed to the future. Thus there is evidence that between 1700 and 1750 the number of people living in Lancashire, Warwickshire and the West Riding of Yorkshire rose several times as fast as that of England as a whole, while Coalbrookdale, the pioneering ironworks area, also grew rapidly at that time.[3] A notably careful calculation of the population of Scotland as 1,265,000, made in 1755 by Dr. Alexander Webster, minister of the Tolbooth Church in

---

[1] See Table I, below.
[2] See the famous description in Samuel Pepys' *Diary* (summer and autumn of 1665).
[3] See below, p. 28.

Edinburgh, suggested an appreciable rise in that country since 1707. After 1750 the pace of population increase quickened, yet only modestly compared with what was to follow.

Around 1780—it is clearly impossible to date precisely—a steep rise started, with rates of increase that may fairly be called 'dramatic'. Three sets of figures illustrate this 'take-off'. First, the total population of Great Britain went from an estimated 8·9 millions in 1780 to 10·5 millions at the first Census in 1801; within the fifty years after 1801 it almost doubled itself; and by 1871 it was nearly three times what it had been in 1780.[1] Such growth meant a high rate of increase never before so long sustained. For most of the 19th century it was growing twice as fast as a hundred years earlier: at its peak, from 1811 to 1821, the rate of growth

Table II *Urban and rural growth, 1801–1971*[2]
(population in thousands)

The following sets of figures show the growth in size of (a) British cities and (b, c, and d) groups of English and Welsh counties.

(a) *British cities*

	1801	1831	1871	1901	1931	1971
London	1117	1907	3890	6586	8110	7452
Aberdeen	27	72	88	111	167	182
Birmingham	71	144	344	522	1003	1015
Bristol	61	104	183	329	397	427
Cardiff	2	6	40	164	224	279
Edinburgh	67	161	197	261	439	454
Exeter	17	28	35	47	68	96
Glasgow	77	202	478	566	1089	898
Leeds	53	123	259	429	483	496
Liverpool	82	202	493	685	856	610
Manchester	75	182	351	544	766	544
Norwich	36	61	80	112	126	122
Oxford	12	21	31	49	81	109
Coventry	16	27	38	70	178	335

(b) *Mainly rural English and Welsh counties*

	1801	1831	1871	1901	1931	1971
Bucks.	108	147	176	197	271	586
Cards.	43	65	73	61	55	55
Devon	340	494	601	662	733	847
Herts.	97	143	192	258	401	922
Lincs.	209	317	437	500	624	808
Suffolk	214	296	349	373	401	545

[1] See Table I, p. 2.

[2] Local government changes in 1974 make it impossible to provide satisfactory figures for 1981.

Table II—*cont.*

(c) *Heavily industrialised English and Welsh counties*

	1801	1831	1871	1901	1931	1971
Glamorgan	71	127	398	861	1229	1255
Lancs.	673	1337	2819	4373	5040	5106
Notts.	140	225	320	514	713	975
Staffs.	243	409	858	1184	1434	1857
Warwicks.	207	337	634	1087	1533	2080
Yorks., West Riding	591	1013	1882	2843	3446	3781

(d) *English and Welsh counties with mixed agricultural and industrial economies*

	1801	1831	1871	1901	1931	1971
Brecon	32	48	60	54	58	53
Cheshire	192	334	561	842	1088	1543
Cornwall	192	301	362	322	318	380
Durham	149	239	685	1187	1486	1408
Leics.	130	197	269	438	542	771
Worcs.	146	223	339	385	467	693

in England and Wales reached 1·8 per cent per annum and in Scotland almost 1·6 per cent. Secondly, those towns and areas which in this same span of time became great centres of industry and trade grew specially fast. Manchester, which had some 9,000 inhabitants when Daniel Defoe saw it in the early 18th century and called it 'the greatest mere village in England', had 75,000 by 1801 and 182,000 by 1831. Birmingham, with perhaps 25,000 in 1740, rose to 71,000 by 1801 and 144,000 by 1831. Glasgow went from 23,000 in 1755 to 77,000 in 1801 and 202,000 in 1831.[1] Yet, thirdly, until the middle of the 19th century most British people still lived in rural areas—and here too the number of inhabitants also rose very fast, even though many of those born in them moved to find better-paid jobs in the London area or the new industrial towns. It has, for example, been estimated that during the fifty years from 1781 to the Census of 1831 the population of such overwhelmingly farming counties as Buckinghamshire, Hertfordshire and Suffolk rose by 50 per cent or more; while that of counties like Cheshire, Cornwall and Worcestershire, with mines or other industry scattered among their agriculture, doubled, or very nearly so.[2]

Why did this 'population revolution' come about? Many reasons have been suggested; few are very convincing. What one scholar said about this question in 1970 remains true: 'at present very little can be asserted with any degree of confidence and much of what has been asserted in the past

[1] See Table II, p. 3.   [2] See Table II, above.

must now be ignored.'[1] It may be that some very deep-rooted causes are involved, especially when we realise that the great upswing was not an uniquely British phenomenon; all Western Europe experienced it at different times and different paces. Perhaps mysterious biological forces were changing the virulence of epidemic diseases at this time; or the fact that Europe's climate by the mid-19th century was better than it had been for six hundred years made it a much healthier place; or there may always be something cyclical about population changes over the centuries, and a great increase was bound to follow the comparative stagnation which had gone before. Certainly one element which must not be overlooked is the cumulative effect of the gradual rise in population between 1750 and 1780. 'Not only were more children born in the thirty years after 1750, but a relatively high proportion of them survived into adulthood, ultimately to become parents themselves.'[2] Hence in the period from about 1780 an unusually large proportion of the British population consisted of young adults. Yet neither this fact nor any of the other possibilities seems likely *by itself* to explain what happened in Britain.

Table III   *Birth and Death Rates in the United Kingdom, 1901–1981*

	1901	*1911*	*1921*	*1931*	*1951*	*1961*	*1971*	*1981*
*Birth	29	25	23	16	16	18	16	13
Death								
Male (infant)	161	138	94	78	35	25	20	13
(all)	18	16	13	13	13	13	12	12
Female (infant)	133	114	73	59	27	19	16	11
(all)	16	14	12	12	12	11	11	12

* The *percentage* of illegitimate births during these years rose from 4 in 1901 to 5 in 1911–51 inclusive, 6 in 1961, 8 in 1971 and 12 in 1981.

Crudely, the number of inhabitants of a country can increase for three reasons only: a rise in the birth-rate, a fall in the death-rate, and immigration from outside.[3] The last of these made little difference to the total British figure in the late 18th and early 19th centuries, even though one-tenth of Glasgow's inhabitants in 1820 were Irish and there were many Irish in Liverpool also. At first glance, change in the *birth-rate* offers a promising line of enquiry for these years. In some places, such as the coalfields and textile areas like Nottinghamshire and South Lancashire,

[1] M. W. Flinn: *British Population Growth, 1700–1850*, p. 50.
[2] N. L. Tranter: *Population since the Industrial Revolution*, pp. 66–7.
[3] The *birth-rate* = the total births per year per 1,000 of the population; the *death-rate* = the total deaths per year per 1,000 of the population. The *fertility rate*, i.e., the total of births per year per 1,000 women of child-bearing age, in fact provides historians with more significant information than the crude birth-rate.

there is evidence that people were marrying earlier and producing more children. Money wages were rising here and in other industrial areas, and child labour was in much demand. As the new factories grew[1] apprenticeship was declining, enabling workers to marry younger. In rural areas, where most people still lived, it was believed that a new method of poor relief, the 'Speenhamland System', which supplemented labourers' wages out of rates from 1795 onwards, encouraged early marriages and large families.[2] Some of these circumstances undoubtedly helped to promote a rise in population. Yet others, for example the Speenhamland suggestion, do not rest on strong evidence; while some fit particular parts of the country well but other areas not at all. As a whole, the birth-rate evidence is inconclusive.

A variety of causes may have brought the *death-rate* down in these years. Some reflected a slow improvement in living conditions which was taking place at this time (and this no doubt affected the birth-rate also). Agricultural change was producing more food and a more varied diet: the enclosures put more land under corn crops, and turnips enabled more cattle to be kept alive through the winter.[3] Hence more people could eat more fresh meat, more wheaten bread, more potatoes; by 1815 wheat was easily the major bread-corn of England, while potatoes were of vital importance to the north and to Scotland. Turnpike roads and canals built in the late 18th century could bring supplies of food to areas affected by shortages.[4] More coal was being hewn, more bricks being made—both developments pointing towards better housing conditions. Technical progress in the textile industry brought cheaper and more plentiful cotton underwear, and in the chemical industry greater manufacture of soap: both these things made possible more cleanliness and better health.[5] To these general improvements in living conditions must be added, many historians have believed, life-saving advances in medicine. It has been calculated that, whereas in the 1730's between four and five of every ten English children died before they reached the age of two, by the end of the 18th century that appalling death-rate had been very nearly halved; and it seems difficult not to connect that change with medical progress. For the 18th century saw the opening of numerous voluntary hospitals and dispensaries in London and other cities; the growth of notable medical schools in Edinburgh and Glasgow; improvements in midwifery; more skilful and frequent use of various drugs; and the development first of inoculation and then of vaccination as a weapon against smallpox.

It is arguable that all these things must have contributed to the great upswing of population after about 1780. Yet historians on the whole are sceptical about the extent of that contribution. They point out that many of the changes in agriculture, transport and textiles came too late to be of much consequence before about 1820; and that anyway most of the indirect benefits, in diet and health, from such improvements as more meat,

---

[1] See below, pp. 40–42.   [2] See below, pp. 65–67.   [3] See below, pp. 18–19.
[4] See below, pp. 47–53.   [5] See below, pp. 37–40 and 42–43.

wheaten bread, soap, and bricks were probably enjoyed by the upper and middle classes rather than by the mass of the population. Further, the medical 'progress' of these years has been sharply questioned. In particular, the hospitals of that age have been attacked on the ground that they were so dirty and inefficient that they possibly increased the death-rate rather than lowered it (though detailed evidence from some hospitals belies this charge). As to smallpox, it is true that vaccination was widely effective within twenty years of its introduction; but it was not devised until 1796, while inoculation, though used as early as the 1720's and notably successful in some areas (like Highland Scotland) met with violent hostility in others, and its effect on the total British death-rate was probably fairly small. In short, as with the rising birth-rate, so with the falling death-rate: clear-cut and firmly-founded conclusions cannot be reached.

2. POPULATION DURING THE 19TH CENTURY

At the beginning of the 19th century the British population was developing in three ways. Its total was rising very fast; towns were growing at the expense of the countryside; and the coalfields areas were rapidly gaining inhabitants. These trends went on after 1801. The total population of Britain almost doubled itself between 1801 and 1851, and again between 1851 and 1911. This rise is the more impressive in view of the fact that for much of the century the death-rate was stationary or actually rising. It had undoubtedly come down before 1800; but it started to go up again after 1820, and not until fifty years later did it begin to fall appreciably once more. The reason for this behaviour of the death-rate is to be found in the second direction of population development in the 19th century, the growth of large towns. Their bad conditions—above all overcrowding, inadequate water supplies and lack of good drains—exposed them to epidemics like the cholera which came first in 1831 and struck again in 1848. Yet people continued to pour into them and to bring up their children—or, rather, those of them who survived infancy—as town-dwellers. Although the numbers employed in agriculture continued to rise during the first half of the century, nevertheless by 1851 half the population lived in towns and by 1901 over three-quarters did so. Moreover, most of these growing towns were on the coalfields. Middlesex indeed remained the most densely-populated county in 1801, for London still went on growing; the journalist William Cobbett called it 'the Great Wen' because he saw it sucking the life-blood of the countryside. But even by 1801 the next most densely-peopled English counties were no longer in the south. They were Lancashire, the West Riding of Yorkshire, Staffordshire and Warwickshire—all of them with coalpits and growing industries. The centre of gravity of the population was moving north-wards, and this change went on all through the 19th century, with the

Clyde Valley, Glamorgan and County Durham taking their places along-side the other industrial areas. Yet London still went on ceaselessly swelling, absorbing about a quarter of a million human beings every ten years from 1841 to the end of the century.

One new feature of 19th century population change was a huge increase in the number of people who moved into or out of Britain. Once the French wars ended at Waterloo British citizens could virtually come and go as they chose, although until 1825 the letter of the law forbade artisans or skilled craftsmen to emigrate.[1] Between 1840 and the outbreak of war in 1914 about 19 millions of people emigrated from the United Kingdom to lands outside Europe, of whom over a quarter were Irish. Their motives for going varied immensely. Yet the main ones were the 'push' of bad conditions at home, notably in such peak periods of emigration as after the Irish Famine of the 1840's and during the late 1870's and early 1880's; and the 'pull' of attractive prospects in newly-developing lands, above all the United States. The number of those who left was large indeed, somewhere about the same as the entire recorded increase in the United Kingdom population over the same period. The importance of this emigration is heightened by the quality of those who departed: well over half of them were young males, and many were skilled artisans. This exodus was to some extent, at any rate for England, Scotland and Wales, offset by those who came in. Thus the Irish Famine sent perhaps 600,000 across the Irish Sea in the 1840's and 1850's, especially to Lancashire and Clydeside, swelling the British labour force in these mid-Victorian years of swift industrial expansion. Also a substantial propor-tion of all British emigrants to North America came home again, sooner or later, for good. Yet in sum, from the mid-19th century to the 1930's, Britain on the balance of migration had a net loss of many thousands of people almost every year.

In 1911, on the eve of the First World War, there were nearly 41,000,000 people in Britain. This figure far surpassed the wildest imaginings of Gregory King, who had prophesied that England might have 22,000,000 inhabitants 'by the year of Our Lord 3500 or 3600 . . . in case the world should last so long.' Yet by 1911 the rate of increase was slowing down. For the middle 1870's saw a great turning-point: the birth-rate began to decline, and the decline grew steeper as the years passed. In 1876 it stood in England and Wales at 36·3; by 1911 it had fallen to 25. The Scottish pattern was almost identical. Why did this happen? It reflected partly a trend towards later marriage, a trend encouraged by harder times in the late 1870's and the 1880's, when the number of unemployed men rose; partly too the early days of the middle-class movement for the emancipation of women.[2] More important, parents were limiting the

---

[1] Many nevertheless did so, among them Samuel Slater, a Lancashire millhand who took with him in his head to the United States the design of new spinning machinery and so helped to establish the American cotton textile industry.

[2] See below, Chapter 23, pp. 231–5.

number of children they had, and the size of Victorian families was dropping. For contraception was beginning to be effectively as well as widely practised, a change stimulated by the publicity from the trial in 1877 of Charles Bradlaugh and Annie Besant for publishing a pamphlet on birth control. And the motives for limiting family size were steadily growing stronger. As Factory Acts were passed to check child labour and Education Acts began to make schooling compulsory, the economic advantages of having more children diminished sharply.

Taken by itself, such a fall in the birth-rate would have led in the early twentieth century to a decline in the total population. But a general fall in the death-rate began about the same time as that in the birth-rate; in England and Wales the former went down by over one-third within the forty years to 1911, and the figures for Scotland ran parallel. This sharp change was almost entirely the consequence of a remarkable drop in the number of deaths from a group of infectious diseases, including tuberculosis, typhus and typhoid, cholera, scarlet fever and smallpox. Compulsory vaccination after 1853 went far towards extinguishing small-pox (already considerably reduced in the first half of the century), while scarlet fever seems itself to have grown less virulent during these years. All the other diseases mentioned were curbed by a general improvement in the supply and quality of foodstuffs, and by the gradual introduction (especially after the Public Health Act of 1875) of such vital sanitary reforms as purer water supplies, more effective methods of sewage dis-posal, and, rather later, better working-class housing. It was these, rather than medical progress, that brought the death-rate down, and thus in effect, so far as the total population of Britain was concerned, warded off the threat offered by the fall in the birth-rate. On the eve of the First World War that total was still rising fast, though a good deal less fast than a century earlier.

3. POPULATION CHANGE FROM THE FIRST WORLD WAR ONWARDS

The population of Britain rose from 41 millions in 1911 to 54,000,000 in 1981, an increase of 31 per cent.[1] Behind these figures lie movements and trends at least as important as the totals. These sixty years brought immense economic and social changes which were quickly reflected in population change. The two World Wars of 1914–18 and 1939–45 had long-term as well as immediate consequences. The Depression of the 1930's and the affluence of the later 1950's and the 1960's had their contrasting results. The swift advance of science and technology involved an extraordinary variety of developments affecting population: among these the spread of the motor-car and motor-lorry, the vastly-increased use of electric power, a great range of new medical techniques, the increased productivity of agriculture, improvements in the variety and quality of foodstuffs and the invention of the contraceptive

[1] For this section see Tables I and III, above.

pill were only the most significant. They were to some extent paralleled by the expansion of the school medical service, the creation of the National Health Service, and the growth of a social security system concerned with welfare from the cradle to the grave. The decline of traditional religious beliefs, already illustrated in the rise of birth control, was further shown by the legalisation of abortion (1967). Finally, there was from the 1950's a radical alteration in the pattern of migration, vividly revealed in the arrival of coloured immigrants from the Commonwealth, notably of West Indians and Pakistanis.[1]

During the First World War three-quarters of a million men from the United Kingdom were killed, the great majority of them young. Simply as a rate of population decline this was 'less than the loss by emigration, mostly of able-bodied young men, which in the years immediately before the war had been running at nearly 300,000 per annum. '[2] But the loss in quality was high, while the annual rate of population increase was halved in the war years. A short 'baby boom' in the 1920s did not persist, and the birth-rate went tumbling down in the Depression years of the 1930's; by 1941 it had fallen to the lowest figure recorded up to that date. At the same time the decline in the death-rate, virtually continuous since the 1870's, came to a halt, reaching stability during the 1920s at about 12.0, a figure around which it has ever since remained. The result was plain. The rate of increase of the population slumped to 0.4 per cent, lower than at any time for almost two hundred years. In the late 1930s it was gloomily assumed that the population of Britain was destined to start falling in the very near future.

In fact the Second World War left a different legacy from the First. Rather under 400,000 British lives were lost, less than one in every hundred—and, as a result of air-raids, many of these were not young men. The birth-rate rose in the later years of the war itself, and this time the post-war boom in children lasted longer. In 1947 the birth-rate was 20.5, and after a fall in the 1950's it rose once more in the affluent 60's—only to drop again in the 70's, to 12.0 in 1975. The upward trend of the early 60's, however, seemed to ensure the maintenance of a rise in total population. And its effect was strengthened by one of the major social and medical achievements of the 20th century, a remarkable reduction in the infant mortality rate.[3] This was 154 in England and Wales at the beginning of the century, 105 in 1914 and 51 in 1939; by 1968 it was down to 18, a phenomenal saving of human life.

---

[1] The number of United Kingdom residents born in 'the New Commonwealth' (i.e. excluding Canada, Australia and New Zealand) rose from 218,000 in 1951 to 853,000 in 1966. By 1971 their number of 1,486,000 was over 2% of the British total.

[2] A. J. P. Taylor: *English History, 1914–1975*, p. 120.

[3] The Infant mortality rate = the deaths per annum, per 1000 live births, of infants under one year old. The fall at this time reflected cleaner milk and improved midwifery; laws against baby-farming (the Infant Life Protection Acts, 1872 and 1897) and cruelty to children (the Children's Act, 1908); and the coming in the early 20th century of infant welfare centres, health visitors, and maternity benefits.

Since 1911 there have been noteworthy changes, too, in the *distribution* of the population. First, it was altering markedly by *region*. Electric power and the internal combustion engine between them set much industry free from the need to be close to coal, and the Depression of the 1930's hit the coalfields hard. Relatively they lost numbers to London and the Home Counties, to the Thames Valley, and to the West Midlands, the areas in which the new 'light' industries established themselves before and after the Second World War.[1] Further, while throughout the 20th century three-quarters of English people had continued to live in towns, by the 1970's that proportion was falling slightly. Moreover, improved transport by train, bus, and car after the First World War led to the outward spread, first from London and then from London and then from other cities, of suburbs. By the later 1960's this process had gone so far that the hearts of cities were losing their residents quite rapidly. Secondly, another and probably more important aspect of the change in distribution was that of *age*. Here the root cause lay in the medical improvements which by surgery, drugs and improved hospital services were prolonging life for most men and women well beyond the chances of earlier ages. In the 1870's a man at birth could on average expect to reach the age of 41 and a woman that of 45; a hundred years later the figures were respectively 60 and 75. In 1901 people of 65 and over formed 5 per cent of the population of the United Kingdom; by 1981 they were 15 per cent—and by this date the proportion of those under 14 was falling. These trends point to a predominantly middle-aged population.

4. SOME GENERAL EFFECTS OF THE INCREASE OF POPULATION

In 1798 a clergyman named Thomas Malthus published *An Essay on the Principle of Population as it affects the Future Improvement of Society*. It was a gloomy book which maintained that population, when unchecked by wars, famines, or plagues, always tends to increase more rapidly than the means of subsistence—the food and other necessities upon which human life depends. Life, even in the most favourable circumstances, must always be for most people a desperate struggle for survival. Malthus had much influence in his own day. His book contributed to a widespread fear of over-population, of a country in which there would always be more mouths than could be properly fed, and in which therefore the mass of the people were condemned to lives of grim poverty.

Malthus was mistaken. His prophecies were disproved by the history of the 19th century. The growth of population meant far more mouths to feed than ever before; but not that the people of Britain came nearer to starvation and extreme poverty than ever before. The very opposite of this was true. The rise in population was one of the factors that stimulated

[1] See below, pp. 244, 250–2.

farmers to make more effective use of Britain's land than it had ever before known. Nevertheless, it led also to a growing dependence on imported foreign foodstuffs—a dependence which by the time of the great wars of the 20th century meant that something like four-fifths of all the food the British people ate came from overseas. On the other hand, the growth of population transformed the productive capacity of the nation; the increasing numbers of the people could—and did—manufacture far more industrial goods than had ever previously been known upon earth. These goods, exported overseas, more than paid for the imported foodstuffs. Moreover, it became possible to make a far wider variety of goods, and to sell these both in England and overseas; and this variety meant an increase in the standard of living for most people in the community. This improved standard of living did not follow automatically from the increase in population. It took place only because that increase was accompanied by revolutionary changes in the techniques of industry—particularly by the invention of power-driven machinery.

There were other, indirect, results. Increasing dependence on foreign food supplies meant greater peril in wartime, and greater importance for the Navy. The crowding together of people in great and rapidly-growing cities created a mass of social problems—of health and housing, of poverty and crime, of education, of transport, of town-planning and local government; and to help solve these problems a succession of reforms was passed in the 19th and 20th centuries. The growth of population stimulated the migration of the British overseas, and was thus a very powerful force in the great extension of the British Empire which took place in the 19th century. In effect the economic and social history of modern Britain is a kind of commentary upon the great increase of its population.

2   Agriculture in the Eighteenth Century

In 1700 most people earned their living from the land. A great many spent all their working days on it; others got their bread-and-butter partly by agriculture and partly by some other job like weaving or carpentry; and yet others, like those who lived in the small market towns, really depended on the land for their income even though they were not themselves tillers of the soil. So agriculture provides the natural starting-point of any account of British economic affairs during the 18th century. Moreover, in this century, especially during its latter part, there were numerous and far-reaching changes in the countryside. Over much of Britain the very landscape itself took on new patterns, losing the appearance it had worn for many centuries. The food grown on British soil rose to amounts never before dreamed of. At the same time, the ancient ways of village life began to break up; new crops were grown, new types of farming tried out, and these developments brought disturbance and often misery to many villagers. These changes had begun before 1700, they went on long after 1800; yet this 18th century saw many of the decisive steps taken.

I. AGRICULTURE IN 1700

Most of us tend to associate the 'Open Field' method of farming with the 'Middle Ages'. 'Open Field' indicates the system of unenclosed farming, with the village lands divided into two or three great fields without hedges, each field lying fallow in turn. The cultivated area was broken up into strips, and each family held various strips scattered about the fields. In fact 'champion' or 'champagne' farming—as the open fields were often called—continued long after the Middle Ages; and in 1700 something like half the total arable soil was still cultivated in this way. But there were great areas where, because of the nature of the soil or the lie of the land, open fields had never existed or had long disappeared; among them were the high ground of the west and north (Devon and Cornwall, Wales and the Marches, the Pennines and the Lakeland counties), Essex with its marshland and Kent with orchards and hop-fields. Here, if the land was farmed at all, stone walls and hedges were the rule. Elsewhere, particularly over the flat lands of East Anglia and the rolling country of the midlands, they were the exception.

Yet already by 1700 agriculture was changing. Here and there all over the countryside the strips were being grouped together in compact holdings, thus eliminating the waste of land and time involved when they were separate. Enclosure itself, the replacement of open fields by the hedgerows familiar to us to-day, had been going on slowly—mostly for sheep-farming—ever since Tudor times. Land was being won to cultivation from forest and moor. Considerable drainage schemes had taken place in the Fenlands of East Anglia in the 17th century; and a handful of farmers were experimenting with field drainage. In this, as in other matters, new ideas were coming in from Holland. Sir Richard Weston, a Royalist in the Civil War, had fled to Holland when the King's cause had collapsed; and when he came back he put into practice on his estate some of the ideas he had absorbed in exile. He grew turnips on his fields, using them as winter feed for cattle; hitherto they had been only a garden crop in England. He sowed clover for hay, yielding better grazing than had previously been possible.

But these were exceptional developments. Over most of Britain farming in 1700 continued in the ways it had followed for centuries; and this routine offered little encouragement to pioneers like Weston. The great fields were ploughed and sown in common in spring and winter; when the harvest had been carried home, the stubble was opened to all the livestock of the village. In most places there could be no winter cropping, nor any gain to the man who grew turnips or cultivated grasses on his strips. The division into strips wasted much land; and it was very difficult to devise an efficient system of drainage. The ancient custom of the manor controlled the farming; usually, all the open-field tenants had to do the same things at the same time. The common pastures around the village also discouraged agricultural progress. They were often overcrowded with ill-fed and scraggy beasts among which disease easily spread. The lack of root crops as winter fodder meant that the great majority of cattle had to be killed off at Michaelmas and Christmas; and any attempt at scientific stock-breeding was impossible.

Such a system of farming, with what to later eyes seem such great disadvantages, had survived for centuries very largely because there had been relatively little growth in the population. It had normally been able, except in years of very bad harvest, to satisfy the needs of villagers and of the comparatively small number of town-dwellers. Even London, which was of course quite abnormal in size, could be fed, by the produce of neighbouring counties, by the sending of boatloads of corn round by sea or down the Thames, and by the journeys of great flocks of cattle and sheep, geese and turkeys which walked and grazed their way from north, west, and midlands to be devoured by the inhabitants of the capital. But the 18th century brought change. A rise in population, at first gradual, then swift, and a growth in standards of living meant far heavier demands for food, especially for meat and corn. To meet them, new methods of farming were essential.

2. THE TECHNICAL IMPROVEMENTS IN FARMING

To these changes some historians have given the name 'the Agrarian Revolution'. This is misleading, for it suggests a sudden and violent upheaval; in fact, the changes were spread over a very long period of time and did not involve the kind of violence which we associate with revolutions. Yet the name is really justified, because the effects of the changes were immense; farming was transformed between 1700 and 1850, and the conditions of life of those who lived in the countryside were radically altered. The revolution involved two closely-related sorts of change happening at the same time. The first was a series of technical improvements in farming —new crops and new implements (though not machines as we know them), new rotations of crops, new achievements in stock-breeding. The second was the gradual replacement of the open fields by enclosures. Each of these stimulated the other; neither would have been very profitable without the other. Moreover, farming during the 18th century became more and more concerned not with growing enough food to keep the farmer and his family alive, but with growing crops and breeding animals to sell at a profit in the market. There was nothing new about this commercial farming in itself; but the rapid growth of towns with their thousands of workers to be fed brought far bigger markets with better prospects of profit than ever before, and did much to encourage agricultural progress.

The technical improvements were of various kinds. For example, the new field crops pioneered by Weston in the 17th century began slowly to find widespread acceptance in the 18th. Clover and other legumes such as sainfoin and lucerne were used both for stock-grazing and for cutting as hay. Turnips provided winter food for cattle and were a key to a new rotation of crops, as was made clear by the experiments of the first great 'improving' landlord of the 18th century, Viscount Townshend (1674–1738). He was Secretary of State when in 1730 he was driven from office by Walpole; whereupon he retired to his estates in Norfolk and devoted his abilities to agricultural improvement. 'Turnip Townshend' was not an innovator: many people had grown turnips long before he did. He spread the ideas advocated by Weston, and grew clover and turnips in his fields; improved his land by drainage, marling, and manuring; and experimented in the rotation of crops, working out what became celebrated as the Norfolk Four Course Rotation. This consisted of wheat; turnips; oats or barley; and clover. This alternation of cereal and fodder crops got rid of fallow, provided food for animals, and kept the soil in good condition. Townshend's example was followed by many of his neighbours on the light soils of Norfolk. Progress outside the county was appreciably slower, particularly on the heavier and wetter soils of the clay vales.

Another direction in which improvement came was that of farm implements. Here an early pioneer was an eccentric figure from Berkshire, Jethro Tull (1674–1741). Tull's contributions to farming progress, described in his book *The New Horse Hoeing Husbandry*, published in 1733, were two—the drill for sowing seeds in rows at a controlled depth and thus avoiding the waste from sowing broadcast, and the horse-hoe for keeping the ground clear of weeds. Some of Tull's activities on his own farm, Mount Prosperous, would not meet with modern approval; for example, he claimed to have grown thirteen successive crops of wheat on the same ground without manure. Tull's reputation, like that of Townshend, has been exaggerated. Yet he was important for his inventions —and also for the example he set of accurate observation and experiment; it was on French vineyards that he had seen the value of deep hoeing and frequent ploughing. Farmers generally were slow to adopt his ideas (the seed drill was not widely used until the 19th century), and he was often regarded as a crank. But he was the forerunner of other developments in agricultural implements. Particularly important among these were changes in the harrow and the plough, both of which, thanks in part to the abundant manufacture of iron in Britain by new processes, were by 1820 normally made wholly of iron.

The work of Tull and Townshend and men like them contributed indirectly to advance in another part of agriculture—that of stock-breeding; and here the results of change were more sensational and the work of the pioneers was more rapidly copied. The most famous of them was Robert Bakewell (1725–95), a tenant-farmer of Dishley in Leicestershire. His aim was to breed both cattle and sheep for meat. His new New Leicester sheep fattened quickly and became famous for their mutton; his Longhorns revolutionised the breeding of cattle, and he also developed a successful type of carthorse. Bakewell was by no means the only successful breeder of his day, and his reputation has been overrated: the meat of the

New Leicesters was excessively fat, and the Longhorns were soon replaced by the better beef animals, the Shorthorns. More significant than the particular breeds that Bakewell produced was his method, which has remained the basis of stock-breeding since his time. He specialised in pedigree stock, selected for a particular purpose; he fed and housed his animals with care; and he kept elaborate genealogical tables of his results. Among his immediate followers were Charles and Robert Colling of Ketton near Darlington, whose great achievement was the breeding of Durham Shorthorn cattle.

The new ideas needed a propagandist, and they found one in Arthur Young (1741–1820), who did much to inflate Bakewell's fame. Young did do well as a farmer, but from 1767 onwards became a highly successful agricultural journalist, publishing many books and pamphlets and travelling round England spreading the new ideas. In 1793 he became the first Secretary of the newly-established Board of Agriculture, and with its President, an enterprising Scottish landlord named Sir John Sinclair, he did much to promote improved farming at a time when it was particularly needed; for the same year 1793 saw the outbreak of a war with France which lasted, with one short interval, until 1815, and which made urgent England's need to produce as much as possible from her own soil. Young records in his account of his journeys the very marked contrast which he found between those regions where the progressive ideas had made headway and those other parts of the country where the open field system with all its defects still remained; and he was himself a highly effective agent in promoting improvement in the more backward regions, and in encouraging the spread of enclosures.

Royal patronage and example stimulated agriculture; George III—'Farmer George'—favoured the new ideas, and turned part of Windsor Park into a model farm. But the most celebrated of progressive landlords towards the end of the 18th century was Thomas Coke (1754–1842). 'Coke of Norfolk' inherited in 1776 great estates at Holkham in that county. At that time much of the land was sandy or marshy, barren and ill-farmed. Forty years later they included some of the finest wheat-producing farms in the country, and carried stock of the highest quality. Coke farmed his own lands on the lines laid down by Townshend and other improvers, and educated his tenants to do likewise, encouraging them by giving them long leases; he used marl and clay to enrich his soil, grew turnips and artificial grasses, introduced bone manure and cattle cake, and protected his estate from the sea by planting trees on the sandhills. For many years he held an annual sheep-shearing festival, originally for his tenants and neighbours but later for guests from all over Britain and beyond; there the visitors could see all the novelties of improved agriculture—improved drills, fat livestock, soil experiments and the like—and could return home to use them on their own estates. Such an event foreshadowed the later agricultural shows. Coke was lucky; the French war of 1793–1815 came just at the time to encourage his work by sending up the price of corn and making farming pay as never before. It was said that 'he saved England by the ploughshare when the sword would have availed nothing'.

3. THE ENCLOSURE MOVEMENT

The work of the improvers would have been in vain, and an estate farmed as Coke's was would have been impossible if there had been no enclosure movement. Well over six million acres (two million hectares) in England and Wales—perhaps a quarter of the cultivated land—were enclosed in the 18th and early 19th centuries, with proportionate figures in lowland Scotland. In the first half of the century there was much extension of pastureland, and a good deal of enclosing was done by agreement, without reference to Parliament. The years after 1760 saw an expansion of wheat farming, with much capital invested in the land. Between 1760 and 1793, 1,355 parliamentary Enclosure Acts were passed, and under the stimulus of the war years from 1793 to 1815 there were no fewer than 1,934. Each of these was a private Act, applying to particular estates or parishes. In 1801 a General Enclosure Act was passed which tried, not very effectively, to simplify the legal procedure involved and to reduce the cost. Just as the enclosure movement had begun before 1700, so it continued after 1800, until by 1850 nearly all the agricultural land of England was enclosed, and the open fields in the rare places where they remained had become a picturesque survival.

What did enclosure mean in practice? And in the first place exactly how was it done? It was normally the work of the leading landowners and the more important tenants in a parish, and any decision to enclose was in fact based upon their agreement. From 1774 it was laid down by the House of Commons that notice of any intention to carry out an enclosure had to be fixed to the church door in each parish affected for three Sundays during August or September. Sometimes those who wanted to enclose called a public meeting of the villagers whose land would be affected, but more often they did not. The next step was to petition Parliament for permission to carry out an enclosure, and to draw up a Bill giving details of the proposed scheme. This Bill was referred to a committee of the Commons, before which those who objected could appear and make their complaints. When the Bill was passed a number of commissioners (customarily three) were named to carry out its terms. In due time they came to the area concerned, mapped the land and examined and checked all claims to a share. They put the Act into operation, awarding the various portions of land to the villagers and giving to the lord of the manor and to the owner of the tithes the special shares which were often awarded to them; occasionally, too, a piece of land was set aside for the poor of the village. It was the commissioners' responsibility to decide all disputes about the cost of fencing, rights of way to the new farms, claims to pasture-land, ownership of woods, and so forth. When their work was done, the village had been permanently transformed. Open fields and strips had gone for ever, and in their place had come hedges and compact farms.

In some ways this procedure was outwardly fair to all those whose lands were enclosed; in fact it undoubtedly worked to the advantage of the richer landowners. Opposition to Bills in Parliament was only effective when it came from some considerable landowner whose interests were adversely affected by the Bill, and who could organise friends in Parliament to oppose it. The right to bring complaints before a committee was a mockery to the poor in those days of slow and costly travel; Westminster was far away. The commissioners appointed under the Acts were often friends or neighbours of the landowners who promoted the enclosure. Finally, many villagers could, when the time came, produce no legally valid title to their land; and most commissioners seem to have had little sympathy with claims based upon custom rather than upon legal documents.

How did this system work in practice? What were its effects? It must be said at once that historians have argued at great length about this subject, and that far more detailed study of the results of particular enclosures in particular areas must be done before any very reliable picture can be drawn. For the effects varied from one locality to another. They were complicated by the results of the changes in industry which were taking place at the same time. The growing industrial towns were not merely a market for the produce of the countryside around them; they were also a magnet drawing peasants to jobs in a factory. Moreover, some of the changes which enclosures stimulated had been going on for some time. For example, one very important development of these years was a change in the way land was owned or occupied. Many freeholders or 'yeomen', men whose ancestors had long held land in their villages by right of inheritance, seem to have disappeared; they were replaced by tenant-farmers whose claim to their farms depended entirely on regular payment of rent. But it is clear that this process had been going on long before the second half of the 18th century; in some areas in the midlands and East Anglia, it has been discovered, much of the land was already in the hands of tenant-farmers. In this and other ways the enclosure movement simply accelerated changes that had previously begun.

Nevertheless, its results were immense. Most obviously, the movement involved (by about 1850) the ending of the open field system over a great area of land, including in the midlands and the east some of the best corn-growing districts of the country. This made possible far more efficient farming, with the use of the new techniques. Change came slowly, and many estates remained backward, especially the smaller ones, where there was less capital available for improvements. But what could be done was shown, for example, in the Lothians of Scotland, which, hitherto relatively neglected, had been transformed by 1830 into one of the most go-ahead agricultural areas. Much waste land on the outskirts of villages, previously untilled, was now put under the plough; generally it was the commons which were enclosed first and the open fields afterwards. The acreage under cereals and potatoes was increased. The improved techniques made possible by enclosure led to an increased yield of crops per acre. Such developments, taken together with the progress in scientific stockbreeding (and also with contemporary improvements in transport), meant a great increase in the amount of food produced on British soil—at the time when the population was rising fast and when the French wars made it vital to produce as much food as possible at home. Finally, the changes were the foundation of further agricultural developments later in the 19th century.

Yet neither food nor efficiency are everything. This agricultural progress undoubtedly brought with it much hardship to great numbers of villagers. Riots against enclosures were not infrequent. They produced scenes like those recorded at Otmoor in Oxfordshire in 1814, when, as the House of Commons *Journal* put it, 'it was found impracticable to affix the notices (of enclosures) on the Church doors . . . owing to large Mobs, armed with every description of offensive weapons, having assembled for the purpose of obstructing the persons who went to affix the Notices, and who were prevented by violence, and threats of immediate death, from approaching the Churches'. Such opposition sprang from a strong feeling that enclosures, despite all the advantages they brought to the nation, bore very harshly on the poorer folk in the areas where they were carried out. Even Arthur Young, who was a great enthusiast for enclosures and who wrote many articles and pamphlets in support of them, came round to the view that they brought much hardship. In 1801 he wrote, 'By nineteen out of twenty Inclosure bills the poor were injured, and some grossly injured. . . . The poor in these parishes may say, and with truth, "Parliament may be tender of property: all I know is that I had a cow and an Act of Parliament has taken it from me." '

The hardship came in various ways. As has been indicated, the whole legal process by which enclosure was carried out favoured the richer landowners. Lawyers' fees were high; and it was beyond the purse of poor men to hire counsel to oppose an enclosure Bill. Yet when the Bill was passed all those whose land was enclosed had to bear their share of the legal costs, including the heavy fees demanded by the officials of the House of Commons. When the village lands were actually divided up, there were surveyors' fees, as well as the charge for hedging and ditching; these last fell more hardly on those whose holdings of land were small, and many of them sold out to the local landlord or to a wealthier neighbour. Others were worse off still, losing their land or their rights altogether. Very often 'squatters', living in rough huts, had established themselves on the waste or commons, tilling a patch of ground and keeping a few hens and geese and a pig or two. They were now turned out, for they had no legal claim to the land. Further, when the open fields were themselves enclosed, a similar fate might befall those villagers who were—like their fathers for centuries before them—'copyhold' tenants, that is tenants who held their land by 'copy of court roll', the roll of the medieval court of the manor; for often the document itself had vanished, and so they had no legal rights to their land. For many villagers whose legal rights were perfectly valid, enclosure meant serious loss of benefits. Before enclosure they could pasture their animals in the common meadow and cut timber or firewood in the woods around the village. Now there was no common meadow and their own new compact holdings were too small to provide sufficient pasture; as for the woods, usually the landlord had taken these as part of his own share and was busy stocking them with game and preserving them for his own shooting.

All in all, the poor probably suffered severely; whereas the rich man, with capital to buy up his neighbours' holdings and to practise the new farming methods, could and did profit greatly. Yet the contrast can be much exaggerated. There is evidence, for example, that at the very period when enclosures were proceeding at so rapid a pace, the number of small holders of land was also rising in most parts of the country, and not least in those areas where enclosures were most numerous. Again, it cannot be maintained that the enclosure movement led to widespread depopulation of the countryside, to a wholesale movement of people from the land into the towns. Where pasture land replaced arable, far fewer workers were needed; but most of the extensive enclosure of waste and commons meant cultivation where there had been none before. The Agricultural Revolution was based on hand labour, not on machinery: more workers, not less, were needed on British farms until after 1850. Moreover, many other factors as well as enclosures brought hard times for the villager in the later years of the 18th century. In particular, the changes in industry which were going on at the same time often affected him directly; the development of spinning machinery meant that work which had brought his women and children extra wages was now increasingly done in factories.[1] Again, the war with France brought a rise in prices, which hit hardest of all the poorest-paid workers in the community—the agricultural labourers. Thus enclosures were by no means the only cause of distress at this time.

3 The Industrial Revolution of the Eighteenth Century

1. INDUSTRY IN THE EARLY 18TH CENTURY

In 1700 England was already an important industrial country, despite the fact that most of her people depended on agriculture for their living. Through the length and breadth of the land, in the small towns and in the countryside, a wide range of manufactures was carried on. Sheffield had long been famous for its cutlery, and in the districts round Birmingham a great variety of small metal goods—firearms and trinkets, nails and hardware—was made. The pits of Tyneside sent regular and increasing supplies of coal to London, and at the other end of the country the tin mines of Cornwall employed numerous workmen. London, which was by far the biggest market in the country for manufactured goods, had itself a mass of miscellaneous industries—glass-making, silk-weaving, printing, brewing, leather-making, pottery and furniture among them—as well as the innumerable activities connected with its position as the port for most of the nation's trade. Cotton manufacture had started in south Lancashire.

[1] See below, pp. 40–42.

Above all, there was the most famous of English industries—the manufacture of woollen cloth. Almost every small town had its cloth weavers: yet three regions were particularly celebrated for it. These were the West Country, especially Gloucestershire, Somerset and Wiltshire; East Anglia; and the West Riding of Yorkshire. Within each woollen area there was a considerable degree of specialisation, with many towns concentrating mainly on particular sorts of cloth—a sign that the woollen industry was far from a simple or primitive affair.

Moreover, although most English manufactures were sold in England, there was a vigorous export trade. English goods went to Europe; to the English colonies in America; to India in the ships of the East India Company, and to Africa as part of the slave trade. Of these markets Europe was easily the most important. Cloth was the chief export. Next to it came leather goods and the countless sorts of ironware. All this overseas trade did much to stimulate the development of English industry.

Nevertheless, we get a false impression of English industry in 1700 if we let the word bring to our minds the pictures of the 20th century—pictures of great factories and thousands of employees working under the same roof, of power-driven machinery and of mass production, of big firms with many hundreds of shareholders. These things, as we know them today, did not exist in 1700. Some industries, indeed, employed many numbers of workers in one place; brewing and some parts of the iron industry provided examples of this. But most industry was domestic—that is to say, the work was carried out in the workers' own homes. This was true of nearly all the operations in the woollen and other textile industries. There were few machines, as we to-day understand that word, although there were some quite elaborate tools of which the weaver's loom is the best example. Power, apart from human power and animal power, played a small part in industry; water power, used for example in corn mills or fulling mills, was the important exception; steam power had not yet been effectively harnessed for industrial purposes. In such circumstances the mass production which is a normal phenomenon of 20th century industry, as illustrated by the standardised parts of motor vehicles or by taps and window fasteners and the like, was a practical impossibility.

There is one other comparison between 1700 and the present day about which it is particularly important to be clear. Nowadays most industrial concerns of any size, apart from those which like the railways or the coal mines belong to the community, are the property of a group of shareholders who have invested capital in them. They are in fact capitalist industries, controlled by owners who are capitalists. Now in the early 18th century factories and large-scale businesses were very rare; but capitalists were by no means unknown. A good deal of capital was necessary, for example, in the iron industry, with its heavy and expensive equipment. And even in the clothing industry, where nearly all the work was done in the cottages of spinners and weavers, much of the trade, especially in the West Country, was in the hands of capitalist employers. These were the merchant clothiers, who bought the raw material, distributed it to the workers and later collected from them the finished cloth, and sold it in the markets at home or abroad. Often they owned the looms on which the weavers worked, and in fact they decided whether the workers were employed or not. Domestic industry certainly did not mean industry in which the ordinary weaver or cloth-worker worked independently and on his own account.

2. WHY INDUSTRIAL CHANGES CAME ABOUT IN THE 18TH CENTURY

A remarkable series of events during the 18th century transformed some industries: there was a 'take-off' then which began the economic growth of modern Britain. The two most important of these events were the invention of various forms of power-driven machinery, and the coming of the modern form of factory. Why did these changes happen at that time? Certainly it is quite insufficient to say that Great Britain in this era suddenly produced a succession of mechanical geniuses who devised a number of remarkable inventions. These inventors, of whom James Watt (1736–1819) was the most celebrated, undoubtedly played a most important role in the story. But in general inventors only invent things when the community wants them. They do not come like manna from heaven: rather they arise in response to the environment around them. What brought about the great changes in 18th-century industry was a series of social factors—developments of various kinds in British society.

In certain ways Britain was a country well equipped by nature for the growth of power-driven industry. The temperate climate encouraged people to work hard: it was not so hot that they became lazy, nor so cold that large-scale industrial development was impossible. An abundant rainfall meant that in hilly areas like the slopes of the Pennines there were swift-flowing streams to provide water-power. Britain had plentiful coal supplies, in Northumberland and Durham, the West Riding and south Lancashire, in the Scottish Lowlands and north Staffordshire, in South Wales and the Black Country. Moreover, in some of these areas there was iron near the coal measures, ensuring the supplies of the raw material most essential to the rapid manufacture of heavy machinery. So far as transport was concerned, no part of the country was far distant from the sea, and much of it was reasonably accessible from navigable rivers like the Thames, the Severn and the Trent which penetrated far inland. In short, the setting for large-scale industrial development was present.

Yet why in the 18th century did British people take advantage of these natural resources so much more than their ancestors had done? One obvious reason was that growth of population which we have already noticed. This meant, for example, many more customers to buy manufactured goods—especially if these goods could be produced in large quantities and at low prices. It meant also many more hands available to make the goods. Both these things—a wider market and bigger labour supplies—were bound to stimulate the growth of every kind of industry, and especially of industries like textiles. Yet the great upswing in population did not start until about 1780: and there were already many signs of industrial change evident by then. The growth of population by itself did not account for them, although certainly the most spectacular industrial progress followed it.

Perhaps the most important single cause of the change was the growth of trade, much assisted by the great series of wars against France during the 18th century. For wars encouraged countries to develop their own resources, for example of iron, coal and wool; they created heavy demands upon industries like armaments, shipbuilding and textiles. Wars and the growth of trade alike had stimulated the growth of banking and finance, leading most notably to the foundation of the Bank of England in 1694. In various areas outside Europe a vigorous English commerce was beginning to expand: the newly established West Indian colonies were growing sugar and demanding slaves, the East India Company was shipping spices and silks from India, and the great Spanish Empire in South and Central America, the Indies, began after 1713 to be open to British traders. All this meant that Englishmen were making money; which meant in turn that money was increasingly available for investment as capital in industrial enterprises. Those who wanted to borrow money in the first part of the 18th century were fortunate, for money was plentiful and rates of interest were falling. Good supplies of capital were an essential basis of the growth of industry in these years.

Many other things, of various kinds, helped to bring about change at this time. The skilled labour which was necessary to handle and develop the new machinery was available; for industry in Britain was highly specialised long before this time, and there was a firmly established tradition of fine craftsmanship. Secondly, the scientific ideas which were to play an important part in shaping the minds of industrial inventors like James Watt were beginning to establish themselves; the Royal Society was founded in 1662, while Sir Isaac Newton was alive until 1727. Thirdly, political conditions favoured industrial development. The long rule of Sir Robert Walpole (1721-42) gave the new Hanoverian dynasty a chance to establish itself, and his deliberate policy as first minister was to let trade flow freely and men grow wealthy and satisfied. The Act of Union with Scotland (1707) not only opened the way for Scotland to develop as an industrial nation, and for Glasgow with its shipbuilding and textile industries and its tobacco imports to become one of the great industrial and commercial cities of Britain: it also allowed many Scotsmen, of whom James Watt and Thomas Telford were merely the most gifted, to play leading roles in Britain's economic history. Finally, even political persecution contributed to economic growth. The law of the land no longer prevented Dissenters, or Nonconformists as they came to be called, from worshipping freely in their own way in their chapels and meeting-houses; but it still shut them out from public life, excluding them from holding offices under the Crown. Naturally enough, they turned their talents to trade and industry—talents which were the more useful because their schools, the Dissenting Academies, were the best in the land in this age. The Nonconformists were numerous and important in such activities as banking and the iron industry.

3. THE GENERAL PATTERN OF INDUSTRIAL DEVELOPMENT

The two really big changes that the 18th century brought to British industry were, as has been suggested, the introduction of machinery driven by power, and the organisation of industry in factories. These things were the heart of the 'Industrial Revolution' which took place in Britain during the second half of the 18th century, and which made Britain 'the first industrial nation' of an entirely new kind never before seen on earth. Henceforward changes in industry took place at an unprecedented rate, transforming the ways of life of countless millions of people.

Since the late 18th century power-driven machinery, factory industry and the other developments which accompanied them have come to be accepted as everyday features of British life. But it is important to be clear about the way in which these changes came; otherwise we may get the story of modern British economic history entirely out of focus. First, they did not come about suddenly. The causes suggested in the previous section worked slowly. Moreover, what they did was not so much to start something quite new, as to accelerate changes which had already begun. For example, the use of power was of course not unknown; water-power had long been used to drive mills for grinding corn, windmills were not uncommon, and many people experimented with steam-power in the 17th century. Secondly, when the changes began, they came at different rates in different industries; and there was nothing remotely resembling a wholesale change-over to power-driven or factory industry in this century. Steam-operated machines were being used to pump water out of mines before 1710; but not until the 1780's were they employed to drive textile manufacturing machinery. As for factories, some very important developments in technique had occurred in the textile industries before 1760, but there were very few factories before that date. Thirdly, there were industries which made very little use of power but which nevertheless grew rapidly at this time; pottery is an example of these.

The central and in a way the key development of the age was the invention by James Watt of a commercially effective steam-engine, first for work in the mines and then, in a different form, for driving textile and other types of machinery. This provided a source of power far superior to anything which man had previously been able to control. Its use involved the predominance of coal and iron—the one the vital fuel, the other the vital raw material for the new machines. The industry in which power made at first most rapid headway was the textile industry, particularly the manufacture of cotton goods; yet it is essential to note that until very near the end of the 18th century 'power' in the textile industry meant water-power. Taken together, the stories of coal and iron, of the textile industries, and of the steam-engine provide the central pattern of industrial history during this period; though other industries like pottery and chemicals deserve brief mention.

What did the change mean in terms of men, of human lives? Here too it is complicated, and it is important to get the picture in focus. The Industrial Revolution of the 18th century, as we shall see, meant very long hours of work in very bad conditions; it meant child labour; it meant slums, bad housing and overcrowding. None of these things was new; all had been common and normal for centuries. But there were two differences. First, the new factories meant a new discipline. The worker could no longer 'knock off' when he liked and then work very long spells in order to make up the time; he spent long hours at his machine, under harsh regulations imposed by his employer. Secondly, the bad conditions were far more obvious in the new industrial towns than they had been in the countryside, simply because the towns were so big.

The owners of the foundries and factories, the new industrial capitalists, were often self-made men who by hard work had built up wealth for themselves. At this stage of industrial history it was not a case of shareholders and managing directors: those came later, in the 19th century. Yet, even though the owners had not infrequently risen from the ranks, a gulf quickly developed between them and their workmen. The latter, in the days before the rise of factories, had themselves been known as 'manufacturers'. This word was now transferred to the owners; the workmen instead became known as 'hands'—a word which itself suggests a decline in their status and importance. Naturally enough the workmen banded together in trade unions to try to secure better conditions, to resist the natural tendency of employers to lengthen hours and keep wages to a minimum. Here again there was nothing original about such organisations, which in different forms had existed before the coming of power-driven industry. But the new conditions, with great numbers of workers herded together in a limited area, made their growth easier, and at the same time provide ample reasons for their growth. Thus the developments of the 18th century sharpened antagonism between masters and men, and opened the way to much industrial strife.

4 Coal and Iron in the Eighteenth Century

I. THE COAL INDUSTRY, 1700–1815

At the beginning of the 18th century almost all the British coalfields of the present day, except that of Kent, were being worked. Coal was already an important item of trade, used for example by metal-workers, brewers, soap-boilers and sugar-refiners as well as in brick-kilns and on the domestic hearth; it was also exported to Europe. But the coal-working was on a small scale. In 1913 the total of coal hewn from British pits was 287,000,000 tons: in 1700 it was only about 2,500,000 tons. Much of the mining was still virtually surface mining, although shafts of over 200 feet (60 metres), were already in existence, and during the next hundred years pits went much deeper than this. The collieries were usually in the countryside, often in remote moorland areas, and other folk regarded miners as a strange wild race, barbarous and frightening. Not infrequently during the 18th century the great landowners on whose property coal seams were found played a leading part in the industry and made handsome profits from it: one of them, the Duke of Bridgewater (1736–1803), was to win renown by the enterprise he showed in developing his pits at Worsley near Manchester. By far the most important coalfield in Britain at this time was the north-eastern one in Northumberland and Durham, which sent steady supplies of coal to London in its fleet of sturdy, roomy boats called 'colliers'.

During the 18th century the output of coal increased considerably, and by 1800 it had risen to about 11,000,000 tons. This growth came about mainly because other industries were beginning to demand more coal as fuel—notably various branches of the iron industry. New pits were opened and deeper shafts sunk. Ponies began to be used for underground haulage; iron rails were first used for surface transport in 1767, and before the end of the century many miles of these iron 'tramways' had been laid down, especially in the north-eastern field; and the widespread construction of canals after 1760 encouraged the development of coalfields. Yet the most important technical invention which affected the industry came quite soon after 1700. The major problem of all mining enterprises was to keep the shafts free from flooding: Cornish tin-mine owners were just as interested in solving this as the colliery owners of the north and midlands. They tried all sorts of methods, among them handpumps and endless chains of buckets: eventually the road to solution was found by experimenting with the use of steam-power. In 1708 a Dartmouth blacksmith, Thomas Newcomen, invented a self-acting atmospheric engine. A great swinging beam was driven by a piston moving up and down in a cylinder as steam was injected and then condensed; to the other end of the beam were connected the rods of the pump which sucked the water from the shaft. Costly, cumbrous, and often ineffective though it was, the New-comen engine came gradually into use, most notably in the north-eastern coalfield, where about 140 of them were at work by 1781.

Coal-mining has always been a dangerous job: and conditions in the pits of the 18th century were by modern standards appalling. Falling rock and subsidence were ever-present perils. Fire-damp, the inflammable gas (methane), caused great loss of life to miners working by candle-light; sometimes as a safeguard two shafts were sunk, and in one a sort of iron cradle containing flaming coals was placed, so as to draw the gas up that shaft and cold air down the other one. Eventually about 1815 a number of inventors, of whom Sir Humphrey Davy and George Stephenson are the best known, devised several forms of safety lamp, the essential principle of which was the surrounding of the naked flame by gauze. In the long run these greatly reduced accidents: yet at first they made little difference, since they merely encouraged owners to work more dangerous shafts and levels. In 1807 John Buddle, the 'viewer' (i.e. manager) at Wallsend Colliery, devised his fan, which was an air-pump to provide the ventilation necessary to get rid of 'choke-damp' (carbon monoxide). Yet human life was little regarded in the pits. Women and children worked long hours underground. Primitive winding gear, worked by horse gins, was another cause of frequent accidents; miners rode up and down in the wooden baskets which carried the coal to the surface, or simply clung to the winding-rope as it rose and fell.

2. THE GROWTH OF THE IRON INDUSTRY

The 18th century saw great changes in the iron industry. The most important reason for these was the growing shortage of timber suitable for making charcoal. Already in 1700 some areas long famous for producing iron, like the Sussex Weald, were not able to supply sufficient charcoal for their iron-foundries; and foundries were being opened in regions where there was still plenty of woodland, like South Wales or even the Scottish Highlands. Another, far more important, result was to encourage iron-founders and others to see whether coal, hitherto found unsuitable, could be used in smelting iron. Again, the 18th century was an age of frequent wars, especially between Britain and France; and these, especially the Seven Years War (1756–63), were a great stimulus to the iron industry. Moreover, in the later years of the century, developments in other industries and in transport brought an increase in the demand for iron goods: cast-iron rails, iron parts for textile machinery, and iron or partially iron ploughs provided three important illustrations of this.

In 1700 the centres for the production of iron—that is, for turning iron ore into pig-iron—were widely scattered over the country; they included not only areas like South Wales and south Yorkshire which were later to develop the industry on a great scale, but also Sussex, the Forest of Dean and Cheshire. The total output by itself was quite insufficient to meet the demands of those areas which manufactured iron goods. The most notable of these was Birmingham and the Black Country, where a great range of iron goods—guns, swords, locks, bolts, bits, chains, buckles, toys and nails—was turned out in many small towns and villages. In general, the manufacture of iron goods took place on the coalfields, for coal could be used as fuel in this process. Yet so long as it could not be satisfactorily used for smelting iron ore, the development of the entire industry was bound to be slow. Moreover, much bar iron had to be imported from Russia, and the cutlers of Sheffield and other manufacturers of steel goods, which required iron of specially high quality, had to get raw material from Sweden.

In such circumstances it is not surprising that ironmasters were anxious to find some way of using coal instead of charcoal in the production of iron. The great drawback of coal—or, strictly, of coke—was the presence of sulphur, which made the pig-iron when it came from the furnace impure and brittle. During the 17th century several inventors experimented in vain to overcome this difficulty. Sucess came at last in 1709, when Abraham Darby, the first of a dynasty of ironmasters working at Coalbrookdale in Shropshire, successfully smelted iron-ore with coke made from local pit coal. He was in a sense lucky, for this coal, the 'clod coal' of Shropshire, was of a type peculiarly suitable for use in a blastfurnace. His example was only slowly followed. The Darbys were Quakers, not given to advertising themselves or their activities. Furthermore, the initial success was limited to the production of pig-iron suitable for casting. The second Abraham Darby considerably improved his father's process and was by about 1750 making from coke-smelted pig relatively small quantities of bar-iron which could be used in forges. Coalbrookdale contributed other important developments as the century went by. In 1766 wrought iron was made there in a reverberatory furnace using coal fuel. The first iron rails were made at Coalbrookdale in 1767, and the first iron bridge was built, across the Severn, by the Coalbrookdale Company in 1777–81.

Between 1740 and 1750 another Quaker, Benjamin Huntsman, a clockmaker of Sheffield who was not satisfied with the quality of metal he was able to obtain, devised an improved method of making steel. The process was a relatively simple one. He took 'blister steel'—that is, bar iron which had been heated in a furnace with charcoal for twelve days and thereby been hardened—and melted it in small clay crucibles placed in a coke furnace so hot that it burned away all the impurities. The finished product, crucible or cast steel, was peculiarly hard yet flexible, suitable for articles like watch-springs and razor blades. But it came only slowly into general use. Huntsman took out no patent; nevertheless he tried to keep the details of his new method a secret. There is a story, probably only a legend, that a rival ironmaster, Samuel Walker, dressed up as a poor beggar and persuaded Huntsman's workmen to let him warm himself near the furnaces, and so discovered the new technique. Whether it is true or not, Walker made a princely fortune for himself in the great foundries he built near Rotherham.

The needs of the Seven Years War (1756–63) did much to hasten the next important technical developments in the British iron industry. The demand for munitions led to the opening of new iron works, like those started at Carron in Scotland by John Roebuck and at Bradley in the Black Country and Broseley in Shropshire by John Wilkinson. 'Iron-mad' Wilkinson (1728–1808) was a person of peculiar interest and importance. The owner of a group of blastfurnaces in the Midlands and of ironworks in France, with extensive shares in Cornish tin and Welsh copper and lead mines, he did much to make Boulton and Watt's commercial development of the steam-engine possible by supplying them with accurate borings and castings.[1] He was the first ironmaster to use the steam-engine to blow the blast of his furnaces and to drive the hammer at his forge. An early

[1] See below, p. 32.

example of a capitalist whose wide business interests formed a sort of industrial empire, he was a ruthless and eccentric man who was eventually buried, as he had directed, in an iron coffin beneath an iron obelisk. His successful career illustrated the growing importance of the iron industry; yet it was a very different character from Wilkinson who was responsible for the next major advance in the iron industry. This was Henry Cort (1740–1800), who in 1783–4 took out patents for two processes known as 'puddling' and 'rolling' iron.

Darby had shown how to use coke to produce pig-iron: Cort went on to use it to manufacture bar-iron in quantity. Hitherto the conversion of pig-iron into bar-iron had been a slow and costly process, involving prolonged hammering of the semi-molten metal, and dependent on the use of charcoal. In Cort's process, the pig-iron was heated in a reverberatory furnace fed with coke; when it became molten it was stirred or 'puddled' into iron rods and thus most of the carbon and other impurities were burned away; later the 'loops' or 'blooms' into which the molten metal collected were again heated, and passed through great iron rollers which pressed out the remaining dross. Previously it had taken twelve hours to hammer a ton of iron; now fifteen tons could be put through the rolling mills in that time, no charcoal was used at any stage in the process, and the finished iron was of good quality. Cort himself, like so many 18th-century inventors, made little profit from his work; he fell into debt, went bankrupt, and died dependent on a government pension. But his invention was revolutionary. Henceforward the industry, freed from dependence upon charcoal, and sure of plentiful supplies of good quality iron for almost any purpose, could go ahead at a pace hitherto undreamed of. In 1788 the output of pig iron in Britain was 68,000 tons: by 1804 it had risen to 250,000 and by 1818 to 325,000 tons.

Three important results followed Cort's work. First, the iron industry, parts of which had previously been widely scattered about the country, moved to the coalfields, where every process of iron manufacture could be carried on within easy reach of the vital fuel, coal. Four areas in particular became the major centres of the industry, with its roaring blast-furnaces, its endless hammering, its swift-growing slag-heaps. They were the Black Country, south Yorkshire, Clydeside, and South Wales. Secondly, Cort's process provided a splendid opportunity for the rapid building-up of a number of large-scale businesses which controlled every process in the industry from the mining of the iron ore and the coal to the sale of manufactured rails or other large iron goods. Typical of these was that of Richard Crawshay of the Cyfarthfa Ironworks in South Wales. He was the first ironmaster to use the puddling process, and his works transformed Merthyr Tydfil from a tiny village to a great industrial centre in a few years. Thirdly, cheap iron was the key which unlocked the door to an era of swift industrial and social change. John Wilkinson's contemporaries thought him mad when he proposed building iron ships: he launched the first one on the Severn in 1787. A year later he made forty miles (sixty-four kilometres) of cast-iron water-pipes for the city of Paris. These were but two examples of the ways in which iron could replace other materials; there were countless others, particularly in building and large-scale engineering. Above all, cheap iron made possible an age of machinery, providing the accurate, strong and lasting material essential to mechanical development. Nineteenth-century Britain was to see an industrial development never previously known on earth: and its basis was iron machinery.

5   The Coming of Steam Power

1. BEFORE JAMES WATT

By tradition, the great name in the story of steam-power in Great Britain is that of James Watt, who took out his first patent for a steam-engine in 1769. But the possibility of harnessing steam as a source of power had been guessed at many centuries earlier. In the first century B.C. Hero of Alexandria had written a book on the subject: lost during the Middle Ages, Hero's writings were rediscovered during the Renaissance and had aroused much interest. The 17th century had seen various experiments on the Continent as well as in Britain. Perhaps the most gifted of these earlier inventors was a French Protestant scientist, Denis Papin (1647–1712). Driven by religious persecution from his own country, he carried out numerous experiments both in England and in Germany. He invented a pressure cooker and a safety valve, as well as a mechanically-propelled boat, which took fifteen years to make and was then destroyed by boatmen who feared that it would take away their livelihood. This kind of experience was to befall many later inventors.

By the end of the 17th century the principles behind the problem of steam-power were fairly widely known. The practical need for some kind of engine was most evident in the tin mines of Cornwall, where the sinking of deeper shafts made flooding an ever-greater hindrance. Two west-countrymen had produced engines which were only partially satisfactory. Thomas Savery's 'The Miner's Friend or an engine to raise water by fire' (patented in 1698; a heat-operated vacuum pump rather than an engine) was not strong enough to cope with the quantity of water to be raised from deep mines. The engine of Thomas Newcomen (patented in 1708) was far more effective than Savery's, and came during the next sixty years into widespread use in the mines. It was also used to blow blast-furnaces, among them that of the Darbys at Coalbrookdale, and to provide drinking water for towns. Its great weakness was that it was extremely uneconomical to run, for it consumed vast quantities of fuel.

2. JAMES WATT (1736–1819)

It was at this point in the story that the genius of James Watt appeared. Watt was a Scotsman, born in Greenock in 1736. His grandfather had been a teacher of mathematics, his father was a shipwright (and builder, contractor, carpenter, and undertaker as well) who repaired nautical instruments as well as ships: he himself was soundly educated at the local grammar school, and then trained as a mathematical instrument maker. After a short apprenticeship in London, where he was forced to spend most of his days indoors for fear of the activities of the press gang, he came back to Glasgow and at the age of 21 set up in business as a scientific instrument maker to the University. In fact he turned his hand to a good many other things besides scientific instruments—violins and flutes among them. His job brought him into contact with professors and students, society which stimulated him to reflect on the scientific questions of the day. He studied chemistry under Joseph Black, one of the ablest contemporary scientists, who was a professor at Glasgow, and investigated the problem of latent heat; and he experimented with a steam-engine of the kind devised by Papin a century before. Thus his mind, with its natural mathematical bent, was well prepared to contribute to a solution of the problem of steam-power. Watt combined scientific study with practical craftsmanship.

Among the apparatus belonging to the University was a model of a Newcomen engine which in 1763 was given to Watt to repair. It set him thinking. Newcomen's engine depended for its effectiveness on the alternate heating and cooling of the cylinder in which the piston moved up and down. The piston moved down because a vacuum was created in the cylinder by injecting first steam and then cold water which caused the steam to condense. The sudden changes in temperature involved a high wastage of energy: great quantities of fuel had to be used in order to reheat the cylinder. How was it possible to avoid this, and thus make the Newcomen engine much cheaper to run? This was the question upon which James Watt pondered. He hit upon the answer one Sunday afternoon in 1765, when he was taking a walk across Glasgow Green. The vital element in his solution was to build a separate condenser to cool the steam, thus avoiding any lowering of the temperature of the cylinder. He also introduced an air-tight cover for the cylinder and drove his piston by the combination of steam pressure and atmospheric pressure.

To make this revolutionary change in a model was a job of a few weeks: to turn the new steam-engine into a commercial proposition was a very different matter. It needed time and money, and Watt was not a wealthy man. His first attempt to find someone who would finance his experiments in the hope of profit was not successful. John Roebuck, the founder of the Carron Iron Works, with whom Watt entered into partnership in 1768, joined him in taking out a patent for the new engine in 1769; and a full-size trial engine, incorporating Watt's improvements, was built in Scotland. It would not work—principally, it seems, because the workmanship of the mechanics (specially imported from England) was defective, and the various parts they had made were inaccurate. Watt fell into debt, and was compelled to turn canal-surveyor to earn his living; and Roebuck went bankrupt in 1773. The prospects of the new engine did not appear to be bright.

In fact, salvation was at hand, in the person of Matthew Boulton (1728–1809). Boulton was a highly successful businessman, the owner of a large works at Soho near Birmingham, where he manufactured a great variety of hardware goods from buttons to clocks, from snuff-boxes to statuettes. His goods had a European reputation, and the Soho works was one of the sights for foreign visitors. Optimistic in temperament, he was an adventurous businessman, prepared to take risks where he saw a chance of profit. He was specially interested in the problem of engines, for the Soho works depended for its power on a water supply which often ran dry in the summer. Roebuck owed him £1200, and Boulton agreed to take over the former's share in the steam-engine patent in settlement of the debt. Thus there began the famous partnership of Boulton and Watt, the firm which gave the world its first really effective steam-engine. The trial engine was taken to pieces and sent to Birmingham, where it was rebuilt with more accurate parts. In particular, it was given a cast-iron cylinder accurately bored by John Wilkinson at his works at Broseley with his cannon lathe (devised in 1774). In 1775, the year after Watt himself moved to Birmingham, the patent was extended for another twenty-five years: and in 1776 the first engines were sent out from the Soho factory. They worked, and quickly won fame throughout the industrial Midlands. The hardest corner had been turned, and the way was open to triumph.

But definite commercial success was slow to come. It was to be ten years before the partners could consider themselves reasonably secure. Skilled workmen were scarce and hard to manage, and Watt, an impatient person who suffered from headaches and indigestion, was not the man to handle workmen wisely. The other concerns of the Soho works ran into difficulties, and for years bankruptcy seemed near at hand. Most of the early orders for engines came from the tin and copper mines in Cornwall, and according to Watt, who spent most of his time there superintending their installation and first operation, the Cornish were peculiarly difficult people to deal with; there were constant disputes over a complicated method of payment for the engines, which was based on a calculation of the amount of fuel which the mine-owners saved by replacing their old Newcomen engines with the new ones, and the mines themselves were often speculative ventures which failed and left Boulton and Watt to face a loss. Finally there were periodic troubles with rival companies who pirated their patent; barely half the engines at work in Cornwall by 1800 had been erected by the Soho firm.

Nevertheless the firm survived these hard years and eventually flourished. It did so not merely because the new engine was bound to establish itself as an essential piece of equipment in the mining areas: but also because Watt's inventive genius led him on to further developments of his engine which opened new fields for use for it. The first Watt engine, that originally patented in 1769, was in effect a reciprocating engine with a to-and-fro motion, suitable for pumping. Huge new possibilities lay ahead if steam power could be effectively used for driving the machinery in textile mills, hitherto dependent on water-power and thus tied to establishment in certain localities only. In 1781 Watt made this possible. He took out his second patent, for rotary motion, incorporating the device known as 'sun and planet' motion, said to have been suggested to him by his foreman, William Murdock. This invention, making it possible to transmit steam power to all sorts of industrial machinery, was at least as important in its effects as Watt's initial improvement of the Newcomen engine. Various other improvements followed. In 1782 he devised the double-acting ex-pansive engine, admitting steam alternately on each side of the piston and thus doubling the duty done by each cylinder; in 1784 he introduced the device of parallel motion which transferred the thrust of the piston-rod, on its upward stroke, to the end of the beam, and a technique for applying steam-power to drive hammers in iron forges; and finally in 1788 he adapted for steam engines the governor, a device which kept their speed constant and thus secured smooth movement. Any one of these inven-tions by itself would have won James Watt distinction; taken together, they make him the central figure in the technical progress of the 18th century. Backed by the capital and business acumen of Boulton, they made him wealthy. When the first patent expired in 1800 the two partners dissolved their original firm and handed over the business to their sons; and James Watt, far more fortunate than other contemporary inventors, lived on in ease and comfort until his death in 1819.

3. THE USE AND IMPORTANCE OF STEAM POWER

In the 1770's there may have been as many as 300 of the old-style Newcomen engines at work, mainly in the mining areas. Between 1775 and 1800 Boulton and Watt, who held the legal monopoly, are reckoned to have erected about 500 of their new engines[1]. They started slowly, and by 1782 there were only about 50 in operation: but the invention of rotary motion altered the situation, bringing a rapid demand from the cotton firms of Lancashire, Derbyshire and Nottinghamshire. To some extent the areas to which they went were limited by the problem of transport: the heavy parts of steam engines were very difficult to carry along boggy and rutted roads, and water was used wherever it was at all possible, for example to Cornwall. The building of canals in the years after 1775 helped to ease the situation. Watt's earliest engines were used mainly in the tin and copper mines of Cornwall and in the iron mines of Shropshire and Staffordshire for drainage and pumping. In the coal mines they found at first less demand, for there the saving of fuel mattered little; but their greater efficiency soon made them essential. In the iron industry they were used to raise water to drive bellows and rolling-mills. Breweries, distilleries, water-works and canal-building schemes also made use of them. Then came the demand from textile manufacturers. A spinning-mill was being driven by steam-power at Papplewick near Nottingham in 1785: after 1790 steam power was applied to drive the 'mules', the

[1] And there were by 1800 at least as many 'pirate' engines, illegally built by other engineers.

standard type of spinning machinery which was spreading rapidly through the cotton industry. By 1800 most of the demand for steam-engines was coming from these sources; perhaps 1200 all told were built during the 18th century, a few of them being exported.

The introduction of steam-power was the greatest revolution in economic history since the discovery of agriculture in prehistoric times. When Matthew Boulton said 'I sell here, sir, what all the world desires to have— Power,' he was pointing the way to a new age. For steam-power opened the way to the transformation of the ways of life of future generations. Steam-power immeasurably extended the range of man's economic activities, freeing him from dependence on water-power by making available to him the vast stored-up energy of coal. From this came economic change in many directions. Steam in the mines and ironworks multiplied many times the supplies of cheap iron as well as of coal; steam in the textile factories opened the way to the mass production of clothes; steam would before long be applied to transport and so produce railways, themselves the chief cause of another vast acceleration of industrial production. In some ways perhaps the most significant result of all, one upon which so much else depended, was the growth of engineering as a highly-skilled industry. The 19th century was to see an almost infinite expansion of machine-driven industry, an expansion in which not the least important part was the construction of machines whose sole function was themselves to make other machines. It origins lay in the successful achievements of Watt the inventor and Boulton the business man, of Iron-mad Wilkinson, of William Murdock and the other craftsmen of the 18th century.

6   Textiles and other Industries in the Eighteenth Century

1. THE TEXTILE INDUSTRY BEFORE 1750

In 1700 the most important part of the British textile industry was the manufacture of woollen cloth. It was the biggest English export; nearly every part of the country was financially interested in its manufacture, and three areas (East Anglia, the West Country, and the West Riding of Yorkshire) drew much of their livelihood from it. The merchant clothiers who, especially in the West Country, dominated the industry, were men of great wealth and substance. The number of workers was very large, even though there was little that could be called 'factory' organisation in the industry; for cloth-making involved a long chain of processes. The raw wool had to be cleaned; then combed, to separate short from long, or carded, to turn it into a workable roll. Next followed the central operations of spinning the wool into yarn, and weaving the yarn into cloth. After these the cloth had to be fulled and washed, stretched and bleached, and dressed, that is, have the nap raised and sheared. At some stage it was dyed. Some of these processes were carried out by men and women working part-time, as a 'by-industry' in the intervals of working on the land: but many operatives in the great woollen areas were full-time and specialised craftsmen.

Moreover, the trade was regarded as so vital to national prosperity that the great cloth merchants formed a powerful pressure group with much influence in Parliament. A whole series of laws was designed to protect the industry and to regulate the quality of the finished product. There were Acts fixing size and weight of pieces of cloth and the methods of drying and dyeing. A law of Charles II's reign declared that every person dying on English soil had to be buried in a woollen shroud: another of William III's time killed the Irish woollen industry by imposing prohibitive export duties on its products. In 1700 and again in 1721 the woollen merchants did their best to destroy the growing cotton trade by forbidding the import of printed cotton fabrics from Asia. This prohibition had effects not wholly favourable to the woollen industry: for the prohibition of foreign cotton goods stimulated the English cotton-manufacturing industry, which just at this time was beginning to take firm root, and thus created a rival which later on would challenge the supremacy of woollens.

The woollen industry was mainly domestic—that is, most of the work was done in the workers' own homes. Some processes, like fulling and dressing, involved the use of mills and some form of power, either horse or water: others, like dyeing and bleaching, used equipment too big for a cottage. But spinning and weaving, the key processes, were normally carried on at home, the spinning by the women (who might or might not be 'spinsters' in the modern sense of that word) and the weaving by men: for spinning wheel and hand loom alike could easily be set up in a cottage room. This did not mean, however, that each family was an independent unit, making and selling its own cloth. For by 1700 the cloth industry was falling more and more under the control of the merchants who bought the raw wool from the farmers, saw it through its several processes, and sold the finished cloth. They were the capitalists, the men who could afford to buy the wool and pay out the wages to the various workers, and wait to collect their profit on the finished article. Their power varied from locality to locality. In the West Country they were supreme, and if one of them went bankrupt his failure would affect the well-being of many families; in East Anglia control of the industry had fallen into the hands of men who governed one of its early processes, the master combers; yet in some parts of the West Riding the working weaver, himself employing five or six spinners to keep him supplied with yarn, was often much more independent. But in general domestic industry was capitalist industry, dominated by a small number of wealthy men: and this was as true of silk and the other textiles as of woollens.

The woollen industry was a conservative one; it did not take readily to new ideas and new techniques. This was mainly because it was established and successful, and prosperous woollen merchants were very ready to argue that if they were doing well under the old methods there was no point in adopting new ones. Thus technical change was bound to come slowly in woollens. By contrast, both the cotton and silk industries were ready to welcome change. Both, differing from woollens, depended on imported raw materials: both had to struggle hard in competition against the established woollen industry. The cotton industry was a relative new-comer to Britain; the silk industry had always to fight against the long-established and highly-developed French industry. Thus it was in them rather than in woollens that technical progress was likely to come.

In fact there was little change before 1750, although what there was pointed the way to vital developments later in the century. The general direction of change was towards an increased use of water-power, as was illustrated by the celebrated silk factory set up by Thomas Lombe on an island in the River Derwent at Derby between 1718 and 1722. This contained silk-throwing machines based on Italian designs said to have been smuggled into England. Its size—it was six storeys high—and its machines, worked by a water-wheel, made a great impression on contemporaries. Daniel Defoe said of it, 'Here is a curiosity of a very extraordinary nature, and the only one of its kind in England. . . . This engine contains 22,586 wheels and 97,746 movements, which work 73,726 yards of silk thread every time the wheel goes round, which is three times in one minute, and 318,504,960 yards in twenty-four hours. The water wheel gives the motion to all the rest of the wheels and movements, of which any one may be stopped separately.' Moreover, Lombe employed three hundred persons. He made £120,000 in fifteen years, and was knighted. Other silk-manufacturers built factories on his model, employing even more workers.

Yet silk in England was destined to remain a minor industry. The main line of factory development, with vast consequences in the growth of new towns, ran through the major textiles, wool and cotton. Here the decade 1730–40 saw two significant technical advances, one in weaving, the other in spinning, neither of them leading to immediate results, yet both pointing to future great changes. The first came in 1733, when John Kay invented the Flying Shuttle: the second in 1738, when Lewis Paul devised a method of spinning involving the use of rollers.

Kay was a native of Bury in Lancashire who in the early 1730's was working for a clothier in Colchester in Essex. He was an ingenious mechanic who had already invented a new carding process. His Flying Shuttle was not in itself a machine at all, but simply a gadget for saving the weaver time and labour at the loom: Kay's device enabled the shuttle to be struck to and fro by hammers which the weaver controlled by strings. The width of cloth need no longer be limited by the length of the weaver's arms. One man could now weave broadcloth, a process hitherto requiring two. It was an admirable invention: it was also most unpopular with the weavers, who complained that it deprived them of their livelihood. Kay, forced to leave Colchester, went to Leeds, where the manufacturers used his patent without paying him; thence to his native Bury, where opposition was so bitter that there was a riot in which his house was sacked. Eventually the wretched man fled to France and died in poverty. The hostility of the weavers undoubtedly slowed down the general introduction of his device, and not until about 1760 did it come into general use.

The second invention of this early period, Lewis Paul's spinning machine patented in 1738, had an obscure history; indeed it is not certain whether Paul, who was the son of a French refugee, or a carpenter named John Wyatt was the real inventor. The patent provided for a machine which was to pass the carded cotton or wool through revolving rollers, and so draw out the thread and make it finer; it was then passed on to spindles which gave it the twist essential to strengthen it. But for reasons which are not clear, the machine failed in practice; small mills set up to employ it, in Birmingham and elsewhere, had to close down. The ideas which, a generation later, were to revolutionise the spinning industry, were present in this invention; the commercial success which was essential to its general adoption was not yet at hand.

2. THE GREAT TEXTILE CHANGES AFTER 1750

A cotton industry was firmly established before 1750 in south Lancashire, a region whose advantages included soft Pennine water; a damp climate with relatively little variation in temperature, providing the humid atmosphere for handling cotton thread; swiftly-flowing streams for processes using water-power; a good port in Liverpool; and plenty of available labour. Competition with the established woollen industry stimulated enterprise. The demand for cotton cloth, for calicoes and muslins, was growing and was capable of great expansion, both at home and overseas: there was a prospect of great profits for enterprising business men here. All these things stimulated efforts to find ways of increasing output—and especially to invent appropriate machinery for this purpose. Moreover, the nature of cotton thread made it more responsive to machinery than the thicker and less even woollen material could be.

The 1760's, like the 1730's, saw two notable advances in the technique of the textile industry. This time, unlike the earlier inventions, they bore fruit at once, producing a great increase in output and leading to further technical progress. In particular, they revolutionised the cotton industry. They were in the first place cotton inventions, and were swiftly adopted throughout the industry: only later, and much more slowly, did they spread to wool. Both were designed to speed up the technique of spinning. It had always been difficult for spinners to keep weavers supplied with sufficient yarn; and now the gradual introduction of the Flying Shuttle was making the situation worse by doubling the pace at which weavers could work. It was therefore urgent to find some means of expanding the output of the spinners, and the 1750's and 1760's saw many ingenious persons in Lancashire attempting to produce new spinning-machines.

The first to meet with real success was James Hargreaves, a Blackburn weaver, who somewhere about 1765 made what came to be known as the Spinning Jenny, a machine which could spin six threads at once. Although it was ultimately constructed to be capable of as many as eighty threads at once, it was originally a machine to be worked by hand, and small enough to be used in a cottage. It was cheap to make, and rapidly came into widespread use in Lancashire: ten years after Hargreaves' death in 1778, it was reckoned that 20,000 jennies were being used in England. Yet the Spinning Jenny, although it greatly increased the output of spinners, did not itself lead directly to the employment of any new form of power, or to the factory system. This development resulted from another invention of this time, the Water Frame or Rollers patented by Richard Arkwright in 1769. This was a device rather similar to Lewis Paul's unsuccessful machine, using rollers to stretch the threads: the yarn it produced was stronger than that from the jenny. But the Water Frame was a big machine and needed power to drive it. Thus its coming meant the setting-up of mills or factories. If any one invention may be called the prime cause of the modern factory age, it is the Water Frame.[1]

Richard Arkwright (1732–92), youngest child of a poor Preston family, died leaving a fortune of half a million pounds. Apprenticed as a boy to a barber, he eventually became a knight and Sheriff of Derbyshire. So ill-educated that even when he was over 50 he spent two hours a day taking lessons in grammar and spelling, he was the first cotton magnate in English history. Carlyle said of him, 'What a historical Phenomenon is that bag-cheeked, pot-bellied, much enduring, much inventing barber!' His claim to have invented the Water Frame is dubious; he may have cribbed the idea from one or more earlier inventors. Although he devised a carding machine (1775) involving the use of cylinders, Arkwright was above all a business man, capable of organising the labour of others and of turning the new technology to swift profit. In partnership with Jedediah Strutt he set up his first major factory at Cromford in Derbyshire in 1771. Like Lombe's mill on which it was modelled, it drew its power from the water of the Derwent. Within a few years he was running more mills in Derbyshire (one of these, at Wirksworth, provides the first recorded use—1780—of steam-power, probably for pumping, in a cotton factory) and also in Lancashire. He got involved in disputes with rivals who wanted to enjoy the benefits of his patents, and finally lost his patent rights in a lawsuit of 1785, when he himself could offer no very convincing account of the origin of the Water Frame. The defeat made little difference to Arkwright, easily the richest cotton spinner of his day, and before his death in 1792 he had extended his existing factories and founded new ones, among them (in conjunction with David Dale) the New Lanark Mills on the banks of the Clyde. Richard Arkwright, the first great modern factory owner, the man whose ambition, so they said, was to pay off the National Debt, was the herald of a new age.

The tale of spinning inventions was not yet done. In 1779 a Bolton weaver, Samuel Crompton (1753–1827), produced a machine which got the name of the Mule because it was a cross between the Jenny and the Water Frame: combining the rollers of the latter and the moving carriage

---

[1] Arkwright's original model, made entirely of wood, may be seen to-day at the Science Museum, South Kensington.

of the former, it produced a yarn which was at once fine and strong. Crompton, a single-minded inventor, in type a marked contrast to Arkwright, took out no patent and made little from his invention. Later he invented a carding machine, but, fearing that others would reap all the profit from this too, he deliberately smashed it; and he died a poor man, having spent most of a parliamentary grant of £5,000 in paying his debts. By that time the Mule had become the most important of all spinning machines. Originally a cottage machine, it was in 1790 harnessed to water-power by William Kelly, then manager of the New Lanark Mills, and its use spread very rapidly. The high-quality yarn it produced enabled English manufacturers to rival Indian craftsmen in the production of fine muslins, a branch of the cotton industry which grew quickly in Glasgow as well as in Crompton's native Bolton. The invention by Richard Roberts in 1825 of a self-acting device finally assured the triumph of the Mule: and Crompton's machine, with modifications, supplied the central elements of cotton-spinning machinery until the coming of ring-spinning from the U.S.A. later in the 19th century.

Steam-power was, as we have seen, first applied to spinning machinery in 1785, and its use spread in the cotton mills in the 1790's. This meant that the factories could leave the banks of country streams and come into the towns: but many millowners in fact preferred to stick to water-power long after 1800. This was true of spinning; it was even more true of the weaving process. The rapid adoption by spinners of the three inventions of Hargreaves, Arkwright, and Crompton, had created a situation peculiarly favourable to skilled hand-loom weavers. Whereas in the early part of the century weavers had often been unemployed because the spinners could not give them enough yarn, now in the 1780's and 1790's there was so much yarn available that weavers could get steady employment at high rates of pay. Those who wove the fashionable fancy muslins were particularly fortunate: at Bolton in 1792 weavers were getting 3s. 6d. a yard, and gave themselves great airs, going about the streets with £5 notes stuck in their hatbands.

This golden age of the weavers could not last. Wages fell partly because great numbers of unskilled men rushed into the trade to try to get the high rates of pay, partly because of the dislocation of business caused by the French Wars which began in 1793. Moreover, there had already been attempts to invent machinery which would restore the balance between the weaving and spinning processes by enabling the weavers to use greater quantities of yarn. Success of a sort came in 1784 to a clergyman, Edmund Cartwright, who was a fellow of an Oxford college and had been Professor of Poetry in the University. He was a brilliant and impulsive man: after falling into a discussion with some Manchester manufacturers who maintained that to make a loom which could be driven by power was impossible, he set out to build one, although he had never seen a weaver at work. His first machines were clumsy, and it was some years before the power loom was working effectively. It met, inevitably, violent opposition from the hand-loom weavers: a factory which Cartwright built to hold 400 looms driven by steam was burned down in 1792. He was no business man, and fell into further troubles, this time with manufacturers rather than with workmen, over another invention of his, a wool-combing machine. The general adoption of the power-loom, even in the cotton industry, came after 1800, at which date there were only a few hundred at work. Cartwright's invention needed various technical improvements. One came in 1803, when John Horrocks of Stockport installed power-looms made wholly of metal; in the 1820s Richard Roberts built what became the standard type of power-loom. Even in 1830 there were still about 200,000 hand-looms at work in the cotton industry: as for woollens, the power-loom did not come into widespread use in the West Riding until the middle of the 19th century.

3. SOME EFFECTS OF THE COMING OF MACHINERY

Power-driven machinery meant the coming of factories, above all to the textile areas of south Lancashire, Lanarkshire, and the West Riding of Yorkshire; yet its spread was slow, and for many years after its first introduction the factory system and the domestic system existed side by side. In woollens the rate of progress towards a machine-driven industry was far slower than in cotton. So factories arose later in Yorkshire than in Lancashire, and hand-workers survived far longer there. Businesses were smaller there, too: only Benjamin Gott of Leeds, the great army clothing contractor, was comparable to Arkwright. Yet during the 19th century power-driven machinery triumphed in wool as it had done in cotton. As a result one of the three traditional homes of the cloth industry far outdistanced the other two, which in fact positively declined. The West Riding had plentiful coal supplies: East Anglia had none at all, the West Country very few. Thus as steam became the predominant source of industrial power, Leeds, Bradford and the other Yorkshire towns became the great centres of woollen manufacture just as the Lancashire towns round Manchester had already become the home of cottons.

What were the general results of this coming of machinery in the textile industries? They were numerous and complicated; yet a few are worth underlining. The first and most obvious were the various social results which followed from the building of the factories essential to house and operate the new machines. Where the power used was water, these tended to be built at isolated places in the countryside, like Arkwright's mills at Cromford: but where it was steam, factories grouped themselves together on the coalfields. The future lay with steam, and so within the space of a few years the population of the textile towns rose by thousands. Slums and terrible overcrowding occurred, with all their hideous consequences of squalor, disease and misery. For there were few laws about town-planning, few public health regulations, and often no effective local government at all: thus paving, lighting, drainage and water-supplies depended largely on chance and were often neglected. In older towns which received a sudden increase of population, like Manchester, tenement houses were crammed with inhabitants from attic to cellar, often with one family per room; in the newly-built ones 'jerry builders' ran up row after row of meanly-built houses, with thin walls and shallow foundations, damp and dismal, often 'back to back' with no through ventilation. Here amid the grime and soot arose a massive social question which later generations would have to answer.

Secondly, conditions within the factories themselves created a whole set of new problems. The factories were big barrack-like places, planned to make the maximum use of the new machines, usually with little regard to the health or safety of the workers. Ventilation was bad: it was bound to be a difficult problem in cotton mills in view of the importance of a humid atmosphere in working the material. There was a serious outbreak of 'factory fever', a disease similar to gaol fever (typhus), in Manchester in 1784. Machines were unguarded. Hours were long, a fourteen-hour day being not abnormal. We must be careful not to judge this state of affairs by later standards alone. There is plenty of evidence to show that in many ways conditions in the new factories were no worse than they had been in domestic industry. Further, wages rose during the latter part of the 18th century; and they rose more for industrial workers than for agricultural ones, and more for factory workers than for domestic industrial workers. On the other hand there is evidence to suggest that this rise in wages was largely offset by a rise in prices. And there was now a vital new element in the factory workers' condition. This was the rigid discipline and the insistence on punctuality: the latter is neatly illustrated by the story of the Duke of Bridgewater who, when his workmen came back late after the midday break one day and said in excuse that they had not heard the factory clock strike one, at once had the clock altered so that thereafter it struck thirteen. Along with strictness about time went severe deductions from wages for such 'offences' as leaving factory windows open or singing at work. All this was peculiarly hateful to workers accustomed to cottage industry.

Thirdly, one item of factory conditions was so striking as to make public opinion regard it as a grave problem. From the start much of the work in textile factories (at firstly largely spinning mills) was done by women and children, who in 1838 were three quarters of the labour force. Spinning was traditionally women's work; and women were better workers than men—more obedient, less likely to be absent after payday. Many of the jobs to be done were well within the powers of quite small children, and some, such as the picking up of bits of thread beneath the machines, could be much better done by children. And above all women and children took less wages. There was nothing new about child labour; Daniel Defoe, at the beginning of the century, had spoken with favour of the sight of children of five or six years of age working alongside their parents. But its large-scale appearance in factories towards the end of the century attracted much attention. Further, the system by which pauper children, often orphans, were handed over to employers was open to scandalous abuse.

Many of the northern mills were in areas where labour was scarce: and so employers contracted with parish overseers of the poor in London and other southern areas to take batches of these so-called 'parish apprentices'. Some employers treated them well: one of these was Sir Robert Peel the elder, the mill-owner from Bury whose son was one day to be Prime Minister. But many of them undoubtedly suffered much at the hands of harsh employers and brutal foremen; and 'their young lives were spent, at best in montonous toil, at worst in a hell of human cruelty'.[1]

One other effect of a compensating kind from the point of view of the wage-earner must be mentioned. The coming of machines was of course eventually to bring a great rise in the standard of living: the textile machines, for example, were to bring supplies of cheap clothes within reach even of the very poor. But this sort of gain was not apparent to the hand-workman who lost his living because of the introduction of machinery, and it was natural enough for workmen to show the kind of hostility towards machines that Kay and Cartwright both experienced. Yet machines had come to stay; and their arrival and the creation of factories gave workmen a new opportunity of combining together to improve their lot. The coming of the factory stimulated the growth of trade unions, whose object was to defend the standard of life which workmen felt to be threatened by the new machinery and all that it brought with it. Their significance at this time is shown by the fact that in 1799 the government felt it necessary to pass the Combination Acts prohibiting the existence of trade unions.[2]

4. CHANGES IN OTHER INDUSTRIES: CHEMICALS AND POTTERY

The great technical changes in the major branches of the textile industry naturally found parallels elsewhere in the same industry; thus, for example, the well-established business of calico printing made an important stride forward in 1783 when Thomas Bell invented copper cylinders which revolved under power and could print two or more colours on the fabric as it was passed between them. Some changes, notably in washing, bleaching and dyeing, were closely related to contemporary advances in the chemical industry. The bleaching of çloth, for instance, had for long been done either simply by letting the material remain exposed to the sun for long periods or by soaking it in solutions of ashes and sour milk and then exposing it. This was very slow, particularly in a period when the quantity of cotton cloth produced from the mills was growing by leaps and bounds. 'There was not enough cheap meadowland or sour milk in all the British Isles to whiten the cloth of Lancashire once the water-frame and mule replaced the spinning wheel.'[3] Clearly it was desirable to find some chemical bleaching process. Similarly the demands of the textile industry

---

[1] J. L. and B. Hammond: *The Town Labourer* (1949 edition), p. 147. Some mill-owners, among them Arkwright and Strutt, built for their workers model communities, including churches or chapels, houses with gardens, schools, and shops. One example, that of the Gregs at Styal near Manchester, has been admirably preserved and displayed by the National Trust.

[2] See below, p. 153.

[3] David S. Landes: *The Unbound Prometheus* (1969), p. 108.

for soap and for dyes increased considerably.

The key to the growth of the modern chemical industry was the production of sulphuric acid, a material essential in numerous processes and especially important in the manufacture of the alkalis and soaps needed for textiles. Several sulphuric acid works had been established in Britain before 1750; the most important of these was at Prestonpans in Scotland and belonged to John Roebuck, who in 1746 devised the lead-chamber process for making the acid. Its essential feature was the burning of sulphur and nitre over water in chambers made of lead sheets, and its use spread rapidly in Britain and elsewhere during the years after 1750. The most important application of sulphuric acid was in connection with the large-scale manufacture of soda and thus of soap. Towards the end of the 18th century many chemists were trying to develop a satisfactory method of converting common salt (sodium chloride) into the soda (sodium carbonate) which was needed by the soap-makers; and in 1790 the French chemist Nicholas Leblanc was successful in inventing the process ever since known by his name. He treated salt with sulphuric acid, thus producing sodium sulphate; this he roasted with coal and limestone; and from the resulting black ash he obtained soda. The Leblanc process was only slowly adopted in Britain, but it did more than anything else to lay the foundations of a great chemical industry during the 19th century, particularly on Tyneside and in the area of St. Helens and Widnes.

Shortly before Leblanc's achievement another French chemist, Claude Louis Berthollet, had discovered (1785) the use of chlorine as a bleach. He told James Watt, who was then in Paris, and Watt brought the information back to Glasgow, whose textile manufacturers at once grasped its importance. This Berthollet process was quickly in use in Britain, and in 1799 Charles Tennant opened in Glasgow a factory for the manufacture of bleaching powder in bulk by passing chlorine gas over slaked lime. This was merely one of the numerous commercial developments of chemistry in the second half of the 18th century. The growth of the industry was closely related to the work of contemporary scientists: Joseph Priestley, for example, one of the discoverers of oxygen, also devised a method of manufacturing ammonia. Chemical works of some size arose in south Staffordshire and, rather later, on Tyneside, producing a variety of commodities including, besides the acids, soda, potash, white lead and alum. Attempts were also made to extract tar from coal, an anticipation of interesting later developments: Britain's dependence on the Baltic countries for supplies of tar and pitch was peculiarly irksome in wartime, and in 1782 a works was opened in Scotland to produce tar. It was, however, unsuccessful, and the manufacture of tar in bulk was left to a later generation.

On one British industry the 18th century stamped a pattern which it has never lost. This was the pottery industry, concentrated in the Five Towns of north Staffordshire now collectively known as Stoke-on-Trent: and the pattern was very largely the result of the work of one quite remarkable man, Josiah Wedgwood (1730–95). North Staffordshire had certain natural advantages for the making of pottery, including supplies of a rather crude local clay and plentiful resources of coal that came to be used to heat the furnaces when supplies of wood ran short; and by about 1760 the industry had made appreciable progress, for in that year the district of the Five Towns is said to have contained 150 separate pottery works, each employing some 40 to 50 workers. This age of increasing population, of growing supplies of foodstuffs and of a slowly rising standard of living offered great prospects of an expanding market to the pottery industry. It was the work of Wedgwood to capture that market: thus he 'converted a rude and inconsiderable manufactory into an elegant art and an important element in national commerce'.[1]

Josiah Wedgwood was the son of a master potter, who left him £20 when he died. He began work as a boy, and was self-educated; at 12 he was attacked by smallpox, and its after-effects compelled him to have a leg amputated in later years. He quickly stamped himself as a man of mark in the industry; and his great triumphs start from 1769, the year when he opened his famous Etruria Works, which soon won a world-wide fame for the excellence and quantity of their products. Wedgwood's success rested upon the combination of three qualities. First, he was a lifelong experimenter, sharing the outlook of the many contemporary scientists who were his friends. His experiments led him not to the development of new machines, but to the invention of new glazes and new types of ware like the famous jasper ware, with its white figures set in relief against a background of blue or other colours. Secondly he was a man of fine culture, widely read and of high artistic taste, setting high standards for English pottery. For his elaborate and expensive ornamental wares he employed fine artists and craftsmen; and his pottery as a result won an international reputation, which was symbolised in the celebrated dinner service which he made for the Tsarina Catherine of Russia, in which each separate piece depicted the estate of a different English country gentleman. Thirdly, he was a business man of genius. The strides made by the Potteries in his day were the result not of any technical changes comparable with those in the textile industry, but of Wedgwood's use of the principle of the division of labour. He realised that the output of the industry would be greatly increased if as large a number of workers as possible became specialists in one particular operation or series of operations. Moreover, although he made ornamental ware for his richer customers, he grasped in the 18th century the idea that was to make Henry Ford's fortune with motor-cars in the 20th century—that there was an immense popular market available for the manufacturer who could turn out large quantities of sound but inexpensive goods; and his profits came from his 'useful' wares, among them the famous 'willow pattern'.

Josiah Wedgwood was a great organiser: he was also a 'character', as his men realised when they saw him stumping round the Etruria Works on his wooden leg, breaking into bits any pot which had a flaw in it, and chalking on the bench 'This won't do for Josiah Wedgwood.' His range of interests was wide. A friend of Boulton, he used the steam-engine for

[1] Quoted by T. S. Ashton: *The Industrial Revolution, 1760–1830*, p. 81.

grinding up his materials, although most operations in the pottery industry remained the work of human hands. He bought up a majority of shares in a Cornish clay company, thus safeguarding his supplies of the vital raw material which had been discovered about 1755 by the Plymouth chemist, William Cookworthy. He extended the activities of his works to include the manufacture of earthenware pipes for drains and water supplies, a commodity for which there was soon to be an enormous demand. Finally, he played the leading part in forming a company to build the Trent and Mersey Canal (opened in 1777): thus opening for the Potteries, an area with no navigable river, an industrial highway to the sea, and one peculiarly suitable for transporting its bulky yet fragile industrial products. No other major English industry has owed so much to the activities of one man as pottery owes to Josiah Wedgwood.

7 Transport before the Railway Age

1. THE EARLY EIGHTEENTH CENTURY

Most of the great changes in agriculture and industry took place in the second half of the 18th century. They brought with them inevitable changes in transport. Farmers, merchants, and manufacturers alike depended on quick and reliable communications; enclosures would be unprofitable unless farmers could get their produce to market in the growing towns, and industries consuming more and more coal and iron could not grow unless these heavy and bulky goods could be easily conveyed across the country. The system of transport which existed in England up to about 1750 was neither quick nor reliable. Yet it was in fact already undergoing important changes, and these were to be much accelerated in the latter part of the century.

Englishmen who wished to travel about their country, or to move goods from place to place, in the first half of the 18th century had three methods open to them. They could use the sea, the navigable rivers, or the roads. Of these the sea, despite its perils, was used much more than we might expect for passengers as well as for goods—a fact which is itself an indication of the deficiences of the alternative forms of transport. But it had obvious advantages for conveying heavy goods like the 'sea-coals' sent from Tyneside to London, or the cattle shipped from Scotland to be fattened on the grazing grounds of East Anglia. No doubt the existence of good coastal services delayed the growth of inland transport facilities.

Secondly, the navigable rivers played a vital part in the carriage of goods. Five river-systems covered much of the country. The Thames, navigable above Oxford as far as Cricklade, and its tributaries served the London area and the southern Midlands. The Severn and the other streams entering the Bristol Channel were trade routes for Somerset, the west Midlands, and the eastern parts of Wales: and by way of Stourbridge the Severn provided to a very limited extent for part of the later Black Country. The Mersey and the Dee opened ways into North Wales and into South Lancashire. The Humber and the Trent, the longest group of navigable rivers, served southern Yorkshire, Nottingham, and Derby. Finally the rivers which empty themselves in the Wash served an area of the eastern counties including Stamford, Northampton, Bedford and Cambridge. To these main groups must be added a number of isolated rivers of special importance to limited areas, like the Tyne in the north-east or the Exe in east Devon.

To the towns on or near these inland navigation systems came food supplies and the raw materials of local industry: from them went the cloth or other manufactured goods and the metals mined or stone quarried in the neighbourhood. Their importance was great, and the growth of commerce in the early 18th century led to improvements like the deepening or straightening of channels, as for example, in the Aire and Calder Navigation in the West Riding. Yet they had obvious limitations. Seasonal variations in water supplies and the silting to which the Dee, for example, was peculiarly liable were two of these; a third was man-made—the jealousies between neighbouring towns (e.g. those between Nottingham and Burton-on-Trent) which led to deliberate obstruction in order to prevent trading competition from towns higher upstream. Most serious of all was the restricted area served by the rivers. Many regions gained little from them: these included the southern coastal counties, most of Wales, most of Lancashire and the north-west, and a great part of the Midlands. This last area, which included both Birmingham and the Potteries, was one of special industrial importance, and it is scarcely surprising that it became in the second half of the century a great centre of canal-building.

One reason for the use of navigable rivers was the badness of the roads. Englishmen, right up to the modern motorist, have always been very ready to grumble about the quality of their roads, and there is plenty of evidence that in the years around 1700 they had ample right to do so. Maps of the time showed a land covered by a network of roads: but the maps were one thing, the reality quite different. This was the unanimous verdict of contemporary travellers.[1] The best of the roads were still those built by the Romans fifteen centuries before, where they survived; for they were wide, and had a hard surface and sound foundations. The others, the great majority, were narrow, with soft surfaces, except where they became causeways to cross a marsh. In summer, when they were at their best, travellers sank deep into smothering dust: in winter, when nobody travelled who could avoid it, they turned into sticky quagmires with potholes of outrageous depth. It was normal for travellers who found the road impassable to take to the open fields instead, and quite possible in these days before

[1] One of the most informative of these was a well-to-do lady named Celia Fiennes, who journeyed about England extensively in the reigns of William III and Anne, and has left an entertaining account of the sights she saw and the roads she endured in a book called *The Journeys of Celia Fiennes*.

enclosure became general; it was notable that some of the roads which caused the greatest difficulty to travellers were in areas like Kent, where enclosure had taken place early, and where hedges stopped the benighted traveller from taking to the fields. No doubt some of the stories told of the roads—of journeys over very short distances taking weeks, of potholes which swallowed up horse and rider entire—were travellers' tales, but they were tales worth telling just because the reality itself was so deplorable.

One result of this state of affairs was that the amount of wheeled traffic was small. There were indeed regular services of stage coaches between London and other towns; there were the post-chaises, patronised by the gentry, with fresh horses available at post-houses on the way; and there were the covered stage-wagons with their eight or ten horses and giant wheels, lumbering along at three miles per hour. But most of the gentlemen who wanted to travel and the business man who had to do so went on horseback: the poor man, if he travelled at all, went on foot. Goods which had to go by land were carried on packhorses or mules, and trains of thirty or forty of them in single file, the leading animal wearing a bell to warn travellers coming in the opposite direction, were a common sight. It was in this way that the great fairs held once a year at certain centres (like Sturbridge Fair held every summer near Cambridge) and the regular markets which took place in every small town got their supplies. Along these roads, too, went the packman or pedlar, that lively but suspect character who supplied the country housewife with all manner of goods from scissors and purses to buttons and ribbons.

As the 18th century went on, the amount of traffic on the main roads increased greatly, and various attempts were made to improve their standard. Since Tudor times the authorities legally responsible for the upkeep of the roads were the parishes: once a year for several days all the inhabitants were supposed to turn out and work on the roads, and the farmers had to supply carts and materials for repair. In fact, this system never really worked, for nobody liked the job and every parish maintained that it was the through traffic and not the local traffic that did damage to the roads; and most parishes did little more than tip a few loads of stones into the deepest ruts and holes, and enjoy an annual holiday. Clearly some other system of repair—and, what was more important, of permanent improvement—had to be devised. There were those who believed that something could be done by controlling the weight, size, and wheels of vehicles; and they had their say, for example, in the Broad Wheels Act of 1753, which fixed nine inches as the minimum breadth for wheels except for those of light vehicles like traps. This type of regulation was based on a fallacy, that broad wheels did less harm than narrow ones: in fact, instead of merely causing ruts, they ground the whole road surface to powder. The real answer lay in another direction—that of the creation of turnpikes.

The first Turnpike Act had been passed in 1663. It empowered the Justices of the Peace in Hertfordshire, Cambridgeshire, and Huntingdon-shire to levy tolls on road-users, and to use the money for the repair and maintenance of the roads. They had to build toll-houses and put turnpike gates at various points on the roads. This idea caught on slowly at first, but it had obvious merits; and in 1706 it was further extended when Parliament created the first Turnpike Trust. This gave power to a body of local gentry to take over from the parish a certain length of road named in the Act, and to improve and maintain it by charging tolls. Other Trusts followed, each set up by a separate Act of Parliament. There were about 400 of them before 1750, most of them dealing with quite short stretches of ten or a dozen miles (sixteen or twenty kilometres) of main road; and the next twenty-five years saw a rapid increase in their numbers.

They were at first very unpopular with road-users, and it is not hard to see why. Local feeling was hostile to having to pay for the use of what a village or parish looked upon as its own roads. There were complaints that village folk were having to pay to keep up the main roads for the benefit of strangers. Some trusts were dishonest, others were inefficient, and both neglected the roads. The tolls charged varied greatly from place to place; there were privileged customers, like stage-coach proprietors; there was a good deal of bribery of gate-keepers. All this meant periodic riots all over the country against turnpikes; as an Act of Parliament put it in 1728, there were 'ill designing and disorderly persons' who 'associated themselves both by day and night, and cut down, pulled down, burnt, and otherwise destroyed several turnpike houses and gates'. One of the most serious disturbances took place at Bedminster, on the outskirts of Bristol, in 1749. Nevertheless the advantages of turnpikes to trade were sufficient to outweigh opposition. They led to a real improvement in the quality of many roads, and their number rose greatly in the second half of the century.

2. THE GREAT ROAD ENGINEERS

Turnpiked roads, of which there were about 22,000 miles by 1830, were patchily distributed over the country, and never formed more than one-sixth of the total road mileage. But they were a real advance, and contributed to encourage other forms of road improvement. There was a notable growth in the number of stage coaches on the roads; their quality improved too, not least in the invention of efficient forms of springing. Coach-building became a very important craft and profitable business, and there was much profit also in the large coaching inns which Charles Dickens, writing in the 1830's and 40's, was to describe so brilliantly in novels like *Pickwick Papers*. These sprang up along all the main roads and enjoyed a period of high prosperity until the railways arrived to take away their customers.[1] In 1836 there were over 3,000 coaches on the roads, providing employment for 30,000 men.

One particularly interesting development was in the postal services. In 1720 Ralph Allen, a citizen of Bath, had been granted a monopoly of

[1] However, prosperity was to return with the coming of popular motoring in the 1920's.

the country (i.e. outside London) posts, and had established a system of cross-country posts conveyed by postboys on horseback. This had not worked too well, partly because the postboys were at the mercy of the highwaymen who abounded in the 18th century, lurking in the thickets by the roadside and especially troublesome on the edges of the towns, in places like Hampstead Heath. Then came the advance of stage coaches and the development of turnpikes; and in 1784 John Palmer of Bath got the government to accept the idea of a Mail Coach service protected by armed guards. These fast coaches carried the Royal Mails—and passengers as well—between the chief towns until they in their turn were replaced by the railways in the 1840's.

The increase in road traffic and in turnpikes opened the way to a new career—that of the road engineer. This age of commercial and industrial advance offered amazing opportunities to the men who had the skill and the imagination to build roads and canals, bridges and docks and harbours. Brindley was one who seized his chance. Another of very different kind was John Smeaton (1724–92), who built harbours, bridges, mills, and canals; among his achievements were a more efficient blowing cylinder for Roebuck's Carron Iron Works and the building (1756–9) of the third lighthouse on the Eddystone Rock off Plymouth.[1] Among such men three road engineers must be numbered—John Metcalfe, Thomas Telford, and John Loudon Macadam.

John Metcalfe (1717–1810) came from Knaresborough in Yorkshire, and had been blinded by smallpox at the age of six. 'Blind Jack of Knaresborough' was a person of remarkable character who contrived, despite his disability, to live an unusually full life, being at various times soldier, farmer, publican, and road engineer. He constructed 180 miles (288 kilometres) of turnpike road, most of them in Lancashire and Yorkshire, doing the surveying himself, tapping his way across the moors which his roads crossed. In areas where the soil was soft and boggy he laid masses of heather as foundation for his roads; and he was a pioneer of drainage, digging ditches along the sides of his roads and giving them a convex surface so that rainwater could run away easily.

Thomas Telford (1757–1834), the son of a Dumfriesshire shepherd, has some claim to be regarded as the greatest of all British civil engineers. He was certainly a man of astonishing versatility. He was a bridge-builder of genius whose work lives to-day in the lovely Menai Straits Suspension Bridge; he was the engineer of the Caledonian Canal in Scotland, of the Ellesmere Canal in Shropshire with its impressive aqueduct at Pont-Cysylltau, and of the Gotha Canal in Sweden; and he built docks and harbours in Scotland. But his greatest work was as a road-builder on the Glasgow-Carlisle road, as Surveyor of Roads in Shropshire, and above all as engineer of the London–Holyhead road, begun in 1815. This road, the greatest of the coaching age, the later A5, revealed Telford's skill, in its

---

[1] The 'Smeaton Tower' now stands on Plymouth Hoe; it was displaced by the present Eddystone Lighthouse in 1882.

strong foundations, its gentle gradients, its moderate curvature, and the width of its surface. Telford, the 'Colossus of Roads', was the first president of the Institution of Civil Engineers, a body whose establishment marked the arrival of a new profession in Great Britain.

John Loudon Macadam (1756–1836) was another Scotsman. He won his early reputation as a road-builder in Cornwall, and in 1815 was appointed Surveyor-General of the roads in the Bristol area, later becoming the leading turnpike engineer in the London region. The foundations of his roads were not so heavy as those of Telford: this meant that they were cheaper, a very important point in the eyes of the Turnpike Commissioners. His most notable contribution to the art of roadmaking was his use of the type of surface which has continued to bear his name—the closely-pressed packing of angular stone fragments which consolidates into a kind of concrete; much of his actual work consisted not so much in the construction of new roads as in the repairing and strengthening of old ones by this kind of surface.

The results of the work of these and other engineers, of the increase in turnpikes and of better coach-building, may be conveniently measured by comparing times of travel in 1750, at the beginning of the real improvements, with those in 1830 just before road-travel was challenged by the railways. In 1750, under favourable conditions, it took ten days to get from London to Edinburgh: by 1830 it could be done in two. To go from London to Dover took more than a day in 1750: by 1820 it took ten hours. The time to Brighton over the same period fell from a day to five and a half hours. To reach fashionable Bath had taken two days in the middle of the 18th century: by 1822 you could get there in just over a quarter of that time. Finally, travellers to Ireland found the Holyhead road a great boon: in 1785 the journey to the port took three days, but fifty years later it could be done in 27 hours. It was, of course, much slower to get from one provincial town to another: London was peculiarly favoured with highly-organised fleets of coaches. No doubt, too, these times indicated only the fastest journeys which the regular services offered, and they represented a high cost in horses. Coaches, like the trains of later days, did not invariably run to time; moreover, many travellers thought of comfort rather than of speed. But to the business men—to whom time was money—speed was beginning to matter greatly. It was the business men, too, who in this year 1830 were giving the warmest welcome to the first important railway undertaking, George Stephenson's Liverpool to Manchester line. Coaches had reached their maximum; industrial and commercial advance was now demanding a swifter and more efficient form of transport.

3. THE GOLDEN AGE OF CANALS

In 1759 an illiterate millwright began to cut a canal for an eccentric Duke. This began a period of about seventy years in which the canal was the most important method of industrial transport in England. An artificial waterway, quite different from a 'cut' which simply improved a natural river, it had clear advantages, which had been appreciated on the Continent, especially in France, long before they were realised in England. It was the cheapest means of transporting heavy and bulky goods, and the safest way of carrying fragile ones; there were adequate water resources in England to keep canals supplied; and they would be specially advantageous to inland industrial areas remote from navigable rivers, provided the gradients were not so severe as to make the construction of locks uneconomical or impossible. The slowness of canal transport did not, in the days before railways, counterbalance these merits.

The first modern English canal was the Sankey Brook Navigation, opened in 1757, which enabled coal to be carried by water from St Helens to Liverpool. But the one that awakened public interest was the Bridgewater Canal from Worsley to Manchester, begun in 1759 and opened in 1761. The Duke of Bridgewater, a wealthy nobleman who—so one tale goes—had been jilted and sought to forget his sorrows by turning all his energies to business, owned collieries at Worsley, some seven miles (eleven kilometres) from Manchester: but the cost of carrying the coal that distance on horseback was so high that it was difficult to find customers. It was decided to cut a canal. The engineer was James Brindley, a Derbyshire millwright, and a self-taught practical genius. Like his noble employer, Brindley was an individualist; when he found a problem difficult, he retired to bed to work it out. His canal was a masterpiece, notably in the celebrated forty feet (twelve metres) high aqueduct which carried it across the River Irwell; and it was immediately successful in its commercial purpose, for the price of coal in Manchester fell by half at once.

The Bridgewater Canal opened an era of canal building. The Duke himself, with Brindley as engineer, followed his initial venture by extending his canal from Manchester to the Mersey, an enterprise completed in 1767. A year before this a great scheme, to be known as the Grand Trunk Canal, joining the Mersey and the Trent, was launched by a group of men among whom Josiah Wedgwood was prominent (he built his Etruria works on its bank); Brindley again was its engineer. He died of overwork in 1772; the Grand Trunk was opened in 1777. These were the early stages of a generation of canal-building. Its main landmarks included the Coventry Canal (begun 1768) and the Oxford Canal (begun 1790) which between them linked the Trent and Mersey to the Thames; the Forth–Clyde (begun 1768, completed 1790); the Thames and Severn (1783–9) which joined London and the Bristol Channel; the Grand Junction (1793–1805) running from the Oxford Canal near Northampton to London; the Leeds–Liverpool (1770–1816) which crossed the Pennines by engineering feats of some magnitude, and thus linked two great industrial areas by water; and the Caledonian Canal (1803–22) in the Highlands of Scotland. The financing of these canals, in which industrialists were prominent, was often highly speculative: and the canal 'mania' of 1791–4, when numerous companies were formed, brought ruin to many rash investors.

By 1830 there were over 4,000 miles of navigable waterways in Britain.

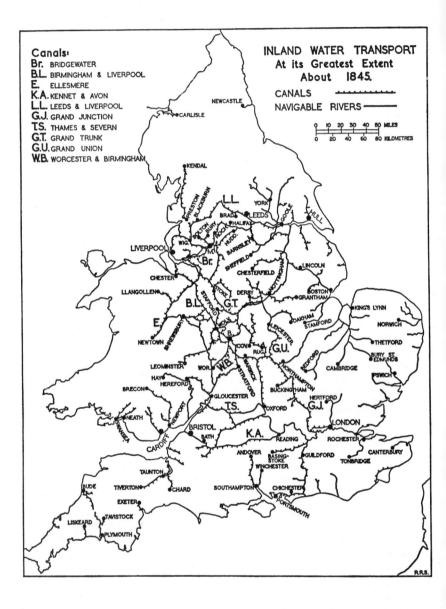

Canals:
Br. BRIDGEWATER
B.L. BIRMINGHAM & LIVERPOOL
E. ELLESMERE
K.A. KENNET & AVON
L.L. LEEDS & LIVERPOOL
G.J. GRAND JUNCTION
T.S. THAMES & SEVERN
G.T. GRAND TRUNK
G.U. GRAND UNION
W.B. WORCESTER & BIRMINGHAM

INLAND WATER TRANSPORT
At its Greatest Extent
About 1845.

CANALS ━━━━━
NAVIGABLE RIVERS ━━━━━

0 10 20 30 40 50 MILES
0   20   40   60   80 KILOMETRES

NEWCASTLE
CARLISLE
KENDAL
PRESTON
BLACKBURN
L.L.
YORK
BRAD.
LEEDS
HALIFAX
GOOLE
HULL
BOLTON
BURY
ROCH.
MIDD.
WIG.
BARNSLEY
LIVERPOOL
M.
Br.
SHEFFIELD
CHESTERFIELD
LINCOLN
CHESTER
STOKE
NOTTINGHAM
LLANGOLLEN
DERBY
BOSTON
GRANTHAM
B.L.
STAFFORD
G.T.
KING'S LYNN
E.
OAKHAM
STAMFORD
NORWICH
NEWTOWN
SHREWSBURY
NN.
B.
LEICESTER
COV.
RUG.
G.U.
THETFORD
BURY ST.
EDMUNDS
LEOMINSTER
WOR.
W.B.
WARWICK
NORTHAMPTON
BEDFORD
CAMBRIDGE
IPSWICH
HAY
HEREFORD
STRATFORD
BRECON
GLOUCESTER
BUCKINGHAM
HERTFORD
G.J.
T.S.
OXFORD
NEATH
SWANSEA
NEWPORT
BRISTOL
BATH
K.A.
READING
LONDON
ROCHESTER
CARDIFF
ANDOVER
BASING-
STOKE
GUILDFORD
TONBRIDGE
CANTERBURY
WINCHESTER
TAUNTON
BUDE
TIVERTON
CHARD
SOUTHAMPTON
CHICHESTER
PORTSMOUTH
EXETER
LISKEARD
TAVISTOCK
PLYMOUTH

R.R.S.

Two areas above all others gained immensely. One was the North Stafford-shire Potteries, with its new water connection with the Mersey and the port of Liverpool. The other was Birmingham (which got its first canal in 1772). To the north it was linked with the Grand Trunk and Liverpool, to the south with London via the Grand Junction; through Worcester it had access to the Severn and the Bristol Channel, and through Warwick to Oxford. Birmingham became and has remained the hub of the English canal system.

The canals, which were above all carriers of goods, did much to promote the Industrial Revolution. Their great age lasted until the 1840s; then, comparatively suddenly, the prosperity of nearly all vanished. They had been built to no plan: they varied in width, and a cross-country journey might involve dealing with half a dozen companies. Their financing was local; often they cost far more than anticipated – partly through wartime inflation up to 1815; their investors took their profits and bothered little about future upkeep of locks and banks. But the main reason for ultimate failure was the coming of another form of transport equally capable of carrying heavy goods, far more adaptable, and much faster—the railway. Some canals indeed (e.g. the Leeds–Liverpool and the Kennet and Avon) carried their maximum goods traffic in the later 1840s, because the railways at first concentrated on passengers; but once the railways developed cheap and effective goods services, the canals were commercially doomed.

8   The Growth of Overseas Trade

1. BRITISH TRADE IN THE 18TH CENTURY

Just as industry grew in the 18th century, so did trade, both at home and overseas, expand. One of the most remarkable features of British economic advance in the century was the growth of imports and exports alike. The money value of imports in 1800 was over seven times what it had been in 1700, and that of exports nearly seven times. Even when we allow for the growth in population by about fifty per cent over the same period, and even when we take into account the rise in prices, which gave an exaggerated impression of the actual increase of trade in goods, it remains true that there was an immense trading development in this hundred years. The growth was not steady; there were times when business fell off sharply, as for example between 1775 and 1780, because of the American War of Independence. The rate of growth, both of imports and of exports, was much faster in the second half of the century than in the first—and it was enormously accelerated after about 1780. In other words, industrial development, demanding more imported raw materials and making more finished goods for sale in the world's markets, was beginning to move fast after about 1750; and very fast after about 1780—that is, in the period when power-driven machinery was first beginning to make its presence felt.

The main items of British trade continued for much of the century to be what they had been in its early part. Woollens, for example, remained in first place: the hardware of the Black Country and the cutlery of Sheffield both remained important. But some notable changes were taking place. Cotton goods rose very fast as an export, and in fact they passed woollens just after 1800. The last decade of the 18th century saw the beginnings of a great rise in the exports of iron and coal. There was one very interesting change in the other direction. At the start of the 18th century wheat had been a major item of export from England, which was looked upon as one of the granaries of Europe; but by about 1750 England had definitely ceased to be a corn-exporting country and had become a corn-importing one instead.

Three other items have to be added into the reckoning of British exports. First, British merchant ships made much money by the work they did carrying other countries' goods: in the 17th century it had been the Dutch who dominated this carrying trade of the world, but now the British had captured much of it. Secondly, British merchants did a big re-export trade in goods from the British colonies in America. The trade regulations laid it down that certain goods from the colonies—and these the biggest items of their exports, like dyestuffs and tobacco—had to be sent to Britain in the first place before being passed on elsewhere. Thirdly, a growing proportion of English shipping was devoted to the Slave Trade, the traffic in negroes from West Africa to the West Indies and to the southern colonies of the American mainland. The takings from this were great, as the dealers of Bristol and Liverpool knew, and were important in the total of British overseas trading profits.

Overseas trade was much regulated by the government, at any rate as far as it could make its regulations effective in practice; for most statesmen, business men and economists believed in what came to be known as 'Mercantilism'. This meant, broadly, that trade should not be allowed to develop on its own and find its own outlets, but that it should be directed into certain channels by the government for the benefit of the community as a whole—or for that part of it which was influential enough to get the ear of the government. Most British governments of the century had certain aims in trade policy. They wished to promote English shipping and to strengthen the mercantile marine; not merely because shipping was profitable, but because it was from the mercantile marine that the Navy, by the odious system of the press-gang, recruited its sailors in wartime; and Britain was much at war during this century. They wished to protect the old-established woollen industry, which at the start of the century accounted for about half of all the exports: hence the regulations against the calico importers that we have already noticed. Agriculture likewise needed special treatment, for most people in Britain depended on the land for their living, and nearly all the M.P.s were landowners; so there was a system of bounties on the export of corn to encourage the growers. The overseas colonies had a very important place in the trade regulations; for they were held to exist for the benefit of the home country, and their trade was to be governed primarily with a view to the well-being of Britain. Therefore there were many laws governing colonial trade and industry—forbidding altogether certain manufactures in the colonies and directing that certain exports should be sent only to Britain.

2. SPAIN AND SIR ROBERT WALPOLE

When the century began, Great Britain was on the verge of war with France; the war came in 1701 and lasted until 1713, being known as the War of the Spanish Succession. From the economic point of view it was one of the most important wars in which Great Britain has ever taken part. It benefited British trade greatly, for both France, Britain's enemy, and Holland, Britain's ally, lost commercial ground during its course, whereas British trade increased. Indeed, it increased so obviously that public opinion, led by the Tories who paid most of the land tax which financed the war, turned against the Whig government on the ground that the merchants, who were mostly Whigs, were doing too well out of the war and were prolonging it for their own benefit. Moreover, it brought several solid commercial gains. The Methuen Treaty with Portugal, signed in 1703, allowed port wine into England at reduced rates of duty in return for similar Portuguese concessions to English hardware and textiles. The Treaty of Utrecht (1713), which ended the war, gave Britain important trading privileges in the Spanish Empire (the Indies) in Central and South America. The 'Asiento' gave Britain the monopoly of selling slaves to the Spanish colonists, and British merchants were given the right to send one ship a year, laden with British goods, to the great fair at Portobello. The French handed over Nova Scotia, recognised Britain's right to Newfoundland, and surrendered claims to vast territories in northern Canada to the Hudson's Bay Company. Finally, as a measure of security in the course of the war, England made in 1707 the Act of Union with Scotland. This gave the Scots free trade, opening to them on the same terms as to Englishmen English markets abroad and in the colonies; thus creating Great Britain as a trading unit.

The waters round the coasts of the Spanish Indies were known to Englishmen as the South Seas, and they provided the background for the celebrated South Sea Bubble of 1720. The attractive possibilities of the trade in those regions had encouraged a group of Englishmen to form in 1711 a company for exploiting it. Nine years later, in return for a monopoly of the Asiento and of the trade in the South Seas, the Company agreed to take over the responsibility for much of the National Debt, amounting at this time to about £50,000,000. This encouraged public confidence in the Company to soar to great heights, and in the first six months of 1720 the value of the Company's stock rose from £130 to over £1,000. A wave of speculation accompanied this, with wild investment in all sorts of schemes, many of them fraudulent or absurd, like those for exporting

Spanish jackasses for unspecified purposes to unspecified regions, or for transforming quicksilver into gold. This was the famous Bubble. It could not last, and it burst when confidence in the South Sea Company suddenly began to fail, and its shareholders started to sell, thus sending the price of shares tumbling down. Many people were ruined, and there was a cry for vengeance, the louder because members of the government had been deeply involved in the scheme.

The Bubble was a disaster—but a disaster of a kind that could only happen in a prosperous community which had money to invest. It was a sign of the growing trading energy of Britain. Further, it helped to open the road to power to a politician who was destined to do much for British trade. Sir Robert Walpole, already known as a capable financier, became in 1721 chief minister, remaining so for twenty-one years. In that time he did much to promote British trade. He kept Britain out of European wars, knowing that however much a war might pay the merchants for a short period, peace was in the long run better for business, and far better for a country like Britain which was becoming increasingly interested in overseas trade. He tried in various ways to help British exporters: he removed the restrictions on the export of some goods, allowed the raw materials for others to come in free of duty, and paid bounties on the export of corn, gunpowder, silks and other commodities. He tried to simplify the Book of Rates which laid down the amount of customs duty payable on various articles, and introduced the bonded warehouse system. Because public opinion was much alarmed about the size of the National Debt, which had risen greatly during the wars against Louis XIV, Walpole made strenuous efforts to reduce it, notably by creating a Sinking Fund, whereby so much was set aside from taxation each year to pay off the principal of the Debt.[1]

The terms of the Treaty of Utrecht which dealt with the Spanish Indies were difficult to enforce. It was possible in theory to limit trade between Britain and the Indies to one ship a year; the government in Madrid, unwilling to abandon the monopoly of trade with its vast American possessions, thought so. In practice things were different. The colonists in the Indies wanted to trade with foreigners, and to buy from them cloth, hardware and trinkets as well as slaves. A considerable illicit trade grew up. English smugglers got involved in affrays with Spanish *garda-costas*, and English seamen were killed and injured and taken prisoner by the Spaniards. Old memories of the Inquisition were revived, and atrocity stories arose, the most celebrated of which concerned a Captain Jenkins, who told how in a fight with the Spaniards his ear had been cut off, and how he had 'commended his cause to his country and his soul to his God'. It seems not impossible that a sea-captain might have said something different from this in such circumstances. Walpole wanted a peaceful settlement but public opinion, fanned by his political opponents, clamoured for war; so did many merchants. So in 1739 Walpole yielded

---

[1] For more information about Walpole's financial policy, see below, pp. 147-8.

and the War of Jenkins' Ear broke out. At first Britain fought only Spain; but before long this war merged into a wider conflict, the War of the Austrian Succession (1740–8), in which the chief opponent was France.

3. AMERICA AND INDIA: WORLD TRADE AND WORLD EMPIRE

During the 18th century Great Britain fought five wars with France. Two—those of the Spanish (1702–13) and Austrian (1740–8) Successions —have just been mentioned. The third was the Seven Years War (1756–1763), which decided that both India and Canada should develop under British and not under French rule. The fourth was the War of American Independence (1775–83), the most notable military defeat in modern British history, involving the loss of the Thirteen Colonies which became the United States of America. The fifth was the Revolutionary War (1793–1802), in which Britain was fighting a new France, a France which turned out its ancient line of kings and became a Republic inspired with revolutionary zeal to convert Europe to its ideas. These wars were fought for a variety of reasons. Some were political, involving quarrels between the two countries over the Balance of Power in Europe. Others were economic: a conflict for empire overseas sprang very largely from trade rivalry. French and British fought one another on the high seas and in the islands of the Caribbean, around the Great Lakes of North America, in Bengal and on the Coromandel coast round Madras. Commercial 'interests', groups of merchants directly interested in the trade with certain areas like India and the West Indies, put much pressure on the government. Thus in the Seven Years War the chief minister, William Pitt the Elder, was on very friendly terms with the wealthy merchants of the city of London. Pitt wanted to extend British power over Canada and other lands beyond the seas by victory over France; behind the vision of world empire was the prospect of solid material gain, of hard cash resulting from more trade.

There was a well-established trade with the Thirteen Colonies of the American mainland, whose principal exports were the tobacco and dye-stuffs of the southern colonies and the timber of New England. A major object of the Seven Years War was to protect these colonies from the French. This is why British merchants wanted to wrest Canada from France, not because they foresaw the possibilities of developing Canada itself, which seemed little more than a wilderness. Only the members of the Hudson's Bay Company, anxious to capture the fur trade from the French, were directly interested in its development. The most commercially attractive of British possessions in the New World lay in the blue waters of the Caribbean. Here Barbados and Jamaica and a handful of smaller islands were bringing riches to those who owned the slave-worked sugar plantations and shipped their valuable produce home to England. The Seven Years War added more to Britain's territory in this favoured area. The 'sugar-interest' indeed was not wholly enthusiastic about this, for the new possessions meant more rivals in the trade, as these former enemy sugar colonies were now protected by British tariffs. But the importance of these West Indian possessions may be measured by the fact that when peace came to be signed in 1763, there was much debate in the Cabinet whether Britain should retain Canada, or hand it back to the French and keep instead the two big French islands of Guadeloupe and Martinique.

The most powerful interest of all was the East India Company. Founded in 1600, this company of London merchants had in the 17th century been forced by Dutch competition to retire from the East Indies to the mainland of India, where it established a handful of widely scattered 'factories', as its warehouses were called, at Madras and Calcutta, at Surat and Bombay. In the early 18th century its interests lay in items of trade from the East which were beginning to become important, like the calicoes and muslins whose import into England was alarming the woollen manu-facturers; or the tea, now becoming a regular, though very expensive, item of trade, coming not from India itself but from China, where by 1700 the Company had secured a foothold in Canton; or the Chinese porcelain which Dutch influence at the English court in the reign of William III made fashionable. These were luxury items, as were the traditional goods of 'John' Company's trade, spices and silks and rich cloths. The Company was highly influential, carrying great weight in Lords and Commons alike.

Its directors needed all their influence as the century wore on, for they had to take up in India a challenge from the French East Indian Company. There was warfare between the two Companies for much of the period between 1740 and 1763. The East India Company maintained its own army and navy, and it also drew much support from the government at home. The conflict did not stop with Robert Clive's victory at Plassey in 1757, which ensured that henceforward Britain and not France should dominate Indian affairs. When in 1778 the French joined the Americans against the British in the War of American Independence, the forces of the Company had to resist a coalition of native princes organised against them by the French from their base in Mauritius. The course of events had made this company of British merchants the rulers of many millions of people in Bengal and other provinces of India. During the next eighty years two developments took place which together left the East India Company merely an interesting relic. First, it gradually lost its political power over the peoples of India, becoming in effect merely the agent carrying out the orders of the British government, until in 1858, a century after Plassey, the Crown took over direct control of those lands in India (by that date almost two-thirds of the entire country) which the Company had conquered. Secondly, in 1813 it lost its monopoly of the India trade, and in 1833 that of the China trade, and in effect ceased to trade at all.

4. THE SLAVE TRADE

The Slave Trade, so far as Englishmen were concerned, began when John Hawkins in the 16th century first picked up a cargo of negroes in West Africa and took them across the Atlantic to sell to the Spanish colonists in the Indies. It grew and expanded in the 17th century as more colonies were developed in the islands of the Caribbean as well as on the American mainland; and it came to embrace British colonies like Jamaica and most of the Thirteen Colonies as well as Spanish and French ones. Virginia, for example, received its first boatload of negroes in 1619. The trade grew more elaborate, affecting other commodities as well as slaves. One version involved exchanging the slaves for molasses in the West Indies, to be carried north to Massachusetts and converted into rum—which was used to buy more slaves. Another involved Virginia rather than the West Indies; the negroes were exchanged for tobacco, which was brought to England and the proceeds of its sale turned into trinkets and various oddments of 'Brummagem ware': these would pay native chieftains on the Guinea coast for another load of slaves.

The basis of the whole business, the actual trade in slaves itself, was as simple as it was diabolical. Every year at a number of settlements on the West African coast, like Cormantine and Cape Coast Castle, there assembled crowds of wretched negroes, men and women alike. They had been captured in the ceaseless tribal wars, and this was the penalty of defeat. The victorious chieftains sold them like so many cattle to the slave-traders, who packed them on board their ships. These were specially fitted for the purpose, with narrow spaces, little more than racks, below the deck, into which the slaves were chained. The effect of a voyage—which might last many weeks—in such conditions upon negroes who had never been on the sea before was terrible, especially if epidemic disease broke out among them. They did not go on deck often: for it was not unknown for the captives to leap into the sea and die by drowning rather than endure the voyage any longer. Losses on the voyage were frequently appalling, sometimes rising to about one in four of all the negroes carried. When this horrible 'Middle Passage' was over, the survivors were sold, usually by auction to the highest bidder. About 1770, 100,000 Africans were exported annually, half of them in British ships.

The profits from this trade went to English merchants, many of them respectable, God-fearing men living comfortable lives in fine houses in Bristol and other towns. Bristol was its leading centre in the first part of the 18th century, but was overtaken by Liverpool, which by the end of the century had about six-sevenths of the trade. The trade expanded considerably in this period; great sums of money were invested in it and thousands of sailors were engaged. Between 1783 and 1793 Liverpool traders carried over 300,000 slaves to the West Indies and sold them for £15,000,000. All told, the trade represented a very powerful commercial interest which it would be very difficult to dislodge.

Not until about the middle of the 18th century did the public conscience begin to be concerned about the horrors of the trade. Then the lead in attacking it was taken by a number of Quakers; and John Wesley also denounced it. In 1772 the legal decision in *Somerset's Case*, in which Chief Justice Mansfield declared that slavery was illegal in England, encouraged a movement against the slave trade; and in 1787 a committee for its abolition was formed, with Granville Sharp and Thomas Clarkson among its leading members. They went to great trouble to collect evidence, finding out precise information about the exact amount of space given to slaves on shipboard and similar details; and they began to publish pamphlets to stir public opinion against the trade. But they quickly came to the conclusion that they would not succeed unless they could get a powerful spokesman in Parliament; and they found him in the man whose name is always most closely associated with the abolition of the slave trade, William Wilberforce (1759–1833).

Wilberforce was twenty-eight when he decided to throw all his energies into a cause which he looked upon as a crusade. He was a wealthy young man, from a prosperous merchant family of Hull; he had entered the Commons at twenty-one, and quickly made a mark; and he was an intimate friend of the Prime Minister, William Pitt the Younger. Hitherto a rather fashionable young man about town, he had lately undergone a religious conversion: he altered his mode of life, dropped his gambling, gave much of his income to charity, and devoted himself to the new cause. At first the prospects looked bright, for public opinion seemed to be favourable; and Pitt spoke strongly in favour of abolition. Then in 1789 came the French Revolution, and the skies darkened, especially after Britain and France went to war in 1793. All reform became suspect. The cause of the slave-traders appeared to be patriotic: for was not the trade, in the words of its defenders, 'a nursery of seamen'? Would it not be disastrous folly in a war in which Great Britain was fighting for life to abolish so rich a trade and one so important to the Navy? And would it really benefit humanity? Would not the merchants of other nations step in and carry on the traffic?[1] These arguments were very strong in wartime. Pitt became lukewarm, and declined to place the government's support behind Wilberforce's proposals for abolition.

Yet abolition was postponed, not cancelled. Wilberforce persevered, regularly introducing his proposals to the Commons. His moral case was very strong, and the evils of the trade were generally admitted: and the public conscience, despite the war, swung round again to his support. In 1806 Pitt died; Charles James Fox, ever a generous supporter of the cause, became chief minister, and introduced in the Commons resolutions abolishing the slave trade in British ships. Fox too died in 1806: but his proposals became law in 1807. The crusade had succeeded—at

[1] They did, particularly Americans both North and South. The transatlantic slave trade perhaps reached its peak in the late 1830s, at about 135,000 Negroes per annum.

the cost of the destruction of an important trade worth millions of pounds a year. For Wilberforce it was only the first stage; he turned his attention next to the abolition of slavery itself within the British Empire.[1]

9 The Great French War (1793-1815) and its Aftermath

1. THE WAR AND BRITISH INDUSTRY AND TRADE

From 1793 to 1815 Great Britain was almost continuously at war with France. The war was longer and more costly than any in which Britain had previously been engaged in modern times. In its later stages nearly half a million men were serving in the army and navy. It was a war against a new France—in its early years against a country fired with enthusiasm for the revolutionary principles of 'Liberty, Equality, and Fraternity', and later against the most powerful military tyranny the modern world had seen, headed by Napoleon Bonaparte, a soldier of incomparable genius. The strain on Britain's economy was greater than ever before: and the morale of the people was severely tested. Twice the country seemed on the brink of ruin: once in 1797 when the Navy mutinied and a financial crisis caused the Bank of England to stop paying cash, and a second time in 1804, when Napoleon was massing his army of invasion on the cliffs at Boulogne. Many factors enabled Britain to survive and ultimately to emerge not only victorious but also more powerful than at any previous point in her history. The strength of her own navy was one; the heroism of the national armies of Spain, Russia, and Prussia, rising against the tyrant, was another. Yet certainly one highly important reason for her success lay in her economic resources.

British naval supremacy, which for practical purposes was complete (except occasionally in certain waters) throughout the war, had two immense economic advantages. First, Britain, unlike the lands of the Continent, remained entirely free from invasion; factories and foundries could work without fear of destruction by invading forces, and British crops were never harvested by foreign soldiers. Secondly, naval supremacy made it possible to drive French and other enemy merchantmen off the seas, and to safeguard British traders. It was always a major object of British naval strategy to keep the seas open for British merchant shipping; to enable British merchants to sell freely to neutrals, and to force, either directly or by smuggling, British goods into enemy-held countries. This policy, after a considerable struggle, was highly successful, and contributed much to the downfall of Napoleon's régime.

[1] See below, p. 132.

The direct effect of the war on British industries varied greatly. In general it accelerated the introduction of steam-power and machinery. Some particular industries benefited greatly: iron most notably. There was a steady demand for iron goods; and the needs of the war encouraged the development of technical processes, so that, for example, Cort's techniques of puddling and rolling were adopted much more rapidly and widely than they might otherwise have been. Other industries that profited included copper and the other metal trades, chemicals, and shipbuilding. The textile industries were affected in various ways. Among woollens the manufacturers of the coarser clothes which could be used for uniforms did well: those whose products were lighter and finer did not prosper so much. This helped to speed the supremacy of the West Riding, where the coarser cloths were made, and to quicken the decline of the West Country and East Anglia where the finer materials were more important. The cotton industry was in some ways upset, principally because the British blockade of Europe led to disputes with the greatest neutral power, the United States, and these involved interruption of the supplies of raw cotton from the southern states. The pottery industry suffered hardship because the European demand for its products fell off. Moreover, development of industry was hindered because capital became more expensive to borrow: the government was raising large loans, which sent up the interest rates. This tended to make things even more difficult for those industries which were already hit by the war, but not to affect those which did well out of it; people were ready to lend their money to a firm that was making guns for which there was a steady demand, but not to invest it in one whose market was uncertain.

One industry that was much stimulated by the war was agriculture. The number of Enclosure Acts increased remarkably during the war years. Wheat prices rose sharply, encouraging farmers to put more land under the plough: much of this land was marginal, pasture or waste which it only paid to till when prices were high. This development did not take place simply or even mainly because continental supplies were cut off; for Britain was still able to supply the great bulk of her own food, and furthermore Napoleon in the later years of the war allowed French farmers, anxious to get rid of surpluses, to export food to Britain. But the population was rising fast; there were soldiers, British and allied, to feed; and transport was bad, often causing very serious local grain shortages. So farmers on the whole did well, and many of them, relying on the high prices, were ready to take longer leases of their lands and to pay higher rents.

Overseas trade was much dislocated by the war, and particularly by the various ways in which British and French attempted to blockade each other's possessions. Quite early in the struggle the French attempted to exclude British goods from the mainland of Europe; while the British for their part declared a blockade of the French-controlled coastline, with the object of stopping neutral shipping from capturing the export trade to France. This type of conflict reached its climax in Napoleon's famous

Continental System and in the British reply, the Orders-in-Council. The Continental System was proclaimed in a series of decrees, of which the most important were those at Berlin (1806) and Milan (1807), issued after a succession of Napoleonic victories which seemed to lay all the powers of Europe at his feet either as conquered foes or submissive allies. In effect they said that the British Isles were in a state of blockade and that no trade with them was permitted; any neutral vessel which allowed itself to be inspected for contraband by the British authorities, or which called at a British port, was to be confiscated. The British Orders-in-Council, first issued between the two Napoleonic Decrees, required all neutral shipping bound for Europe either to call at a British port or submit itself for inspection by the British naval authorities.

The economic warfare which these measures provoked lasted until about 1812. Napoleon's aim was not to starve Britain into submission by cutting off supplies. It was rather to bring the 'nation of shopkeepers' to their knees by preventing them from selling their goods overseas: the British were to be *'vaincus par l'abondance'*, destroyed by a glut of goods which they had made but could not sell. This policy caused much hardship at certain times and in certain areas in Britain, notably in the bad winter of 1811–12. But in the long run it failed. British control of the sea made possible widespread smuggling of British goods into Europe from a number of bases—either small islands off the coast like Heligoland and Malta, or, in the later stages, mainland ports like Gothenburg and Salonika. Moreover, it enabled Britain to extend her export trade considerably in other parts of the world, like the United States, South and Central America (which had at this time risen in revolt against Spain) and the West Indies (including the former French colonies there). The peoples of Europe who wanted British goods hated the Continental System: and in 1811 Tsar Alexander of Russia refused to operate it any longer, thus provoking Napoleon's disastrous invasion of Russia in 1812, which led to a widespread European revolt against the tyrant and so to the collapse of his power.

The most unfortunate consequence of the Continental System, so far as Britain was concerned, was that it led to a serious quarrel with the United States, whose trade was much interfered with by both British and French regulations. Other factors helped to make a difficult situation into an occasion of war. Sailors from the British Navy deserted in large numbers to the American mercantile marine, where pay and conditions were superior, and the activities of British naval search-parties in recovering them from American vessels—and taking off American seamen instead—led to bitter disputes. There was a lively and outspoken group of American politicians who were anxious to attack Britain while she was involved with Napoleon, and so seize part of Canada. In 1812 Britain and the United States went to war (the so-called War of 1812) over these things. This war lasted for two years and brought no decisive result.

Yet on the whole it is probably true to say that British trade and industry made progress during the long wars. Certainly the new techniques both in food production and in industry contributed powerfully to enable Britain to withstand Napoleon and to play a leading role in his defeat. Certainly, too, the total amount of trade rose during the war. Exports in particular expanded substantially. There were good times and bad, booms like those in 1802 and 1809–10 and slumps like that of 1811–12. On balance Britain's economic life stood the strain reasonably well.

2. THE WAR AND CONDITIONS OF LIFE

In what ways did the war affect the conditions in which people lived? This sort of question is always difficult to answer precisely, because large-scale wars are ruinous for some civilians, taking away their jobs altogether, and yet bring fat incomes to others whose work happens to be vitally necessary in wartime: and it is specially difficult for the French War of 1793–1815, for this particular war coincided in time with the revolutionary changes in agriculture and industry. It is impossible to decide how far conditions of life in those years were changed by the war and how far the same changes would have come about anyway because of the coming of machinery and the spread of enclosures. All that can be done is to record the chief changes of the war years and indicate how the wars at least helped to bring them about.

The most obvious change of this period which affected everybody in the country was a great rise in prices, which at once went sharply upwards on the outbreak of war, and were by its end almost double what they had been. Wheat prices, the most important of all, which had averaged 53s. 8d. per quarter over the years 1790–5, were 94s. 3d. for the years 1811–15; and they had been even higher in some single years, touching 126s. 6d. in 1812. This sort of rise is an economic phenomenon which normally accompanies wars, when certain types of goods which everybody wants become scarce. The rise of population of this period was also partly responsible for it. Moreover, the government's financial policy during the war helped to cause an inflation of prices. In the first few years of war the government, whose head was William Pitt the Younger, chose to borrow heavily from the Bank of England rather than to raise taxes. This helped to cause a drain of gold from the Bank, which in 1797 was compelled to suspend cash payments[1] (which were not resumed until 1821). Payments were henceforth made in paper notes: and large numbers of small country banks sprang up, each issuing its own notes. The result was an increase in the amount of paper money in circulation, which stimulated the rise in prices. Nevertheless the situation in Britain was nothing like so serious as it was in France, where the revolutionary paper money, the *assignats*, became almost worthless.

As prices rose, so did wages, so far as we can tell with the rather insufficient information we have. But they rose more slowly, and they rose much more unevenly over the country as a whole and in different sorts of

[1] i.e., payments in coin and not in notes. See also p. 143.

jobs. Skilled workers did well, and best of all in London: they came nearest to keeping pace with prices. Among the unskilled workmen it paid better to be in a town than in the country: for the wages which rose least of all were those of the agricultural labourer. Farmers passed on to their work-men in higher wages little of what they were getting in higher wheat prices. There can be no doubt that times were desperately hard for many people during the war, like the farm-labourers in Sussex whose wages appear to have risen only from 9s. a week in 1790 to 13s. in 1810, and then actually to have fallen to 12s.; or the handloom weavers of Bolton (the town where they had not so long before gone round with £5 notes stuck in their hats) whose wages dropped from 25s. to 15s. between 1805 and 1808; or the nail-makers whose working day in 1812 apparently started at four in the morning and went on until eleven at night.

The distress caused to farm-labourers by rising prices was evident in the countryside quite early in the war: it was aggravated for them by the fact that the coming of power-driven machinery was at this very time killing the by-industries, particularly the spinning, which had long added to the family income of agricultural labourers in many areas. In 1795 the Berkshire magistrates, meeting at the Pelican Inn in the parish of Speen, near Newbury in Berkshire, discussed how to deal with this distress. They decided to fix rates of wages according to the price of bread, giving an allowance varying with the size of the labourer's family: and they pro-vided that where the farmers did not pay a sufficient wage a supplement should be given out of the local rates. This 'Speenhamland System', a local measure for Berkshire, spread over much of southern England, and remained a feature of agricultural life there until it was abolished in 1834. Other countries and parishes adopted their own, often similar, plans for coping with the poor.[1]

'Speenhamland' confused the problem of wages with that of parish relief or the Poor Law. In 1782 Gilbert's Act had provided that parishes might join into 'unions' to build poor-houses, to which only the aged and infirm were to be sent. What was to be done with the able-bodied poor who could not or would not get work? Presumably they would have to be given some sort of outdoor relief, and this was what the Berkshire magistrates were doing. Their action turned out in the long run to be a disaster for the community as a whole and for the agricultural labourers in particular. At a time when Britain's population was rising very fast (in the 30 years 1791–1821 it increased by about 46 per cent) there was surplus labour; and wages were low. 'Speenhamland' kept them low: farmers were in effect subsidised from rates. These rose alarmingly; they had been under £2,000,000 in the 1780s, but by 1815 they were about £6,000,000. When the war ended, prices fell and farmers went bankrupt, the pinch of the rates was felt—and the Speenhamland system was blamed for demoralising the poor, making them

[1] A variation upon it was the 'Roundsman' system, used in the Thames Valley: by this labourers were 'sent the round' of the parish with a ticket which enabled the farmers to employ them: part of their wages came out of rates.

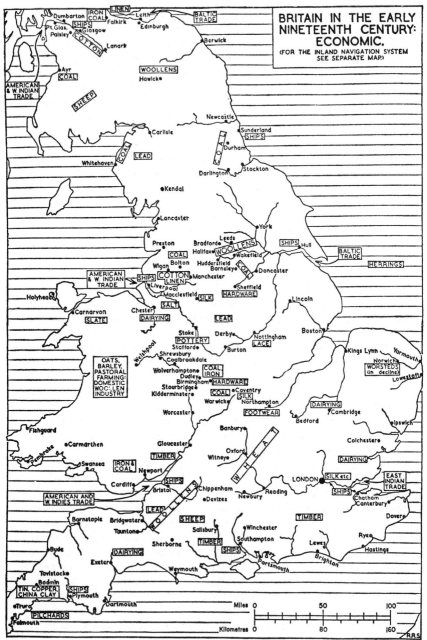

BRITAIN IN THE EARLY
NINETEENTH CENTURY:
ECONOMIC.
(FOR THE INLAND NAVIGATION SYSTEM
SEE SEPARATE MAP.)

idle and encouraging large families. The one thing to be said in favour of the system was that it did guarantee a subsistence wage to the poor, though the subsistence was at a very low level. Some historians think this may have prevented the spread of revolutionary ideas among the poor at this time.

The system did not catch on in the new industrial areas of the north and midlands as it had in the more rural southern counties. But the industrial areas had their own troubles during these war years. One of them was the attitude of the government to trade unions. Although the French Revolution of 1789 had at first been enthusiastically welcomed by many Englishmen of all classes, who saw it in a great move towards freedom for the people of France, this attitude soon changed. The growth of violence and the 'Reign of Terror'; the intention of the leaders of the Revolution to thrust their doctrines upon other peoples, by force if necessary; the execution of the French King in January, 1793—all these things swung the ruling class in Britain towards the outbreak of war with France later in 1793. The effect of this was quickly felt in Britain. Pitt's government turned against all movements of reform. Various societies demanding parliamentary reform were attacked and their leaders tried for sedition: *Habeas Corpus* was suspended, and laws passed restricting the right of public meeting. In such circumstances working-class movements were bound to fall under suspicion, and by a piece of panic legislation, supported by the great influence of Wilberforce, trade unions were declared illegal by the Combination Acts of 1799 and 1800.[1]

The later years of war witnessed outbreaks of violence in the industrial areas. These were the Luddite Riots, so called because they were said to have been directed by one Ned Ludd, a mysterious figure with headquarters in Sherwood Forest. 'A single General Ludd there was none, though hopeful magistrates occasionally thought they had caught him.'[2] If he lived at all he may only have been a half-witted boy who one day smashed up some machinery. But the riots were real enough. They reflected the natural hostility felt by uneducated men towards machines which were putting them out of work, as well as the unemployment caused by wartime fluctuations of trade. In 1811–12 rioters in Nottinghamshire smashed a thousand stocking-frames which, they claimed, the employers were using to make low-grade goods. Parliament retaliated by making frame-breaking a capital offence, despite a great speech against the bill by the poet Lord Byron. Further riots followed in Cheshire, Lancashire, and Yorkshire: the workers attacked power-looms and shearing-machines, and in Lancashire, where the cotton trade was in depression, they demanded cheaper potatoes. The government, believing that a widespread conspiracy was plotting revolution, took stern measures. The conspiracy was a myth; and many details of the 'revolution' were invented by government spies and by *agents provocateurs* who deliberately stirred up

---

[1] For details about the Combination Acts and their effect, see pp. 152–3.
[2] Malcolm Thomis: *The Luddites* (1970), p. 120.

risings in order to get evidence. But some twenty persons were put to death for various offences: among them was a lad of sixteen who had acted as sentry while his brothers were burning down a Lancashire mill. The Luddite movement was a warning of more serious trouble to come in the years after the war.

3. THE POST-WAR YEARS (1815–22)

The Battle of Waterloo was fought in June, 1815. The allied victory marked the end of Napoleon's power. But it also marked the opening of one of the grimmest periods in modern British history, years of distress and class hatred, darkened by sullen discontent and periodic riots in the industrial areas and by a policy of savage repression by the government. The mere catalogue of events makes a bitter tale. In 1816 there were riots in Spa Fields in London: and in 1817 a stone was thrown through the window of the Prince Regent's coach. The government suspended *Habeas Corpus* in 1816, and in the following year passed the Gagging Acts, forbidding public meetings except under licence from magistrates. This same year saw the 'March of the Blanketeers', when a group of cotton workers from Manchester set out to march to London to present a petition to the Prince Regent, carrying blankets with them to sleep in on the way: the march was broken up by the authorities. 1817 was also the year of the Derbyshire Insurrection, a pathetic outbreak of unemployed framework knitters, deliberately stirred up by Oliver the Spy, an *agent provocateur*: three poor men were hanged and eleven transported for life. The next year was quieter apart from a serious strike in the cotton area: but 1819 brought the terrible episode of the Peterloo Massacre. An orderly reform meeting, attended by many thousands in St. Peter's Fields, Manchester, was broken up by a charge of yeomanry: eleven were killed and hundreds injured. The government congratulated the magistrates responsible and Parliament passed the Six Acts: these extended the authorities' right of search of private houses, further suppressed public meetings, and imposed what was intended to be a crushing tax on all periodicals. Finally in 1820 a group of desperate men, extreme Radical reformers, hatched a plot, the Cato Street Conspiracy, to murder the entire Cabinet. It was discovered, and the principal conspirators were put to death.

These were only the more serious episodes. As a constant background to all this there were numerous strikes, the work of what was officially an illegal trade union movement; great meetings demanding parliamentary reform and the extension of the right to vote to the working class, addressed by powerful orators like Henry Hunt; and a lively Radical press, whose leading figure was William Cobbett, backing the reform movement and denouncing the ruling class in strong and frequently abusive language.[1]

What were the causes of this discontent, and of the distress that drove

---

[1] For further information about Cobbett, see below, pp. 98, 162.

men to act in this way? At bottom, no doubt, discontent and distress alike reflected the great changes in agriculture and industry. Factories and enclosures meant for many millions of people a harsh process of adjustment to new conditions—to the discipline of the factories, to the disappearance of the common land, to the machines which put men out of jobs. But there were other causes at work as well in these post-war years. There were, for example, bad harvests in Britain in the years 1816-19, and these contributed powerfully to distress in days when most British food was still grown at home. Not only did they send up the price of bread: they also helped bring about industrial depression, with falling trade and unemployment, for when the poor had to spend more on bread they could spend less on other things, which meant less demand for the products of mills and factories. Again, there was in these years a considerable migration of Irishmen to Lancashire and, to a smaller extent, to other British industrial areas; and this reduced the standard of living for British workmen, because the Irish, coming from a land of poverty much worse than that of Britain, were ready to accept very small wages, thus lowering the general level of wages in the areas affected. These things were not unimportant. Yet the main factors which increased distress after 1815 can be grouped under two headings—the results of the ending of the war, and the results of the policy of the government.

The ending of the war involved the sudden demobilisation of about 300,000 men, thrown on to the labour market (and the Poor Law rates) all at once. It meant also the closing down of many munitions and other factories. Those industries that had prospered most because of the war, like the iron industry, now felt the most serious shock when the government ceased to need their products. Government expenditure fell by a half within the year 1815. It is true that the end of this war, like the end of most large-scale wars, was followed by a short industrial boom, in which industry was turning out in large quantities those goods of which people at home had for some time been deprived on account of the war; and there was also a brief but high demand from overseas for British exports, which in 1815 reached the value of £51,000,000, higher than the previous record figure of £48,000,000 in 1810. But the boom collapsed, as the government orders fell off, as the number of unemployed grew, and as foreign countries, impoverished by the war and anxious to develop their own industries, sharply reduced the number of British goods they bought. This last point was especially important to a country like Britain that was becoming more and more sensitive to what happened to its growing export trade. There followed a period of depression—of bad trade and widespread unemployment—which, apart from a short-lived boom in 1818, lasted until 1821-2.

Perhaps the most striking feature of the depression was the sharp fall in prices. In 1814 prices had in general been about twice what they had been before the outbreak of the war: by 1816 they were only about one and a third times the pre-war figure, and apart from a temporary recovery in 1818, they continued to fall. This fall had serious effects upon industry: it checked the expansion of businesses, and it discouraged the borrowing of capital. Moreover, it had an unfortunate effect upon the burden of the National Debt. This had grown by the end of the Napoleonic War to the staggering figure of £834,000,000: just over thirty years before, at the end of the American War of Independence, it had been under £241,000,000. So heavy a load of debt meant that taxes had to remain high after the war in order to pay the interest: and the fall in prices meant in effect that the burden of that interest was greatly increased.

A fall in wages followed the fall in prices. Yet as far as we can tell wages as a whole do not seem to have fallen as sharply as prices: and there is some evidence to suggest that by 1830 at any rate the *real* wages of the town work-man—that is, the amount his wages would buy for him when considered together with the prices of the time—had in fact risen quite appreciably. But as always much depended on where the workman was and what his job was; and it seems pretty clear that wages were low for a very large number of workmen in these first few years after the war. This was bound to be so when there was much unemployment, as in the cotton trade: when times improved in 1818, the cotton operatives went on strike in order to bring wages back from the low level to which the employers had reduced them in the depression. The coming of Irishmen sent wages down; and it seems likely that the rise in population must have had the same effect. Between 1801 and 1831 the population rose by 50 per cent.; there was more labour available, and a good deal of it was juvenile labour, which was cheap. At the extreme end of the scale were the handloom weavers, whose plight was now worsening from year to year; those in Bolton were getting only eight shillings a week in the early 1820's. If things were difficult in the towns, they were undoubtedly worse in the countryside, where Speenhamland kept wages down, and where the enclosure movement continued to deprive many cottagers of their right to keep a cow or a pig on the common—or to take away their land altogether. Wage rates seem to have fallen appreciably in the agricultural areas in the post-war years.

The second major factor in the distress was the attitude of the govern-ment, throughout these post-war years a reactionary one, with Lord Liverpool as Prime Minister and the much-hated Lord Castlereagh, the Foreign Secretary, as its leading spirit. Its members were men of property, most of them lords of great estates; men born in the later years of the 18th century, whose adult lives had been overshadowed by the French Revo-lution and the twenty years of war which it had brought. Two things governed their attitude towards politics: one was a lasting fear of revolu-tions, the other a desire to defend the interests of the landowning class whose members filled nearly all the seats in Parliament. They feared that revolution might come to Britain, that the British working class might one day rise and do what the revolutionaries had done in France—seize the property of the wealthy, execute many of the nobility, destroy the monarchy, proclaim a republic, and apparently deluge the land with blood.

This was a fantastic vision, unsupported by evidence: the only revolutionaries of that kind in Britain were a handful of extremists who were quite out of touch with the opinions of the ordinary workpeople. But its possibility seemed to the members of the government to justify a policy of repression. Moreover, one practical fact gave ministers much ground for fears of disorder, though not of revolution. There was at this date no police force in England apart from such a special body as the Bow Street Runners. Any disturbances had to be quelled either by the yeomanry, which represented the upper and middle classes, or by the regular troops; the latter were not numerous, were sometimes more inclined to sympathise with rioters than to fire upon them, and were indeed generally drawn from the worst elements in the population.

To quell riots and disorders was reasonable, and the maintenance of law and order was a notable achievement. The weakness of the government's policy was its failure to adopt any constructive measures to deal with the ills that caused the riots. Instead, it turned to crush all reform movements, in the belief that the reformers were dangerous revolutionaries. Hence came the suspension of *Habeas Corpus*, which enabled the government to detain prisoners as long as it liked without bringing them to trial; the breaking-up of working-class meetings, and the enforcement of the Combination Acts; and the passage of measures like the Six Acts. Hence, too, came those uglier steps—the use of spies and *agents provocateurs*. Closely connected with these methods was the enforcement of the savage English penal code of that day, with its provision of capital punishment for over two hundred offences and its extensive use of transportation for life.[1]

These things revealed the fears of the governing class. Its economic policy seemed to show its intention to govern in its own interests, not in those of the whole community. The most famous illustration of this occurred in 1815. In that year wheat prices, which had been 126s. 6d. a quarter in 1812, fell to 65s. 7d.; for now that the war was over British ports lay open to the corn of France and of eastern Europe. Such a fall caused widespread alarm among the farmers and landowners, who had sunk much capital in developing inferior land during the war and now saw the prospect of heavy losses. So Parliament in some haste passed the Corn Law of 1815, which said that no foreign wheat was to be imported into Britain until the price of home-grown wheat reached 80s. a quarter. This law to protect the farmers and landowners was defended on the ground that agriculture must be protected lest Britain should become dependent on foreign foodstuffs, which would be disastrous in wartime: also that the amount of arable land must not be allowed to diminish, for the rural population traditionally supplied most of the nation's soldiers. Yet the real object was to defend an interest of the landowning class. The actual benefit of the Corn Law to farmers was not as great as its supporters had hoped;

[1] For further information about the penal code, see below, pp. 226-7.

the extremely high prices of wartime did not return, and there was in fact a good deal of bankruptcy among farmers at this time. Yet corn prices, aided by poor harvests, remained high: wheat prices did not fall below 70*s*. a quarter until 1820. Bread prices were too high for the poor, at least in the sense that they had to spend too much of their wages on bread and less on other necessities. For this they blamed the Corn Law and the Parliament which passed it.

In 1816 Parliament took another step which indicated its attitude, abolishing the Income Tax. When this had first been imposed by the Younger Pitt in 1798, he had promised that it would be removed as soon as the war was over; and Parliament now insisted that Pitt's successor, Liverpool, should fulfil that pledge. This meant that the fairest of taxes, which was based on a man's ability to pay, was removed. Its abolition threw an increased burden on the indirect taxes, which fell on the whole community and were proportionately most severe on the poor. What made the situation worse was that much of the taxation went to pay the interest on the National Debt—which meant that it went into the pockets of the well-to-do, the very people who benefited from the abolition of income tax.

One other example which illustrates the narrow policy of the post-war government is the maintenance of the Game Laws. These were the laws which limited the right to shoot or take game—not only pheasants and partridges but also hares and rabbits—to the landowners. The enclosure movement had encouraged many landowners to extend their parks and warrens, and had led to a stricter preservation of the game. The laws against poaching were made much more rigorous; in 1816 the labourer found at night with a net in his possession became liable to transportation for seven years, no matter whether he was actually found poaching or not. Moreover, many landowners began to protect their estates with spring-guns and man-traps, though these were abolished by law in the 1820's because they had caused so many casualties among gamekeepers. In the bad years after Waterloo, many a villager existing on the meagre wages of a labourer was only too ready to take a hare or a pheasant for the pot if he got the chance, and village opinion sympathised with him, regarding the Game Laws as cruel and unjust.

In these various ways the policy of the government, added to the effects of the ending of the war, made a bad situation worse. The hard times lasted for six or seven years: then there was a real but slow change for the better in Britain's economic circumstances. A gradual recovery followed the depression of 1819, aided mainly by a marked rise in the export trade; the quantity of British exports rose by 40 per cent. between 1819 and 1824. Wheat prices came down, bringing bread more within the grasp of the poor and thus enabling them to purchase other commodities in greater amounts. These economic changes were accompanied by changes in the membership of the government, when younger men, alert to the new problems of industry and trade, took the places of the 'Old Tories' who had ruled since before Waterloo. Among these 'New Tories' were Robert Peel the Younger, son of the Bury cotton millionaire, and William Huskisson, M.P. for the great trading city of Liverpool and a notable commercial reformer. There were plenty of hard times ahead; and the countless social problems created by the changes in industry had scarcely been tackled at all at this date. Nevertheless, at no future time in the 19th century was a great war to complicate the solution of such problems; nor was Britain to have again a government so out of touch with the needs of the people as that of the years after Waterloo.

10   Railways before 1914

Between 1830 and 1850 the main pattern of the railway system of Great Britain came into existence. This was an event of high importance, perhaps even the most important event in the whole 19th century. For the coming of the railways vastly accelerated the rate at which Britain was becoming an industrial country; it is not impossible to claim that the railways began a second Industrial Revolution. Their immediate economic effects were immense. Their building gave employment to great armies of men—for they were built almost entirely by direct human power, by thousands of muscular navvies with pick, shovel, and wheelbarrow. They made colossal new demands on the iron industry and on the coal mines. Vast sums of money were invested in them—£150,000,000 of it in the years 1846–50 alone. Their coming led to the building of new towns, to the speeding-up of trade and business, to the expansion of industry, to a huge increase in Britain's export trade. Thus they were vital to the prosperity of Victorian Britain. In social, as distinct from economic, life their influence was equally great. They opened a new world to millions of humble folk simply because, as the Duke of Wellington grumbled, they 'enabled the lower classes to move about'. Moreover, the rapid spread of railways made men used for the first time to power-driven machinery as a familiar thing of daily existence; and thereby accustomed them to change and swift material progress. 'Middle-aged Englishmen, travelling from place to place at speeds thought impossible in their youth, found it easier to assume a quickened rate of change, and of change for the better, in other matters.'[1] There is ample justification for calling the middle years of the 19th century 'the Railway Age'.

I. THE EARLY RAILWAYS

The modern railway is the outcome of a union between the iron rail and the steam-driven locomotive; and of the two the iron rail came first. 'Tram roads' of plain wooden rails to carry horse-drawn wagons were

[1] E. L. Woodward: *The Age of Reform*, p. 41.

known in the middle 17th century, and were a commonplace on some coalfields by about 1730. Iron rails were first made at Coalbrookdale in 1767. Experiments were made with cast-iron plate rails, with a flange on their inner side to keep the wagon-wheels from falling off: these had the advantage that the trucks which used them could also be run on an ordinary road, but on the other hand stones and grit accumulated in the angle of the rails, and they fell out of favour. By about 1790 rails made wholly of cast iron, with the wagons kept on by flanges on the wheels, were being used. The growth of mining and ironworks at this time led to improvement, and wrought-iron rails were being used by 1810. The Bedlington type of wrought-iron rail, which came later into general use, was first patented in 1820.

The locomotive presented a far more complex problem for the engineers to solve. Before its coming horse-drawn traction was widely employed on the wagonways and railways which were built in the mining areas, particularly in the north-eastern coalfield. There were also other devices for traction, like the self-acting inclines on which laden wagons running downhill pulled empty wagons up to the top, or on that unique wagonway in South Wales where wagons were driven by sails. Outside the mining areas railways were scarcely used at all before 1800: Ralph Allen's wagonway, built about 1730 to bring stone to Bath from his quarries at Combe Down nearby, was quite exceptional. There were one or two considerable engineering feats in this pre-locomotive age, like the famous Tanfield Arch in Durham, the first railway viaduct, with its span of one hundred feet, built in 1726. The areas most interested in the development of improved methods of traction were likely to be the growing mining districts, with their heavy and bulky commodities for which there was an inexhaustible market if they could find some more effective means of transport.

After James Watt's successful improvement of the steam engine, it was natural to look to steam as a source of locomotive power; indeed, in the year in which James Watt took out his first patent (1769) a French inventor, Nicholas Cugnot, built a steam carriage in Paris. In Britain it was Watt's enterprising Scottish foreman William Murdock (1754–1839) who first constructed a model steam-engine. This was in Cornwall, where he was superintending the erection of Watt's engines in the local mines, and there is a pleasing tale that he took it out along a local lane and terrified a vicar, who thought this fiery creature was the Devil. But Watt himself, aware of the difficulty of building boilers capable of the necessary high pressure, saw little future in steam traction, and discouraged Murdock, who seems to have dropped the idea after a few years. A Cornishman, Richard Trevithick (1771–1833), made a full-size steam carriage in 1801, and on Christmas Eve took a load of passengers for a run along the highway. Three years later, in 1804, he built the first locomotive to run on rails, at the Pennydaren Ironworks, near Merthyr Tydfil. But this does not seem to have been very successful: and although a third engine of Trevithick's, named 'Catch Me Who Can', caused a sensation when it was exhibited on a circular track in London in 1808, Trevithick, an erratic and impulsive man, soon gave up locomotive engineering. By this time north-countrymen, from Tyneside and the West Riding, were turning their energies to the problem. A Leeds firm of engineers was responsible for the building about 1812 of a group of locomotives designed by John Blenkinsop, whose distinctive feature was the use of a gear-wheel fitting into a toothed rack laid alongside the rails; for Blenkinsop doubted the power of smooth driving wheels to pull any great weight. On Tyneside, William Hedley and Timothy Hackworth were starting to build locomotives for the collieries, and one of Hedley's engines, *The Puffing Billy*, is among the most famous of all the early British ones.

Meanwhile the number of railways had appreciably increased. In 1801 an Act of Parliament had authorised the construction of the Surrey Iron Railway from Wandsworth to Croydon, the first to be built in the neighbourhood of London: it had a double track, was 24 feet (just over 7 metres) wide, and was intended to carry freight of all sorts from coal to agricultural produce. In the coal- and iron-mining area of South Wales almost 150 miles (240 kilometres) of line had been built in the twenty years after 1791; and at other points throughout Britain there were odd isolated lines, none of them more than a few miles in length. About 1815 the railways were still of much less importance than canals in the industrial world. Their progress was very slow, and there was considerable caution about them, for they were costly to build. Yet it was clear that the successful development of the locomotive might rapidly change the outlook.

2. STEPHENSON, BRUNEL, AND THE 'RAILWAY MANIA'

It was at this point that George Stephenson (1781–1848) appeared on the scene: his first engine was set to work at the Killingworth Colliery near Newcastle in 1814. George Stephenson is the most famous of British railway engineers: indeed, the *Dictionary of National Biography* calls him 'the inventor and founder of railways'. Such a description is inaccurate, and unfair to men like Trevithick and Hedley; in any circumstances, so elaborate an invention as the railway must clearly owe much to great numbers of men. Moreover, George Stephenson was lucky in his generation. By his time the engineers were beginning to be able to make with accuracy the stronger boiler plates and the more precise tools which were denied to his predecessors. Nevertheless, his achievement was immense. By qualities of character and determination as well as by his genius as an engineer, he laid much of the foundation of the modern British railway system.

George Stephenson was the son of a colliery fireman in Northumberland, and started life by working as a cowherd: later he drove the engine horse which wound up the colliery coals. He had no formal education; he learned to write in his late 'teens, and always hated both reading and writing. But as a young man he made himself an expert in the knowledge of the Watt steam-engines which were commonly used in the Northumberland pits for pumping and winding, and in 1812 he was appointed engine-wright to the Killingworth colliery. In 1814 he built his first locomotive the *Blucher*, to carry coals to the Tyne six miles (about nine kilometres) away; and during the next few years he widened his knowledge of everything to do with railways, from the improvement of the locomotive to the surveying and constructing of the track. In 1821 the colliery owners of Darlington, wanting a cheaper and quicker means of getting coal to the coast at Stockton, got an Act of Parliament empowering them to build a railway, and George Stephenson was appointed its engineer. This Stockton–Darlington line was opened in 1825. It was laid out primarily for horse-drawn traffic; at first stationary engines were used for certain gradients; and when steam locomotion was employed it was for years used only for the coal trains. Moreover, the line was leased for passenger traffic to the owners of horse-drawn coaches, who in effect paid toll to the railway. It could not therefore be properly called a public railway. Nevertheless, it seems to have left one legacy to the British railway system. It is said that the chairman of the directors, Edward Pease, ordered Stephenson to make the width of the track equal to that of ordinary country carts in the neighbourhood; and that Stephenson had about a hundred local carts measured and took the average of their widths, which turned out to be 4 feet 8½ inches (1.4 metres), the gauge on which all Stephenson's later lines were built and which has become the standard of all British lines.

The triumph of George Stephenson, marking the true start of public railways in this country, was the Liverpool to Manchester line, to which he was appointed engineer in 1826. Its building involved a tunnel of 2 kilometres, the deep Olive Mount cutting, and a 'floating embankment' across the great marsh of Chat Moss. The directors held a competition for a prize of £500 for the best locomotive. There were five entries for this Rainhill Trial, held in 1829, and the prize was won by George Stephenson's *Rocket*, which reached a speed of almost 30 m.p.h. (48 km/h). In 1830 the Liverpool to Manchester line was opened. Its immediate success settled all doubts about the use of steam locomotives. It carried a great passenger traffic during the first few years, far more than had been anticipated: and it stimulated a rush to promote railway companies, get private Acts of Parliament passed, and start building the lines. By 1843 London had been linked by rail with Dover, Brighton, Southampton, Bristol, Birmingham, Lancaster, and York: there were also lines from Newcastle to Carlisle, Darlington to Rugby, Liverpool to Hull, and Derby to Gloucester, besides other smaller ones. The era of railway building had been fairly launched—not on any nationally-planned basis, but by a series of private and sometimes competing companies.

George Stephenson continued to play an important part in this develop-ment and must rank with Telford and Brindley among the outstanding civil engineers of British history. Only less notable than his father was Robert Stephenson (1803–59). He was a particularly gifted locomotive engineer and the builder of some magnificent railway bridges—the tubular bridge across the Menai Straits, carrying the London and North Western line to Holyhead, the high-level bridge across the Tyne at Newcastle, and the superb stone viaduct of the Royal Border Bridge at Berwick-upon-Tweed. Yet perhaps his greatest achievement was the construction of the London to Birmingham Railway, noteworthy, for example, by the digging of the Kilsby Tunnel near Rugby, where by determination and courage as well as by high technical skill he drove the line through a bed of wet quicksand covering several square miles.

Comparable with the Stephensons in genius was Isambard Kingdom Brunel (1806–59), who at the age of twenty-seven was appointed chief engineer to the Great Western Railway. His work for the company included the construction (1835–41) of what was in many ways the finest main line in Britain, that from London to Bristol, with its slight gradients, gentle curves, and the mile-long straight of the Box Tunnel, and a further extension at the end of his life involved the building of the lovely Royal Albert Bridge across the Tamar from Devon to Cornwall. This was a major feat of engineering, made the more difficult because the Admiralty refused to permit the channel below the bridge to be obstructed even by temporary scaffolding. Brunel built his bridge in a viaduct of two main spans of 445 feet (139·7 metres) long, which were assembled on the riverbank and then hoisted into position on the single deepwater pier in the middle. Brunel was a many-sided genius. Clifton Suspension Bridge, which carries a road high across the gorge of the Avon at Bristol, was his work; so was the early steamship *The Great Eastern*; and so was the harbour at Milford Haven, which he envisaged as a port to rival Liverpool. These last two were failures at the time, for Brunel had much of the visionary in him. So was another of his railway experiments, the atmospheric railway which he constructed in South Devon (from Exeter to Newton Abbot). This was in theory an admirable device. No locomotives were used: instead, stationary pumping engines were installed at intervals along the line, and these were used to pump out the air from a continuous pipe, fifteen inches in diameter, which was laid between the rails. On the train a piston was suspended from one carriage to the pipe, and the suction created in front of this was powerful enough to haul the train along. This was excellent, for there was no smoke and little dirt, and trains could travel at speeds up to 70 m.p.h. (112 km/h). The practical snag which wrecked the project—thus costing the directors half a million pounds—was the leather flap which was necessary to connect the piston and the pipe: the sea air, and rats, destroyed the leather, and at times the lack of vacuum stopped the trains: and within two years the scheme was abandoned. Another failure of Brunel's—though a failure from whose general adoption Britain would probably have profited—was his employment for the Great Western of the broad gauge of 7 feet (2·1 metres). He insisted on this despite the otherwise general use of Stephenson's 4 feet 8½ inches (1·4 metres), on the ground that it would make possible higher speeds and greater comfort, and there can be little doubt that he was right; but contemporary opinion was against him, and in 1846 Parliament refused to sanction any further extension of the broad gauge. This settled the 'battle of the gauges', although the Great Western did not finally change over to the narrow gauge until as late as 1892. Nevertheless, it would be quite unfair to measure Isambard Brunel by his failures. He was an engineer of superb genius who has left a legacy of masterpieces, and often where he was a failure he was in fact merely in advance of his time.

The first edition of Bradshaw's famous *Railway Guide* was published in 1839; its appearance showed that railways had come to stay—although it contained no details about the arrival times of trains. In the 1840's there took place what has come to be called the 'Railway Mania'—a sudden violent outburst of railway company promotion and of speculation in railway shares. The most prominent figure in this movement was George Hudson, a linen-draper of York, who in a very few years became the 'Railway King' and was the effective founder of the North Eastern Railway. He made a great fortune, much of it by fraudulent juggling with the shares of various companies, until he was found out in 1849, when his fall from power was even more rapid than his rise. Although much of this activity was mere speculation and some of it very bogus, it was responsible for adding much mileage to British railways. In 1843, 1,952 miles (3128 kilometres) of railway were open, by 1848 about 5,000 miles (8000 kilometres) were in use, and by 1855 nearly 8,000 (12800 kilometres). By this date nearly all the main routes from London had been built or planned for most of their length. This huge development had been undertaken by a large number of different companies, without any national plan. Each new company required a private Act of Parliament to give it powers to buy land and construct its railway, and Parliament also governed the railways' development by various general regulations. The most celebrated of these was contained in the Railways Act of 1844, providing that each company had to run at least one train in each direction over its lines every day, stopping at every station, travelling at a rate of at least twelve miles per hour, and charging a penny per mile.[1] This was the 'parliamentary train', notorious to Victorians for its slowness and inconvenience, and much satirised, for example, by W. S. Gilbert in his opera *The Mikado*.[2] The same Act also contained a clause which gave the state the right to buy up after twenty-one years all railways built in or after 1844. This right was never exercised; and so Britain's lines developed haphazardly and with little regulation.

There was great opposition to railways, for a wide variety of reasons.

---

[1] Strictly, this part of the Act applied only to companies founded after 1844, or to old ones which wanted new legal powers.

[2] The idiot who, in railway carriages,
   Scribbles on window-panes,
     We only suffer
     To ride on a buffer
   In Parliamentary trains.

In the first place many landowners were bitterly hostile to them. There were pitched battles between farmers and gamekeepers on one side and surveying parties on the other. Sometimes surveyors worked at night with dark lanterns: sometimes they carried out elaborate stratagems, as in the story of the landowning parson on the London to Birmingham line, whose land was surveyed while he was conducting a Sunday service. Many landowners compelled the railways to make costly and difficult detours, as on the Liverpool to Manchester line; others imposed very troublesome conditions, like the sixth Duke of Devonshire, who would only allow the railways to come near his great estate in Chatsworth in Derbyshire under a covered way (the fifth Duke had banned it altogether). Yet landlords in general did well out of the railways. They got handsome compensation, and usually the value of their lands was increased rather than diminished by the greater trade and the quicker agricultural development which the new communications made possible.

Established interests like canals and coaching companies had very natural objections to the new form of transport which stole their traffic. The Liverpool to Manchester Railway, for example, was built to compete with the Bridgewater Canal. In practice, many of the canals were bought out by the railway companies, and often allowed to fall into ruin by neglect. The road interests were hit hard, and the blow was often immediately fatal. Turnpike trusts were ruined; one toll-bar on the Manchester to Liverpool road which was let for £1,700 in 1830 found no takers at £800 in 1831, after the railway had been opened. Cabs and carts flourished with the coming of the trains to and from which they conveyed passengers and their luggage; but coaches, and the famous coaching inns with their stables and their ostlers and their romantic memories, perished. No coach left London for Bristol after 1843, within two years of the completion of the Great Western Railway; and this was merely one among the many which vanished.

For a variety of reasons the main-line railways avoided certain towns, whose inhabitants have regretted it ever since. Among them were Northampton and the Five Towns of the Potteries; the latter felt their needs too well catered for by the existing canals. Neither Oxford nor Cambridge welcomed the new invention, and kept it safely distant from any colleges. Eton College strongly disapproved, and stopped the Great Western Railway from building a station even at Slough, over a mile away from Eton. This last piece of opposition was based upon snobbery. A wider and more popular hostility founded itself upon ignorance, as revealed, for example, in the pages of *John Bull*, which was a most vigorous and outspoken railway-hater. Travellers, it was said, would be suffocated in tunnels, made nervous wrecks by the noise, or blinded and deafened by the appalling speeds at which they hurtled along: stones on the track would infallibly wreck trains; cinders from the engine would set fire to cornfields and woodlands, noise and smoke and sparks would terrify grazing animals out of their senses. Then there were powerful attacks from

EARLY RAILWAY DEVELOPMENT

0 10 20 30 40 50 MILES

0   20   40   60   80 KILOMETRES

BUILT BEFORE 1844 +++++
BUILT 1844 - 1846 ————
BEGUN BY 1846 - - - - -

Berwick

to GLASGOW

to EDINBURGH

Carlisle
Wigton
Maryport
Windermere
NEWCASTLE
Tynemouth
South Shields
Sunderland
Stanhope
Durham
Bishop Auckland
Barnard Castle
Darlington
Middlesb.
Stockton
Whitby
Richmond
Pickering
Scarborough
Bridlington
Fleetwood
Lancaster
YORK
Selby
HULL
Goole
LEEDS
Bradford
Blackburn
Burnley
Clitheroe
Huddersfield
Grimsby
Preston
LIVERPOOL
Wigan
Bolton
M'ster
Glossop
Rotherham
Gainsborough
Birkenhead
SHEFFIELD
Macclesfield
Lincoln
Holyhead
Chester
Crewe
DERBY
NOTTINGHAM
Stafford
Swannington
Kings Lynn
NORWICH
Shrewsbury
Tamworth
Leicester
Peterborough
Lowestoft
Wolverhampton
B'HAM
Rugby
Ely
Bury St. Edmunds
Coventry
Huntingdon
Cambridge
Ipswich
Droitwich
Warwick
Bedford
Colchester
Worcester
Hereford
Monmouth
Aylesbury
Dunstable
Bishops Stortford
Gloucester
Oxford
Hertford
Chelmsford
Fishguard
Carmarthen
Merthyr
Newport
Cirencester
Swindon
LONDON
Greenwich
Gravesend
Rochester
Whitstable
Margate
Swansea
Pembroke
CARDIFF
BRISTOL
Bath
Hungerford
Reading
Basingstoke
Woking
Reigate
Tun. Wells
Canterbury
Deal
Bridgwater
Guildford
Ashford
Dover
Folkestone
Taunton
Yeovil
Salisbury
Winchester
Crediton
Dorchester
Poole
Southampton
Chichester
Portsmouth
Lewes
Brighton
Hastings
EXETER
Bridport
Weymouth
Wadebridge
Bodmin
Devonport
Redruth
Hayle

    This map shows clearly that by the middle of the nineteenth century London, Lancashire and County Durham were adequately served by railways, and that new construction was proceeding energetically. Wales and Cornwall, however, remained almost without railways.

sabbatarians, denouncing Sunday travel: in 1841 a poster of the Newcastle to Carlisle Company, advertising a Sunday trip to Carlisle, found itself competing with another poster headed 'A Reward for Sabbath Breaking' which proclaimed that passengers would be 'taken safely and swiftly to Hell next Lord's Day by the Carlisle Railway for 7*s.* 6*d.*'

Early railway travel was certainly not without its perils and discomforts. Speeds were uncertain and railwaymen unskilled; signalling was primitive, being operated at first by 'policemen' by hand, and accidents were not infrequent. The carriages were, by later standards, desperately uncomfortable, even for first-class passengers; very often second-class coaches had roofs but were not enclosed at the sides; and the third class at first were open boxes on wheels, with no seats but space for sixty standing passengers, until the Railway Act of 1844 compelled better conditions. There was no efficient means of foot-warming for half a century after passengers began to travel by rail: and there were no communication cords until a murder in a compartment led to their installation. Yet the advantages of railways were so great and so obvious, once they had fairly begun to develop, that neither danger nor inconvenience could check or hinder their growth, or deter the Victorians from making ever-increasing use of them.

To describe their results is almost to write the economic and social history of the period which followed the opening of the Liverpool to Manchester Railway. Their construction stimulated trade after the 'Hungry Forties'; their devouring need for huge supplies of capital multiplied investment. Their building made enormous demands upon the metal and coal industries, and promoted new techniques, e.g. by the development in the 1860's of rails made of Bessemer steel. By reducing transport charges they lowered the costs of industry, and thus made British exports cheaper. In rails, locomotives, and the engineering skill which built them, railways themselves were a most valuable export: British contractors like Thomas Brassey (1805–70) built them in four continents. They transformed the methods of marketing livestock and gave farmers much wider markets, while opening to them the technical and commercial resources of the cities.

For people in town and country alike, railways meant new possibilities of movement. New towns grew rapidly, like the railway towns such as Crewe and Swindon and the holiday resorts of Bournemouth, Southport and Weston-super-Mare. Holidays—the day excursion or the annual trip to the seaside—were for the mass of the population a habit largely created by the railways. Railways made Southampton a major port, and transformed the fish trade from Grimsby. They began the use of the electric telegraph (Paddington was connected to West Drayton in 1838 and to Slough four years later); transformed the postal services and the distribution of news; and led to the national adoption of Greenwich Mean Time in the 1840s. Anti-Corn Law men could spread their gospel far and wide; trade unionists started to develop a national movement; London police arrested Chartists in Birmingham. The isolation of the remoter country areas was in many ways broken down. Finally, the Public Schools, the large boarding schools for the sons of gentry, grew greatly in number from the 1840s onwards – partly at least because railways made it a comparatively simple matter to convey large numbers of boys with their trunks and boxes about the country six times a year.

3. RAILWAYS FROM 1860 TO 1914

By 1860, the year after the deaths of Brunel and Robert Stephenson, it is probably true to say that the great creative days of railways in Britain were over. Nevertheless, there has been very considerable progress in many ways since that time. Among these have been further extensions of the system and important changes in organisation; a great variety of technical developments in every branch of railway activity; and notable increase in the comforts and amenities provided for passengers. Even a bare summary of the principal changes indicates very considerable progress. In the second half of the 19th century the railways enjoyed almost un-challenged supremacy as a means of transport. But the 20th century brought the effective development first of the electric tramway and then of the internal combustion engine; the motor-car, the omnibus, and the lorry between them cut deep into the supremacy of railways, and compelled them after the First World War to face economic problems of a kind unimagined by Victorian railway directors.[1]

With one or two exceptions the extensions of railway in Britain after 1860 were in directions already foreshadowed. The 1890's saw the building of one new main line, the Great Central, whose London terminus, Maryle-bone, was opened in 1899. Considerable geographical difficulties had to be overcome in some of the new developments, for example in the con-struction of the lines in the Scottish Highlands and in the driving of the Midland Railway through the Pennines from Settle to Carlisle. Moreover, the extensions involved two of the most notable engineering feats in British history. The first of these, the Severn Tunnel, which runs for $4\frac{1}{4}$ miles (7 kilometres) beneath a tidal estuary, was begun in 1873; the perils caused by flooding during its construction were very great,[2] and it was not opened for traffic until 1886. The second, the Forth Bridge, was first used in 1890; built of three great cantilever girders, it was a novel design for a railway bridge; and its construction at that date was all the bolder in view of the disaster of 1879, when the first Tay Bridge, opened only the year before, collapsed in a December storm and hurled a train and its eighty passengers to destruction. At this time the mileage of railways increased very considerably: yet most of the increase was on branch lines

---

[1] For details see below, pp. 253–4, 269–70, 298.

[2] At its lowest point its roof lies 45 feet (13·7 metres) below the bottom of a channel in the river which carries 95 feet (29 metres) of water at high tide.

and in suburban areas. Another feature of 19th-century development was a good deal of amalgamation of neighbouring lines; the costs of running tended to rise, and it was an obvious economy to cut down the expense of management by uniting with other companies.

Technical development over these years took many forms. The 1870's saw the general changeover from iron to steel rails. The broad gauge finally disappeared in 1892 from the Great Western Railway, its last stronghold. The apparatus and systems of signalling were vastly improved: the Block System, whereby the line is divided up into sections and only one train is allowed in each section at a time, first used in the 1840's, was made compulsory in 1889. Bogie carriages and automatic brakes came into normal use. Locomotive power was very greatly increased, a step that became vitally necessary as traffic became denser and trains heavier in the later years of the 19th century; and the years round about 1900 saw the beginning of the design of the most effective modern locomotives, with longer boilers of higher capacity, and with the use of superheated steam. The standard 4-6-0 type was first introduced for passenger traffic on the North Eastern Railway in 1899. Higher speeds were the most obvious result of the improvements in locomotives. In 1895 a train ran on the West Coast route from London to Aberdeen at an average of 67 m.p.h. (107 km/h): in 1904 a Great Western train travelled from Bristol to London at an average of 70 m.p.h. (112 km/h). But these were exceptional performances, not equalled until the 1930's.

Over most routes, and especially over long distances, steam remained supreme as the source of traction power: the coming of electrification was of special importance in suburban areas. It was first introduced on surface lines in London in 1898, as a result of the growing competition from electric tramways: thence it spread to other cities, such as Manchester, Glasgow, Liverpool and Newcastle-on-Tyne. Its use on the London Underground was rather earlier. The first London underground line, the Metropolitan, had been opened in 1863, using steam locomotives: despite the many discomforts—the clouds of smoke in the tunnels, the stench of oil lamps in the carriages—10,000,000 passengers travelled by 'Metro' in its first year. The Metropolitan was a shallow underground line: the first modern deep level 'tube' railway in London was opened in 1890, and was powered by electricity from the start. Others quickly followed, including the famous 'Twopenny Tube', the Central London Railway from Shepherd's Bush to the Bank of England, in 1900, and the Bakerloo and Piccadilly Lines in 1905.

The second half of the 19th century saw also a great advance in the services and amenities supplied to travellers. For many years the companies were reluctant to provide for the poorer passengers—hence the 'Parliamentary train' of 1844: but in 1872 the Midland Railway took the lead by putting third-class coaches on all its trains, even its fastest expresses, and two years later it provided upholstered seats for its third-class passengers. The other lines soon followed suit when they saw that the Midland was

profiting by its revolutionary steps. The Cheap Trains Act (1883) introduced workmen's fares. Sleeping cars were first used in 1873, though not
for third-class passengers until 1928. Pullman cars came in 1876; the first
daily all-Pullman train was the *Southern Belle*, started in 1908, which did
the run from Victoria to Brighton in one hour. The first restaurant car
appeared on the Great Northern in 1879. It was a very luxurious affair.
'Passengers were charged half-a-crown over and above the cost of their
meal for the privilege of travelling in the car! The kitchen was fitted with
a coke-burning range, and the scullery boy peeled the potatoes and did
other menial tasks out on the open platform at the rear.'[1] Corridor trains
began in 1892. The heating of compartments long remained a problem.
Early foot-warmers were simply oblong boxes filled with hot water. In the
1880's one company used vessels containing sodium acetate; porters came
in at the stations to shake them up and re-start the chemical reaction which
gave off latent heat. Steam heating was first used in 1884.

The years round 1900 saw railways at their peak in Great Britain. They
were the predominant form of transport for goods and passengers alike;
the internal combustion engine was little more than a cloud on the
horizon. British industry, commerce, and agriculture revolved round them;
they carried the coal from the pits to the foundries and factories, the raw
cotton and wool from the ports to the mills and the manufactured textiles
from the mills to the ports, the imported food from the docks to the cities,
the milk and vegetables from country to town, the business men from the
provinces to London, the clerks from suburbs to city, the commercial
travellers on their endless journeys. They gave employment to great
numbers of men; and the railway trade unions were among the most
important in the land.[2] The long miles of permanent way, the cuttings,
embankments, viaducts and tunnels, the fine bridges—at Saltash and
Berwick-upon-Tweed, and across the Menai Straits and the Firth of
Forth—created a new landscape. Imposing railway buildings, like Euston
in London, Temple Meads at Bristol and the handsome station at Newcastle-upon-Tyne, lent distinction to cities; while the countless small
country stations represented the changes which the Victorian age had
brought to British life. Taken as a whole, the railway system was the most
remarkable material achievement of the British people in the 19th century.

---

[1] O. S. Nock: *The Railways of Britain*, p. 86.
[2] See below, pp. 158–9, for events showing the importance of the Amalgamated
Society of Railway Servants.

11   The Growth of Free Trade

In 1776 a professor at the University of Glasgow wrote the most notable book on economics that has ever been written in English. His name was Adam Smith and his book was *The Wealth of Nations*. 1776 was a year of importance in the history of freedom, for on July 4th the Americans issued their Declaration of Independence, proclaiming themselves free from British rule. Appropriately enough, Adam Smith's book was also a challenge on behalf of freedom—but freedom of a very different kind from that demanded by the Americans. What *The Wealth of Nations* claimed was freedom of trade—freedom from the tariffs and bounties, prohibitions and monopolies and all the other restrictions which governments imposed upon manufacturers and merchants. The book, with its superb style and its profound argument, became a classic, for it contained much else beside a defence of free trade. It began the modern science of economics, and Adam Smith has been hailed as 'the father of political economy'. It had considerable influence on the Continent, especially in France under Napoleon and in Prussia in the early nineteenth century, as well as in Britain. Five editions were published in Britain before Adam Smith died in 1790.

For centuries before 1776 it had been taken for granted, in Britain as elsewhere, that it was the task of the government to regulate trade in what it thought to be the best interests of the community: and we have already noticed some examples of how this kind of trade regulation worked in practice.[1] The most obvious feature of this Mercantilism, as the system of regulation came to be called, was an elaborate and complicated structure of tariffs, i.e. of lists of Customs duties on the export or import of particular commodities: and the most important part of Adam Smith's attack was launched against tariffs, and the name 'Free Trade' has come to be given to an economic policy whose central feature is the absence of tariffs. But there were many other features of mercantilism, like the trade regulations imposed on the American colonists; or like monopolies given to certain groups of merchants, as, for example, that given to the East India Company. Both these Adam Smith attacked with some vigour.

By the time Adam Smith wrote, mercantilism was already weakening, and many types of regulation were simply being ignored. The most obvious domestic example of this ignoring of regulations was smuggling. The 18th century was the golden age of smugglers: most of the smuggling stories, whether they concern adventure on the Portsmouth Road or the lonely salt marshes of Essex or in the rocky coves of Cornwall, belong to this period. The reason for this is not that people in that century were

---

[1] See above, pp. 35, 54–55.

more than normally dishonest about defrauding the revenue, but that there were far more trade regulations than could be effectively enforced, and that on the whole Customs duties were so high that the temptation to smuggle was irresistible. It is clearly impossible to estimate how much of any given commodity which entered Britain from abroad during the century was smuggled, but there is abundant evidence that tea, tobacco, and French wines and brandies were all smuggled in very large quantities indeed. The purchase of smuggled goods was a perfectly normal activity about which few folk made any scruples.[1] Those unfortunate men, the revenue officers, who seem to have spent most of their days being out-witted by a sort of unholy alliance of smugglers and public opinion, were too few and too badly paid to have much chance of being successful. Smuggling went on mainly because the laws which the smugglers defied were impossible to enforce in face of a hostile public opinion. Not until the next century, when the trade regulations became less elaborate and, in particular, the Customs duties on the great majority of imports were abolished altogether, so that there was little profit in evading the law, did smuggling die away and become an occupation which most of the population regarded as criminal.

The colonies provided another example of the ignoring of regulations, and one of great historical importance. Even while Adam Smith was writing his book (it took him ten years to do it) a quarrel was brewing between Britain and the Thirteen American Colonies partly because a minister of the Crown, in order to make the Americans pay part of the cost of their own defence, was trying to enforce commercial regulations which had long been a dead letter. As in commerce, so in industry: many regulations were more honoured in the breach than in the observance, like those which insisted in a wide range of employments upon an apprenticeship period of seven years. Free trade was in reality developing fast: and it was only to be expected that it should in this age of economic expansion. For as industry and trade grew, they went further afield for markets and raw materials; they dealt in a greater range of commodities, and in larger quantities of them; and they became more elaborate and complicated. Supervision by the state became more and more impracticable, in days when there was almost no trained civil service at all; here again what happened in the Thirteen Colonies showed up the defects of the system, for it proved impossible to enforce across 3,000 miles (4800 kilometres) of ocean restrictions which the Americans did not intend to obey. Further, the aim of mercantilism was to force trade into the channels that the government wished it to enter: but this was no longer so easily possible now that Britain was beginning to develop a great and varied export trade. The woollen manufacturers had been able to get Parliament early in the

---

[1] See on this point references in the entertaining *Diary of a Country Parson* kept by the Rev. James Woodforde (1740–1803), a respectable clergyman who held livings in Somerset and Norfolk. He bought tea direct from smugglers—although he did it late at night.

eighteenth century to pass laws restricting the cotton trade: but it was not possible to enforce them when the sending of cotton textiles to the Far East began to be an important item in the export trade. The defences of mercantilism had been undermined and breaches made in its walls before Adam Smith delivered his assault upon them.

The general ideas which he put forward in place of mercantilism are sometimes summed up in the French phrase *laissez-faire*, meaning 'let it alone'. Adam Smith himself was mainly, though by no means entirely, concerned with trade proper, that is the exchange of goods. *Laissez-faire* was often used in a much more general way. For example, many manufacturers were strongly opposed to any attempt to limit hours of work or to control conditions in factories, even on behalf of child workers. They based their opposition on *laissez-faire* grounds: they said that these things were no concern of the state, that manufacturers could manage them much better themselves, that any government interference with the hours of work would spell ruin to the industry—in short, that the state ought to let things alone. *Laissez-faire* in fact itself became the basis of a rigid economic doctrine. This argued that there were certain iron laws of economics which were bound to operate. The best example of them was the law of supply and demand. If goods were plentiful and demand was limited, prices would be low: if goods were in short supply and the demand for them was high, prices would be high: it was useless for the state to attempt to regulate prices. If jobs were plentiful and the supply of workers was small, wages would be high: if work was scarce and there were plenty of workmen, wages would fall: it was no good for the state to try to fix wages, and the mere attempt would only make things worse for the workmen in the long run. In short, the only thing for the state to do was to keep out of economic affairs—a view readily acceptable at a time when there was no incorrupt civil service, no efficient system of local government. Quite apart from this rigid doctrine, *laissez-faire* tended to become, so to speak, the normal intellectual climate of the early 19th century. People came to take it for granted that there should be no state interference at all in economic affairs unless some very overwhelming case was made out for it—as was, for example, to be made out in favour of limiting the hours of work for small children in factories. Admittedly they were not always very logical about this. Thus M.P.'s were quite ready to overthrow *laissez-faire* and interfere with trade unions by the Combination Laws—but then they argued in defence of this action that trade unions themselves were breaches of *laissez-faire*, for *they* were interfering with business! But then people as a whole are not very logical when what they regard as their interests are involved. On the whole, the idea of *laissez-faire* was the normal approach to economic problems for most Englishmen in the early part of the 19th century.

2. PITT THE YOUNGER AND HUSKISSON

Here we are not concerned with *laissez-faire* in general, but more narrowly with the history of free trade, in the sense of the setting free of trade from various types of regulations of which tariffs were the most important. The abandonment of mercantilism and the definite establishment of free trade as a national policy was a slow process. It was started in the last twenty years of the 18th century, and then sharply interrupted by the French war and its aftermath: resumed by a group of notable statesmen in the 1820's, it was practically complete by about 1860. Great Britain remained a free-trade country for seventy years thereafter, only abandoning the policy under the very different conditions of the 20th century.

Walpole had taken some very modest steps in the direction of reducing commercial regulations; but the first 18th-century statesman to move towards freer trade as a policy was William Pitt the Younger, who became Prime Minister in 1783. The extent to which he could put the precepts of *The Wealth of Nations* into practice was much limited by circumstances. He took office at the end of the disastrous War of American Independence which had done much damage to British trade, swollen the National Debt, and lost a large part of the colonial empire. In such a situation his first duty was to set the national finances in order, and his tariff policy reflected this situation. Six years after he took office the French Revolution broke out, and the war which followed in 1793 shattered Pitt's commercial policy and so cut across the movement towards free trade, for wartime meant much extensive regulation of trade. Thus Pitt's actual achievement as a free trader was bound to be small.

In 1784, mainly as an anti-smuggling device, he reduced the heavy tea duties; and he developed in this and the next few years more effective governmental machinery for collecting customs and excise duties. As part of this policy, in 1787 he consolidated the tariff: that is to say, he reorganised the methods by which duties were calculated. These were often very elaborate, involving perhaps six or eight different financial calculations which had been added to the original duty over the years, and Pitt replaced them by a single rate of duty for each article, laid down in the new Book of Rates which he issued. Meanwhile he tried to extend foreign trade by the abolition of restrictions. In 1785 he proposed to Parliament the formation of a commercial union with Ireland, which at that date had a separate trading system, and one which was designed to give the maximum advantage to British rather than to Irish merchants and manufacturers. This would have involved lowering customs duties on both sides of the Irish Sea, and would in particular have benefited the Irish linen industry. The project raised strong opposition, led by Boulton and Watt, among British manufacturers who feared that their businesses would suffer from competition from Ireland, where wages were notoriously low; and Pitt had to withdraw it. He was more successful next year (1786) when he carried through a commercial treaty with France, the Pitt-Vergennes Treaty (sometimes called the Eden Treaty, after its chief English negotiator, himself a friend of Adam Smith). By this Britain agreed to let French wines and spirits come in at lower rates of duty: in return the French reduced their duties on British textiles and hardware. The treaty encouraged the drinking of claret in Britain; but the French Revolutionary government dropped it in 1793, and in any event it was most unpopular with French manufacturers who found their goods being undersold in France by those from Britain.

Pitt's work was halted by the French war; and afterwards came the years of distress, which were scarcely the right time for experiments in free trade. Not until 1823 did a successor to Pitt appear in this field of action, when William Huskisson became President of the Board of Trade. Much had happened in the long interval to make the arguments for free trade more powerful. When Pitt came to office in 1783, the use of power-driven machinery in British factories was in its infancy. The forty years that followed saw a very great increase in the output of industry and in the manufacturing capacity of British mills and foundries—an increase that cried out for an expansion of international trade to provide it with new markets and new sources of raw materials. In some directions the events of wartime had blazed the trial for this expansion: under the spur of the Continental System, British traders had extended their markets in the New World, both in the United States and in the rebellious Spanish colonies to the south. During these forty years British territory in India had been widely expanded: the peace treaty of 1815 had given her outposts all over the world, like Ceylon, the Cape of Good Hope and Trinidad; even Australia, 'that land of convicts and kangaroos', as a contemporary wit called it, was beginning to become something more than a penal settlement and to sell wool to Bradford merchants. Here were vast opportunities for trade and industry. Moreover, Britain at this stage of her history was fitted to seize them. Her geographical position in relation to Europe and the New World; her large mercantile marine, developed under the shelter of her naval strength; her natural resources of coal and iron, the twin keys to this new age of steam power; and, most significant of all at this stage, the fact that in the development of the new machinery she had obtained about a generation's start over other countries—all these things were immense advantages.

To use them fully, she needed free trade, the sweeping away of all barriers and obstacles to international commerce. Manufacturers wanted their raw materials to enter Britain free of duty. Except in certain special circumstances, like those of the manufacturers of silk goods, most of them could afford not to bother about protection for their own goods on the British market. Merchants naturally favoured the removal of any restricttions on the amount of trade. Shipowners were anxious not to throw open the trade with the colonies to the ships of other countries, for they were nervous of the growth of the American merchant navy; but in the European trade they were comfortably supreme. All told, the demand for free trade was powerful and certain to become more powerful so long as Britain was able to maintain the trading supremacy which she held in 1815. In 1820 the London merchants sent a petition to the government. It declared that 'freedom from restraint is calculated to give the utmost extension to foreign trade, and the best direction to the capital and industry of the country', and it asked for the freeing of imports from all duties except those imposed for revenue. This last qualification was not unimportant in 1820, for the government, thanks to the heavy load of debt incurred in the war, was spending more than it was getting by way of income from taxation; and so any attempt to reduce duties would add to its financial difficulties. The improved trade of the early 1820's altered this situation, and by 1823, when William Huskisson took office, positive steps towards free trade became possible.

Huskisson was M.P. for Liverpool and was very popular with the merchants; and in collaboration with the Chancellor of the Exchequer, F. J. 'Prosperity' Robinson, he carried out a group of reforms, each of which in a different way helped to free and to encourage trade. First, they undertook a general lowering of Customs duties. As with Pitt, part of the aim was to discourage smuggling. Duties on many raw materials used in the textile and metal industries were reduced. As for manufactured goods, prohibitions were scrapped: the maximum protective duty was fixed at 30 per cent. *ad valorem* (i.e. on the worth of the goods). Silk goods imported had to pay the maximum duty; hitherto they had been prohibited—and therefore much smuggled. In line with this policy of freedom, Huskisson allowed the export of raw wool, which had previously been forbidden; and similarly he repealed the law which forbade the emigration of artisans abroad, a law which half a century before Boulton and Watt had strongly supported lest their skilled mechanics should be lured abroad by foreign agents and take the secret of the steam-engine with them.

Secondly, he got Parliament to pass in 1823 a Reciprocity of Duties Act, which gave authority to ministers to make trade treaties with foreign countries providing for mutual reduction of tariffs—something similar to the method of the Pitt-Vergennes Treaty of 1786. In the course of the next few years treaties on these lines were signed with most European countries. Holland would not accept the British proposals: this provoked the famous instructions in verse, sent by Canning, then Foreign Secretary, to the British Ambassador at The Hague.

> In matters of commerce the fault of the Dutch
> Is giving too little and asking too much.
> The French are with equal advantage content,
> So we clap on Dutch bottoms just twenty per cent.[1]

Thirdly, Huskisson was anxious to encourage trade with the British Empire, and to promote its development as a source of raw materials. So he

[1] 'Bottoms' here = ships.

gave an advantage to colonial producers by letting certain goods enter Britain at lower rates of duties than those imposed on similar goods from foreign countries. Among these were West Indian rum, Indian silks, Canadian corn, and Australian wool. This policy of Colonial Preference, gradually dropped by later 19th century governments, returned in the 1930's.[1]

Closely connected with his ideas about the Empire was the fourth and in some ways the most revealing of Huskisson's reforms, his alteration of the Navigation Code. This was the code of regulations designed to promote English trade and shipping which had been built up since the middle years of the 17th century, when it had been first aimed at the Dutch. Its general purpose had been to ensure that goods coming to England were carried in ships which were English-built and mainly English-manned, or in the ships of the country from which the goods came: thus attempting to exclude Holland from the carrying trade of the world. Certain trades were limited wholly to English vessels: these included the fisheries and the trade with the colonies. The world 'English' in the Navigation Code included colonial as well as home shipping. By the beginning of the 19th century the code had outrun its purpose, for Holland was no longer a great sea-power, and British merchant shipping was now firmly established. Moreover, it had became very complicated in its details. Nevertheless, it had its defenders. Among them had been Adam Smith, who justified it on the ground of national safety: 'As defence, however, is of much more importance than opulence, the Act of Navigation is, perhaps, the wisest of all the commercial regulations of England.' So Huskisson was cautious in his dealings here, and did not abolish the Code entirely. Instead, between 1823 and 1825 he modified it, getting rid of most of its restrictions: the most important one which he left concerned trade within the Empire, which was still to be reserved 'entirely and absolutely' to British and colonial shipping—another indication of Huskisson's concern for imperial development. Not until 1849 was the Navigation Code entirely abolished.

These four achievements met with the approval of the merchants and manufacturers. With one other class in the community, however, Huskisson ran into trouble. These were the landowners, who found Huskisson's liberal views on the Corn Laws not at all to their liking.[2] In 1827 they **resisted his proposals for revising the Corn Law of 1815, and in 1828 he** resigned from the government. In 1830 he was killed by a locomotive when crossing the line at the opening of the Liverpool to Manchester Railway.

3. PEEL, GLADSTONE, AND COBDEN: FREE TRADE COMPLETED

The next great free trade minister was Sir Robert Peel, who had been a colleague of Huskisson's in the 1820's, when as Home Secretary he won

---

[1] See below, p. 245, for the Ottawa Agreements.

[2] For a full account of the Corn Laws, see Chap. 12, pp. 95–98.

lasting fame by establishing the Metropolitan Police Force as well as by reforming the Penal Code.[1] It was as Prime Minister (1841–6) that he carried free trade a stage further towards completion. His Lancashire inheritance—he was the son of the cotton millionaire of Bury—as well as his own intellectual brilliance qualified him to grasp the economic problems of the age, and this Peel Ministry was perhaps the most important of the century from the point of view of economic and social development. Apart from free trade, its reforms covered a wide field, including mines and factories, railways, and the banks.[2] When Peel took office, times were hard, and he determined to pursue a policy which would serve to promote trade: thus he deliberately used his budgets as means to that end, taking charge of them himself in the Commons. His aim was to set trade free from duties which sent prices up and so reduced the sales of British manufacturers at home and overseas. He realised that the reduction of duty would mean, at any rate at first, an appreciable loss of revenue from indirect taxation: to offset this he re-introduced the Income Tax.[3]

In 1842 he reduced the tax on all imported raw materials to a maximum of 5 per cent.: by 1846 all raw materials except timber and tallow were admitted free of duty. For semi-manufactured goods he set, in 1842, a maximum of 12 per cent: by 1846 many of these, too, were admitted duty-free. On manufactured goods he brought the maximum tax down from Huskisson's 30 per cent, first to 20 per cent, and then to 10 per cent, with the exception of silk, which had to pay 15 per cent. The Budget of 1842 reduced the duties on 750 commodities in the official list: that of 1845 abolished those on 520. He did much to make food cheaper and thus to encourage its consumption: the duties on imported sugar, cheese and butter came down, and those on live stock, meat and potatoes were abolished. Another step in line with this policy of destroying all obstacles to trade was the removal in 1843 of the prohibition on the export of machinery from Great Britain. The crowning achievement of this ministry came in 1846, when Peel abolished the Corn Laws after one of the most desperate political struggles ever fought in this country. This not only freed from taxation the most important item in the diet of the people: it also defeated the last powerful group of protectionists, the landowners.[4]

Free trade was for practical purposes completed by a fourth great statesman, William Ewart Gladstone, while he was Chancellor of the Exchequer (1853–5, 1859–66). Like Peel, Gladstone had a business inheritance, for his father was a Liverpool merchant. He had served under Peel in the 1840's, and learned much from him: as Vice-President of the Board of Trade, he had done much of the detailed work of tariff revision. Like

---

[1] See below, pp. 223, 227.
[2] See above, p. 78, for Railways, and below, pp. 180–1 (Mines and Factories) and p. 144 (Banks).
[3] See below, p. 149.
[4] For fuller details about the Corn Law struggle, see below, pp. 95–98.

Peel, he used his budgets as means of stimulating trade and industry. As a financier, he surpassed his master. His general object was to abolish all duties on goods coming into Britain, except for small duties on a few articles in widespread use: these he kept simply in order to provide revenue for the Exchequer. The object he attained in a series of masterly budgets, of which the most important were those of 1853 and 1860. In 1853, he removed all duties from imported soap and cotton yarn, and halved those on fruit and dairy products: in 1860 the fruit and dairy produce duties vanished altogether, as did those on almost all manufactured goods. Other steps taken by Gladstone included the abolition of the duties on imported paper and on timber. In effect, free trade was completed. Apart from duties collected solely for revenue purposes, the government of Great Britain raised virtually no tariff barriers whatever against trade with nations overseas. The pattern completed by Gladstone remained for seventy years, until in 1932 Great Britain returned to a policy of protection.

It would be wrong to leave the establishment of free trade without mentioning the most notable 19th century advocate of this policy, Richard Cobden (1804–65). Cobden was a principal figure in the Anti-Corn Law League formed in 1839, and supplied many of the most powerful arguments against the Corn Laws, playing a leading role in the debates in the Commons that led to their abolition. In 1860, on behalf of Gladstone, he negotiated what has become known as the Cobden Treaty with France, a treaty similar to the Pitt-Vergennes Treaty of an earlier period. By it France agreed to reduce duties on a wide range of British goods, including coal, steel, tools and machinery; in return, Britain was to admit all French manufactured goods duty free, to admit French brandy at the same rate as colonial-produced brandy, and to reduce the duties on French wines. Like the earlier treaty, it was far from popular with French manufacturers: from the British point of view it represented a considerable success for the idea of free trade. Cobden was the leading figure of what came to be known (from the town where it got its strongest support, and where the Anti-Corn Law League had been founded) as the Manchester School of economists, which flourished in these middle years of the 19th century. The Manchester School believed ardently in complete free trade. They pointed to the success British manufacturers and merchants were enjoying under free trade conditions; between 1840 and 1847 British imports rose by 44 per cent, and exports by 34 per cent. They condemned the growth of an empire, because empires in practice involved trade restrictions. Finally they maintained that free trade should become the normal practice of nations, not just because it would bring increased prosperity and a higher standard of living: but also because the more nations traded with one another, the more they were likely to be able to live together at peace. For Cobden and his supporters, free trade was the road to universal peace.

4. THE CHALLENGE TO FREE TRADE: JOSEPH CHAMBERLAIN
AND TARIFF REFORM

The policy of free trade was not seriously challenged until the early years of the 20th century, and then the challenge came from an unusual politician in unusual circumstances. Between 1899 and 1902 Great Britain fought the South African War against the Transvaal and the Orange Free State. The war was the climax of a period marked by much enthusiasm for the extension of the British Empire. The most prominent champion of imperialism among politicians was Joseph Chamberlain, the Colonial Secretary. When the war was over he paid a visit to South Africa, and he returned convinced that every possible step must be taken to promote the unity of the Empire. With this end in view he launched in 1903 a Tariff Reform campaign, in which he proposed that Great Britain should abandon free trade and revise her system of tariffs, in order to give greater preference to goods from the self-governing dominions and the colonies. His proposals were not supported by a majority in the Unionist (in effect, Conservative) party to which he belonged, and so he resigned from the Cabinet in order to push his campaign.

He found at first a good deal of support in the country. This came partly from those who were convinced imperialists like himself, and believed that the Empire should be strengthened by economic bonds. But there were quite different reasons which led many people, if not to support Chamberlain, at least to be critical of the established policy of free trade. One was the fact that Britain was now (1903) alone among the great industrial countries in holding to free trade. At first the others had tended to follow Britain's example, but they had swung over to protective tariffs, partly to defend their manufacturers against British competition: and now Germany, the United States and France were all protectionist nations. A second lay in the relative decline in Britain's trading position in the world. The long lead of the early and middle 19th century had gone, and both Germany and the United States had overhauled Britain in many branches of industrial production. The struggle for markets overseas was now far more keen than at any time in the 19th century. Many people were inclined to think that a protective tariff might help to strengthen British industry and thus equip it better for the struggle for overseas trade. A third reason was that when Chamberlain put forward his proposals Britain was passing through something of a slump. Times were bad, and many manufacturers wondered whether it would not pay to give tariff reform a trial. It would at least, so they thought, prevent the 'dumping' of cheap foreign goods on the British market: there was much feeling at this time about the quantity of low-priced German goods, for example toys, which were on sale in British shops.

Such arguments as these helped to win Tariff Reform some support, especially among the business men. But there was one difficulty about Chamberlain's proposals which these arguments did not touch, and which was to be fatal to him. The manufacturers were thinking in terms of a tariff on foreign manufactured goods, which would help them by protecting the home market. Yet such a tariff would not achieve Chamberlain's end. He wanted to help the Empire by tariff preferences, which meant putting lower rates of duty on those things the dominions and colonies produced. Now these things were not manufactured goods at all, but raw materials like the wool of Australia and the timber of Canada—and above all foodstuffs, corn and meat and dairy produce. Here was the weakness of Chamberlain's policy upon which his free-trading opponents seized at once. To make Tariff Reform work—at least Chamberlain's sort of Tariff Reform—foreign-produced foodstuffs would have to be taxed, and food prices would have to go up, a prospect which the majority of the population did not relish at all. In 1906 a general election was fought in which the main issue was Tariff Reform: and Chamberlain's policy was decisively rejected by the voters. The Liberals won the biggest electoral victory known up to that date. This was not entirely the result of Tariff Reform: the pendulum had already been swinging against the Conservatives. But Chamberlain's policy had split his own party from top to bottom, so that some fought as Free Traders and others as Protectionists. The Liberals could truthfully warn the voters 'Your food will cost you more': they proclaimed themselves the party of the 'big loaf' against the 'little loaf' that would be the result of Tariff Reform. And Chamberlain was in one way unlucky. By 1905–6 the slump of 1903 had gone: times had improved, and manufacturers were doing much better. The argument for protection by tariffs had lost much of its force: voters had no enthusiasm for tariffs to help business men who were doing well anyway. With Chamberlain's defeat and retirement from politics in 1906, the movement for Protection died away, not to be resumed until the First World War of 1914–18. Thereafter, in a world which had become much less favourable to British trade, Great Britain at last abandoned in the 1930's the policy of free trade.[1]

12 Agriculture, 1815-1914

1. THE CORN LAWS, 1815–46

In 1815, as we have seen, a Corn Law had been passed which prohibited the import of foreign wheat until the price of homegrown wheat had reached 80s. per quarter. The purpose of this law was to protect farmers and landowners against the effects of the fall in prices which would follow if foreign-grown grain were allowed to enter Britain freely—a fall which had in fact appeared already, immediately the ports were opened after the end of the French War. They had prospered under the high prices of

---

[1] See below, pp. 245–6.

wartime. Rents had risen: much capital had been invested in ploughing up poor land and extending the area of cultivation: and neither farmers nor landlords were anxious to face the losses that lower prices would bring. Therefore they demanded protection, and they got it because a majority of M.P.s were themselves landowners. Yet the results of the Corn Law of 1815 did not really satisfy anybody. The poor in the towns hated it because it kept up the price of bread: the agricultural labourers found it made no difference to their wages, which remained very low. The rising manufacturing class disliked it because they saw no good reason why the landlords should receive this special measure of protection. As for the farmers and landlords themselves, they found that the law did not work miracles. There was in fact a good deal of depression in agriculture in the years after the war, with many farmers being forced to sell out. Corn prices remained high on the whole, but they varied considerably.

During the 1820's various efforts were made to revise the Corn Law, with Huskisson playing a prominent part in them. He was anxious to make the law more flexible because in its existing form it was an obstacle to foreign trade: and he put forward proposals for a sliding scale of duties on corn. Instead of a rigid prohibition of imports until home-grown corn reached a definite price, duties were to be put on foreign corn, varying according to the price of home-grown corn: if corn prices rose the duty was to fall, and if they fell it was to rise. Such a method would, it was believed, keep corn prices reasonably stable. But the strongly protectionist landlords did not like Huskisson's sliding scale: they rejected it and accepted another, put forward by Wellington in 1828. This did not work well. It did very little to make prices steadier: furthermore, it encouraged corn dealers to hold back corn from the market when prices were rising, because they thereby got higher prices when they sold and also benefited by being able to import the foreign corn at a lower rate of duty. In 1842 Peel modified the sliding scale, lowering the rates of duty all along the line.

By this time a vigorous propaganda against the Corn Laws had arisen. In 1839 an Anti-Corn Law League had been formed in Manchester, led by Richard Cobden and by John Bright, a Quaker cotton manufacturer from Rochdale. It won its main support from manufacturers, who were strongly in favour of free trade and looked upon the Corn Laws as the greatest single obstacle to its establishment. They argued that the Corn Laws prevented Britain buying foreign corn, and therefore prevented the corn-producing countries from buying British manufactured goods: this argument appealed powerfully to industrial Lancashire, dependent upon the maintenance of a high export trade in cotton textiles. The League, well supplied with funds by the manufacturers, attacked the laws cease-lessly and energetically, holding public meetings throughout the country and printing pamphlets by the thousand, which it could now distribute by the Penny Post (started in 1840). Cobden and Bright entered Parliament and developed the attack there: both were fine speakers, Cobden a master of convincing argument and Bright swaying the emotions of his hearers in beautiful Biblical English. The Protectionists took up the challenge of the League, crying that the manufacturers wanted corn prices lowered not to help the poor but to enable them to cut wages. The struggle was between two great 'interests'—a duel for economic power between landlords and manufacturers, especially the cotton manufacturers.

Chance had decreed that the Prime Minister, when the struggle reached its height, was a Lancashire manufacturer's son who was leader of the party of the landlords. Peel had come to power in 1841, as head of the party pledged to maintain the Corn Laws. But his Budgets showed him to be a free trader, and the League was convinced that sooner or later he must come round to their views—and realise that the needs of the landlords must take second place to those of the community as a whole. In fact, Peel seems to have been convinced by 1845 that the Corn Laws would have to go: there is a famous story of him listening to one of Cobden's speeches in a debate on the Corn Laws, and crumpling up in his hand the paper on which he had been taking notes, as he turned to a colleague and said, 'You answer this: I cannot'. Already the landed gentry in his own party were mistrustful of him, and had found a voice in a young Jewish novelist, Benjamin Disraeli, who defended the laws in ardently protectionist speeches. Then in 1845 came events which forced decision upon Peel. It was a wet summer, and the English corn harvest was bad: in Ireland the rains brought catastrophe, for blight struck the potato crop, which meant the prospect, unless relief came speedily, of a terrible famine throughout the land. The League led the demand that the ports should be opened to foreign corn: they knew, Peel knew, the protectionists knew that once the ports were opened the Corn Laws would never come back again.

There followed a short but extremely bitter political struggle in the House of Commons, while Irishmen in thousands were dying of starvation. Peel resigned, but the Whigs, the opposition party, would not form a government: so he came back and proposed the repeal of the Corn Laws. He was attacked with great savagery by the protectionists in his own party, Disraeli in a tremendous series of speeches denouncing him as a traitor. Ultimately in 1846 the Repeal of the Corn Laws went through. The night the Lords passed the Bill, the protectionists in the Commons joined the Whigs and voted against Peel on another issue, so compelling him to resign. It was the end of his ministry: he died in 1850, without regaining office. He had, as Thomas Carlyle put it, done 'a strenuous, courageous, and manful thing': he had also shattered his party. The immediate results of Repeal are difficult to assess. Certainly it came too late to help the Irish. Certainly bread prices did not come down. But Repeal no doubt stopped them from rising higher. Certainly, too, agriculture was not immediately ruined by Repeal, for farmers prospered in the 1850's as never before. Yet it was undoubtedly the greatest of the victories of free trade. It meant the triumph of the manufacturer over the landowner: it meant also the triumph of the townsman who wanted cheap food over the countryman who was no longer the dominant figure in England. Perhaps more than anything

else, it shows that Great Britain had become a country governed by towns-
men and by the needs and interests of the urban areas.

2. THE DEVELOPMENT OF AGRICULTURE, 1815–75

As we have noted, after 1815, and despite the Corn Laws, British agriculture fell upon troubled times, and its difficulties lasted for much of the
first half of the century, although by the accession of Queen Victoria (1837)
signs of improvement were already visible. Farmers who had taken out
long leases on high rents during the war were in difficulty when peace came.
Prices fluctuated so widely that farmers lacked confidence. Bad harvests
in the immediate post-war years brought hardship: yet when good harvests
came, as in 1822, corn prices fell so low that there was something of a
slump. The rise in the poor rates was greatly felt: for it was agriculture
that carried most of the burden of the Speenhamland system. Altogether
this meant that bankruptcies among farmers were by no means infrequent
in the first twenty years after Waterloo.

Yet by far the greatest hardship fell upon the agricultural labourer. His
wages were the lowest in the land: he shared in none of the benefits of
protection. The development of enclosures meant that he was now usually
landless. In the south he was the victim of the Speenhamland policy. The
potato, cheaper than bread, was beginning to play a larger part in his diet:
for meat he was often dependent on poaching. Some observers of the time
believed that the hard lot of the labourer was leading to the depopulation
of villages. One of these was William Cobbett (1762–1835), the greatest
journalist of his time. Born the son of an innkeeper in the country town of
Farnham in Surrey, he was a Radical who spent much of his career
demanding parliamentary reform and fighting for the freedom of the
Press.[1] But he was essentially a countryman at heart, and in 1821, 1826,
and 1829, he made a series of journeys around the countryside of southern
England, which he described in the book known as *Rural Rides*. It was a
lively book, noting all manner of things—new agricultural methods and
stately country-houses, men working on the roads, men out shooting, fine
landscapes and good crops of turnips: it was a book full of attacks on the
many sorts of people Cobbett hated—the stockbrokers and bankers who
swindled the honest men, the parsons who lived well on tithes paid to
them by hard-working farmers, the Londoners who bought land just for
the shooting, the 'agriculturasses' as he nicknamed the landlords who stood
out obstinately for protection. Cobbett described villages through which
he had ridden, where cottages were falling down and land was running to
waste: and he concluded that the inhabitants were being drained from
rural areas to increase the population of the industrial districts. Certainly
there was migration from many villages: yet it seems equally certain that
the total population of the rural areas did not decline at this time. The

[1] For these parts of his career, see below, p. 162.

poor law records, in fact, suggest much unemployment in the countryside.

This distress found a tragic outlet in 1830, when there took place what has been called 'the last Labourers' Revolt'. Often during the post-war years there had been outbreaks of rick-burning and riots against the high price of bread: but this movement of 1830—the so-called 'Swing Riots', allegedly led by a mysterious Captain Swing—was far more widespread and serious than anything that had previously occurred. Through most of the south from Kent to Dorset, in East Anglia and the southern Midlands, labourers burnt ricks and destroyed threshing-machines: they demanded higher wages and higher rates of poor relief, together with a lowering of rents and tithe. There was little violence: some unpopular farmers and overseers of the poor were ducked in horseponds or chased out of villages but no one was killed. The government took brutal measures when they had put down the disorders. The special commissions of judges appointed to try the labourers used the full authority of the law. Nine men were hanged (one was a lad of nineteen who had knocked off the hat of a wealthy landlord) and 457 transported: many more were imprisoned, including some farmers who had sympathised with the labourers. The episode left bitter memories behind it in the countryside of southern England.

Yet distress did not mean that there was no advance in agriculture in these years. Enclosure went on, and by 1850 the vast majority of the open fields had gone for ever: the process was accelerated by two Enclosure Acts of 1836 and 1845, the second of which did something, rather late in the day, to safeguard the remaining commons and open land in the neighbourhood of villages and towns. Wars in the Crimea (1854–6) and the U.S.A. (1861–5) cut foreign competition in wheat. There was technical progress too: the threshing-machines the labourers had destroyed were one sign of it. Perhaps most important of all, there were major advances in land drainage, the result of the inventions (1840's) of cheap machine-made cylindrical pipes and of the mole plough—aided by government grants.

These improvements foreshadowed more considerable advances around the middle years of the century. Gloomy prophets foretold that the Repeal of the Corn Laws (1846) would ruin British agriculture. The Repeal certainly showed that agriculture was less important in Britain now. Yet in 1851 one in every six males over the age of ten was a farm labourer— a sign that farming was still highly important. In reality the thirty years which followed Repeal were a golden age of farming, in which prices were stable and profits good. Numerous factors contributed to the prosperity of this period of 'high farming'. The abolition of the Speenhamland System in 1834 and the adjustment in 1837 of the method by which tithe was calculated (so that henceforward it was related to price-levels) removed two burdens from the shoulders of agriculture, or at any rate adjusted them so that they were distributed more evenly. The discoveries of new goldfields in California in 1849 and in Australia in 1851 made it possible to increase the amount of currency in circulation, and this stimulated prices and wages alike, which brought an increased demand for foodstuffs. The rapid growth of the railway system in Great Britain in the 1840's was an immense boon to agricultural producers, bringing them in quicker contact with their markets and extending the range of their sales.

There was considerable progress in the production of fertilisers. Peruvian guano was first imported in 1839 and rapidly came into widespread use, while the work of scientists led to the production of superphosphates (1842) and other artificial fertilisers. The Rothamsted Experimental Station for research in agriculture began in 1842. The work of various agricultural societies and the production of agricultural shows (the Royal Agricultural Society was founded in 1838) set higher standards of farming. The introduction of machinery in agriculture was relatively slow, for labour was cheap, and the 'gang' system survived long: under this gangs of labourers, often including women and children, were hired out for field work for long hours in bad conditions. Nevertheless, new machines began to come into use in the second half of the century: one of these came from America —the earliest mechanical cutter, developing out of the McCormick Reaper, to which an effective self-binding device was added in the 1870's.

3. THE DEPRESSION AND ITS RESULTS, 1875-1914

The golden age lasted for about thirty years. While prices of farm products remained reasonably high and competition from overseas foodstuffs was not yet severe, Britain's farmers produced about half the wheat and six-sevenths of the meat which British people ate. Landlords and farmers did well: the remains of their prosperity may be seen in rural England to-day, in the many substantial farm-houses with solid barns, stables and other outbuildings which were put up in this mid-Victorian age. But it was short-lived prosperity, and its end was sudden. Disaster came to British farmers from events across the Atlantic. Railways in Britain had done much to help the farmer, giving him a wider market for his goods, bringing him fertilisers and the new machines, and so increasing the value of his land. Their development in the United States in the 1860's and 1870's opened for arable farming the virgin soils of the prairies, carrying thousands of settlers to turn this new land into the world's greatest cornfields. At the same time the improvement of the combine-harvester made it the ideal tool for working these endless level spaces: and the coming of the steamship opened the way for rapid bulk transport of grain across the ocean. Thus it came about that the crops of the prairie lands could be planted, grown, harvested, threshed, carried across the Atlantic and sold in Britain at prices well below those at which British-grown corn could be marketed. The invasion of American wheat began in the 1870's, with dramatic effects on prices. During 1870-4 the average price of wheat in England was 55s. a quarter: by 1895-9 it had tumbled to 28s. These two figures are a summary of the disaster which struck British agriculture, bringing bankruptcy for many farmers and driving thousands of labourers off the land into new jobs in the towns or across the sea to the United States and Canada.

Times were bad generally in the later 1870's, when an industrial depression threw many town workers out of jobs. Nature herself, too, seemed to take a hand in damaging British agriculture at this time. There were rains and bad harvests: 1879 was the wettest year on record, ruining the home crops—yet still prices fell because of the American imports. There were serious outbreaks of foot and mouth disease and of liver-rot in sheep (about 3 million sheep died): these struck sharply at those farmers who were turning over to stockbreeding and to animal husbandry, aiming to produce meat if wheat could no longer be made to pay. Nor was this all. Technical progress came again to add to the damage. In 1880 the steamship *Strathleven* docked in London from Australia. She had on board the first successful cargo of refrigerated meat (beef and mutton) to reach Britain. It was not long before cargoes of frozen meat were coming regularly and in increasing quantity from New Zealand, Australia and Argentina. Although the harm done to British agriculture by this second 'invasion' was neither so great nor so sudden as that caused by the opening of the prairies, it was a severe blow; and to many a farmer it was fatal.

Wheat prices did not recover for the rest of the 19th century: they reached rock bottom, 22s. 10d. a quarter, in 1894. In 1874 there had been 3,630,000 acres under wheat in Great Britain: by 1900 the total was only just over half that figure. Great areas of land, especially in the arable farms of the east and in the midlands, had been given over to grass. Rents had tumbled. In thirty years some 300,000 agricultural labourers had left the countryside. Moreover, the depression forced farmers almost everywhere to economise. Fences fell into disrepair: ditches got choked: repairs to buildings were neglected, and here and there farms were entirely abandoned. The fields were worked less thoroughly and cleaned less carefully. All this meant that the value of the land itself, the basis of agriculture, inevitably declined. Landowners began to sell estates as never before.

The depression had started in the late 1870's. Twenty years earlier the farmers and landlords might have been able to get Parliament to pass a new Corn Law to protect them against imported wheat and so perhaps avert disaster. But now it was too late. For a majority of the voters were town-dwellers, for whom cheap food from abroad mattered more than rescuing the British farmer. Moreover, Great Britain was dependent on exporting great quantities of manufactured goods: and overseas countries could pay for these by sending foodstuffs in bulk to feed the townsfolk who operated the machines in the factories. So little was done: no tariffs were placed on imported foodstuffs. By an odd twist of fortune the Prime Minister when the agricultural depression began was Benjamin Disraeli, the very man who thirty years before had led the Protectionists in the defence of the Corn Laws against Peel. But he had accepted Free Trade, and so had most of the electors—especially those town workmen to whom he had himself given the vote in 1867.

On the whole, agriculture remained a depressed industry in Britain until the First World War of 1914. Certainly the prosperity of the days of high farming never came back. Yet the picture of difficulty must not be over-painted. Certain areas, especially the great corn-growing region of Lincolnshire and East Anglia, were hit far harder than others: in south-western England, for example, where pasture land had always been more important than arable, things were much less bad. Everywhere times improved and prices rose after about 1900: farming could clearly be made to pay again, though it did not pay as well as in mid-Victorian days. Those farmers did best who were most easily able to adjust their activities to the needs of the market. Most obvious among these were the dairy farmers, supplying milk and butter (and vegetables too) to the growing populations of the great cities: thus the farmers of Cheshire prospered by feeding the townsfolk of Merseyside, Manchester and the Potteries. In some regions, such as the Vale of Evesham, there was great expansion of market garden-ing and fruit-growing in these years. Near London too, in Kent, Middlesex and Hertfordshire, many acres were put under glass to supply food for the giant market of the capital. These last developments were no doubt exceptional, the result of very favourable circumstances. They were yet another sign that Great Britain had become an overwhelmingly industrial country, and that British agriculture was having to adjust itself to this state of affairs.

13   Mid-Victorian Prosperity

1. ECONOMIC PROGRESS AFTER THE REPEAL OF THE CORN LAWS

In 1851 the Great Exhibition took place in Hyde Park. It was opened by Queen Victoria's husband, Albert the Prince Consort, who was an enthusiast for the project. A huge building of iron and glass, the Crystal Palace, was specially constructed to house the exhibits; designed by Joseph Paxton, it was so large that tall trees stood beneath its roof. Within were displayed the products of British craftsmanship and industry, to-gether with a representative array from other lands. There was much opposition to the plan. Many people distrusted the activities of a German prince. Protectionists disliked it because they were still smarting from their defeat over the Corn Laws. Others disapproved of the new-fangled developments of an industrial age. Yet the Exhibition was a great success, attracting thousands of visitors from overseas and bringing a flood of orders to British manufacturers. The Prince had hoped for more than this; he believed that by improving trade between the nations it would promote world peace; but the Crimean War which broke out three years later destroyed that dream. Nevertheless the Exhibition symbolised for all the world to see the rapid strides which were being made by British industry.

It was held in the early years of an era of remarkable economic progress and prosperity. The period which began in the middle 1840's, about the time of the Repeal of the Corn Laws, and ended with the depression of the 1870's, was a high noon of economic advance. The difficulties of the dark years after Waterloo and of the earlier 'hungry forties' seemed to have vanished and to have given way to a new and brighter age in which the majority of the people shared. Even before the Repeal of the Corn Laws in 1846 there had been signs of better times. At bottom the improvement rested upon Britain's natural resources, especially of coal, iron, and skilled and adaptable man-power, and upon the lead that the industrial developments of the late 18th century had given her over all rivals in the race towards industrialisation. Other factors played a part as well. A stable form of government and a secure banking system encouraged investment. Her naval strength guarded vital overseas trade routes. The growth of population—which in England and Wales increased by over a quarter in the twenty years after 1851—gave manufacturing a swiftly-increasing home market as well as a sure supply of workers. The policy of Free Trade, to which Britain was committed after 1846, encouraged overseas commerce. The rapid extension of railways after the 'mania' of the 1840's accelerated industrial and commercial development of every kind. Two great gold discoveries—in California in 1849 and in Australia in 1851—immensely increased the world's supplies of money and thus effectively stimulated trade.

The extent of economic advance was very great. We have already seen that these years were a golden age in British agriculture. A few figures will illustrate the development of industry and trade: they will also reveal that the Great Exhibition was a sign of the beginning of an age, not its climax. Coal output, which was some 45 million tons in 1846, had risen to 65 million ten years later and to over 100 million in the early 1860's. Iron output had been 1 million tons in 1833: by 1855 it was 3 million; by 1875 it had gone up to 6 million. Steel in the early 1850's was a costly material used only for specially fine products, and the annual output was only 40,000 tons: remarkable technical advances in this period multiplied this figure sixfold by 1870, and brought it to a million and a quarter tons by 1880. Railway mileage, 2,044 (3272 km) in 1843, was 14,000 (19600 km) thirty years later: the number of passengers carried by the trains had increased fourteen-fold in the same thirty years. In shipping the advent of the steamship brought a revolution. In 1847 the British mercantile marine totalled about 3 million tons, of which little more than 100,000 tons were under steam: by 1875 the total was well on the way to 5 million—and of these nearly 2 million were steamships. All these figures are small ones when set against later advances: but these were the years when the first great strides were made—and the period, too, when Great Britain was making them alone, virtually unchallenged in industrial supremacy in the world.

For this last reason, one feature of this period needs special emphasis. These were the days when Britain justly laid claim to the title 'workshop of the world'. The great industrial and transport developments were the basis of a swiftly-growing export trade, which carried British-made goods all over the globe. Cotton goods from Lancashire—and also from the Scottish lowlands—had been the most important of British exports since the beginning of the 19th century, and they remained so now, going in great quantities to the United States, to India and to China. Woollen goods came second only to cotton: between them these two textiles made up 60 per cent of the total value of British exports in 1850, showing that Great Britain was becoming the clothing shop of an increasing proportion of the world's inhabitants. Yet although the total of exported textiles was increasing fast, the share they took in Britain's entire export trade tended to fall in these years. This was because other exports were growing, some of them very rapidly. One was the raw material, coal: another was machinery, whose export had been prohibited until 1843: a third was iron and steel goods of every kind. There were many others, some established earlier, like pottery and the countless different copper and brass goods of the Birmingham area, and some just starting to become important, like the tin-plate of South Wales. Of these varied exports, about a third went to the British Empire at this time, a high proportion of them to India. The United States, whose own infant industries could not keep pace with the needs of a fast-expanding population, was another great customer, for machinery as well as for textiles. Most of the exported coal went to Europe and to the Mediterranean lands.

Increase of exports meant increase of imports to pay for them. The most important import was foodstuffs, to feed a growing population more and more of whose members were factory-workers. By the end of the 1870's Britain was importing over half the cereals from which her bread was made. In the first part of the century most of the imported wheat had come from Russia, but now an increasing quantity was coming from across the Atlantic, most of it from the United States. Other foodstuffs also were being imported in greater amounts, including meat, sugar, butter, cheese, and tea. Another vital import which was growing in leaps and bounds was raw cotton, the majority of which came from the United States. The people of Lancashire were harshly reminded how serious it was to be mainly dependent on a single source of supply when the American Civil War broke out in 1861. For the Union navy imposed a tight blockade on the ports of the Southern States, from which the cotton came: and by 1863 most of the Lancashire mills were idle and many thousands of people were unemployed and near to starvation. The desperate attempts to find alternative sources of supply in India and Egypt were not very successful, and after the Civil War was over Britain again went back to dependence on the American crop. Wool was another major import, for the factories of the West Riding. Here Australia had begun to send supplies early in the 19th century, and by its middle years had become the chief source of raw wool.

Timber, tobacco, and various metals added to the list of imports.

What was the relation between exports and imports? Which was the greater? In fact, imports were greater than exports, and the difference between them grew larger still during this mid-Victorian era, so that by the middle 1870's the balance of imports over exports was about £70,000,000 per annum. On the face of things, Great Britain had a large and growing adverse balance of trade. But this did not mean national bankruptcy: on the contrary it was accompanied by a growth of prosperity on a scale which had never previously been seen. This was because certain 'invisible' exports more than outweighed the adverse balance in the 'visible' articles of trade mentioned above. These invisible exports were of two main kinds. First there were the payments for the services rendered by British shipping, carrying the goods of other nations to ports all over the world. The last days of wooden sailing ships saw heavy competition in the Atlantic between British and American-built vessels. But with the coming of steam and of iron (and, later, steel) ships, Britain went far ahead in shipbuilding and in the control of the carrying trade between foreign ports. Secondly, Great Britain was drawing a large and growing income on capital which British firms and individuals had invested abroad. By 1875, it has been estimated, something like £1,000 million of British capital was invested overseas. It went to a wide variety of countries, particularly to western Europe, the United States, South America, and India. A good deal of it was spent on the construction of railways: a fair amount went to foreign governments, to be spent on public works of various kinds. In practice much of the money came back to Britain to buy locomotives, rails, machinery, ships and other heavy equipment; while the interest on the loans provided a lasting revenue for British investors, and helped to give Britain a comfortable surplus in her total balance of trade.

2. COAL, IRON AND STEEL

Perhaps the most striking thing about the British coal industry in the 19th century, apart from its immense increase in output, was that it remained almost entirely a hand industry throughout the century. There was indeed some technical progress. Metal cages bearing iron coal tubs carried the coals and the miners up and down the shafts, and wire rope for the winding engines was introduced from Germany in the 1840's, gradually replacing the hempen ropes and wrought iron chains previously used. But the vital process, the hewing of the coal from the ground, continued to be done by miners with picks and shovels: and this was so despite the deepening of pits, especially in the most important northeastern coalfield. Even by 1900 machinery was scarcely used at all for undercutting coal. One reason for this was that a great many pits were comparatively small; another was that the seams worked were already beginning to grow thinner. Nor was there any national plan for the extraction of coal. British mines remained under a very large number of private owners.

By contrast the iron industry, the other pillar on which Britain's industrial progress rested in these years, underwent great technical changes. The expansion of iron output owed much to two inventions made slightly earlier. John Neilson's invention (1828) of the hot blast, allowing the use of raw coal in the furnaces, cheapened the production of iron by halving the quantity of coal employed: this led in particular to a rapid development of the iron industry in the Scottish county of Lanarkshire. Then in 1840 James Nasmyth invented the steam-hammer, making possible the large-scale manufacture of the great iron bars needed for the new railways and steamships. But the major developments here concerned not iron but steel, that blend of iron and carbon which provides a metal far tougher and more serviceable than iron itself. Its properties had of course long been known, but the cost of its manufacture had prohibited large-scale production. Now, just as Henry Cort's discoveries of the 1780's had opened the way to cheap iron, a series of inventions brought cheap steel and thus promoted a further stage of the Industrial Revolution.

The first in chronological order was the converter devised by Henry Bessemer in 1856. Bessemer (1813–98) was a versatile genius. 'As a young man he made all manner of things—cardboard copies of medallions; a perforated stamp impossible of forgery, which the Government appropriated without acknowledgment (for the rest of his life he hated Government departments); an embossed Utrecht (i.e. worsted) velvet, which found its way to the exalted chairs of Windsor Castle and to the lowly seats of London cabs and omnibuses; a mechanically produced bronze powder, the secret of which he kept during twenty years of manufacture; a sugar press—the outcome of a casual conversation with a Jamaica planter but which none the less won the Prince Consort's Gold Medal in 1851; and finally plate glass, which brought him without knowing it to the verge of his conquest of steel.'[1] He was employed during the Crimean War in making cannon, and realised the superiority of steel for this task. His converter was a cylindrical vessel into which he poured molten pig-iron, driving a hot blast through it to burn out the silicon and other impurities, and adding the appropriate amount of carbon afterwards. The resulting product was known as semi-steel or mild steel. The Sheffield manufacturers scorned it: but Bessemer founded a company to manufacture it, and soon found customers in the railway companies. The process was simple and cheap, and within the years after 1856 the output of steel multiplied several times, while the price was halved.

Ten years later, in 1866, William Siemens, a member of a famous German engineering firm who had settled himself in England, invented another steel-manufacturing process. This was the Open Hearth Process. In this the hot blast on its way to the furnace passed through regenerative cham-

---

[1] C. R. Fay: *Great Britain from Adam Smith to the Present Day*, pp. 273–4.

bers which brought it up to a very high temperature: gas was used as the source of heat, thus making it possible to use any type of coal and to control the temperature very easily. Like the Bessemer process, the Open Hearth made it possible to produce mild steel in bulk and cheaply: and the parallel development of the two rival processes further stimulated the output of steel and its use to replace iron in many types of manufacture. Siemens' genius, like that of Bessemer, was applied in other fields than steel. In 1879 he invented the electric furnace, and in 1883 he was the first man to use electric power for traction purposes in the British Isles.

Yet both these new processes, successful though they were (as was shown by the fact that the British railway systems changed over to steel rails in the 1870's), suffered from one common defect: they could not use iron ores which contained phosphorus. This was a serious drawback for Britain, for most of the native ores (apart from the Cumberland ironfield) were phosphoric: to extend the range of their activities the new steelworks had to import increasing quantities from Spain and Sweden. There was obvious need for a further invention which would make it possible to use phosphoric ores, and in 1878 this next step was taken. It was the work of a London police-court clerk aged 28, Sidney Gilchrist-Thomas, and his cousin: he had studied metallurgy in evening classes and solved the problem in a tiny laboratory in his backyard. He put a basic lining in the converter which would exclude the phosphorus from the metal and deposit it in the slag: it was a device applicable both to the Bessemer and the Open Hearth Process. When he first announced his achievement in 1878 nobody believed him; the following year he gave a demonstration in the growing iron-town of Middlesbrough, and within a few weeks he was world-famous. For if the new technique was valuable to Britain, it was far more so to foreign countries, especially to the United States and to Germany, each of which had rich fields of phosphoric iron ores. The rapid exploitation of these by the Gilchrist-Thomas process marked the beginning of a new era in which Great Britain's economic supremacy was successfully challenged.

3. MACHINERY AND MACHINE TOOLS

It was to be expected that the change from hand-work to the use of power-driven machinery would make rapid progress during such a period of industrial expansion. For example, the power-loom, the vital machine in the weaving process, which had almost extinguished hand-loom weavers in the cotton industry by the middle 1840's, now went on to triumph in woollens as well. It had been unusual in this industry as late as 1840: thirty years later it was clearly supreme. Another advance here was the general use of combing machinery to separate the long wool from the remainder. Edmund Cartwright had invented a machine for combing as early as 1789, but a really effective one did not come into use until that devised by S. C. Lister and James Noble about 1850, which spread rapidly through the woollen industry of the West Riding. In the textile industries, too, steam finally drove out water as a source of power, as a result of the abundant supplies of cheap coal in areas within easy rail distance of the mills. In other industries not hitherto mechanised the change began in these years. Thus the sewing-machine, invented in America by J. M. Singer about the middle of the century, began in the late 'fifties to come into use in tailoring and boot-and-shoe factories in Britain; although until later in the century the power used to drive it was normally not steam but hand or foot.

But the most important developments in machines at this time were of a different kind from those just mentioned. They concerned the manufacture of the first accurate machine tools and standardised parts of machines. Later generations have come to take mass production of great numbers of identical articles for granted. Such production depends on the existence of machine tools, devices like the mechanical drill or mechanical cutting machines which have become a commonplace of 20th-century factories and which succeed only because they are precise to within the minutest fraction of an inch. These machine tools, whose role in the Industrial Revolution is of immense importance, were first devised by a succession of outstanding craftsmen and engineers in the early 19th century. The first of them, indeed, was properly an 18th-century figure, a contemporary of James Watt, the parts of whose steam-engines, it will be recalled, had to be constructed with tools made by the variable hands of workmen. He was Joseph Bramah (1748–1814), who devised a patent lock, and made machine tools in order to be able to reproduce it accurately. Bramah was indeed a benefactor of the human species, inventing an improved water-closet and also the pull-over tap long used in public houses. Trained by Bramah was Henry Maudslay (1771–1831), who in the years round about 1800 invented a heavy screw-cutting lathe, which produced the first standard screw, and a slide-rest for holding the metal-cutting tool. Among Maudslay's pupils were Joseph Whitworth (1803–87) and James Nasmyth (1808–90), each of whom began to manufacture machine tools in Manchester in the early 1830's. It was Whitworth's work, based on that of Maudslay and Bramah, which helped to quicken industrial advance in the mid-Victorian era. He set out to build standardised gauges and measuring machines and to turn out a series of exact and classified screws and screw-threads, and to get them generally adopted. His work was highly commended at the Great Exhibition, and by 1870 he had gone far towards achieving his object. Engineers and manufacturers who depended on the use of machines were beginning to realise the enormous advantages of standardised parts in saving time and labour.

4. TRANSPORT AND COMMUNICATIONS

Much the most important development in land transport in these years was of course the swift growth of the railways, which has been dealt with elsewhere.[1] Here it is worth noting their effects on other means of land transport. They ruined the canals except in certain areas: what tended to happen was that the railway companies bought up the canals and neglected them. By 1865 about one-third of all the canals in the country belonged to railway companies. As for the roads, their long-distance traffic fell into the hands of the railways: and as a result the turnpike trusts went bankrupt in large numbers. By the middle of the century they were decaying fast, and control of the English roads was falling back into the hands of the rate-payers of the parish. In the towns horse-drawn omnibus services were firmly established by 1850: in 1855 an omnibus company, which later grew into the London General Omnibus Company, was organised in the capital —by Frenchmen. The surfaces of London streets began to show signs of more advanced engineering, and asphalt was introduced as a road surface from Paris. Both in towns and along country roads telegraph poles began to become familiar things in these years. The telegraph had been first patented in Britain in 1837; for the first few years it was used only by the railways, but after 1850 various private companies opened telegraph services. In 1868 these were taken over by the Post Office. Two years earlier the laying of the Atlantic cable had been completed by the steam-ship *Great Eastern*, after a failure in the previous year; and by 1870 Britain was linked with India by cable.

Among the relatively small-scale changes that did much to stimulate economic progress in these years, a high place must be given to the Penny Post. This had been started in 1840, and replaced the old system under which letters were charged by weight and distance, and payment was made by the receiver, not by the sender. Rowland Hill (1795–1879) devised the new system, under which every letter, irrespective of distance, was charged one penny postage in the form of an adhesive stamp fixed to it by the sender: the first stamps were the famous Victorian 'penny blacks'. It was immensely successful, and the idea spread at once to other countries. Coinciding as it did with the coming of railways, of which the Post Office took prompt advantage in order to speed up mail deliveries, it was an enormous boon to business enterprise. Another significant Post Office development of this period was the opening in 1861 of the Post Office Savings Bank, promoted by Gladstone, then Chancellor of the Exchequer.

The great export trade of these years depended upon the development of shipping, and here the mid-Victorian era saw notable changes. Steam-ships, indeed, were well-established before the 1840's. A Scottish engineer, William Symington, had been experimenting with marine steam-engines before the end of the 18th century, and in 1803 his *Charlotte Dundas* had

---

[1] For railways, see above, Chap. 10.

successfully steamed 19 miles (30 kilometres) along the Forth–Clyde Canal. Several regular coastal services with steam-vessels had been opened in 1816, and two years later the Dover–Calais service started. The first crossing of the Atlantic under continuous steam power was made by a cross-channel steamer of 703 tons, the *Sirius*, in 1837, taking 18 days 10 hours from Cork to New York. In 1839 Samuel Cunard obtained the government contract to carry the North Atlantic mails, and so began the Cunard Line. Various other steamship companies arose about the same time. Nevertheless, steam did not replace sails at all rapidly. Steamships were costly, and could at first only operate profitably in such favourable conditions as those provided by regular cross-Channel services. Their consumption of coal in their early stages was extremely high, which meant either that their trips could only be short ones, or that the space available for passengers and cargo was restricted.

At this time, too, the sailing ship reached its highest peak of achievement in the famous 'clippers'. This type of ship, built for speed with its great length and vast area of canvas, was originally developed by American shipbuilders in the early years of the 19th century; although probably the most famous of them were the British-built ones employed in the 1850's and 1860's to carry the tea crop from China to the Thames. The competition from American-built and also Canadian-built sailing ships was fierce; so far as sailing ships were concerned, the American mercantile marine was growing faster than the British, especially in the Atlantic trade; and it must be remembered that steamships were a very small proportion only of the world's shipping in 1850. What gave victory to steam (and enabled Britain to defeat the American challenge) was the development of iron, and later of steel, ships, and the invention of engines more economical of coal.

Iron steamboats were in use on rivers in the 1820's, but there were serious doubts about their ocean-going capacity. In 1839 the East India Company bought its first iron ship; the Cunard Line did not launch one until 1865. The early iron vessels were paddle-driven, but the screw-propeller came gradually into use in the 50's and 60's. One of the most celebrated of the early iron steamships was the gigantic *Great Eastern*, the work of that versatile genius Isambard Brunel.[1] She was 680 feet (207 metres) long, far bigger than any other ship of her time: equipped with both screw and paddle, she was launched in 1858, but she proved a commercial failure and was turned into a cable-laying ship. A more successful invention of 1854 was the compound engine, devised by John Elder, which made possible a great economy of fuel. Despite such developments, many wooden ships and many sailing ships were launched in the 1860's. In the next decade, thanks to the work of Bessemer and Siemens, steel hulls would come into more common use: they would supersede iron, and for commercial purposes complete the destruction of the sailing ship.

---

[1] Who had earlier built the *Great Western* (1837), the second ship to cross the Atlantic wholly under steam, and the *Great Britain* (1843).

5. RISING STANDARDS OF LIVING: EMPLOYERS AND EMPLOYEES

Such changes as those described in this chapter—an expanding industry and export trade, a growth of transport and of overseas investment—meant a rising standard of living for the people of mid-Victorian Britain. Those who most obviously benefited were the middle-class manufacturers and merchants, the men who made the goods and those who sold them. It is worth noting that most business firms in this age were still comparatively small: generally speaking, they were family concerns or partnerships, private companies which had not yet expanded into larger enterprises with numerous shareholders. Yet change was on the way. Some of the most important Victorian businesses had from the start to be companies with many shareholders, for they needed more capital than the resources of one or two families could supply. This had been true in earlier times, for example, of the overseas trading companies like the East India Company: now there were among these 'joint stock' companies the railways, the bigger shipping lines, some of the firms in heavy industry like iron and steel, and some of the banks. Moreover, the device of 'limited liability' became legally established in this period. Hitherto any one partner in a business could be made responsible for the entire debts of the firm if it went bankrupt—and a great many firms did go bankrupt every year; now a series of acts from 1855 to 1862, of which the first was the Limited Liability Act of 1855, enabled persons to take shares in companies without becoming liable for more than the amount of their own holding. This eventually encouraged the growth of giant business concerns with many hundreds of shareholders: but its use spread very slowly before the 1870's. In the mid-Victorian era, apart from such businesses as the railways, the typical 'employer' was one man or a family partnership. Factories varied so greatly in size that 'averages' do not mean very much: yet it is probably fair to say that a cotton mill which employed 250 hands was a large one, and that in most other industries, apart from such enterprises as ironworks and shipbuilding yards, the general size of factories was much less than half that figure.

Thus there was a considerable and growing class of well-to-do employers: and with them may be ranked the bigger merchants and agents, the railway directors and managers, the bankers and stockbrokers and others who in various ways controlled Victorian industry and trade. They prospered mightily in these years. They built for themselves, in these days when materials and labour were cheap, large and substantial mansions and villas—then on the outskirts of the industrial towns which provided the money for them, but now usually enveloped by later suburbs. They lived in solid comfort, filling their living-rooms with heavy furniture in oak and mahogany; often they employed two or three domestic servants; they ate meals on the lavish scale indicated in that most typically Victorian work, Mrs. Beeton's *Cookery Book*, which was published in 1859: and they kept their carriage and pair. Their sons went to the growing Public Schools. Yet despite all this expenditure they were thrifty: for they contrived usually to extend their businesses out of profits, setting aside enough to install new equipment, add another section to the factory, or open a new branch overseas.

What about their employees, the working people who formed the majority of the population? Did they share in the prosperity? The answer to this is undoubtedly that most of them did, though the gain made by the individual workman was nothing like so great as that of the average employer. There were bad times like the economic crisis of 1857–8, which caused a good deal of unemployment: there were troubles affecting particular areas, like the cotton famine caused in Lancashire by the American Civil War. There were important groups in the population which benefited very little if at all from the general progress, such as the agricultural labourers: and there was a large body, perhaps one in ten of the entire working class, consisting of tramps, casual labourers, dockers, and workers in various 'sweated' trades, who remained in desperate poverty on the edge of starvation, inhabiting the slums of London's East End and of industrial cities like Glasgow and Newcastle, or drifting in and out of the workhouses in the rural areas. But for the majority these years brought an appreciable improvement in living conditions, especially after 1865. The best evidence for this comes from a comparison of prices and wages. Prices rose considerably between 1850 and 1875, probably on account of the great increase in the world gold supplies: yet the wages of most British workmen, and particularly those of the more skilled men like the engineers, more than kept pace with them. It has been estimated that 'real wages'—that is, the power of the workman to buy goods at current prices—rose by about one-third between 1850 and 1875. What this meant in practice is revealed by the fact that the average consumption per head of meat, tea, sugar and tobacco rose considerably in the same years.

Various other factors helped in this period to make life less harsh than it had been in the first half of the 19th century. Trade Unions, beginning with the Amalgamated Society of Engineers in 1851, effectively established themselves. The Co-operative Stores spread fast in the industrial districts of the north, bringing cheaper yet purer food to working-class households.[1] The movement for Factory Reform, after a long struggle, achieved limited hours, and better conditions, safeguarded by government inspection, in many important industries by 1870.[2] Local authorities up and down the country were at last beginning to tackle the various problems connected with Public Health.[3] Sundry minor benefits of various kinds were beginning to be available in some degree to working-class folk. Some local authorities were opening public parks, others public baths and wash-houses. Soap was cheaper: matches and paraffin were coming into common use: and some working-class wives managed to afford one of the new Singer sewing-machines. Cigarettes came in after the Crimean

---

[1] For Trade Unions and Co-ops, see below, Chap. 17.

[2] For Factory Reform, see below, Chap. 18.

[3] For Public Health, see below, Chap. 19.

War. The railway companies were running cheap excursions to the seaside. Such things were beginnings, no more. It would be quite wrong to suppose that the average mid-Victorian workingman thought of himself as living in a sort of golden age. His housing conditions often remained appalling. The threat of unemployment was nearly always present, and he had no security against its effects except what he might obtain through his own savings in a Friendly Society. Old age was inevitable, but there were no old age pensions in the 19th century. Nevertheless, it is broadly true that the era of mid-Victorian prosperity brought substantial benefits to the majority of English people.

14 The Challenge to British Economic Supremacy, 1875-1914

I. WHAT THE CHALLENGE WAS

During the final quarter of the 19th century Britain ran into rougher economic water than she had met since 1850. The reasons for this were in part international—a country so dependent on overseas trade as Victorian Britain was bound to be much at the mercy of international developments in trade and finance. The usual symptoms of bad times appeared: prices fell, factories closed down, the number of unemployed went up, there was widespread distress. Agriculture was in special trouble.[1] The fluctuations of good and bad spells in these years make it misleading to talk of a 'Great Depression' at this time. Nevertheless the *rate* at which industry grew slowed down appreciably, and profits were lower than they had been. British businessmen were often reluctant to introduce new processes or machinery, for example in chemicals or in the application of electricity. There is a good deal of evidence that the difficulties of the 1870's and 1880's undermined the confidence and optimism which had marked mid-Victorian manufacturers and merchants.

In truth the writing was on the wall—the sign of the end of an era and the warnings of difficult times to come. For the age of British economic supremacy was over. Henceforward Great Britain was to be challenged, and to a great extent successfully challenged, in the markets of the world by countries which were in many ways more amply equipped in natural resources; and most notably by the United States and by Germany. The United States, once the Civil War (1861-5) was over, entered upon an era of astonishing economic development. Railways were thrown across the continent, mines dug in the Rocky Mountains, and thousands of acres of virgin prairie soil put under the plough, while in the great cities of the eastern states there arose innumerable factories and businesses. Every year many thousands of immigrants from Europe brought their muscles

[1] See above, pp. 100-2.

and their brains to this new country: yet there were never enough people for the jobs to be done, and so there took place a swift development of machinery of every kind. In Germany the situation was very different, yet the challenge to Britain was as great. The German Empire achieved political unity in 1871. The German people were gifted and industrious: they had vast resources for the age of power-driven machinery, including in the Ruhr the richest coalfield in Europe, and also the great ironfield of Lorraine: and their rulers during the generation after 1871 protected German manufacturers by tariffs, and stimulated many of them by building up great armaments.

Coal was one key to industrial progress in the modern world: steel, thanks to Bessemer, Siemens and Gilchrist-Thomas, had become the other. Not until 1899 did American coal output exceed that of Britain, and British output at the time was still more than double that of Germany. But in steel the position was very different. American production had passed that of Britain by 1890; six years later the Germans, having more than doubled their own output in that time, overhauled Britain; and by the end of the century the total steel production of Germany and the U.S.A. together was well over three times that of Britain. In short, by 1900 Great Britain had been far outdistanced in the production of the most important industrial commodity in the world, the metal which was by this date vital to all heavy machinery and engineering, in addition to its use in armaments. This event was no doubt inevitable once Germany and the United States started rapid industrialisation, for both countries had far greater supplies of iron ore than Britain: yet its coming could scarcely be welcome to men who had grown accustomed to the comfortable supremacy of the mid-Victorian 'workshop of the world'.

The situation in steel was in itself only one element in the challenge, although the most significant one. There were many others. One was the relative supplies of man-power of the three countries. Both Germany and the United States had more inhabitants than the United Kingdom in 1870—and in both the rate of increase during the next forty years was higher. The population of the United Kingdom rose from 31·8 millions in 1871 to 45·3 millions in 1911, an increase of 42·4 per cent: Germany went from 41 millions in 1871 to 64·9 millions in 1910, an increase of 58·2 per cent: the U.S.A. in the same years rose by no less than 138 per cent, from 38·5 millions to 91·7 millions. A second element in the challenge was the use of tariff barriers; whereas Great Britain stuck to free trade, Germany erected a protectionist tariff in 1879, and the U.S.A. in 1890; and both countries, in common with most of the rest of the world, put them higher still in later years. Their aim was to protect their own manufacturers—at the expense of British ones. A third element in the German and American challenge lay in the facts that they could learn by Britain's earlier mistakes, and that, starting up new industries, they had no capital tied up in existing plant and machinery: thus their equipment could be and very often was—e.g. in the steel industry itself—more up-to-date and better planned than that of Britain. And a fourth was the superiority of Germans and Americans in technical education: their technical schools and colleges were more numerous and on the whole more progressive than those of Britain.

These things foreshadowed a world economic map in which Britain's place would be very different from that which she held in mid-Victorian days. She would lose markets and leadership alike. Nevertheless, the speed of this change must not be exaggerated. The market open to the great exporting countries was practically unlimited: there was ample room for all to do business in the less-developed areas of the globe—which in the late 19th century meant virtually the entire world outside western Europe and the United States. It was certainly not a question of British trade declining automatically because that of Germany and the United States was growing. Rather it was that all three countries were expanding their business at different rates, all of them fast but that of Britain appreciably less fast than the others. Nor must the change be dated too early. As late as 1889 Great Britain's foreign trade was still greater in amount than that of Germany and the United States combined; so, even in 1900, were British exports of steel. In the years immediately before 1914 British shipyards were building over 60 per cent of all the world's mercantile tonnage. None of these figures suggests a nation in decay: rather they seem to indicate that Britain's supremacy was in certain ways long maintained.

2. THE DEVELOPMENT OF BRITISH INDUSTRY AND TRADE, 1875–1914

Whatever conclusions are drawn from a comparison with the economic expansion of other lands, one thing is unquestionably true of British industry in the forty years before 1914—namely, that it expanded and developed its activities on a great scale. The basic and traditional industries —coal, iron and steel, shipbuilding, woollens and cotton—increased their output. Others already established on a comparatively small scale grew far bigger: these included such enterprises as boots and shoes, chocolate, biscuits, brewing, soap and tobacco. Then there were new fields opened by various technical inventions and discoveries into which British business began to enter—electrical engineering, bicycles and motor-cars, aluminium, rubber, margarine, ferro-concrete, artificial silk; and a new source of power, electricity, had come into use, especially in certain areas like the north-east coast. There were many notable individual developments of particular firms: it was in these years that such new names as Lipton, Dunlop, Boot, Selfridge and Lever became household words. Taken as a whole, the figures of production and export available for the study of British trade in the years before the First World War reveal a swiftly-advancing industrial and trading community. Between 1893 and 1913 coal production rose by 75 per cent and steel production by 136 per cent: exports of manufactured goods went up by 121 per cent, those of raw materials by

238 per cent. Over the same years the outward clearances of shipping, both British and foreign, from British ports were considerably more than doubled.

Such expansion of industry demanded a great increase of capital, and thus contributed to another striking development of these years—a general rise in the size of firms. For all large-scale industry joint-stock companies, often with many shareholders, became the normal practice, even where, as was not uncommon, the new company retained the name of the private firm out of which it had grown. This development provided the new funds necessary for expansion; yet it brought with it dangers and disadvantages. The old paternal management of the family firm had sometimes been benevolent, sometimes tyrannical: it had always been direct and intimate, in contrast with the new situation in the 'limited company', where policy was directed in the interests of numerous share-holders who never saw the works or the workers and who were solely concerned about the size of their dividends. So management might become more impersonal and harsher. Moreover, this process of enlarging was soon taken far beyond the range of single firms. For there were obvious advantages in combining a group of separate companies which were competing in the same line of business: costs (such as those of offices, advertising, and marketing) could be considerably reduced, and the price-cutting 'wars' avoided. If the group of companies was so large that they virtually controlled the market in the particular commodity they sold, then a combine or union of these companies could in effect fix prices at its own level. So there arose in Britain (as in Germany and the United States) about this time a number of giant combines, resulting from amalgamations of firms. The first, not very successful, was the Salt Union, started in 1888, which claimed to control 91 per cent of the salt output of the United Kingdom: others which came into being before 1914 included the thread-making combine organised by J. and P. Coats of Paisley, the Imperial Tobacco Company, and the vast steel and armaments business of Vickers-Armstrong.

One further feature of British industry and trade in these years deserves special mention. As we have noticed, Britain's export trade, upon which so much of her prosperity depended, was well maintained in this period. Despite tariff barriers, British goods were still going in large quantities to the United States, Germany and to other European countries; more were going to Argentina than before; and there was a great increase in the goods going to the British Empire, especially to India, Canada, Australia and New Zealand. On the whole British merchants seemed to have no difficulty in selling their wares. But a most significant change was taking place in the kind of wares they sold. Britain's 19th-century prosperity had been built up on exports of manufactured goods like the cottons of Lancashire, the woollens of Yorkshire, and the hardware of the Black Country. Now the proportion of these goods in her exports was falling—while machinery, coal, and ships were becoming more prominent in the export

IRON AND ITS USES: The Iron Bridge at Coalbrookdale, Shropshire, built in 1777–81. Interior of a smelting house at Broseley, Shropshire, about 1790.

TWO ASPECTS OF THE EIGHTEENTH CENTURY. English Taste at its best; a teaset produced by Josiah Wedgwood in 1784 (pp. 43–45). (*Below*) The Slave Trade; a descendant of a slave demonstrates the iron collar used to prevent escape, and manacles; also the model of a slave ship used by Wilberforce to show the House of Commons the way in which slaves were stowed (see pp. 60–61).

FOUR CREATORS OF MODERN BRITAIN: (*Top, left*) Thomas Telford, 1757–1834, maker of the Caledonian Canal and the London–Holyhead Road (see p. 49). (*Right*) James Watt, 1736–1819, the father of steam power (see pp. 30–33). (*Bottom, left*) George Stephenson, 1781–1848, the father of the railway engine (see pp. 75–77). (*Right*) Sir Henry Bessemer, 1813–1898, whose steel-making process created the modern industry (see pp. 106–107).

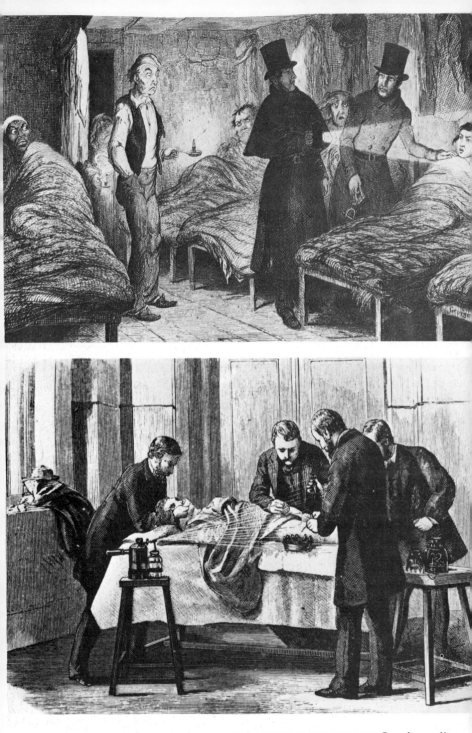

LAW AND ORDER AND MEDICAL SKILL IN THE NINETEENTH CENTURY: London policemen arrest a suspect in a common lodging house. (*Below*) The Lister antiseptic
spray in use at an operation in the 1870's (pp. 196–197): the standard of steri-
lisation remained very primitive.

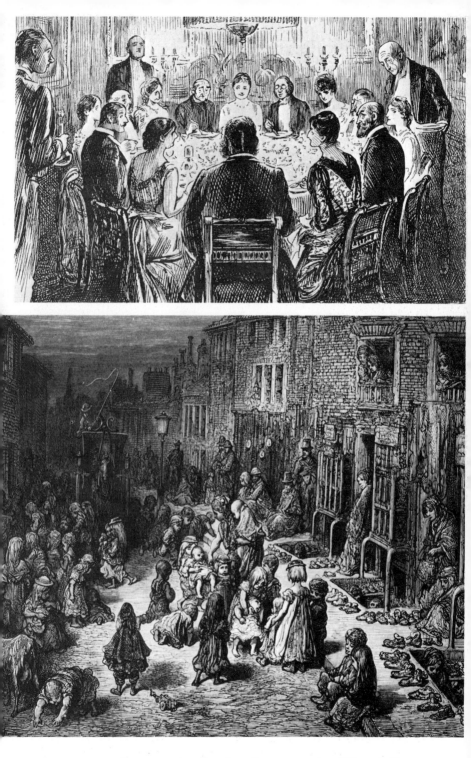

THE TWO NATIONS: An upper-class London dinner party in 1886, and Gustave Doré's picture of Dudley Street, Seven Dials, London, in the 1870's.

TWO SORTS OF EDUCATION: The spacious playing-fields of Victorian Rugby (pp. 205–206) contrast with the asphalt yard of a London elementary school in the 1900's (p. 208).

PUBLIC TRANSPORT: Swindon station on the Great Western Railway in the 1880's, showing the means by which both Brunel's broad gauge (p. 78) and also narrow gauge trains were served. (*Below, left*) London buses, horsedrawn in the nineteenth century, with (*right*) motor buses coming in the early 1900's (p. 118).

VOTES FOR WOMEN AND THE RIGHT TO STRIKE: (*Above*) A suffragette arrested for demonstrating outside Buckingham Palace (see pp. 233–234) (*Below*) Ben Tillett addressing strikers in 1911 (see p. 158).

trade. This was a dangerous omen for the future: for all these commodities could be used to build the industry and trade of other countries. They were in fact means by which Britain's customers were turned into Britain's commercial and manufacturing competitors.

There was another dangerous aspect of the situation. Britain had become during the 19th century overwhelmingly dependent on foreign trade. By 1914 the swift expansion of her industries had far outrun her own natural resources. By that date she was importing over half her foodstuffs; and—if we leave coal out of the reckoning—almost seven-eighths of the raw materials used in her industries. All the cotton and most of the wool, all the oil, nearly all the tin and other non-ferrous metals, a great deal of the iron—all came from overseas.

British investment overseas grew fast in these years, apart from occasional fluctuations during periods of slump. Between 1865 and 1914 the total amount of British capital invested overseas was over £4,000 million. It was invested overseas rather than in Britain because it brought in more profit: there were new areas with rich possibilities like the prairies of Canada, and in many places overseas labour was cheaper than in Britain. Most of the investment went to temperate regions of recent settlement, notably the U.S.A., Canada and Australia. A good deal went to the British Empire, which grew fast in these years,[1] and a fair amount to South America. As always, much of the money thus loaned by British capitalists came back to Britain; and a growing fraction of it was spent on machinery and other equipment, which would one day enable these less-developed countries to produce their own manufactured goods instead of buying them from Britain. This process was inevitable, for Great Britain could not indefinitely have remained the workshop of the world. But it should enable us to understand the change which was coming over Britain's economic position. Meanwhile, the proceeds from overseas investment continued to give Britain a favourable balance of trade right up to 1914; aided, as before, by the money brought in by British shipping companies; and also aided by the financial services rendered by British bankers to customers all over the globe in these days when London was the main financial centre of the world.

3. TRANSPORT AND COMMUNICATIONS, 1875–1914

This was a great age in the history of British transport. Besides the developments on the railways which we have already noticed,[2] it witnessed the dawn of the bicycle age, the manufacture of the first British motor-cars, and the beginning of greatly-improved roads; the application of electricity to trams and trains; an outstanding invention in marine engineering and great progress in ship-building; the coming of telephone and wireless telegraphy; and the first hesitant beginning of the aeroplane.

---

[1] See below, pp. 135–40.   [2] See above, pp. 82–85.

Bicycles, in sundry shapes which appear odd to later eyes, had existed since the early 19th century. The 'penny-farthing', with its great front wheel and its tiny rear one, was in vogue in the 1870's: yet it was two developments of the next decade which made cycling easy and popular. In 1885 the first 'safety' bicycle was built at Coventry; and in 1888 J. B. Dunlop (a Belfast veterinary surgeon) invented his pneumatic tyre. Cycling caught on at once, among people of every class. Its effects were various. It created a new industry in the Coventry area and stimulated the rubber trade. It gave to many thousands of workmen and their families a chance, hitherto rare, to get easily into the country from the smoky cities. And it helped to revolutionise women's dress by killing off the heavy petticoat.

The petrol engine was a German invention, the work of Gottfried Daimler and Carl Benz: it first drove a vehicle in 1885. The early movements of the motor-car in England were hindered by a law which required any horseless carriage on the roads to travel at a maximum of four miles an hour and to be preceded by a man bearing a red flag—a law not wholly unwise when the lives of horses and of droves of sheep and cattle needed protection against steam-traction engines of various kinds, some very experimental. This was not completely repealed until 1896,[1] when the law permitted 'light locomotives' to travel at up to fourteen miles per hour. By the end of 1904 there were some 20,000 motor-cars in Britain. Many of them were foreign-made, although a number of British firms had begun to build; the Rolls-Royce was started in 1906. Progress was slow until after the First World War, and the motor-car remained very much a rich man's luxury.

The roads of Britain at this time were far from ready, in many areas, to receive motor traffic even when its speed was limited to fourteen miles (twenty-two kilometres) per hour. The turnpike trusts had nearly all died by 1888, when the newly-formed County Councils took charge of the main roads. These bodies spent a good deal of money on road-making and repairs before 1914. Yet most roads were not main ones; in 1894 these secondary roads were handed over to the Urban and Rural District Councils. Such roads remained narrow, treacherous and—above all—dusty and muddy until after the First World War. Action on a national scale to deal with roads did not come until 1910, when, as a result of Lloyd George's 'People's Budget', a central Road Board was set up. This was created by money from motor-car licences and from taxes on petrol; and it began at once to enable the County Councils to tackle the principal immediate problem—that of tarring the surfaces of main roads.

In the towns new forms of public transport arrived in this period to compete with the cab. One was the motor-bus. London had 1,000 on its streets by 1908, and 3,500 five years later, when nearly all its horse-buses had gone; while in the provinces several motor-bus companies, like the Midland Red in Birmingham and Crosville in the north-west, were well-

---

[1] Although the red flag was not compulsory after 1878.

established by 1914. A second was the electric tram. It was German in origin, and continental cities were far swifter to develop it on an extensive scale than British ones. By 1914, however, there were over 2,500 miles (4,000 kilometres) of electric tramlines in Britain. Buses, trams and—in a few cities only—underground railways enabled the growing urban areas of the 20th century to cope with their daily 'rush hour' problem of passenger transport: they also enabled more people to live at a greater distances from their places of work.

In shipping this was a period of much progress. The total tonnage of British steamships rose from 1,700,000 to 11,300,000 between 1873 and 1913—a gigantic rise, even when allowance is made for the fact that sailing shipping fell over the same forty years from 4,100,000 tons to a mere 800,000. The new steamships included some celebrated passenger vessels, like the Cunarders *Mauretania* and *Lusitania*: the latter was to be sunk by submarine in 1915, but the former held the 'blue riband' for the fastest Atlantic crossing for twenty-two years after her maiden trip in 1907. Such great new liners gave a splendid opportunity of growth to the port of Southampton, with its deep water and four daily tides, and these years saw a rapid expansion of docks and quays there. Manchester too developed as a port at this time, thanks to the construction of the Manchester Ship Canal; opened in 1893, this new deep waterway enabled ocean-going steamers to dock in the capital of the English cotton industry. Further, Britain made in these years one highly important contribution to marine engineering. This was the invention of the steam-turbine by Sir Charles Parsons (1854–1931). It was applied to drive marine engines from 1894 onwards. The greater speeds it made possible were obvious at once, and within ten years it was being adopted both in naval vessels and in large liners.[1]

Yet perhaps the most important single change in shipping at this time was the introduction of oil as a fuel. It was used in two ways—first to drive steam-engines, and secondly to drive internal-combustion motors. The second of these uses was of very slight importance before 1914 in British shipping: Diesel heavy-oil engines were being manufactured in Germany from 1897 onwards, yet not until 1912 was a ship of any size fitted with one. But the use of oil fuel for raising steam had begun to develop fast. It had great advantages over coal: it saved space and labour, it was cleaner, and it produced much more steam in proportion to weight. The British Admiralty quickly grasped its possibilities, and warships as well as liners began to convert to oil before 1914. For Britain, which had abundant coal but virtually no oil resources at home, this represented yet another part of the challenge to her economic supremacy. The oil industry, beginning

[1] Parsons turned his small experimental *Turbinia* loose at the 1897 Jubilee Naval Review at Spithead. 'To the consternation of the Navy's top brass, the little *Turbinia* tore between the assembled ranks of flag-bedecked ships. The fleet's fastest destroyers were ordered to intercept the intruder, but in vain. As she was capable of the hitherto unheard-of speed of 34½ knots, *Turbinia* showed them a clean pair of heels.' L. T. C. Rolt: *Victorian Engineering*, 1974 ed., p. 205.

in the United States, had by now become an enormous international business with wells in Russia and Borneo, Texas and Mexico; and private British companies like Shell were prominent in it. A measure of its importance may be seen in the fact that when (1909) the Anglo-Persian Oil Company was formed to exploit a newly-discovered oil field in Persia, the British government itself became a major shareholder in the company. 'It was only the second or third time that the British Crown had acquired shares in a joint-stock company since Queen Elizabeth put money into Drake's privateering voyages and other enterprises of her subjects, or King Charles I put money into a trading venture to the China Seas.'[1]

The telephone was a Canadian invention, patented by Alexander Graham Bell in 1876. It came into use in Britain in the 1880's, operated by private companies and later by a number of municipal councils. It spread fairly slowly, with some opposition from those who held that telephone wires and poles would spoil the appearance of the countryside. In 1892 the Post Office took over the main trunk lines; it later extended this control to the privately-owned National Telegraph Company, and thus from 1912 onwards became responsible for the telephone services of the entire country.[2] Some years before this event the first steps in wireless communication had been successfully taken. The pioneer was an Italian scientist, Guglielmo Marconi: the Post Office gave him intelligent support. Early experiments took place across the Bristol Channel: and at the end of 1901 the first wireless message was successfully sent from Poldhu in Cornwall across the Atlantic to Newfoundland. In its first years the use of wireless telegraphy was practically limited to shipping, and even by 1914 less than 1,000 British steamships carried wireless. One of them had been the unlucky *Titanic*, the great liner which on its maiden voyage in 1912 had struck an iceberg and gone down with the loss of over 1,500 lives: wireless alone had made it possible to rescue some survivors.

The aeroplane was not in any sense a British invention. Its chief pioneers were the brothers Wilbur and Orville Wright in the United States, and Louis Blériot in France: and Blériot made the first cross-Channel flight, landing in Kent in the summer of 1909. Nor was it yet of any economic importance. It early uses were military and its first cargoes were bombs.

4. NEW MATERIALS AND NEW POWER

Great Britain's industrial strength in the hundred years which followed the great changes of the 18th century depended upon a few comparatively simple materials. Coal, iron and steel, wool, cotton—these were the major elements in it. To them of course must be added timber, the various clays from which factory bricks and Wedgwood china alike were made, other metals like tin and copper, chemicals such as sulphuric acid and the alkalis,

---

[1] Sir John Clapham: *An Economic History of Modern Britain*, Vol. III, p. 276.
[2] Except for the local telephone services in Hull, which have continued to be a separate undertaking, controlled by the city itself.

and so on: but these remained subsidiary to the small main group. Equally, the provision of power was a relatively straightforward matter. At first it was water-power; then this was gradually—not by any means entirely— replaced by steam in the course of the 19th century. The success of the mid-Victorian 'workshop of the world' thus rested almost entirely upon a small number of foundations—upon the steam-engine and the iron and steel of the blastfurnaces, upon the textile goods of Lancashire and the West Riding, and upon the coal which lit the furnaces and drove the engines, the locomotives and the steamships. Broadly, this state of affairs remained overwhelmingly true until the last quarter of the 19th century. Then changes began to show themselves. It was not that coal, iron and steel, wool and cotton and the steam engine lost their central places in British industry: in fact they retained them right on into the 20th century. What began to happen in the last years of the 19th century was something quite different—namely, that new materials of various kinds and new sources of power began to be discovered and developed, and to take up positions in the industrial picture. Although these new things were relatively unimportant at first, it was plain that they would become very important in the not too distant future. Their arrival upset the existing industrial balance, and this was disturbing for Great Britain. For some of these newer materials were not easily available to her, whereas her industrial rivals were often well endowed with them. Here in fact was yet another part of the challenge to British industrial leadership. One result of this problem of new materials was to encourage the more industralised countries to look for them in the less-developed parts of the globe, for example in Africa; here was one source of the rivalry among the European powers for overseas empires in the last quarter of the 19th century.

The newly-developed industrial materials were of very varied kinds. They included such different things as aluminium, rubber, the oils used in the manufacture of soap and of margarine, a wide range of synthetic dyestuffs, and other chemical products, ferro-concrete, petroleum, and the earliest plastics like celluloid and artificial silk. The part which Great Britain played in their use and manufacture varied greatly. Some, like rubber and palm oil, came from tropical countries. Rubber had begun to be used in the middle years of the 19th century, but it was the development of the bicycle, and later, of the motor-car industries which created a heavy demand for it; by 1914 over 20,000 people were employed in the British rubber-manufacturing industry. Aluminium was later to become an everyday item of kitchen equipment, and later still to be vital to a vast aircraft industry; but before 1914 it was the basis of only a tiny industry in the United Kingdom, which had very little of the bauxite clay from which the metal is obtained. The synthetic dyestuff industry had its origins in the discovery by a young British chemist, William Perkin, of a method of manufacturing a mauve dye (1856); but since that time German chemists had gone far ahead, and by 1914 Great Britain was a long way behind Germany in this great and highly-important industry which was built very largely on materials derived from coal-tar. Celluloid had first been made (in Britain) in 1855: artificial silk had followed (in France and in Britain) in the 1880's, and the first English factory for manufacture of this early example of plastics opened in 1900. By 1914 about a quarter of the world's total output—an output still very small—was made in Britain. Finally ferro-concrete, which had been tried out as a building material in various countries during the 19th century, began to be extensively used in Britain about 1900.[1] It was quickly and naturally followed by the coming of steel-frame building.

These things were newly-developed materials, whose use in industry was in innumerable ways starting to alter people's ways of life. At least as important was that new source of power which began its effective career in Britain during these years—electricity. Scientists in Britain and other countries had investigated the nature of electricity long before; the story goes back to the 18th century when the American Benjamin Franklin had devised his lightning conductor and when an ingenious Frenchman had diverted the court of Louis XV by transmitting an electric current along a wire held at intervals by a series of friars, thus making all the friars leap simultaneously into the air. It was an international study, as the names of electrical units like volt, ohm, and ampere indicate. Its first distinguished pioneers in Britain in the early 19th century had been Michael Faraday and Charles Wheatstone, and out of their work had come the earliest practical applications of electricity in Britain—the telegraph (patented by Wheatstone and first used by Brunel's Great Western Railway in 1838) and the submarine cable (first laid across the English Channel in 1851). The next developments followed in the 1870's. They included the invention of the telephone in 1876 by the Canadian Graham Bell; and the first application of electricity to lighting, the result of the invention of the incandescent electric lamp by the American Thomas Edison and the Englishman Joseph Swan. These changes were naturally followed by the application of electricity for power, as distinct from lighting or the sending of messages. In 1881 the first electric tram ran near Berlin; and two years later William Siemens pioneered the building of the light electric railway at Portrush in Ireland.

Britain in fact made an enterprising and early start in the use of electricity. But thereafter this new form of light and power was slow to extend its hold in this country. Most towns had by this time a well-established system of cheap gas lighting; for this had been invented by William Murdock and installed in Boulton and Watt's Soho Works as long ago as 1803; and now an incandescent gas burner was quickly devised to compete with the electric lamp. Where a municipal council owned the gas works, opposition to the introduction of electric lighting was naturally strong. Electricity was bound to be costly at this stage, and it was made more so by the detailed regulations about underground mains and similar precautions laid down by Acts of Parliament and by local by-laws. As for the use of electricity for power in industry, most manufacturers tended to

[1] The Royal Liver building on the Liverpool waterfront, completed in 1910, was an early example of its use. '

argue that steam-power had been so satisfactory for so long that there was no sound reason to change over; the coal to drive the engines was cheap and plentiful. So progress was slow.

There was one man of genius among the electrical engineers, Sebastian de Ferranti (1864–1930). By the age of nineteen he had devised a generator, an arc lamp, and a meter; and at twenty-five he devised for the London Electric Supply Corporation a great power station at Deptford capable of supplying sufficient current to light all London. His system of supply, using high-pressure alternating current, was ultimately to triumph throughout the world; but in 1891 those who favoured low pressure distributive current from small stations won the day in London, and the company dropped Ferranti's scheme.[1] There were also some exceptional areas, notably Tyneside, where the big engineering firms and shipyards were quick to install electrical plant. This was probably connected with the influence in that district of Sir Charles Parsons who in the 1890's further improved his turbine for use in electrical as well as in marine engineering. In many places, too, numerous small workshops—those of joiners, boot-repairers, coach-repairers, tailors and others—installed electrical power. But the major industries made on the whole little use of it. In the larger cities electric power was used to drive trams; yet even here Britain was slow and cautious in development. In London the new 'tubes' were driven by electricity, and in the provinces one or two stretches of railway were electrified, e.g. on Tyneside and between Liverpool and Southport. Yet for all these purposes much of the equipment and machinery had to be imported, usually from Germany or from the United States; and naturally the new experiments and developments tended also to come from overseas. In electric lighting the carbon filament lamp, the Ediswan whose name indicated its two inventors, was unchallenged until about 1906: then improved lamps began to come from abroad, notably the gas-filled lamp from the U.S.A. in 1913.

5. THE CONDITION OF THE PEOPLE, 1875–1914

How did these rapid and remarkable economic changes affect standards of life? Did the challenge to Britain's economic supremacy, and the loss of that supremacy in many important matters, reduce the material well-being of the British people? What sort of differences did these technical and other advances make to the average man's way of life? It is always dangerous to answer questions like this in a general way; for it is very unusual for any important economic change to benefit everybody connected with it. There will nearly always be exceptions, people who get hurt by the change, as for example the hand-loom weavers who had been driven down into desperate poverty and finally extinguished by the gradual introduction of the power-loom in the woollen industry during the 19th century. What is progress for most people may be ruin for a few. Again,

[1] 'He was, indeed, the Brunel of electrical engineering'. L. T. C. Rolt: *Victorian Engineering*, (1974 ed.), p. 226.

particularly in an industrialised country dependent as Great Britain had become on foreign trade, economic progress is uneven. Times are not always good; there are periodic slumps. Thus there were four very bad years from 1884 to 1887, with many thousands of people out of work and with widespread poverty and suffering. Nor in good times were the benefits of prosperity by any means equally shared in the community; some people invariably gained much more than others, and many undoubtedly did not gain at all. So any *general* answer to questions like 'Did the standard of living improve?' must be regarded with caution.

Bearing this warning in mind, we are pretty safe in saying firmly that the average person in Great Britain was a good deal better off in 1914 than in 1875. All sorts of things contributed to this, and many of them were not very directly connected with economic developments. Thus there had been considerable progress in medicine, and the average man was living longer and his life contained less pain.[1] Public education had made notable strides; it had been compulsory since 1880, and now a rather higher proportion of the population could read and write.[2] This, incidentally, had helped to make profitable the introduction of cheap newspapers appealing to a reading public much wider than that catered for by the old-established papers like *The Times*: the *Daily Mail*, started in 1895, was the first of the new type in Great Britain. After the Third Reform Act (1884) nearly 60 per cent of adult males were qualified to vote in parliamentary elections.[3] This had compelled Parliament to pass laws which directly promoted the welfare of many of the new voters. Such laws included, to take the most notable examples, the development of Workmen's Compensation for injuries received at work; the creation in 1908 of Old Age Pensions; and the establishment in 1911 of a system of National Insurance against sickness and unemployment.[4] Such changes were specially important because they gave to many people the beginning of a security against old age and misfortune which had never previously existed. Finally, over the great majority of occupations the daily hours of work were much reduced in these years. The Coal Mines Act of 1908 gave miners an eight-hour day; while the Shops Act three years later secured a weekly half-holiday for all shop assistants.

Yet the economic developments themselves had directly and in countless ways made life easier for the majority of the population. There were, for example, many more retail shops in 1914 than in 1875, and they sold a wider range of goods. Necessities like clothes, boots and shoes and soap were more plentiful; minor luxuries like chocolate, jam and biscuits were coming more within the reach of working-class shoppers. The big stores, with their countless departments, had begun to come into existence in London: both Harrods and Selfridge's began in these years. So did Boots

---

[1] Below, pp. 197–201.
[2] Below, pp. 206–9.
[3] This was about 30 per cent of the total adult population; no women had the vote until 1918. Most of the unqualified men were excluded because of a complicated system of registration.
[4] Below, pp. 187–9.

the chemists and Lipton's the grocers; while in London at any rate people could now have tea at an A.B.C. or at Lyons'. More important than any of these to the working-class housewife, especially if she lived north of the Trent, were the Co-operative Stores, which grew mightily in size and in the range of the goods they sold in these years.

The transport developments, especially the bicycle, the railway and the tram, were in various ways making life easier; fresh air, seaside excursions and visits to football matches and similar entertainments were among the benefits brought by improved transport. The development of trade and of shipping meant a wider variety of imports as well as greater quantities of them: the coming of refrigerated meat and butter is an illustration of this. Electric light no doubt was still rather a luxury before 1914; but gas was not; the output of gas had gone up, and gas-fires and gas-cookers had come in, as well as the incandescent mantle. Clothes were being ready-made in large quantities by 1914—and their quality had risen. Finally, and not least important, bread itself, still the staff of life for millions, came down in price during these years. The average price of a 4-lb. loaf in London was 8*d*. in 1870, and nearly 10*d*. in 1872: but between 1887 and 1914 it only once went over 6*d*. Here was the effect of the American development— imports of wheat now came in all the year round, and thus stabilised the price as well as removed that fear of famine which had always been a possibility, locally if not nationally, so long as Britain depended on her own or European harvests.

Thus there are plenty of signs that life was becoming easier and less uncomfortable for most British people at this time. This evidence is to a large extent confirmed by the movements of wages and prices during these years. Broadly, wages, after a slight drop in the late 1870's, rose fairly steadily until 1900; the retail prices of goods on the other hand fell steadily until 1895, when they began to rise very slightly. Thus 'real' wages, the amount of purchasing power available to the wage-earner, in fact rose appreciably until about 1900. Wages were rising because the country was on the whole prosperous; prices were falling because of plentiful foreign imports, especially of foodstuffs. But after 1900 the picture, from the wage-earner's point of view, was not so satisfactory. Roughly wages between 1900 and 1914 failed to keep pace with rising prices. Thus the workman's earnings would not buy quite so much as before for himself and his family. This is reflected in the figures which are available about commodities in common use like meat, tea, sugar, tobacco and beer; whereas in general the average consumption of these per head of the population had risen greatly between 1850 and 1900, it remained stationary or fell a little between 1900 and 1914. This probably shows that a rapid improvement in working-class conditions had slowed down—although it must be remembered that there were now many more things available on which wages could be spent than there had been in 1875. One sign that wage earners were not so satisfied with conditions came in a long series of **strikes** by great numbers of workers—railwaymen, miners, dockers and many others—in 1911–12. They believed that in a time of rising prices wages ought not to lag behind.

Finally, several other items must be taken into account in measuring the change in living conditions in this period. There had, for example, been a considerable increase in house rents, which undoubtedly absorbed a fair amount of the higher wages; yet this increase was itself largely the result of higher rates, which went to pay for the better paving and scavenging, for the draining and lighting improvements which had taken place in all the large cities in these years. Housing conditions had improved, but much more slowly than might have been expected;[1] there were enormous areas of slums where the overcrowding was appalling. Even in 1914 nearly one-third of all the inhabitants of Newcastle-on-Tyne and Sunderland were living more than two to a room; the situation was at least as bad in parts of London, like Bethnal Green, Stepney and Shoreditch; and in Scotland it was far worse, for there the proportion was 45 per cent. There were mining villages in Glamorgan, Durham and Staffordshire which were almost entirely without drains and whose unpaved streets were often thick with filth. Over the country as a whole, too, there was everywhere a great deal of poverty, as two notable social surveys made during this period revealed. The first was organised by Charles Booth, a wealthy shipowner; he investigated conditions in London and issued his results in a series of volumes called *Life and Labour of the People of London*, published 1889–1907. They suggested that nearly one person in every three lived in continuous poverty, and revealed appalling slum conditions in the East End. About one-tenth of London's people, the so-called 'submerged tenth', many of them driven to crime, lived perpetually on the edge of starvation. The second enquiry was made by Seebohm Rowntree; he made a house-to-house survey of York, a relatively prosperous town whose main industry was the railway works. His survey, published in 1901 under the title of *Poverty: A Study of Town Life*, showed that in York nearly 28 per cent of the entire population of the city earned less than the minimum necessary to meet the bare physical needs of a household; and it was obvious that the situation in the bigger industrial cities was undoubtedly much worse. Thus although on balance there was a notable improvement in the average standard of living in Britain between 1875 and 1914, it was not a uniform improvement, nor one about which British people could be complacent. For most people life was a little easier than it had been: for many it still remained grim, poverty-stricken and wretched.

[1] For further information about housing, see below, pp. 200–1.

15 The British Empire and Trade since 1783

During the 17th and 18th centuries England built up a vast overseas empire.[1] Thirteen colonies grew up along the eastern coast of North America, and by 1776, when they declared themselves independent of British rule, they contained some two and three-quarter million people. Canada was taken from France in the Seven Years War (1756–63). The East India Company, beginning as a group of merchants, had established trading factories at several points on the coastline of India; then, in that same Seven Years War, they conquered wide territories and thus laid the foundations of British rule over many millions of people in Asia. Oliver Cromwell's capture of Jamaica in 1655 was one of the first steps in the conquest of a succession of profitable West Indian islands. Gibraltar was taken by English forces in 1704. A string of small British settlements arose along the Guinea Coast of West Africa. Finally, Captain Cook's first voyage of exploration (1769–71) opened a British claim to Australia, the last of the habitable continents of the globe. Thus Great Britain became an imperial power.

Men went to the colonies for various reasons. The Pilgrim Fathers crossed the Atlantic in 1620 because they wanted to be free to worship God in their own way; and soon thousands of other Puritans followed them to Massachusetts for similar religious reasons. By contrast, numerous colonists went, or were sent, overseas because they were ne'er-do-wells who had made England too hot to hold them. But for the great majority of individual settlers in the colonies the reason for this hazardous venture of a new life in far-off lands was simply that they wanted to better the conditions in which they lived. For some, like the first settlers in Virginia, it was the lure of supposed goldmines that attracted them; for others it was the prospect of making a fortune out of sugar or tobacco plantations; and many saw profitable possibilities of becoming successful traders. Yet most colonists seem to have been humble folk, peasants and craftsmen anxious above all to escape the poverty which had been their lot in Britain. After the early years of colonisation, many went out to the North American mainland or to the West Indies as 'indentured servants', binding themselves, in return for their passage money, to work for a term of years for some plantation-owner or farmer already established in the colony. Merchants and others at home were ready to finance colonial settlement, in

---

[1] Strictly, it was an English empire until 1707, and a British one after the Union with Scotland in that year. In many ways—as soldiers and settlers, merchants, colonial administrators and missionaries—Scotsmen played a very large part in imperial history.

return for grants of land or a share in trading profits, and formed companies to do so; ship-owners, too, obviously stood to gain by the development of colonies.

Many colonies of course—like Jamaica and Canada—were not British-founded: they were captured in wars. Just as settlers had different motives for going out to the colonies, so the British Government had several reasons for conquering overseas possessions. Sometimes these reasons were strategic; Gibraltar was captured and retained because it guarded the entrance to the Mediterranean. But here again the most important ones were economic—the areas concerned were valuable for trade. Even where the colonies had in the first place been founded from other motives, governments at home were interested in them for economic reasons. Massachusetts and the other New England colonies which had begun as places of refuge for Puritans were to 18th century British governments mainly valuable as sources of timber and ships' stores and as the home of a flourishing shipbuilding industry. The West Indian islands were the most valuable of 18th-century colonies on account of the sugar they supplied. The later West African colonies, with some exceptions, grew out of the small trading settlements of the 18th century: settlements whose trade was not in cocoa but in slaves. Most striking of all, England's interest in India was at first, and for well over a century, wholly economic; English merchants founded the East India Company in 1600 in order to trade, not to conquer India. Only in the middle of the 18th century did they begin to conquer land and to govern it.

British governments in the 18th century attached much importance to the development of colonial trade. This was not because they wanted the colonists themselves to prosper, but because they wanted to be sure that the economic development of the colonies was on lines profitable to Britain. Hence there grew up an elaborate group of laws and regulations which came to be known as the Old Colonial System. The most important item in it was the Navigation Laws, which had begun in the second half of the 17th century, as part of an attempt to stop the Dutch from getting control of the world's 'carrying' trade between one country and another. They decreed that all goods shipped from any country to Britain or to British colonies must be carried in vessels which were British or colonial or belonged to the country concerned, and which were mainly manned by British or colonial sailors or by sailors who were nationals of that country. The trade between Britain and the colonies themselves was strictly confined to British and colonial ships. These and other regulations tried in various ways to ensure that the profits of colonial trade came into British pockets. For example, the most valuable goods produced in the Thirteen Colonies, such as tobacco and dyestuffs like indigo, were classified as 'enumerated articles' and could not be shipped direct to Europe; they had to come first to British ports. Manufacturing industries in the colonies were restricted in the interests of British producers; English woollen manufacturers were particularly nervous of colonial competition. This led to a number of regulations which were absurd and irritating; hence, for example, no felt hats were to be made in the colonies. The colonists were restricted in the goods they bought as well as in those they sold. The Molasses Act of 1733—passed as the result of pressure from the sugar 'interest' in the British West Indies—imposed heavy duties on sugar imported to the American Colonies from the French West Indies, which produced cane-sugar much more cheaply than the British islands. All these regulations led to wholesale smuggling and similar methods of evading the law. After the Seven Years War ended in 1763 an attempt was made to tighten up the Old Colonial System, and this was one of the main reasons why the people of the Thirteen Colonies broke into open revolt against Britain in 1775.

These developments of the 17th and 18th centuries suggest several ways in which throughout modern British history the Empire has been of economic importance to Britain. First, the Empire has been to an important extent peopled by *emigration* from Britain. The families which went out in large numbers to Canada, Australia and New Zealand in the late 19th and early 20th centuries were merely a few of the countless successors of the first settlers of Virginia and of the Pilgrim Fathers. Secondly, colonies and the later dominions alike have been important as sources of *raw materials and foodstuffs* useful to British people and profitable to British merchants. Tobacco from Virginia, sugar from the West Indies, wool from Australia, jute from India, corn from Canada, gold from South Africa—these are important examples of colonial commodities which at various times in the last two hundred years have been vital elements in British trade. Thirdly, the lands of the Empire have been *markets* for British manufactured goods. This has been strikingly so in the 19th and 20th centuries, with the development of factory industry in Britain and the great improvements in overseas transport. Much of the wealth of the Lancashire cotton manufacturers in the 19th century depended on their exports to India; the railways, roads and dams of the dominions and colonies were largely built by British contractors; in effect the payment for colonial produce (foodstuffs and raw materials) was made in British manufactured goods. Finally, the Empire became an important area of *investment* for British capital. In the early days there were companies like the Virginia Company which financed the early settlements in Virginia (although there the investors lost their money). In the 17th and 18th centuries great sums were invested in the East India Company and the process continued in the Empire as a whole during the 19th and 20th centuries.

2. THE ECONOMIC DEVELOPMENT OF THE BRITISH EMPIRE, 1783–1850

In 1783 the treaty of Versailles ended the War of American Independence and confirmed the loss of the Thirteen Colonies of the American mainland. At first this seemed a crushing blow. The shipyards of New England, the tobacco plantations of Virginia, most of the great expanding market of North America seemed to be lost to Britain. The possession of Canada, gained from the French twenty years earlier, offered poor compensation. For Canada was an empty and seemingly barren land, economically of small significance except for the fur trade of the Hudson Bay region, and most of its people were poverty-stricken French-speaking peasants scraping a living from small holdings in the St. Lawrence Valley. Yet in reality the blow was not economically disastrous; for the United States continued to do most of her trade with Britain. The new country was an important market for the textile manufactures and the hardware which British industry, under the impact of the 18th-century changes, was beginning to pour out in increasing quantities. Moreover, cotton provided a peculiarly important link between the two countries. The invention of the cotton gin by the American Eli Whitney in 1793 made it possible to remove the cotton fibres from the seed far faster than had previously been known: hence there came about a remarkable increase in the amount of raw cotton exported from the southern states of the U.S.A. Lancashire became almost entirely dependent upon the American crop.

The failure of the American War caused the death of the Old Colonial System as well as the loss of the Thirteen Colonies. This was in itself no bad thing, for the system was proving impossible to carry out in practice. It was also true that the American victory led British politicians to distrust the whole imperial idea. It came to be taken for granted that the fate of the American colonies would be the fate of all colonies: sooner or later they would shake off British control and declare themselves independent. If this were to happen, what then was the point of acquiring or establishing colonies? They were costly, for they required soldiers and sailors to defend them as well as officials to govern them: and they might involve Britain in disputes with other powers. They had, no doubt, certain limited uses. Australia, for example, could be used as a penal settlement: the first boatload of convicts, 717 in number, had landed at Botany Bay in 1788. But on the whole colonies were considered more of a liability than an asset. One indication of this attitude is the fact that the Colonial Office was not established as a separate department of state until 1854: before that date colonial problems were dealt with by the Secretary for War.

Other developments elsewhere in the Empire at about the same time strengthened this attitude towards colonies. The West Indies, hitherto the most commercially profitable part of the overseas empire, lost much of their prosperity as a result of the French Wars (1793–1815). There was much fighting in the islands, with frequent raids and wrecking of plantations, before Britain's naval superiority enabled her to overrun the French West Indies. Moreover, the French Revolutionary doctrines of 'Liberty, Equality and Fraternity' spread to the West Indies and very naturally led to large-scale slave risings among the coloured peoples, and these caused great damage to the property of the slave-owning ruling class, with widespread destruction of crops and buildings. The abolition of the Slave Trade by Britain in 1807 was a serious threat to the economy of the islands, for they were not self-supporting in slaves.[1] So the prosperity of the West Indies fell off. And across the world in India too the wars brought great difficulties to the East India Company, which had to maintain an army and a navy in order to defend its possessions, and was nevertheless expected to pay a dividend to its shareholders. The American War and the French Wars alike meant heavy fighting against leagues of Indian rulers organised by the French; and the struggles in effect bankrupted the Company. At home its methods were under heavy fire from critics who claimed that it was wrong for a company of merchants, whose aim was to make profit as traders, to accept responsibility for governing many millions of those with whom they traded. The government began to take over a share of direct responsibility for the government of India: and the criticism found an outlet in the prolonged impeachment (1788–95) of Warren Hastings, the Governor-General who had saved India for the Company during the American War. There was a growing demand that the special trading privileges of the East India Company should be taken away: for this was the age when *laissez-faire* was growing strong.

At the peace treaty signed at Vienna in 1815 Great Britain made a number of colonial gains. They included Ceylon, the Cape of Good Hope, Mauritius, Malta, Heligoland, Trinidad, Tobago and St. Lucia. None of these was of immediate economic consequence. Some of them, like Malta, Mauritius and the Cape, were justified on strategic grounds—which meant in fact that they were excellently placed to defend Britain's overseas trade routes. Ceylon with its tea and Trinidad with its asphalt were in later years to provide important items of trade, and one of the gains, the Cape of Good Hope, was at the end of the 19th century to be of immense economic importance to the world for reasons entirely unsuspected in 1815.

A widespread lack of enthusiasm for colonies remained until after the middle years of the 19th century. William Huskisson's policy of Colonial Preference in the 1820's was a small exception to the general rule. So were the activities of a small group of Radical politicians, including Lord Durham, Charles Buller and Edward Gibbon Wakefield, who wanted to see an energetic programme of colonial development undertaken by the government. Wakefield (1796–1862) was the most prominent figure among these 'Radical Imperialists'. While he was serving a sentence in Newgate Prison (1827–30) for abducting an heiress, he started to write his *Letter from Sydney*, in which he advocated planned colonisation, based on systematic emigration of suitable settlers and careful financial investment; later he was the leading spirit in the establishment of South Australia in the 1830's; and he worked zealously to promote the early development of New Zealand, where he died in 1862. Yet active public interest in the Empire remained small; and the great majority of emigrants who left the United Kingdom went not to British colonies but to the United States.

Nevertheless, there occurred in the 1830's a series of events which were of high importance in the history of the British Empire. These events

[1] See above, pp. 59–61, for details.

were the Emancipation of Slaves (1833); the Great Trek in South Africa (1836 onwards); the Canadian Rebellions (1837) and the Durham Report (1839); and the annexation of New Zealand (1840). None of them proceeded directly from economic causes: yet each was to have important economic results, often in ways unsuspected at the time.

The Emancipation of Slaves in the British Empire (1833) was the result of a long struggle whose main motives were humanitarian and religious. The Evangelical reformer William Wilberforce, after victory in the abolition of the slave trade in 1807 (above, pp. 59–61) had gone on to attack slavery itself. When in 1823 he had retired from active leadership—to be succeeded by Thomas Fowell Buxton—the anti-slavery campaign was already on the way to victory; for the public opinion of the educated classes in Britain was growing more Evangelical in outlook and ready to respond to the challenge of social reform. In economic terms, competition from the cheaper sugar of Brazil and Cuba, and slave risings in the 1820's, both encouraged Jamaican and other British West Indian planters to give up the struggle for slavery. Success came to the reformers in 1833, Wilberforce living long enough to know that the cause had triumphed. The Act of that year ordered that all slaves in the British Empire should be set free. All under six years old were to be freed outright; the others were to remain as 'apprentices' to their former masters for six years if they were field slaves, four if domestic, and then to be free to stay or leave as they pleased. Parliament provided £20 million as compensation to their owners.

Emancipation was a notable and humane action, a great moral advance; although the slave-owners might observe that they themselves—not the members of Parliament—had to carry the burden of its results. These results were serious in those two areas in the British Empire where slaves were numerous. In the West Indies the entire economy of the islands was dislocated, for the free slaves in effect refused to work on terms acceptable to the former slave-owners. The sugar-growing industry, already damaged by the earlier troubles, fell into further decline—a decline accelerated in the later years of the 19th century by increasing competition of beet-sugar grown in Europe. In South Africa, where slaves were not so numerous (three-quarters of the compensation money had gone to the West Indian planters), Emancipation helped to touch off an explosion which was to have far-reaching results.

When Great Britain finally took possession of the Cape of Good Hope in 1815, she found there as inhabitants a population of Dutch farmers, the so-called Boers. British settlers were slow to go to South Africa, and the Boers resented the arrival of those who did come. From the start the attitude of the two white peoples towards the native Africans differed. The Boers regarded them as inferior creatures, and enslaved them. The British, while employing the Africans as servants, were prepared in certain ways to treat them as equals. The British government, powerfully influenced by missionary opinion which sympathised with the coloured people, ruled that in the law courts of the Cape Colony the word of an African

should be treated as equal to that of a white settler. This decision antag-
onised the Boers; and Emancipation, which was clearly in line with it,
angered them still further. Moreover, there was a serious land shortage
in the colony. Boer farms tended to be very large; most of South Africa
was very dry, and the farming was nearly all pastoral. So 6,000 acres (2500
hectares) was by no means an abnormal holding, and it was taken for
granted that every son of a Boer household should be provided with a farm
of his own. Further, the government restricted Boer encroachment on
lands already occupied by African tribesmen. All these factors—of which
Emancipation was only one—led to serious dissatisfaction with British
rule; hence in 1836 there began the Great Trek, the Exodus of Boer
history. Large numbers of Boer families during the next few years trekked
northwards with all their possessions, out of the Cape Colony into the
thinly-peopled lands to the north. There they set up two new states, later
recognised by the British government as independent republics—the
Orange Free State and the Transvaal. They took with them a strong dis-
like of the British, and their belief in the inferiority of coloured people
was totally unchanged. For the present the two republics remained
struggling communities of simple farmers, negligible in the world's affairs.
But the day was to come when the world's richest goldfield would be discovered in one of them.

In Canada, as in South Africa, Great Britain found herself by right of
conquest ruling a group of another European nation—the French settlers
of the St. Lawrence valley. For a variety of reasons two rebellions broke
out in Canada in 1837, one in French-speaking Quebec, the other in
English-speaking Ontario. They were quickly quelled. But in 1839 Lord
Durham, sent over as Governor-General to deal with the situation created
by the risings, published a famous *Report* on Canada which has had far-
reaching influence in the history of the British Empire. In it, among other
things, he recommended that Canada be allowed to develop 'responsible
government'—that the Canadian people should govern themselves through
ministers responsible to a majority in an elected parliament. This recom-
mendation became a fact in the 1840's and led to the establishment of
Canada as the first self-governing dominion of the British Empire. What
is of special interest here is that one of the earliest uses to which the
Canadian people put their new independence was economic. The growth
of free trade in Britain under Gladstone meant the abandonment of the
policy of Colonial Preference which had benefited Canadian producers of
timber and wheat. This led the Canadians to pass their first tariff of
Customs duties against British goods; and to sign in 1854 a Reciprocity
Treaty with the United States, which opened the American market to
Canadian timber and farm produce.

Meanwhile, far across the Pacific Ocean the foundations of two other
future Dominions were being laid. In the middle years of the 19th century
Australia changed from a mere penal settlement into an area of world
economic importance. No more convicts were transported to New South

Wales, the first and most important of the early Australian settlements, after 1840, although they continued to be sent to Tasmania and Western Australia for some years longer. By this date a great sheep-rearing industry had come into being in Australia. It had begun from experiments in sheep-breeding carried out in the 1790's by John MacArthur, an officer stationed at the convict settlement. The vast empty spaces north of the Blue Mountains in New South Wales proved to be superb pasture lands for sheep; and the mills of the West Riding of Yorkshire provided a continuous and rising demand for wool. Thus by 1850 Australia had become the world's greatest producer of wool. This economic development was in itself remarkable enough; and suddenly there was added a second—the discovery in 1851 of a goldfield in Victoria. It led to a gold rush comparable with that which had occurred two years before in California. A few 'diggers' made fortunes; most made little or nothing, and many were ruined. Yet on balance the gold discoveries brought increased prosperity and economic development to Australia—partly by increasing the population, which more than doubled within ten years of the first gold 'finds', reaching over 1,100,000 by 1861. Thus sheep and gold between them put Australia clearly on the world's economic map within a century of Captain Cook's first voyage.

In 1840 by the Treaty of Waitangi a group of Maori chieftains surrendered to the British Crown sovereignty over the islands of New Zealand, whose coasts Cook had charted in 1769. This new territory was annexed in order to forestall the French who were also interested in it. Much smaller than Australia and with far fewer economic resources, New Zealand was of little importance until the later years of the 19th century, despite the growth of a trade in wool with Britain. Immigrants were not numerous, and the white population remained comparatively small. Moreover, there was serious and prolonged conflict with the native Maoris, an intelligent and courageous people. Despite the promise contained in the Treaty of Waitangi that the Maoris should keep their lands, millions of acres were sold to white settlers; and this led in the 1860's to a series of fiercely-fought Maori Wars.

Finally, British trade with India made great strides during these middle years of the 19th century. This was in part the result of the ending of the monopoly held by the East India Company, which ceased its trading activities and became instead simply the organisation through which the British government ruled India. The East India Company lost its monopoly of trade with India itself in 1813, and in 1833 it gave up its control of the profitable trade, mostly in tea, with China. India's imports more than trebled in the twenty years after 1833. Moreover, British trade grew with British power. By the time of the Indian Mutiny of 1857 Britain was the direct ruler of two-thirds of India, the remaining third being governed by native princes who accepted the British Crown as their overlord. Here was a vast area containing many millions of people, more than in the whole of the rest of the British Empire put together. To the merchants and manufacturers of industrial Britain it offered an immense market, and they were not slow to take advantage of it. The most striking development was in the export trade in cotton goods; India became the biggest customer of the mills in Lancashire. In return India began to be exploited as a source of raw materials—including raw cotton, dyestuffs, hides and jute. The first cargoes of Indian jute were landed at Dundee in the 1830's, and the growth of this trade was rapid. About the same time, too, tea, hitherto a product of China, began to be planted in India itself, and after the 1850's the Indian tea industry developed swiftly, bringing down the price of tea and thus converting what had previously been a luxury into a household drink throughout industrial Britain. Furthermore, the expansion of India as a market and as a source of raw materials demanded the development of transport; and so in the 1850's and afterwards the railways came to India, financed by British investors and built by British engineering firms. By 1870 some £70,000,000 had been invested in railways in India, and there had been at least as much again in many other fields of investment like public works, plantations and mills. Here, clearly, was an important portion of those invisible exports which, as we have seen, were so vital in the prosperity of mid-Victorian Britain.

3. IMPERIAL EXPANSION, 1870–1914

About 1870 public opinion in Britain, hitherto rather unsympathetic towards the Empire, began to change. By the 1890's the tide of imperialist enthusiasm was flowing strongly, and the 19th century was to end with Great Britain engaged in the most obviously imperialist of all her wars, the South African War of 1899 to 1902 against the Boer Republics of the Transvaal and the Orange Free State. The effects of this swing of opinion were very great, not least in economic matters; and the last quarter of the century saw notable imperial developments, in tropical and temperate regions alike, in colonies as in self-governing areas.

The reasons for the new attitude of public opinion were various. One was the interest provoked by the activities of the great 19th century explorers, and especially by those who like David Livingstone began to open up the 'Dark Continent' of Africa. A second, in some ways closely related to the first (Livingstone himself was a missionary), was the growth of missionary concern for backward peoples. This reflected the deep evangelical zeal of Victorian Britain; and missionaries in the field not infrequently became advocates of the extension of British rule, on the ground that only thus could native peoples be protected from ruinous exploitation by unscrupulous traders. A third reason was the rise of a group of writers whose work spread propaganda for the imperial idea; the most influential of these was Rudyard Kipling, whose short stories and verse did much to awaken the British middle class to a romantic and heroic sense of imperial responsibility for 'the White Man's Burden'. A fourth factor, in the field of politics, was the rise to power of two statesmen who, in very different ways, championed the idea of imperialism as no front-rank politician had done since the time of William Pitt the elder nearly a century and a half earlier. They were Benjamin Disraeli, Earl of Beacons-field (Prime Minister 1874–80), and Joseph Chamberlain (Colonial Secretary 1895–1903). All these things in their several ways contributed to the awakening and spreading of a new concern for the British Empire.

These were the years when Britain's economic supremacy first began to be challenged by other countries; when her competitors were fast over-hauling her lead in manufactures and trade, making inroads into the world's markets and protecting their own industries by tariff barriers. The lands beyond Europe, undeveloped and in great part unknown, offered prospects of commercial development, both as markets for factory-made goods and as sources of raw materials. This situation encouraged an international scramble by the Europeans for new trading areas—for special 'spheres of interest' open only to the traders of a particular nation, for 'concessions' extorted from native rulers, and ultimately for colonies conquered by the superior weapons of European armies. Politically, once the scramble had fairly started, it was difficult for any power to allow itself to be left behind, to afford to lose prestige. Among the countries of continental Europe, Germany, France, Italy, Belgium and Portugal were prominent in the movement, especially in Africa, the one great continent where, as it seemed, great areas of land could be had for the taking. European rivalries were reflected in Africa: thus hostility to Russia in the eastern Mediterranean meant that Britain was sure to be interested in Egypt. Britain was bound to take a leading role for two compelling reasons above others. One was that her economic position was peculiarly vulner-able, with a great population largely dependent for their well-being on a world-wide export trade; the other, that her navy dominated the seas and so put her in a position of special advantage in colonial conquest.

The tale of British annexations of territories in the undeveloped tropical areas is a long one, but it can be briefly summarised. Almost everywhere the story began with individual traders or explorers—the traders on the coast at first, the explorers striking far inland; although in some areas, as for example in West Africa, there were old-established British settle-ments. The growth of trade and the discovery of unknown lands full of potential wealth led to demands that the government should take control, either directly or by setting up a 'protectorate'. The native African rulers, primitive and ill-equipped with weapons of defence, had no alternative to accepting the orders of the white man. In some places conflict between traders out for quick gains and native tribesmen brought demands from the traders that the government should take over and establish orderly conditions in which trade was possible; sometimes missionaries urged the government to intervene in order to protect the native peoples. A slightly later stage of the process in some areas was the creation of the char-tered company, formed by well-to-do shareholders in Britain to exploit vast areas of new land, and given special privileges by the government. The most famous of these were the Royal Niger Company (working in Nigeria and chartered in 1886), the British East Africa Company (Kenya and Uganda, 1888), and the British South Africa Company (Bechuanaland and the Rhodesias, 1889). Their activities were later followed by the establishment of Crown control. As a result of this process—the flag following trade—the area of the British Empire expanded enormously between 1870 and 1914, especially in Africa, where Britain acquired some 5,000,000 square miles (8 000 000 square kilometres) of land inhabited by perhaps 90,000,000 people. The period of most vigorous expansion was in the 1890's. The territories taken included Nigeria and lands behind the earlier coastal settlements (e.g. the Gold Coast and Sierra Leone) in West Africa; Bechuanaland and Rhodesia in the south; Zanzibar, Kenya and Uganda and part of Somaliland in the east. At the same time France, Belgium, Germany, Portugal and Italy all acquired or added to their empires vast tropical lands, mainly though not entirely in Africa.

Two other features of this movement deserve stress. First, it was not confined to the annexation of territories. In 1875 Disraeli's government bought from the Khedive of Egypt nearly half the shares in the Suez Canal Company. The Canal, built by French engineers and opened in 1869, had shortened the route to India and the Far East by thousands of miles, and from the start most of the shipping passing through it had been British. It was obviously a vital trading highway for the nation which ruled India. Moreover, British interest in the Canal led within a very few years to British intervention in the government of Egypt. In 1882, Britain took control of Egypt's finances and set up military bases there, thus beginning a form of occupation which lasted in one form or another until the middle years of the 20th century. Secondly, the process was not limited to Africa, although that continent was the scene of the greatest activity and annexations. Starting with Disraeli's occupation of Fiji in 1875, innumerable Pacific islands fell under British control. So too did Malaya, where Singapore, built in the 1820's by Sir Stamford Raffles on an uninhabited island, had become by the late 19th century one of the great commercial centres of the globe. Closely related to this development was a considerable extension of British trading and naval interest in China. There Hong-Kong had been British since 1842, taken in the so-called 'Opium War', fought with the purpose of forcing an increase of British trade upon the reluctant rulers of the Chinese Empire. Britain had acquired special rights and privileges in a large group of Chinese ports, notably Shanghai and Canton; and now in the 1890's she obtained a further naval base at Wei-hai-wei.

One episode of the movement deserves more detailed mention because of its peculiar importance—namely, the story of events in South Africa. In 1885 gold was discovered on the Rand near Johannesburg in what was then the independent Republic of the Transvaal. It soon became clear that the 'find' was a very rich one: it was in fact at that time the world's richest known goldfield. Prospectors, most of them British, poured into the Transvaal in great numbers, and trouble very quickly arose between them and the Afrikaans-speaking farmers, the Boers, who were the rulers of the republic. The Transvaal government denied to the Uitlanders, as they called the newcomers, any right to vote or to share in the government, although it was not long before there were as many Uitlanders as Boers in the Transvaal; meanwhile they imposed heavy taxes on the miners, and by these and other methods, like the control of dynamite supplies and of the only railway to the mining area, they drew a great revenue from the goldfields. The mines rapidly fell under the control of a small number of companies, with their headquarters in London and headed by a group of very wealthy men, of whom Cecil Rhodes, already a diamond millionaire and chairman of the British South Africa Company, was the chief. Naturally the mining companies wanted the Transvaal to be put under British rule, and put great pressure on the government in London to interfere on their behalf; equally naturally the Boers wanted to keep control of the Transvaal for themselves. The stakes in the conflict were immense and the result after a long series of incidents and tension was the outbreak in 1899 of the South African War between Great Britain and the small states of the Transvaal and its Boer neighbour, the Orange Free State. It took three years for Great Britain to defeat the republics of farmers. Peace was signed at Vereeniging in 1902, and under its terms the Transvaal and the Orange Free State passed to the British Crown. The gold of the Rand was in the British Empire.

What was the general economic importance of these new lands to Britain? Most obviously, they offered new markets for British manufacturers—markets not only for consumers' goods like cotton clothes, hardware and metal goods, pottery and the like, but also for the heavy equipment needed to open up the new territories and develop their resources, for locomotives and rails, steamships, mining machinery and large-scale tools of various kinds. Next, they provided raw materials—new supplies of well-known materials, and in some areas sources of new or virtually unknown ones. Such raw materials included the vegetable oils of West Africa, valuable for the tin-plate industry of South Wales and also for the manufacture of the new commodity of margarine as well as of soap; the cocoa of the same area which enormously expanded the chocolate industry; the rubber and tin of Malaya, the one vital for the new-born bicycle and motor-car industries, the other adding greatly to the world's supplies of a very ancient raw material; coffee and cotton, hardwood and tropical fruits. Sometimes these new supplies had damaging effects upon the existing economic pattern; thus the tin of Malaya, which was alluvial and produced by poorly-paid native labour, was cheaper, even with the cost of transport across half the world, than that dug from the old-established Cornish mines, and so brought the English tin-mining industry almost to a close, causing depression and unemployment in Cornwall. But on the whole they did promote industrial development in Britain itself; they also widened and improved the standard of living for many of her people by increasing the range of goods available to them. Bicycles, chocolate, margarine, soap and canned foodstuffs all in their several ways reflected this development.

Another element in the economic importance of the new lands was the opportunity for investment which they provided. The development of these areas was dependent upon the readiness of investors to lend money for it. In certain areas and forms of enterprise there was heavy investment almost from the start; the gold-mines of South Africa provide the most striking example of this. Some British firms, for example those manufacturing chocolate or soap, extended their capital considerably by colonial investment. Yet the quantity of investment in the colonies remained limited, and the total invested in these new areas was relatively small in proportion to the amount of territory acquired. People with money to lend preferred to invest it in countries more fully developed and with more secure law and order than could yet exist in these new colonies. During the half-century before the First World War some 40 per cent of the total British overseas investment went into the British Empire. Yet it must be noted that the bulk of this was in the self-governing dominions and in India, not in the new tropical colonies. Thus Australia attracted a heavy flow of British money in the 1880's, and so did Canada after 1900.

The profits from these investments went to a fairly small number of British people as shareholders in the companies whose business lay in the colonies. The benefits which came from the new supplies of raw materials, the new sorts of goods which could be bought in the shops of Britain, went to a far wider group, in fact to the majority of the British people. Yet it must be remembered that what made both the interest and the new range of goods possible was the cheap native labour in the new colonies. Plantations, mines, railways and roads—all depended upon the employment of large numbers of native workmen whose wages were extremely low and whose living conditions were primitive by British standards.

The new interest in imperialism stimulated the growth of the self-governing areas of the Empire as well, and gave them a greatly increased economic importance. Technical progress assisted this development. For example, the construction of railways threw open the Canadian prairies to agriculture—just as it did the American Plains; and grain elevators and steamships made possible the marketing of their produce across the Atlantic. The Canadian Pacific Railway, begun in 1871, was completed in 1886. The prairie provinces of Manitoba, Saskatchewan and Alberta became great wheat-growing regions within a single generation. Immigrants from Britain flocked into them—though still in smaller numbers than went to the United States at the same time. Winnipeg, in 1870 an outpost with two hundred settlers, was by 1921 a city with 179,000 inhabitants. Thus Canada took her place as one of the world's great wheatlands; and parallel with this development went increased cultivation of other resources, in lumbering, mining and fruit-farming.

Railways and steamships also helped to develop Australia and New Zealand. Another technical advance was of special importance here. This was the invention of refrigeration. The first cargo of frozen mutton arrived in England in 1880. After a slow beginning, the trade in chilled and frozen meat and in dairy produce from overseas grew swiftly in the 20th century. It was Argentina (and British investors in that country) that made profits from the beef trade; but New Zealand with its Canterbury lamb and butter, and Australia with mutton both became great exporters to Britain. Here as in Canada the number of immigrants rose considerably at the end of the 19th century. In Australia, too, both woollen production and cattle farming increased greatly, as a direct result of the extension of railways which took place especially in the 1870's. Yet perhaps the most interesting development in Australia was the rapid expansion of the great cities, especially Sydney and Melbourne. Australia's exports were mainly agricultural products; but the growth of the cities indicated the arrival of industry and pointed to the trend of Australian development in the 20th century.

16   Finance and Taxation

1. BANKING BETWEEN 1694 AND 1815

The story of modern banking in England goes back to the middle of the 17th century, to the troubled years of the Civil War period. At that time merchants, anxious to take particular care of their money, began to entrust it to the goldsmiths for safe keeping in their strong rooms. The goldsmiths in their turn began to use this money to make loans. Moreover, their customers developed the practice of writing letters instructing the gold-smiths to pay out sums on their behalf—the starting-point of the modern cheque; and the goldsmiths themselves issued promises to pay—the fore-runners of the later banknotes. The goldsmiths were fulfilling the main functions of the modern bank. They received money on *deposit*, paying interest to the depositors: they made *loans*, for which they charged interest; the difference between the two rates of interest provided their profit. They cashed cheques, and they issued *notes*. By about 1675 such 'goldsmith bankers' were well established in London.

Among those to whom the goldsmiths lent money was the government. Before the 'Glorious Revolution' of 1688–9 this was a risky business; the King might use the loan to free himself from dependence on Parliament, or he might repudiate it and stop paying interest. After that date, when Parliament finally established its control of national finance, goldsmiths and others with money to lend felt more confidence in government. There had for some time been discussion of projects for creating a national bank, to which the government could go when it needed loans. Such a body would be useful in peace time, and quite invaluable in war. In 1689 England under William III began the first of two long and costly wars against Louis XIV's France; and it was the government's need for money in this war which led in 1694 to the creation of the Bank of England.

The Bank of England was founded by a small group of business men who collected a 'joint stock' of £1,200,000 and lent it to the government at 8 per cent. At first there was much opposition both by the goldsmiths and by a group of landowners who in 1696 tried to break the new bank by forming a rival Land Bank. But this project was a complete failure, and the Bank of England quickly grew into a privileged and unique institution. It became in effect the government's banker, making a steady profit out of the loans it raised for the government, and handling most of the National Debt. In 1708 Parliament decreed that no other corporate body or partnership of persons exceeding six in number should carry on banking business in England—thus making the Bank of England the sole joint-stock note-issuing bank in England. Besides its special relationship with the government, it carried on ordinary banking business, just like the goldsmith-bankers, accepting deposits, making loans, and issuing notes; it lent funds to the East India and Hudson's Bay Companies; and it soon began to attract investment from foreigners, especially from Dutchmen. This last development was a sign of the times. During the 17th century Amsterdam was the great money market of western Europe and the financial capital of the world; the course of the 18th century was to see London take its place.

The Bank of England helped to make the national finances more secure, and thus indirectly it promoted the industrial changes of the 18th century.[1] Yet the direct effects of its establishment were in some ways limited. On the one hand, its existence did not prevent wild financial speculation; as we have already seen, the South Sea Bubble took place in 1720. On the other, the Bank's activities were concentrated upon London, and it did little to help finance the expansion of industry or to assist agricultural progress. These things were left to the private bankers in the smaller towns.

|As industry grew during the 18th century, manufacturers came to need more money for a variety of purposes. They had to buy raw materials, and to meet the cost of holding the finished goods; often they had to wait twelve months until they were themselves paid for their wares. They

[1] So did another important monetary event of the same time—the great re-coinage carried out in 1696–8 by Sir Isaac Newton as Warden of the Mint. This replaced the thin and clipped silver coins then in circulation by good money of reliable weight and metal, with milled edges as a precaution against clipping. Nevertheless, during the first half of the 18th century gold, rather than silver, became the standard coinage for all considerable transactions, with the gold guinea (first issued in 1663, made of gold from the Guinea Coast of West Africa) as the basic coin.

wanted to install the new machinery and to build factories. And of course there was the regular weekly problem of paying their workmen's wages. This last item led to great difficulties, for there was a serious shortage of small coin in the 18th century. Manufacturers adopted various devices to solve this problem. Some paid their men in 'truck', that is in goods, a method peculiarly unfair to the workmen. Others—John Wilkinson among them—minted their own token coins, which were accepted for payment in the neighbourhood of the works. 'One cotton-spinner of the early 19th century met the situation by staggering the payment of wages. Early in the morning a third of the employees were paid and sent off to make their household purchases; within an hour or two the money had passed through the hands of the shop-keepers and was back at the factory ready for a second group of workers to be paid and sent off; and in this way before the day was over all had received their wages and done their buying in.'[1] Clearly there was a growing need for the development of banks which by organising and accelerating the flow of money would help to overcome these difficulties.

In 1716 a soap and tallow dealer of Bristol, James Wood, started what is believed to have been the first private bank outside London. During the next hundred years many more such banks came into existence, the great majority of them after 1760. By 1815 there were over 600. They were not joint-stock concerns. Many were very small; they had insufficient resources to meet any serious emergency and were thus very liable to go bankrupt; in fact, 240 provincial banks failed between 1814 and 1816. Some of them were started by manufacturers themselves, as a means of helping their own business, and one or two of these were in a later age to become nation-wide banking concerns. Ironmasters in particular needed considerable quantities of capital and employed large numbers of men, and so it is not surprising to find that both Lloyds and Barclays Banks had their roots in the iron industry. In the country areas too, as the enclosure movement spread and the scale of farming increased, there was a growing need of banks. Here they were often started by corn-merchants. At Aberystwyth there was the pleasantly named Bank of the Black Sheep, whose £1 notes carried a picture of a black sheep and 10s. notes that of a black lamb.

Banks as a rule lent money to landowners or mill-owners for short periods only. Long-term investment, particularly important in trade and industry, came not so much from the banks as from private persons with money available. Investment, in one way or another, was an important feature of 18th-century life; its increase, like the growth of banks, was a sign of the economic changes which were afoot. The government, with the National Debt; the overseas trading companies, like the East India Company; landowners anxious to improve their estates, mine-owners and ironmasters; turnpike trusts, house-builders, canal-builders—all these and many others needed money. Lending it might be risky business, as the crash of the South Sea Company had shown. At this time there was no

[1] T. S. Ashton: *The Industrial Revolution, 1760–1820*, pp. 99–100.

such thing as limited liability; a man was liable with every penny he possessed for the debts of a company in which he invested. Nevertheless, people were ready to invest, as the comparatively low interest rates of the 18th century show; money was cheap because it was plentiful. It was plentiful because, among other reasons, taxation was low and England was secure from foreign invasion.

Most of the investment was local, and the sums involved were usually small, for business concerns in the main were small and local compared with those of to-day. Thus landowners put their money in local ironworks, or merchants invested in nearby coal-mines. Much industrial development, once the factory-owner had got started (perhaps by borrowing from friends) seems to have supported itself; profits were ploughed back into the business. Yet wider investment grew during the century. Established businesses drew their money from farther afield; thus the Darbys of Coal-brookdale were much financed by Bristol merchants. Moreover the government, the overseas trading companies and the early insurance companies which started in this century attracted well-to-do investors from all over the country and from abroad. Hence a regular market in stocks and shares of these kinds grew up, handled by the 'stockbrokers' who made their first headquarters in Jonathan's Coffee House in Change Alley and in 1773 moved to a new building which they called the Stock Exchange. Towards the end of the century its members began to deal in canal shares; yet not until the railway boom of the 1840's did the activities of the Stock Exchange extend very widely through the community.

The French wars at the end of the 18th century had important effects upon banking, and especially upon the Bank of England. Fear and uncertainty of the future led men to hoard money and to exchange their notes for cash: this strained the resources of the private banks, and many of them became insolvent. Yet it was mainly government action that brought the Bank of England into difficulties. In the early years of the wars Pitt's government borrowed very large sums from the Bank, which was also lending heavily to Britain's allies on the Continent. This policy, added to the steady withdrawal of cash by private customers, soon threatened to drain the Bank of its gold reserve. An attempted French invasion of Ireland in 1796 caused much alarm and led to further withdrawals of gold, and so in 1797 the government by the Bank Restriction Act took the drastic step of suspending cash payments from the Bank of England. This eased the immediate difficulties. But it seems clear that the increased issue of paper money which followed did much to encourage the wartime inflation, the considerable rise in prices which took place at the time and which added greatly to social distress among the poor. It is probable that the paper money of the private banks contributed more to the inflation than the increased note-issue of the Bank of England. In 1810 a Bullion Committee appointed to consider the problem recommended the resumption of cash payments by the Bank, but the government decided not to act upon its report.

2. BANKING SINCE 1815

The fifty years after 1815 saw important changes in the English banking system turning it in directions which it has followed ever since. The first of these changes was a series of alterations in the laws governing the Bank of England. The growth of trade and industry in the 19th century led naturally to discussion of the place of the Bank in the nation's economic life. Controversy at first raged round the question of cash payments. The chief champion of a return to gold was David Ricardo (1772–1823), the ablest British economist since Adam Smith, and the author of *Principles of Political Economy and Taxation* (published in 1817). He had strongly supported the views expressed by the Bullion Committee. Cash payments were eventually resumed in 1821. A serious commercial crisis in 1825, accompanied by many bankruptcies, led to the passing of the Bank Act of 1826. This modified the privileges of the Bank of England by permitting the formation of joint-stock note-issuing banks outside a radius of sixty-five miles from London. A second step in the same direction was taken by another Act of 1833, which allowed the formation of joint-stock banks even in London itself, provided they did not issue notes.

In 1844 Sir Robert Peel's government introduced the Bank Charter Act. This had three main provisions. The Bank of England was divided into two separate departments—one for the issue of notes and the other for ordinary banking business. It was allowed to make a 'fiduciary' issue of £14,000,000 worth of notes, that is, an issue backed by securities rather than by bullion; every note issued above was to be backed by an equivalent amount of gold in the vaults. Finally, the issues of all other note-issuing banks were not to be increased in future: and any bank which went bankrupt, or amalgamated with another bank, was to lose its right to issue notes. The object of this last clause was to give the Bank of England a monopoly of issuing notes in England and Wales (the last surviving private note-issuing bank, Fox, Fowler & Co. of Taunton, amalgamated with Lloyds Bank in 1921 and so lost its right of note-issue). The banking system on the whole worked well, though there were serious banking crises in 1847, 1857 and 1866; on each occasion the government restored confidence by giving the Bank permission to go beyond the 'fiduciary' limit. During the First World War and for some years afterwards the Treasury itself issued £1 and 10s. notes to replace gold sovereigns and half-sovereigns. In Scotland the banking system developed on lines wholly separate from those of England, since the foundation of the Bank of Scotland (1695) and the Royal Bank of Scotland (1727); the several Scottish banks have each continued to issue their own distinct notes.

A second important development in the 19th century was the great growth of the joint-stock banks. This was much encouraged by the Acts of 1826 and 1833 mentioned above, and by 1842 there were 112 joint-stock banks in operation. Their rise involved the decline of the private banks; these were more limited in their scope, and less stable than the big joint-stock concerns, which were capable of financing the expanding businesses of Victorian England. Gradually during the 19th century the joint-stock concerns absorbed the private banks. This process was accelerated by another banking development of the time—the greatly increased use of the cheque. As a method of paying large sums this was far more convenient than the notes issued by the private banks. The advantages of the cheque were extended in 1854, when the joint-stock banks joined the London Clearing House. This was an institution which had come into being in the late 18th century, arising out of the daily meeting together of clerks from the various banks to collect cheques drawn on each bank, and to settle the balance. Settlement had formerly been made in notes and cash: now, from 1854 onwards, payment was made by cheques drawn on the Bank of England, where the banks henceforward kept their reserves. In 1864 the Bank of England itself joined the Clearing House, in order to simplify the working of the system.

These two major banking developments of the 19th century—the several laws affecting the Bank of England and the rise of the joint-stock banks—between them helped to create in England a unified system of banking. At its head is the Bank of England, at once the government's bank and 'the bankers' bank', with its notes the everyday method of payment throughout the country. The great extension of business since the days of the Bank Charter Act led to a gigantic rise in the 'fiduciary' issue of notes: the £14,000,000 of 1844 became £260,000,000 by an Act of Parliament of 1928. The relationship between the Bank of England and the government became much closer in the 20th century, with the government using the Bank in various ways to control the financial policy of the country. Until its nationalisation in 1946, however, the Bank remained in name at least a private company. Below the Bank of England, and working in very close harmony with it, is a small group of very large joint-stock banks, owned by private shareholders and with branches all over the country. They came into being through a long series of amalgamations, first of private banks and then—particularly after the First World War—of groups of joint-stock banks. The largest and most powerful of them—the Westminster, the Midland, the National Provincial, Lloyds and Barclays—were known as the 'Big Five', and dominated day-to-day banking in England and Wales.[1] They have not been without competitors, including some smaller joint-stock banks (strongest in northern England) the Co-operative Wholesale Society (bank founded in 1872), Building Societies (for savings) and since 1969 the National Giro.

3. THE NATIONAL DEBT

The Bank of England was founded in the course of a great war, the War of the League of Augsburg (1689–97). This was the first of the seven wars

---

[1] Two of the five, National Provincial and Westminster, combined to form the National Westminster in 1968.

which England fought, with France as the principal enemy, within little more than a century. The others were the Wars of the Spanish Succession (1701–13) and of the Austrian Succession (1740–8); the Seven Years War (1756–63); the War of American Independence (1775–83); the Revolutionary War (1793–1802); and the Napoleonic War (1803–15). Such a series of conflicts, fought in Asia and North America as well as on the high seas and in Europe, had profound effects on the economic life of the country, and not least upon the nation's finances. For wars were costly, in money as well as in human life and well-being. They were—and are—by far the greatest single item of government expenditure; and in the 18th century their cost rose considerably. At all times wars have to be paid for out of taxation, or by means of government borrowing. Borrowing only puts off the day of reckoning, making later generations responsible for the debts of their fathers; loans bear interest, and interest must be met out of taxation. It is therefore scarcely surprising that the great wars of the 18th century brought about important developments in the national finances and system of taxation—some short-lived, others more permanent.

The most important single result was the creation of the National Debt in 1696. There was nothing new about the government raising loans in order to finance wars: that had been done for centuries past. But until the later part of the 17th century these had been 'short-term' loans, raised to meet a particular emergency and repaid out of taxes at the time. What was new was the setting up of a 'long-term' debt, to be handed on from generation to generation; the interest became a permanent annual charge, to be paid out of taxation. This National Debt had its origins in the £1,200,000 raised by the Bank of England on its foundation in 1694, and lent to the government at 8 per cent. To this there were quickly added later loans, so that, for example, by 1713 the total Debt stood at £56,000,000. This was a large increase, and it caused widespread alarm. Many people believed that the country was on the road to financial ruin. In fact, it showed exactly the opposite—that the country was wealthy enough to afford such great expenditure. For the Debt had come to stay because it had two great advantages. From the national point of view, it enabled the government to raise the money it needed by tapping the wealth of its citizens; for the individual, it provided an attractive form of investment, offering a secure rate of interest.

During the 18th century the National Debt grew prodigiously as a result of the wars. It was £75 million in 1748; £132 million in 1763, after the Seven Years War; £241 million in 1783, when the American War ended; and £834 million in 1815, after Napoleon had been defeated at Waterloo. The annual charge on the debt, the interest which had to be paid to those who had invested in it, and other costs involved in managing it, stood at over £32 million in this last year. By the side of this enormous increase, the efforts to reduce it were modest. Walpole set up in 1717 a Sinking Fund into which he paid money out of taxation every year, so that it might accumulate at interest and reduce the capital of the Debt: and even though he several times raided the fund for other purposes, he had by 1739 got the Debt down to £46 million. Pitt the Younger also employed this same method, starting in 1786 another Sinking Fund into which £1,000,000 a year was to be paid out of taxation. But the outbreak of the Revolutionary War in 1793 killed all hopes of reducing the Debt. Pitt kept the Sinking Fund going, because he believed it gave confidence to the people: yet he did so at a loss, for the money paid into it during the war was itself borrowed. In reality, from the middle of the 18th century onwards the National Debt was no longer regarded with anxiety; despite its huge increase, it had become a safe and profitable investment, and part of the accepted order of things.

4. TAXATION BEFORE 1815

What were the taxes which Englishmen had to pay in order to meet the costs of the great wars? The later years of the 17th century brought big changes in taxation as in other features of the national financial system, and three of these deserve mention here. First, the old-fashioned custom of 'farming' the taxes finally disappeared. Under this system, syndicates of business men (the tax farmers) paid the government a lump sum for the right to particular taxes, and then made what profit they could by collecting them at the rates laid down by Parliament. It was a wasteful system, and before 1700 it had gone, the farmers being replaced by 'Commissioners'. Secondly, an important new tax came into existence in 1698. This was the Land Tax, on the value of land. In years of peace it normally stood at 1s. in the £, when it was reckoned to bring in £500,000: in wartime it went up to as much as 4s. It was highly unpopular with the country squires, upon whom its main burden fell; yet it provided a convenient means of raising a steady revenue. Thirdly, this period saw the beginnings (1689) of the famous Window Tax, whose consequences may still be seen to-day in the bricked-up windows of old houses. Elaborated in later years, it continued until 1851.

The Land Tax and the Window Tax were *direct* taxes, paid directly to the Exchequer. Most of the national revenue came from *indirect* taxes on goods—from the Customs and Excise duties. In the 18th century Customs duties were collected on a few exported commodities, but they fell mainly on imports—tea, wines and spirits, tobacco, coffee, chocolate, and a wide range of foreign manufactures, mostly luxuries. Customs were numerous, complicated, and high enough to encourage widespread smuggling. Sir Robert Walpole, in order to check this, began to extend the use of bonded warehouses, to which dutiable goods had to be taken on landing in Britain. There they were kept until they were taken out for sale by the retailer, who then paid duty on them. This was not a Customs duty but an Excise, similar to that payable on many goods produced inside Britain, like beer, malt, candles, soap, leather, starch and other commodities. Shopkeepers who sold these things could be compelled by the government excisemen to produce a receipt, showing that tax had been paid on them; and the extension of this system to imported goods offered more chance of defeating the smugglers.

In 1723 Walpole applied the Excise system to tea, coffee and chocolate. The results were encouraging; within seven years the receipts from taxation of these goods had gone up by £120,000 per annum. Therefore in 1733 he decided to extend the system to wine and tobacco, and introduced into Parliament an Excise Bill for this purpose. This time the result was an uproar. The whole excise system was unpopular with the poor, for it taxed necessities; and the opposition in Parliament seized the chance of whipping up an outcry—aided by those numerous persons who made handsome illegal profits on smuggled tobacco and wine. Rumours were put about that this was merely the opening move of a scheme to put excise duties on everything—bread, beef, mutton and bacon included. Ballads and broadsheets told how an army of excisemen would come prying into every shop and every house in the land. Mobs paraded the streets of London yelling, 'No slavery, no excise, no wooden shoes.' In face of such noisy opposition Walpole, saying, 'This dance will no further go,' dropped his plan.

The next major developments in taxation came between 1783 and 1793, when William Pitt the Younger was in power. Some of these reflected his free trade policy. Others were moves in the direction of more efficient management of the nation's finances, like the Consolidation of the Revenue in 1787. This reform provided that henceforward all taxes should be paid into a single consolidated fund, from which all the permanent charges on the national revenue would be met. In the same year he greatly simplified the Customs by introducing a new Book of Rates. One object of this was to discourage smuggling; and with the same purpose in view he carried out —this time without protest—Walpole's plan of half-a-century earlier, extending the bonded warehouse system to wines and tobacco. Pitt's measures pointed the way to a much more efficient system of taxation.

But in 1793 his work was sharply interrupted by the outbreak of war with Revolutionary France. At first Pitt met the costs of war mainly by borrowing; then from 1797 onwards taxation was considerably extended. Not only were indirect taxes, in the form of Customs duties, much increased. In 1799 Pitt introduced for the first time an Income Tax, whose amount was based upon details of income supplied by the taxpayer. The rate of tax was 2s. in the £: incomes below £60 per annum were wholly exempt: and deductions were allowed for children and for life insurance premiums. Thus from the start Income Tax had several features which it retains at the present day. It brought in about £6,000,000 in its first year. Apart from the short interval of peace in 1802–3, it remained in force throughout the war years, being eventually abolished in 1816. By 1815 it was yielding nearly £15,000,000 per annum. Thus began what in later years was to become the most important of all burdens upon the British taxpayer.

5. TAXATION BETWEEN 1815 AND 1914

In 1820 Sydney Smith wrote an article for the *Edinburgh Review* in which he described the number and variety of taxes which the Englishman of that day had to pay during his lifetime. He ended, 'The dying Englishman pouring his medicine which has paid 7 per cent into a spoon that has paid 15 per cent flings himself back upon his chintz bed which has paid 22 per cent, makes his will on an eight-pound stamp and expires in the arms of an apothecary who has paid a licence of a hundred pounds for the privilege of putting him to death. His whole property is then immediately taxed from 2 to 10 per cent. Besides the probate, large fees are demanded for burying him in the chancel. His virtues are handed down to posterity on taxed marble, and he is then gathered to his fathers to be taxed no more.' It was an appropriate finale. For in the years after—as well as before— the victory of Waterloo an extraordinary range of articles were subject to taxation, by Customs, by Excise, by stamp duties on legal documents, by licences, by the Post Office, and by other forms of tax. Drinks of every kind, from wine to tea and from cider to cocoa; hops and malt; tobacco, candles, paper, glass, stone, slates, bricks and tiles; dogs, stage-coaches, hair-powder, newspapers, coats of arms; domestic servants and hawkers; windows and houses; wills and letters; upon these and many other articles the tax collectors fastened. The abolition of Income Tax in 1816 made the situation worse rather than better, for the large sums collected through this direct tax now had to be obtained from other sources. Further, whereas Income Tax was paid by the well-to-do, the indirect taxes, except those on luxuries, were spread over the whole community, and fell harshly on the poor; and this just at the very time when the Corn Laws were sending up the price of bread. It was reckoned that in the 1840's the working man paid about 16 per cent of his small income in taxes of one sort or another.

The middle years of the 19th century brought a change in the pattern of taxation. For several reasons the financial situation became easier. The long spell of peace after 1815 lightened the burden of armaments. The expansion of industry in the railway age increased the nation's taxable wealth, and increased it even faster than the rate at which the population was growing; thus the prosperous England of mid-Victorian times could bear taxation much more easily than the England of Peterloo. Finally, the growth of the doctrine of free trade led to the reduction of tariffs. Huskisson in the 1820's began on a modest scale the lowering of Customs. Peel in the 1840's carried out a wholesale slashing of duties, setting free raw materials and most foodstuffs and scaling down taxes on imported manufactured goods to a maximum of 10 per cent. (15 per cent on silk goods). His object was to promote trade and industry; his policy in fact did much to lighten the burden of taxation on the poor. It had another highly important consequence. The removal of so many duties meant a loss to the Exchequer. This was offset by the re-introduction in 1842 of the Income Tax, this time at 7*d.* in the £. Peel's original intention was that it should last for three years only. But it was renewed in 1845, and it has remained ever since—at rates which have come to differ greatly from Peel's 7*d*.

The 19th-century pattern of taxation was perfected by W. E. Gladstone, Chancellor of the Exchequer 1852–5 and 1859–65, and perhaps the greatest of all holders of that office. Gladstone was a great Victorian, not least in his attitude towards money. He believed in economy, thrift and efficient handling of the nation's funds. For the Income Tax he had little enthusiasm, promising in 1853 that he would eventually abolish it by a seven-year plan which brought it down by a penny each year. But the Crimean War (1854–6) wrecked the scheme, and by 1860 the tax stood at 9*d*. As Prime Minister (1868–74) he made another attempt, and in 1874 it was 2*d*., the lowest point it has ever reached. Towards indirect taxation Gladstone had a clear and effective policy, reducing the articles taxed (by Customs or by Excise) to a very small number of things which were in widespread use—principally tea, sugar, beer, tobacco, wines and spirits. This greatly simplified the collection of taxes and discouraged smuggling. The absence of Customs duties on other commodities, particularly raw materials, stimulated trade and industry and thus promoted prosperity. The results of Gladstonian finance were highly encouraging. The national revenue was buoyant and prosperous, reflecting the rising prosperity of the Victorian Age.

Yet even while Gladstone's long political career was running its course, changes were taking place which would ultimately upset his system of finance and lead to developments in taxation at which he would have been horrified. Government was becoming more expensive; in the forty years from 1853 to 1893 the annual national expenditure rose from £55 million to £91 million, and by the end of the 19th century it had passed the £100 million mark. Some of this increase was accounted for by the rise in the population. But there were other reasons too. One was a great rise in the expenditure on armaments: the cost of the Navy—largely because of rapid technical improvements in guns and armour—more than doubled in the last fourteen years of the 19th century. A second was a gradual extension of the range of government activity. As more reforms were passed, so the government found itself spending more money. Public Health Acts, Education Acts, Factory Reforms—all these involved increased expenditure. Before 1900 this was on a modest scale. But it pointed the way to the vast 20th-century developments of the social services, in housing and education, pensions and health.

Inevitably the Budgets presented each year by the Chancellors of the Exchequer to the House of Commons grew in size; and equally inevitably the Chancellors began to look for new sources of revenue. One of the most important of these first appeared in 1894, when Sir William Harcourt introduced Death Duties. These were direct taxes paid on the total capital value of a person's property at death; they were graduated, so that the higher the value of the estate, the higher became the rate of duty. In

1894 Harcourt reckoned they would bring in about £1,000,000 to the Exchequer; forty years later they were yielding some £70 million per annum. Although by the 1930's they were in fact only a small part of the taxation of the rich, death duties had important social consequences. Many reformers welcomed their introduction because they would make the wealthy classes contribute more to the general needs of the national community. Among the wealthy, great landowners were from the start hostile to them, on the ground that they would be particularly penalised; and although this did not at first appear to be true, the extension of Death Duties during the first half of the 20th century did in fact lead to the sale and breakup of many great landed estates in the English countryside.

Rising government expenditure led also to the most famous Budget in British history, that of 1909, introduced by David Lloyd George, then Chancellor of the Exchequer in the Liberal government. He had to find £15 million additional revenue for two main purposes—first, for the building of eight new battleships of the *Dreadnought* class, and second, for the Old Age Pensions introduced in 1908.[1] He was himself a Radical social reformer, ready to place extra taxation on the rich in order to benefit the poor; and his Budget by the financial standards of that day appeared revolutionary. In it he increased Death Duties, Income Tax (from 1s. to 1s. 2d.), tobacco and spirit duties, stamp duties and the charge for liquor licences. Taxes on petrol and motor-car licences were to be used to start a Road Fund which was to finance improvements in the roads made necessary by the new motor traffic. He levied a super-tax on very high incomes, those over £3,000 per annum. Finally he imposed duties on Land Values, in particular one on the 'unearned increment' of land, to be paid whenever it changed hands.

Since 1909 British taxpayers have become accustomed to paying taxes on a scale far higher than that proposed by Lloyd George. Nevertheless, this 'People's Budget' caused uproar among the well-to-do, and led to a long and serious political crisis from 1909 to 1911. This began when the House of Lords threw out the Budget by 350 votes to 75. The Lords contained a great Conservative majority, and since 1905, when the Liberals had taken office, they had used it to defeat some of the government's bills. Action of this kind by the hereditary peers was hard to justify in a democratic community, especially since the electors had in 1906 given the Liberals and their allies (the Irish Nationalists and the new Labour Party) a majority of over 300 in the Commons. To throw out the Budget was a final defiance of the elected representatives of the people—a challenge which the government could not ignore. They accepted it at once, dissolving Parliament and appealing to the verdict of the people. A general election held in January 1910 gave the Liberals and their allies a decisive majority. The Conservatives accepted the position so far as the Budget was concerned, and the Lords passed it at last. So Lloyd George's taxation

---

[1] For Old Age Pensions and the social reform policy of the Liberal government, see below, pp. 188–9.

proposals became law. A further result of this conflict was the passage of the Parliament Act in 1911, which reduced the power of the Lords, and in particular laid it down that they could neither reject nor amend any Bill which the Speaker of the House of Commons declared to be a money Bill: thus the traditional right of the people's representatives, the Commons, to control taxation was confirmed.

The People's Budget, itself easily the biggest budget up to that time, emphasised two developments in taxation. One was an increase in its total amount; the second was the opening-up of new sources of taxation. Events after 1914 violently accelerated these two developments, carrying them by the time of the Second World War (1939-45) to lengths which made Lloyd George's proposals appear to have been merely trifling demands on the taxpayer.

17   Working Class Movements

One important result of the development of industry in Britain was the growth during the 19th century of a strong working class movement. This took a variety of forms. Some parts of it had only limited objectives, like the *Friendly Societies*, whose aim was to enable their members to have funds available to meet unusual expenses in time of need; or the *Mechanics' Institutes* which set out to enable working men to fit themselves by education for more skilled jobs in industry. Some began with limited objectives but widened their aims as they grew in strength; the *Co-operative Movement* started as a modest attempt by a group of Lancashire weavers to provide themselves with cheaper food, but later extended beyond retail trade and even beyond wholesale trade into politics and education. The *Trade Unions* began with strictly economic ends—shorter hours and higher wages; yet almost inevitably they turned to political activity and grew into the biggest single force behind the establishment of a working-class political party, the *Labour Party*. Finally, there was always an important section of the working class movement which threw its energies directly into politics—and especially into parliamentary reform; as, for example, did the *Chartists*. Between these different parts of the working class movement there was always a good deal of overlapping. In order to make the story of their development clearer it is helpful to trace the history of each by itself; yet it is always important to remember that these separate parts are in fact elements of one movement.

1. THE TRADE UNIONS. (*a*) THE COMBINATION ACTS

In the days of domestic industry there were no bodies that could properly be called trade 'unions'. Nevertheless, there were in many towns firmly-established 'trade clubs', containing the workmen in a particular occupation. These ran sickness and burial funds for their members; they did their best to restrict the number of apprentices in their trade so as to make themselves more valuable to the masters, and—as the names of some public-houses like the *Plasterers' Arms* or the *Jolly Bargemen* suggest—they met of an evening and celebrated their joys or drowned their sorrows in beer. In the second half of the 18th century these clubs tended to join together over a wider area and thus became more like trade unions. As they grew bigger, they grew more powerful, defending their wages when the masters tried in bad times to reduce them; and they became capable of staging a successful strike. It was probably this advance in their power that led to the attack that was launched on them at the end of the 18th century.

In 1799 the master millwrights of London and district presented a petition to the House of Commons against the activities of a 'combination' of their journeymen. The great French war was in progress; the ruling class in Parliament was inclined to panic about any organisation which it suspected might contain revolutionary elements; and so the Combination Act of 1799 was passed, forbidding the establishment of any combination of workmen to try to decrease hours of work or increase wages. A second Act of 1800 made one or two slight changes in the first one. Such combinations could already be prosecuted under the common law; these new Acts made it possible to proceed against them quickly (although the maximum penalty provided was three month's imprisonment). The Acts could also be used against combinations of employers: but there seems to be no record of any prosecution of employers under them, although there were undoubtedly many occasions when employers met together and agreed to force down wages. Historians differ about the effects of these laws. Some point out that the absence of prosecutions of employers shows that the Acts were interpreted with a bias unfavourable to the workmen. But others show that many trade unions seem to have been formed in these years despite the law; and that some of them appear to have functioned quite openly. It is certain that whereas some unions went on quite happily without interference by the authorities, others were driven underground, to become almost secret societies. This meant that their members were often ready to turn to violence.

The Repeal of the Combination Acts came in 1824. This achievement was the result of an agitation managed by an extraordinary man, the Radical leader Francis Place. He was a tailor with a shop in the Charing Cross Road: his back room became the centre of Radical discussion in London at this time. He found an ally in a Radical M.P., Joseph Hume, and a parliamentary committee was appointed to investigate the working of the Combination Acts. Place carefully coached the working class witnesses who were to appear before it; and in 1824 Parliament repealed the Combination Acts. The result was an outburst of strikes, and so in 1825 Parliament passed another Act, tightening up the law about trade unions. It was now legal for workmen to combine. But they had to limit their activities to peaceful bargaining about hours and wages; and they were not allowed to 'molest', 'obstruct' or 'intimidate' others, either employers or fellow-work-men, in any way. Trade unions were in fact left in an uncertain position. Their most important weapon, the strike, was a very doubtful affair under the law: everything depended on how judges interpreted vague works like 'intimidate'.

1. THE TRADE UNIONS. (*b*) ROBERT OWEN AND THE G.N.C.T.U.

After 1825 several large unions came into existence. Prominent among their leaders was an Ulsterman named John Doherty who had migrated to Lancashire: he did much to create a Spinners' Union in 1829 and a Potters' Union in 1830, and he also set up a short-lived National Association for the Protection of Labour, whose aim was to cover all the trades in the country. For a time in the early 1830's the attention of the working class was mainly directed towards getting the Reform Act passed. Then came the sudden rise of the most sensational trade union movement of the century—the famous Grand National Consolidated movement. Its inspirer was Robert Owen (1771–1858), a Welshman from Newtown in Montgomeryshire, a man whose ideas have been influential in the British working-class movement ever since his lifetime. He was a draper's apprentice who had made good: at 28 he had become managing partner in the Scottish mills which he made the most famous in the world, the New Lanark Mills, and here he made a considerable fortune. There were plenty of manufacturers who did well by ability and hard work in these early days of the factories. What was remarkable about Robert Owen lay in his criticisms of the industrial system under which he had made his fortune, and in the varied ways in which he tried to establish a different system. He came to believe that men are made by their environment, by the sort of surroundings in which they grow up; as he put it, 'Man's character is made for, and not by, him'. Give a child good conditions of upbringing, and he will have every chance of becoming a good citizen: send him to work when he is small, in a pit or crowded factory, and make him live in a cellar or a squalid tenement in a slum, and you run great risk of turning him into a wastrel or a criminal. Such ideas have to a large extent come to be taken for granted nowadays: but they were unusual in the early 19th century, and Owen spent much of his life in trying to persuade people of their truth. He published his views about society and the ways in which it should be reformed in his *New View of Society* in 1813–14. But his practical work was far more important than his writing.

He was a reformer first in the kind of conditions which he created in his own factory at New Lanark. Here he became a model employer. He paid high wages; he refused to employ children under ten (most factories took them at seven or younger), he provided schools for the children of his employees, and he built houses with good sanitation; and he opened stores where his workpeople could buy goods at low prices. What amazed his fellow factory-owners was that despite all this he made the New Lanark

Mills pay well—contrary to the supposed 'economic laws' of the age. New Lanark became a show-place for visitors from all over the world. Owen himself extended his efforts at factory reform in later years, backing the Factory Act of 1819 which attempted to limit hours of work in textile mills.

But Owen was not merely a model employer. He wanted to find some new basis for society which should be better than the existing system of competition—competition between manufacturers for markets and between workers for jobs. He turned to co-operation instead, and many co-operative movements grew up on Owenite principles, most of them quite small stores for mutual trading. The largest experiments were made by Owen himself in America, where he went in 1824 and set up the community of New Harmony. This, an ambitious attempt to found a 'Village of Co-opera-tion', failed, partly at least because it attracted too many scoundrels and too few hard workers. Yet when he came back to Britain he found a new opportunity to put his ideas into practice in the trade union movement. His beliefs were scorned by the upper and middle classes—because he rejected the capitalist organization of industry, and because he attacked established religions; but he had won considerable support among working men.

There was nothing moderate about Owen's plans. They led to the crea-tion of a giant trade union to include workers of every kind—miners, farm labourers, bakers, sweeps and gas workers among them. For a time this Grand National Consolidated Trades Union (G.N.C.T.U.) founded in 1833 was very successful; in 1834 its membership reached over half a million. Owen envisaged the surrender of all industry by the owners to the workers, who would set up a new co-operative system throughout. This was the merest dream. The employers resisted firmly, and did much to destroy the movement by what became known as 'the Document': they compelled their employees to sign a statement that they were not members of the G.N.C.T.U. and sacked those who refused. This often began strikes or lock-outs, which ended with the men giving in for lack of funds. The dramatic episode of the Tolpuddle Martyrs was another factor in the failure. Six men of the Dorset village of Tolpuddle were charged with administer-ing an illegal oath when planning to join the G.N.C.T.U., and in March 1834, they were sentenced to seven years' transportation. By the end of that year the great union was virtually extinct. Owen's ideas have won him the title of 'Father of English Socialism'; he contributed much to the growth of the working class movement. But so ambitious a scheme as the G.N.C.T.U. was impracticable in the 1830's, when the vast mass of workers were illiterate. Working class interest now turned away from trade unionism and towards other forms of activity—to the Ten Hours Movement for factory reform, and to the exciting political agitation of Chartism.

I. THE TRADE UNIONS. (c) THE A.S.E. AND 'NEW MODEL' UNIONISM

The next turning-point in trade unionism came in 1851, when the Amalgamated Society of Engineers was founded. The A.S.E. was as little like the G.N.C.T.U. as any union could be. Its members were skilled men, those engineers who were the key technicians of the new industrial age; it was limited to a single craft; it had a high subscription, of a shilling a week; it had a considerable series of 'friendly' benefits like sickness and unemployment allowance; it had a full-time paid secretary; and its policy was cautious and non-revolutionary. It accepted the existing organisation of industry, taking it for granted that there were bound to be two distinct groups, employers and employed. Strikes so far as possible were to be avoided. The A.S.E. was in fact a moderate and fairly well-to-do body, wishing to make unions a normal and respectable part of society. In all these things it was typical of what came to be known as the 'New Model Unionism' which grew up in a wide range of skilled trades—e.g. the boilermakers, the carpenters and the bricklayers—during the 1850's and 1860's. Many of these unions had their head offices in London, and their paid officials—men like William Allen, Secretary of the A.S.E., and Robert Applegarth, Secretary of the Carpenters and Joiners—came to form what was called the 'Junta', a small group which tried to guide trade union policy throughout the country. The Junta did not win universal support among unionists; and miners and other unions which were stronger in the northern industrial areas than in the London region remained very critical of it. Nevertheless the Trade Union Congress, which represented a wide range of unions and later became the central organisation of the entire movement, had its beginnings in these years; it held its first official meeting in 1868.

Trade unions needed to develop their strength at this time, for there was much public opposition to them. In 1866–7 there took place the notorious Sheffield Outrages, murders and explosions in Sheffield which were found to be the work of rival unions of cutlers, and these much alarmed respectable Victorian opinion. Moreover, a legal decision threatened the very existence of trade unions. In the case of *Hornby* v. *Close*, brought by the Boilermakers' Union to recover funds which a local official had embezzled, the judge declared that trade union funds were not covered by the law, and that unions could not therefore secure themselves against dishonest officials. A Royal Commission, appointed in 1867, investigated the activities of trade unions very thoroughly; and on the whole they came out well from the enquiry. It was made clear that the A.S.E. was far more typical of trade unionism than the murderous cutlers of Sheffield, and that trade unions had a very strong case indeed for the protection of their funds by law. This prepared the way for an important group of laws about trade unions in the next ten years.

In 1871 Gladstone's government passed two Acts dealing with the unions. The first, the Trade Union Act, met with approval from trade union members, because it gave full legal protection to their funds. But the second, the Criminal Law Amendment Act, was extremely unpopular with them, for it forbade peaceful picketing and repeated the old warnings against 'molestation', 'obstruction' and 'intimidation'. It appeared that men could be sent to gaol not only for striking, but also for getting ready to strike. At the election of 1874 trade unionists helped to put Disraeli and the Conservatives in office. In 1875 the new government rewarded the unions for their support. First they repealed the Criminal Law Amendment Act and passed in its place the Conspiracy and Protection of Property Act. This legalised peaceful picketing, and provided that no action taken by a group of men in the course of a trade dispute was to be punishable as a conspiracy unless it was already a crime when done by one person acting on his own. Secondly, they passed the Employers' and Workmen's Act: whereas workmen who broke a contract could hitherto be sent to prison for committing a crime, now (like their employers) they could only be made to pay damages.

This activity by Parliament did a great deal to encourage the growth of trade unions. In 1874 the T.U.C. claimed to represent 1,100,000 members. The majority of these belonged to crafts or to semi-skilled trades; yet there were already signs of the spread of unionism far beyond the ranks represented by the Junta. One notable illustration of this occurred among farm labourers, certainly the hardest to organise of all workers. In 1872 Joseph Arch, a labourer of Barford in Warwickshire, started an Agricultural Labourers' Union. It spread rapidly at first, and although its mere existence shocked landowners, it succeeded in getting from the farmers some increase in wages. But it was most unlucky in its timing: for there fell upon it in 1874–5 the full effect of the great agricultural depression. As the price of farm produce tumbled, down came the wages of the labourers; and the union practically collapsed, not to be revived until the 20th century. Yet by the middle 1870's trade unions had become one of the accepted and respectable institutions of Victorian Britain.

1. THE TRADE UNIONS. (*d*) TRADE UNIONISM FROM 1889 TO 1914

The next step forward came with the spread of unionism among the worst-paid unskilled workers, previously neglected by the organisers of 'New Model' unionism. In 1888 the match-girls employed by Messrs. Bryant and May, who made a bare living in appalling conditions by dipping matches in phosphorous, came out on strike, encouraged by Annie Besant, the Free Thought lecturer. They won increased wages, and were followed in 1889 by the London dockers, who struck for a minimum wage of sixpence an hour (a rise of one penny). It was a good time to come out—a warm summer, and trade was booming. For nearly four weeks the port of London was closed. The strike was skilfully organised and led by the dockers' leaders, John Burns, Tom Mann and Ben Tillett. The middle class of London, at first frightened by the organised processions of dockers through the city, came round to sympathy with them; nearly all the great writers of the day supported them; and funds came in from many sources, notably from Australia, whose people sent £30,000. The dock owners, at first wholly against yielding, were forced to change their attitude; the Roman Catholic

Cardinal Manning acted as mediator in the dispute; and eventually the owners gave way on all the main issues, granting the dockers their 'tanner'. It was a turning-point in the history of trade unionism, for it led to the organisation in the next few years of great numbers of other unskilled workers as well as of the dockers. Despite considerable ups and downs caused by trade slumps, the total membership of trade unions rose considerably: the 1,500,000 members of 1892 had gone up to over 2,000,000 by the end of the century.

But numbers were not everything. Just as in the 1860's the rising trade union movement had run into troubles caused by industrial violence and by legal decisions, so the same thing happened in the twenty-five years between the Dock Strike and the outbreak of the First World War. Partly because of the successful example set by the dockers, partly because for workers in many industries real wages were not so good after 1900 as they had been before that date, strikes were frequent in this period. There were various industrial troubles in the 1890's, of which the most notorious was the Miners' Lock-out of 1893, in whose course two miners were shot dead by soldiers called out to preserve order. The development inside the trade union movement of a more extreme set of beliefs called Syndicalism, largely imported from France and the United States and stressing the need for a general strike, sharpened hostility between workmen and employers. The troubles reached a climax in a great wave of strikes between 1910 and 1914, in which miners, railwaymen and dockers were the main groups of workers involved. It was a wave so severe that foreigners, seeing these strikes, the activities of the suffragettes and the prospect of civil war in Ireland all occurring at the same time, began to think that the British system of government was breaking down.

Two legal decisions gravely affected the trade unions in these years. The first was the Taff Vale Judgment of 1901. A strike had taken place on the Taff Vale Railway in South Wales: the railway company had lost money as a result, and had sued the Amalgamated Society of Railway Servants for damages. It was awarded £23,000. Here was a new peril for the unions: even if they won a strike, the costs might be quite ruinous. There was a strong demand among union members that Parliament should alter the law; and after 1906 their demand had greater force, for that year brought for the first time an appreciable number of Labour M.P.s. So in 1906 the Trade Disputes Act was passed, reversing the Taff Vale decision and providing that the funds of trade unions were not liable for actions for damages for civil (i.e non-criminal) wrongs; now, if a union called out its members on strike and thus persuaded them to break their contracts with their employers, the union could not be held liable for damages. The Trade Disputes Act thus put trade unions in a privileged position.

In 1908 a railway worker named Osborne, a member of the Amalgamated Society of Railway Servants, who was in politics a Liberal, objected to the system by which a part of every subscription to his union was given to the Labour party. All the large unions adopted this 'political levy', for a majority of their members supported the Labour party, which was thus able to finance working-class M.P.s who would otherwise have been unable to sit in the House of Commons. The courts decided in favour of Osborne: and this Osborne Judgment, confirmed by the House of Lords in 1909, threatened the existence of that party one of whose main objects was to provide for trade unionists a means of political action. In 1911 part of the difficulty created by the judgment was removed by the decision of Parliament that members of the House of Commons, hitherto unpaid, should receive a salary of £400 per annum. This was followed by the Trade Union Act of 1913, which made the political levy legal, provided that it was approved of by a majority of the members of the union; but any member who wished not to pay it could refrain from doing so by 'contracting out' of it when he paid his subscription. This was advantageous to the Labour Party; indeed, without the political levy the growth of the party would have been much hampered. On the face of it this seemed fair enough, for both the majority and the individual appeared to be safeguarded; in practice it might lead to difficulty, with great pressure being put on individual workmen by their mates not to contract out.

2. THE WORKING CLASS AND PARLIAMENTARY REFORM.

(a) THE LONDON CORRESPONDING SOCIETY

At various times in the late 18th and in the 19th centuries a great many workers agitated for the reform of Parliament. They believed that no improvement in their conditions of life was possible until control of Parliament passed from a narrow ruling class to the majority of the people. For until 1832 political power in Britain belonged to the landed gentry, headed by a small group of wealthy peers. Their ownership of land, which remained the most important form of wealth until the profits of industry and commerce surpassed it during the 19th century, was the basis of this power. The system of election and representation ensured the supremacy of the landowners. The right to vote belonged only to a small section of the population. In the counties (electing 92 of the English and Welsh M.P.s) it belonged to those who held freehold land worth 40s. per annum; in the boroughs (with 417 M.P.s in England and Wales) the qualification varied greatly, but nowhere—except in a handful of 'potwalloper' boroughs, where every householder could vote—was it at all democratic. All voting was open, and it was easy for landlords to put pressure on their tenants. Many boroughs had decayed in size, and had fallen into the 'pockets' of the local landlord; and everywhere landlords could exercise great influence. The south and west of England were heavily over-represented, in contrast to those areas of the north and midlands which grew swiftly in population with the industrial changes: whereas towns like Birmingham, Manchester, Sheffield and Leeds had no M.P.s at all until 1832, Wiltshire had 34 and Cornwall 44.

This system was first seriously challenged in the latter part of the 18th century, when a movement for parliamentary reform grew up. It was not a working class movement; its members were landed gentry who were dissatisfied with the existing system, or merchants and business men who felt that their wealth entitled them to take a share in government. It might have won success, had not the French Revolution occurred in 1789. At first English people of all classes welcomed this event; it looked as though the French were going to carry out a great programme of reform, giving themselves a genuinely representative form of government. But it was not long before English opinion changed. The Revolution grew increasingly violent: French aristocrats were deprived of their land, driven into exile, guillotined. In 1792 the French went to war with Austria and Prussia, deposed their King and proclaimed a republic, offered help to other peoples struggling to be free and conquered Belgium (the Austrian Netherlands): in 1793 the Republican Government guillotined Louis XVI and declared war on Great Britain. This series of events was disastrous to the reform movement in Britain. In 1790 the politician Edmund Burke, hitherto a supporter of moderate reform, published his *Reflections on the Revolution in France*, denouncing the whole French movement as a threat to property and order. Led by such ideas as those of Burke, and terrified by what was happening across the Channel, nearly all the landowners and property-owners abandoned the cause of parliamentary reform. As things turned out, this meant that the British parliamentary system remained unchanged for another forty years until the great Reform Act of 1832.

Nevertheless it was the French Revolution that led to the establishment of what has been called 'the first distinctively working-class political body in English History'.[1] This was the London Corresponding Society, founded in 1792. Its aims were to promote parliamentary reform and to win the right to vote for all adults. Most of its founders were skilled craftsmen, workmen who were better off and probably better educated than their fellows. Its secretary was a shoemaker, Thomas Hardy; and he and his supporters set out to create a national movement by holding meetings, by publishing leaflets, and by 'corresponding' with workmen in other parts of Britain. The ideas it was championing were expressed by Tom Paine, who in 1791–2 published (in two parts) his book *The Rights of Man* as a counterblast to Burke's *Reflections*. Paine defended the actions of the French on the ground that they had every right to set themselves free from a tyrannical government: Burke, he said, 'pitied the plumage and forgot the dying bird'—he sympathised with the wealthy aristocracy and overlooked the sufferings of the mass of the French people. Tom Paine's writing, vigorous and simple in style, inspired the English working class reformers.

The life of the London Corresponding Society was short. The policy of the government, whose leader was William Pitt the Younger, moved towards repression, the deliberate destruction of all societies which might be considered revolutionary. It was a policy based upon a nightmarish fear that the Terror which had taken place in France might occur in Britain.

[1] G. D. H. Cole: *A Short History of the British Working Class Movement, 1787–1947*, p. 29.

There is no evidence that the working class reformers in Britain, with the possible exception of a tiny handful of unimportant extremists, were out for revolution. Certainly the London Corresponding Society was careful to avoid any steps that might be considered violent. But lack of evidence did not deter the government. In 1792 they launched an attack on Paine, who fled to France: he was outlawed and the sale of his writings was forbidden. In the next year the leading Scottish radicals were arrested, tried by notably unfair judges, and sentenced to long terms of transportation. Finally in 1794 the government turned on the English reformers. Hardy and other leaders of the London Corresponding Society were arrested: so were Horne Tooke and prominent members of the Society for Constitutional Information, a middle-class Radical society. They were kept for some time in gaol, where attempts were made to extort confessions from them, before being brought to trial for sedition. There was intense excitement in London where the Radicals were numerous: the tension expressed itself through the foreman of the jury at Hardy's trial, who fell down in a faint when he had uttered his verdict. That verdict was 'Not Guilty', and Hardy was released.

After other similar acquittals in London the government dropped the series of cases. But the main policy of repression went on. *Habeas Corpus* was suspended in 1794, enabling the government to detain prisoners indefinitely without trial. The Seditious Meetings Act of 1797 sharply restricted the right to hold public meetings: and, as we have seen, the Combination Acts of 1799 and 1800 were intended to extinguish trade unions. In 1799 a Corresponding Societies Act, forbidding the existence of such bodies, finally killed off the London Society. This marked the end of working class agitation for parliamentary reform until after the French wars were over. Thomas Hardy and the skilled workmen who supported him were political pioneers: the goal they fought for, parliamentary reform, was not attained until many years later.

2. THE WORKING CLASS AND PARLIAMENTARY REFORM.

(b) WILLIAM COBBETT AND THE YEARS AFTER WATERLOO

When Napoleon had been defeated at Waterloo in 1815, British people of all classes expected a period of prosperity. But peace brought not plenty but poverty. Times were very hard for some seven or eight years after Waterloo. It was natural enough for middle and working class men to expect some remedy for their ills from Parliament; and, when no remedy was forthcoming, to demand once again the reform of the system by which Parliament was elected. Two actions of Parliament particularly embittered the working class—the Corn Law of 1815, and the abolition of Income Tax in 1816, both of which added to the burden of the poor. If these two measures were the best that the unreformed Parliament could do, then, argued the Radicals who wanted change, the case for a reform of Parliament was overwhelmingly strong.

This renewed agitation for reform found some support from the middle class, yet it was strongest among the workers. Mass meetings were held: pamphlets were distributed by the hundred: agitators rode up and down the land, rousing public opinion. Tom Paine's writings were reprinted despite the ban on them, and a vigorous working class press sprang up, defying the attempts of the authorities to suppress it. The most notable paper of the day was the *Political Register* of William Cobbett (1762–1835), the most celebrated of English Radical journalists. Cobbett had already had an adventurous career which had involved him in trouble with the authorities. He had been a sergeant-major in the army, and had fled to America to avoid prosecution after he had protested against a sentence of ten thousand lashes imposed on a fellow-soldier. On his return to Britain he started (1802) the *Political Register*, a weekly newspaper which was quickly successful. Cobbett had a blunt style and abundant common sense. He had always been a champion of the agricultural labourer. Now he turned his heart and pen to parliamentary reform, issuing weekly from 1816 onwards a special cheap *Register* at 2d. a copy. This avoided the stamp duty—which would have made it too expensive for the working class—by containing no news: it contained only Cobbett's 'Addresses to the Journeymen and Labourers', exhorting them to demand parliamentary reform. It was immediately successful, selling nearly 50,000 copies a week.

Among those who took up the cause of parliamentary reform were Henry Hunt, a powerful mob-orator, and Francis Place the Charing Cross tailor. Some believed that the reform of Parliament was by itself no solution to contemporary ills: the most prominent of these was Robert Owen with his belief in co-operation. A small group known as the Spenceans (taking their ideas from Thomas Spence, a radical writer who died in 1814) advocated common ownership of the land. But the most popular cause, the cry which went nearest to uniting the working class, was parliamentary reform. In detail this meant a complete overhaul of the existing system—a redistribution of parliamentary seats, votes for all men, and the secret ballot.

The course of events in the years after Waterloo did not encourage the reformers, and it revealed how deeply hostile the landowning class was to change. The various disturbances—the Spa Fields Riot (1816), the Peterloo Massacre (1819), the Cato Street Conspiracy (1820)—provided the government with a good case for a repressive policy. With no police force and a small and unreliable army, the government was alarmed at the possibility of revolution, and the steps it took were away from, not towards, reform. *Habeas Corpus* was suspended, Radical leaders were arrested, meetings banned, and reform literature seized. Cobbett, in fear of arrest, fled to America—but continued to send his articles for publication in Britain. Spies and *agents provocateurs* were employed. A series of Acts of Parliament, especially the Six Acts of 1819, restricted both the rights of public meeting and the freedom of the Press. Against such a background of fear and repression there was little chance of a successful reform movement.

2. THE WORKING CLASS AND PARLIAMENTARY REFORM.

(c) THE GREAT REFORM ACT, 1832

During the 1820's, however, the prospects grew brighter. Trade improved and brought with it better times. A more enlightened group of Tory ministers, including William Huskisson and Robert Peel the younger, made important reforms in the law, like the abolition of the spy system, the creation of a Metropolitan Police Force, and the repeal of the Combination Laws. The Whig opposition, which had been small in number and out of favour with the voters since the early days of the French Revolution, began to recover ground. The middle class, with its growing number of wealthy factory owners and merchants, began to be more actively anxious to gain a share of political power. To do this it was essential to dislodge the landowners from their control of Parliament. This was the object of working class reformers too, and thus in these years there arose a stronger reform movement based upon an alliance between the middle class and the working class. It was this alliance that carried through the great triumph of the reformers, the Reform Act of 1832.

In June 1830 George IV died, and was succeeded by his brother William IV. A general election took place in August. Meanwhile in July the French had risen in revolt and expelled their king. This news caused great excitement in Britain, encouraged the reformers, and helped the Whigs to win more seats in the election, leaving the Tories still in power but with a somewhat shaky majority. It was clear that the problem of reforming Parliament could not be shelved for much longer. Then in November the Duke of Wellington, the Prime Minister, declared that 'the legislature and the system of representation possesses the full and entire confidence of the country'. The result of this extraordinary statement was a widespread public outcry: Wellington, lacking confidence in his majority, resigned, and the King sent for the Whig leader, Lord Grey, and invited him to form a ministry. In 1831 the new government introduced a series of proposals for the reform of Parliament.

The fight for reform was now fairly joined, and the working class took a powerful part in it. They were prominent in the Political Unions which were formed at this time to promote the cause: the first of these was founded in Birmingham under the leadership of the banker Thomas Attwood, and in 1831 a National Political Union was set up. Its principal organiser was Francis Place, it had local branches in all large towns, and half the places on the central committee were filled by working class men. In March 1831 the Whig proposals for reform were carried by one vote in the Commons; they were later defeated by the Tories in committee, and in April the King dissolved Parliament. The general election gave the Whigs a clear majority. They introduced a second Reform Bill, which passed the Commons, and then, in October, was thrown out by the Lords. This provoked a crisis, in a country which had been simmering with excitement throughout the summer. There were great meetings throughout the land in support of the government: the Political Unions declared for 'the Bill, the whole Bill, and nothing but the Bill', and talked of non-payment of taxes until it was passed. More ominous, there were riots at Derby, where the gaol was sacked; at Nottingham where the Castle, the property of a leading Tory peer, was burned; and at Bristol, where rioters for some time were in control of the city, broke into the prisons, sacked the Mansion House, and burned the Bishop's Palace. The country was close to revolution, closer than in the dark years after Waterloo. Against this sombre background the Whigs in December 1831 introduced their third Reform Bill. The Lords held it up: Grey tried to get William IV to promise to create enough new peers to guarantee its passage through the upper House, and resigned when the King declined to do this. Wellington made an unsuccessful attempt to form a Tory government, amid signs of widespread disapproval: the leading Radicals in the Political Unions planned a general refusal to pay taxes, and Francis Place advised a run on the Bank of England with the slogan 'To stop the Duke, go for gold'. Grey came back to office within a week, when the King had pledged himself to create sufficient peers. The pledge alone was enough: the Tories in the Lords retreated, and in June 1832 the first—and greatest—Parliamentary Reform Act became law.

Its passage was in great part the result of pressure by the working class. But they got no immediate benefit from it. The political gains went to the middle class. The right to vote was given not to all men, but only to the £10 householders in the boroughs and to 40s. freeholders, £10 copyholders and £50 short-lease-holders in the counties—that is, to the upper middle classes, the merchants and business men, the professional men and the more well-to-do farmers: and there was no secret ballot. On a long view the Act of 1832 meant that the door which had for so long been shut had at last been opened, and would before long be pushed open wider still, to give the right to vote to men of every class. But in the 1830's, once the immediate excitement was over, the working class who had fought for the Bill began to feel disillusioned with its results. Within a few years another working class campaign for political reform had begun—the struggle for the People's Charter.

3. THE CHARTIST MOVEMENT

In 1836 a group of politically-minded working men formed the London Working Men's Association; its secretary was a Cornishman, a skilled cabinet-maker named William Lovett. Its object was the reform of Parliament, and in 1838 it issued what became known as the People's Charter. This demanded six political reforms—annual parliaments, vote by ballot, equal electoral districts, abolition of the property qualification for M.P.s, payment of M.P.s, and universal manhood suffrage. The Charter won support from meetings held throughout the country, especially in the industrial areas; and from Birmingham came the suggestion of a great national petition to Parliament asking for the immediate adoption of the Charter.

So began the Chartist Movement. From the start its rank and file were working men, although a number of middle-class leaders played important parts in it. The Charter itself was mainly the work of Lovett, although Francis Place had a hand in revising it for publication. Lovett was a craftsmen who had belonged to one of the Owenite Co-operative Societies. The others who played prominent parts in the Chartist Movement were a very mixed lot. From Birmingham came Thomas Attwood the banker, who believed that currency reform was the answer to all economic problems, and Joseph Sturge, a wealthy Quaker corn-merchant; from the north of England came John Fielden, a textile manufacturer, and Richard Oastler, a land agent, both of them keen factory reformers; from Ireland came Fergus O'Connor, a journalist who was quickly to become both the outstanding figure and the evil genius of the movement. In the local branches up and down the land middle-class men often took the lead, like John Frost the Newport draper and that impressive and unusual figure Dr. Wade, the sixteen-stone Vicar of Warwick.

Why did the working class turn so enthusiastically to support of the Charter? In the first place, it reflected dissatisfaction with the actual results of the 1832 Reform Act: many working men felt that they had been deceived and betrayed. Secondly, Robert Owen's gigantic trade union, the G.N.C.T.U., had failed, and in its turn left behind it a legacy of discontent and frustration. Thirdly, the Whig governments of the 1830's had done little for the poor, and after 1835 they passed no major reform. It was true that they had passed the first effective Factory Act in 1833; but in the opinion of most working men they had more than counterbalanced this by passing the Poor Law Amendment Act in 1834.[1] This Act had brought great hardship to many a poor family by its abolition of outdoor relief and by its establishment of the hated workhouses, the 'Bastilles'; and this 'New Poor Law' turned many a workman into a Chartist. Fourthly, Chartism provided an outlet for local grievances: the falling wages of the handloom operatives of the West Riding and the decaying weavers of Wiltshire, the ambitions of the skilled craftsmen of London and Birmingham, the radical views and harsh conditions of the miners of Monmouthshire. Fifthly, and most important of all, poverty and hunger, recurrent hard times, did more than anything else to breed Chartism. When times were bad, as in 1838–9, 1842 and 1847–8, Chartism flourished.

The winter of 1838–9 was a bad one, and great meetings took place, many of them by torchlight in the industrial areas: huge crowds hailed the Charter as the beginning of a new era, and there were wild words about revolution. Early in 1839 a Chartist National Convention assembled in London. The delegates talked of proclaiming a 'sacred month' or general strike, and collected signatures for a great petition to Parliament. But the convention was an unlucky body: from the start there was serious disagree-

[1] For details of these reforms, see below, pp. 179–80, 182.

ment between those who said that moral force alone would compel the government to grant the Six Points, and more extreme members who called for physical force. It took time to arrange the petition, and this gave opportunity for the divisions in the Chartist ranks to grow. The Convention moved to Birmingham, and then back to London again, in time to see the petition rejected by 235 votes against 46 in the Commons. Thereupon the Convention proclaimed a general strike: then cancelled its proclamation a week later; and ignominiously dissolved itself. The government meanwhile had taken firm measures. Additional troops had been sent to the areas where Chartism was strongest; Sir Charles Napier, appointed to command in the north, gave the Chartist leaders a practical warning of what revolution would involve by inviting them to attend an artillery demonstration. Disturbances in the Bull Ring in Birmingham were severely handled by London Police sent for the purpose, and Lovett was arrested there. There was in fact no Chartist rising, apart from a tragic affair in Monmouthshire, when a group of miners marched on Newport, led by John Frost, an ex-Mayor of the town. This Newport Rising was quickly quelled by a handful of troops, and its leaders were transported for life. It was the end of the first, and most serious, outburst of Chartism.

There were two others. In 1842 the petition was again presented to Parliament, and again rejected, this time by 287 votes to 49. Its rejection was followed by strikes and riots, especially in Lancashire, where there took place the Plug Plot, so called because the strikers went round the mills removing the plugs from the boilers which supplied the power. Peel's Conservative government arrested many hundreds of Chartists, and quickly crushed the movement. The divisions in the Chartist ranks now became sharper than ever. Most of the middle class sympathisers were frightened away by the strikes, while Lovett abandoned the cause and turned his energies to promoting working class education. The field was clear for the leadership of Fergus O'Connor. O'Connor was a capable journalist whose paper *The Northern Star* did much for the Chartist cause: he was also an orator who could rouse a crowd. But he was a muddled thinker and irresolute when it came to action. In 1845 he founded a land company to start Chartist settlements of smallholders;[1] in 1847 he was elected M.P. for Nottingham; and in 1848, under the impulse of the European revolts of that year, a third and last Chartist petition was drawn up. It was to be presented to Parliament by a procession, marching to Westminster, from a great meeting on Kennington Common. The government, overestimating the Chartists' strength, took elaborate military precautions, entrusting the defence of London to the Duke of Wellington (now nearly 79) and enrolling 150,000 special constables. They forbade the procession to cross the river, and the petition was taken to Parliament in three cabs instead. It was found to contain not the 5,000,000 signatures which O'Connor had claimed, but under 2,000,000, many of which were bogus. Parliament

---

[1] Several were begun: their cottages may still be seen at Charterville near Burford in Oxfordshire and at Snig's End near Staunton in Gloucestershire.

declined to discuss it. Thus Chartism ended in a fiasco, although the movement lingered on in name for another ten years. O'Connor went out of his mind and died in an asylum in 1855.

Obviously the failure of Chartism was in part the result of the disagreement of its leaders. But there were deeper reasons too. Middle class folk were frightened of Chartism, and feared the triumph of the working class: thus the alliance of 1832 was not repeated. Many workmen were attracted away by other movements—the Co-operative Societies, the Ten Hours Movement for Factory Reform, and, above all in the early 1840's, the Anti-Corn Law League. Further, the Poor Law Amendment Act now began to be somewhat less harshly administered. Yet the most important factor in the Chartist failure was the simplest of all. Bad times had promoted Chartism; good times undermined it; and from the middle 1840's onwards trade was beginning to improve, thanks partly to Peel's free trade policy. Chartism was outwardly a political movement, aiming at a political end, the radical reform of Parliament: yet its real objective was economic, the creation of better conditions of life and work. When those began to improve, the attraction of Chartism was bound to diminish. One further point must be made. Chartism was in advance of its time. All the Six Points save one (annual Parliaments) have since become law. The property qualification for M.P.s was scrapped in 1858, the secret ballot came in 1872; M.P.s were paid from 1911 onwards, universal manhood suffrage was attained in 1918; and a series of reform Acts since 1885 have done about as much as can be done to provide electoral districts of equal size. Thus by later standards the Chartist demands were neither fantastic nor revolutionary. But to the middle-class voters of the 1840's they were quite out of the question.

4. THE RISE OF THE LABOUR PARTY

In one way the Chartists, as a principally working class political movement, were the forerunners of the Labour Party. But there was no direct connection between the two. The Labour Party dates its official beginning from the foundation in 1900 of the Labour Representation Committee, whose object was to promote the election to Parliament of working class men committed to a definitely socialist programme. Yet during most of the half-century between the last Chartist petition and the foundation of the L.R.C. the working class were not strongly interested in politics—and certainly, until the 1890's, not in the creation of a special working class party. Chartism had failed. Now other movements—notably Friendly Societies, the Co-operatives, and the trade unions—grew strong in the pursuit of their various objectives. And the second half of the century saw a fairly steady advance in the standard of living for most of the population. So long as the two existing parties, Liberals and Conservatives, continued to offer gradual reforms there was not likely to be any early demand for the creation of a separate working class political party.

Yet the years after 1850 saw developments in parliamentary reform which strengthened the position of the working class. In the early 1860's a renewed agitation sprang up, very different from the Chartist Movement. It was in no way revolutionary; it was backed by the 'New Model' trade unions; it was much influenced by the growth of political freedom in the United States, and it acted in close conjunction with middle class Liberals like John Bright, the great orator of the Anti-Corn Law League. Trade Union leaders and ex-Chartists joined in forming in 1860 a National Reform League, which in July 1866 arranged to hold a great demonstration in Hyde Park. The government closed the gates of the park on the day of the meeting: a great procession surged against the railings, which collapsed, and the crowd poured in and held meetings in defiance of the police. It was a warning to the rich inhabitants of Park Lane that the time had come for a further reform of Parliament, and in 1867 Derby's Conservative government, stimulated by its opportunist Chancellor of the Exchequer, Benjamin Disraeli, carried the Second Reform Act. This gave the vote to all male householders in the towns and to the £12 ratepayers in the counties. In effect this 'leap in the dark', as the Prime Minister himself called it, almost doubled the electorate, and gave the vote to the town workmen, the artisans. Five years later, in 1872, the Ballot Act made voting secret. In 1884 came the Third Reform Act, passed by a Liberal government headed by Gladstone, which extended the right to vote to all male householders in the countryside, thus putting the agricultural labourer on level terms with the artisan. Thus the Acts of 1867 and 1884 made the working class in town and country the majority of the British electorate. Yet for the rest of the 19th century, some local exceptions apart, they used their votes to support Liberals and Conservatives.

This widening of the franchise helped to prepare the ground for the rise of the Labour Party in the last years of the century. From the start this new party was essentially connected with socialism—the doctrine that the community should own and develop for the benefit of all its members the main sources of national wealth like the coal-mines, the railways and perhaps the land itself. Among the most important of its ancestors in Great Britain was Robert Owen; the Owenite ideas continued to win adherents among working men, especially among the craftsmen of the more skilled trade unions and in the swiftly-developing Co-operative movement. Moreover, the second half of the 19th century brought an increasing number of laws by which Parliament interfered with private freedom in order to benefit the community as a whole—laws like the various Factory Reforms and the Public Health Acts. Such 'collectivist' laws were not socialist: they did not involve ownership of national resources by the community. Yet they accustomed people of every class to the idea of state interference, and so prepared the way for further extension of socialist ideas.

Two very different books contributed to the development and spread of socialism. The first was one of the most influential books of all history—*Capital*, by Karl Marx, the first volume of which was published in 1867.

Marx was a German-Jewish refugee living in London. His book was a profound and difficult analysis of history whose purpose was to demonstrate the overwhelming strength of economic motives in human affairs: he went on to maintain that the rise of communism in all industrial countries was inevitable and that its coming would be heralded by a revolution of the working class against its masters. His influence was far greater on the Continent than in Britain, and greatest of all in Russia, where Marxism became the gospel of the Bolsheviks who carried through the October Revolution of 1917. In Britain, *Capital* found few readers. In this as in other ways it contrasted notably with a second book *Progress and Poverty*, published by the American, Henry George, in 1879. George was a man of one idea: he believed that all economic difficulties would be overcome by imposing a single tax, on the 'unearned increment' of land. 'Single-Tax' George was incomparably less profound and less important than Karl Marx, yet he won many adherents in Britain in the 1880's, and indirectly at least encouraged the growth of socialist ideas.

In 1881 a somewhat unusual London stockbroker named H. M. Hyndman, who had read a French version of *Capital* and been converted to communism, founded the Social Democratic Federation. This body advocated a socialist programme, including such measures as the nationalisation of land, railways and banks: the most celebrated of its early members was the poet and craftsman, William Morris. It was never large; most of its members were middle class; quarrels in its ranks were frequent, and in one of them William Morris and others broke away to found a rival organisation, the Socialist League. Yet the S.D.F. and the Socialist League, too, have their place in the history of the Labour Party because they helped to spread socialist ideas among working class leaders.

A second socialist organisation was in strong contrast to the S.D.F., both in methods and achievements. This was the Fabian Society, founded in 1884 by a small group of middle class intellectuals. Their early leaders included such gifted thinkers and writers as George Bernard Shaw, H. G. Wells, and Sidney and Beatrice Webb. Their ideas owed little to Karl Marx, and there was nothing violent about them. They wished to spread socialist ideas by gradual means: hence their name, taken from the Roman general of old who had destroyed the Carthaginian armies by delaying tactics. They did not think in terms of revolution, but of the gradual capture of the state for socialism by winning votes at elections. At first their influence was small, but it grew rapidly; Fabian pamphlets were of high quality, and members of the Society played a prominent part in local government, especially on the London County Council, established in 1889. They were ready to try to get their policies about particular problems taken up by the established parties, Liberals and Conservatives. The ideas and writings of Sidney and Beatrice Webb have had an influence on 20th-century laws comparable with that of Jeremy Bentham on the laws of the 19th century.

The Fabians were even more middle class than the S.D.F.: and both groups were very small. To form an effective Labour Party numbers were essential, and these could come only from the working class. They could come most effectively through the biggest working-class organisations, the trade unions; and after the Dock Strike of 1889 socialism gained ground in the unions. Scottish working men in this same year 1889 founded a Scottish Labour Party whose aim was independent labour representation in Parliament. There had been working class M.P.s already, like Henry Broadhurst, an Oxfordshire stone-mason who held office in Gladstone's ministry of 1886, or Joseph Arch, the agricultural trade union pioneer who was for a time an M.P. for Norfolk: they had been members of the Liberal party, and were known as 'Lib-Labs'. But in 1892 three independent Labour M.P.s were elected. One was John Burns, a great figure in the S.D.F. and a leader in the Dock Strike: another was Keir Hardie, a Scottish miner elected for West Ham. Hardie arrived at the House of Commons wearing a cloth cap and accompanied by a brass band, and his election was a sign that a new age had begun. Hardie was a very British type of revolutionary; he was a kindly, commonsense Scotsman, believing firmly in the need for a separate Labour party, and seeing socialism not as a system of economics but as a humanitarian necessity—as 'life for the dying people'.

It was Keir Hardie who led the movement that followed for the creation of a separate party. In 1893 he was in the chair at the Bradford Conference, at which representatives from local bodies throughout Britain met together and formed the Independent Labour Party. Its policy was avowedly socialist—'to secure the collective ownership of the means of production, distribution, and exchange'; and its programme demanded a wide range of social reforms, like the eight-hour day, state provision for the aged, the disabled and the orphans, and the reform of taxation. During the next few years the I.L.P. developed considerably, winning support especially among the younger trade union leaders. Much of its success was due to Robert Blatchford, a lively journalist who edited its journal *The Clarion* and wrote a popular book on socialism, *Merrie England*, which was first published in 1894 and eventually sold over a million copies. But the I.L.P. did not itself mark the beginning of the 20th-century Labour party; and in the general election of 1895 all its 28 candidates, Keir Hardie included, were defeated. In a way, a more serious failure was the inability of the I.L.P. to convert the Trades Union Congress to socialism. The T.U.C., which represented the majority of organised working men, was cautious and unwilling to commit itself—and its considerable funds—to the all-out support of a socialist programme.

Not until 1899 did the turning-point come. In that year the socialists at the T.U.C. got a resolution passed for the calling of a special conference of representatives from 'Co-operative, Socialist, Trade Union, and other working class organisations' in order 'to devise ways and means for the securing of an increased number of Labour Members in the next Parliament'. This conference met in 1900, containing representatives from the Fabians and the S.D.F., from the I.L.P., and from the trade unions. There was much difference of opinion; but eventually Keir Hardie put forward a compromise proposal which was accepted, providing for the creation of 'a distinct Labour group in Parliament', with its own whips, through the formation of a Labour Representation Committee. The new body was known almost at once as the Labour party, though it did not officially adopt that name until 1906. Its first secretary was a young Scottish journalist, James Ramsay MacDonald; and in the election of 1900 it got two members elected, one of them being its chairman Keir Hardie, who was chosen for the Welsh mining town of Merthyr Tydfil.

So there began a new political party. Before half a century had passed it was to find itself governing Britain with a large parliamentary majority (1945–50). Yet until the First World War it grew relatively slowly. In 1900, 63,000 Labour voters returned 2 M.P.s; in 1906, 323,000 returned 29 (besides some 26 who could fairly be classed as Lib-Labs); and in December 1910, at the last election before the war, 371,000 returned 42. In these initial stages of Labour party history, the strongest support for the new movement came from the areas of mining and heavy industry, like South Wales, Durham and Clydeside, and also from areas of great poverty, such as parts of the East End of London. The party owed most of its early financial strength to the trade unions, whose members provided a solid body of Labour voters. Hence its policy was closely related to the needs of the unions. Thus in the years before 1914 Labour members gave steady approval to the social reform programme of the Liberal governments, backing such measures as the Workmen's Compensation Act (1906), the Eight Hour Day for Coal Miners (1908) and Old Age Pensions (1908). Yet they reserved their full force for issues like the Taff Vale Case and the Trade Disputes Act (1906), which involved the very existence of trade unions; and the Osborne Judgment and its effects, which threatened the survival of working class M.P.s and thus of the Labour party itself.

5. OTHER WORKING CLASS ACTIVITIES. (*a*) THE CO-OPERATIVE MOVEMENT

Trade Unions and the Labour party were only the most important working class organisations to grow up in the 19th and early 20th centuries. There were many others of varied kinds. The Victorian age believed strongly in self-help, regarding it, for example, as a man's own duty to safeguard himself and his dependants against misfortune or old age. This was not difficult for the prosperous middle class; but for the average working man it was a desperately hard task. As times improved after 1850 it became a little easier; and in particular the rather better-paid workman, the skilled artisan, took the lead in developing various organisations whose main purpose was to encourage thrift. The most notable of these were the Co-operative Movement and the Friendly Societies.

During the first half of the 19th century many small Co-operative societies were set up, most of them under the impulse of the ideas of Robert Owen.

They were of various kinds. Some were producers' co-operatives, whose aim was to cut down the costs of production of goods which they sold on the open market; others were consumers' co-operatives, which bought goods wholesale and sold them to their members at prices below the ordinary market level. Scarcely any were successful. The continuous history of the modern co-operative movement in Great Britain began in 1844, when 28 weavers of Rochdale invested one pound each in setting up a co-operative store in T'Owd Lane in that growing Lancashire cotton town. This Rochdale store prospered and its example was followed elsewhere in Lancashire and the north of England. The secret of its financial success lay in the combination of two devices. One was the 'dividend': the members of the T'Owd Lane Co-operative bought their goods wholesale, sold them at the ordinary market price, and then distributed the surplus to purchasers in proportion to the amount of goods they had bought. The second was the use of capital provided by shares: interest was paid from the start to shareholders, and members were encouraged to leave their dividends in the business to accumulate as shares. This provided a steady growth of capital, enabling the store to expand. It also gave the individual member a convenient and painless means of saving money.

Thus the co-operative society encouraged thrift. Another reason for its success was that it sold pure food at reasonable prices. These years were the golden age of adulteration, when scoundrelly shopkeepers mixed sand with sugar and chalk with flour; and of the 'tommy shops' attached to factories, charging outrageous prices for rotten foodstuffs to customers who were compelled to buy from them. The co-operative store was a welcome contrast to these; and the movement spread swiftly, particularly in the north of England, in the 1850's and 1860's. In 1863 a North of England Co-operative Wholesale Society was established, to provide goods for various retail societies—which were themselves the members of the wholesale society, at once shareholders and dividend receivers. Ten years later, when it set up its first factories, the 'North of England' was dropped, and the company became henceforward the Co-operative Wholesale Society (C.W.S.).

Thereafter the movement greatly extended its enterprises. By 1913 the C.W.S. owned, among other things, flour-mills and tobacco factories, ironworks and boot factories, printing works and biscuit factories; there was a considerable C.W.S. Bank; and other 20th-century enterprises of the society were to include the management of a fleet of tramp steamers and the organisation of a travel agency. It had in fact become one of the major businesses of a great industrial country. As for membership of the movement, that had risen to numbers of which the original Rochdale Pioneers can never have dreamed. In 1881 there were 546,000 co-operators; by 1900 there were 1,703,000 and by 1915 over 3,000,000. Its activities went beyond the range of business. From its earliest Owenite days its aims had not been merely cheap food and thrift. It was a pioneer of adult education in Britain, providing lectures, tutorial classes and eventually a Co-operative College for its members. For a long period the movement kept out of politics.

Yet the natural sympathies of many of its members in the early 20th century were with the rising Labour party; and in 1917 the governing body of the movement, the Co-operative Congress, founded the Co-operative party. This was officially separate from the Labour party but worked in close harmony with it; and Co-operative funds went to secure the election of M.P.s who received the Labour whip in the Commons.

5. OTHER WORKING CLASS ACTIVITIES. (*b*) FRIENDLY SOCIETIES

Friendly Societies of various kinds have been a feature of British working class life since the 18th century, when, for example, some of the bigger 'Orders' like the Oddfellows and the Foresters had their beginnings. But their great development came in the 19th century, when the industrial changes brought workers together in large groups in the towns. Their purposes were very various. Most of them set out to enable their members, by some plan of mutual insurance and self-help, to obtain benefits in the event of sickness, accident, or death. Burial clubs, to enable a poor man's dependants to give him a decent funeral, were very common. By contrast there were deposit societies, to provide a fund against a rainy day; and 'goose clubs' and local 'slate clubs' of many kinds, whose object was to save for some festive occasion. Good fellowship and conviviality often went hand in hand with mutual insurance, especially in some of the larger, nation-wide societies, like the Foresters and Oddfellows (both of which were reorganised in the 1830's) and the Hearts of Oak (founded in 1841). Members of these bigger societies indulged in a certain amount of pageantry and ceremonial, with banners, aprons and the like; and also in a certain amount of liquor, in contrast to such teetotal societies as the Rechabites. Outside these national societies with their local 'lodges' (the Rechabites however had 'tents') was a multitude of small-scale local bodies.

The Friendly Societies were much regulated by Parliament in the 19th century. This was in their own interest, for they were readily open to fraud by their own officials; moreover the financial basis of many societies was very insecure because insufficient statistical information was available to make mutual insurance calculations reliable. A whole series of Friendly Societies Acts was passed, of which the most important were those of 1846, setting up a Registry of Friendly Societies to which they had to belong, and of 1875, codifying the law about them. They continued to grow throughout the 19th century, particularly in the industrial areas and most notably of all in Lancashire. By 1872 they had 4,000,000 members (four times as many as the trade unions), and by 1913 6,500,000. By this time an important change had affected their position. Under the National Insurance System, first established by Lloyd George in 1911, the 'approved' Friendly Societies were appointed as agents to carry out the new scheme and to distribute its benefits. Inevitably, as more and more of the population fell under the government schemes of insurance, the role of the Friendly Societies would become less important in the 20th century than it had been in the 19th. They represented the 'self-help' of Victorian England; the National Insurance scheme of 1911 heralded the 'welfare state' of a later age.[1]

5. OTHER WORKING CLASS ACTIVITIES. (c) WORKING CLASS EDUCATION

A third field in which working class people were active to help themselves was education. There was no universal system of elementary education in England until 1870; and the government made no grant of public money to education until 1833. Many upper class people in the early 19th century were opposed to giving the working class any education at all, on the ground that to do so would encourage the spread of revolutionary ideas; others considered that they should only receive such elementary education as would fit them to carry out the menial tasks of the community. But men like Robert Owen and William Lovett grasped at once the vital importance of education, and gave much of their energy to developing it among the working class. Intelligent working men of the early 19th century realised the opportunities which the new industrial development offered to skilled men, especially to engineers; hence there arose a powerful demand among artisans for some kind of technical education which would enable them to better themselves.

Three examples of movements directed to adult education are particularly worth mentioning. In 1823 a Mechanics' Institution was started in London by Thomas Hodgskin. Its central purpose was to provide technical education, especially in engineering, for working men. Similar institutions were founded about the same time in other large towns; they were supported by Lord Brougham (Lord Chancellor, 1830–4) and middle class Radical leaders as well as by working class leaders like Cobbett. Ultimately the London Institution became Birkbeck College and a part of the University of London. Secondly, in 1899 Ruskin Hall (later Ruskin College) was founded at Oxford to provide an opportunity of residential education for working men who seemed likely to become leading figures in trade unions and similar movements; this received much of its financial support from a group of trade unions. Thirdly, in 1903 the Workers' Educational Association was started. In a sense this was an offshoot of the University Extension system, begun in 1873, under which universities began to send lecturers out to give evening courses to adult students. The W.E.A. aimed to go rather further, and to encourage the student not merely to listen to lectures but actively to co-operate in his own education; and the method of tutorial classes which it evolved was highly successful in doing this. At first its students were mainly interested in such studies as economics and economic history, but gradually its range extended to include modern languages and philosophy, music and the arts, as well as many practical courses.

---

[1] For details about the National Insurance scheme, see below, pp. 188–9.

18 Parliament and Social Reform, 1815-1914

The Industrial and Agricultural Revolutions created for the people of Britain ways of life in which good and ill were blended. The new environment of the factory town or the enclosed village held high possibilities of material well-being—of more food and better clothing, of more comfortable houses, of improved transport. Historians differ sharply in their views about the 'standard of living' in the early 19th century. Some point to the increased consumption of foodstuffs like sugar, to the great sale of cotton clothes to the working class; others to the grinding poverty of farm labourers, to the sufferings of those like the handloom weavers, driven out of work by the new machinery. The evidence from statistics, of wages and prices, is very incomplete. A modern investigator has noted that improvement was 'more marked among industrial than agricultural workers and stronger in the north than the south of England', and that 'though the long-term trend was upward, progress was intermittent and there were years of retreat as well as advance.'[1] There was real gain for many, yet the coming of good things was for most people desperately slow. Meanwhile the ill-effects were for millions immediate and clear. The long hours of disciplined work in mills; the brutalising physical toil of women and children in pits; the slums, with the crowded tenements and their jerry-built cottages; the new towns, with their foul water supplies and inadequate drains, their lack of paving and lighting; the tumbledown hovels of the landless labourer in the countryside—these seemed the obvious results of the changes. Out of them arose other social problems—of the organisation of the Poor Law, of the planning of local government, of relations between employers and workmen, of public health, of education. In effect the great changes in agriculture and industry set a vast series of complex social questions which the men of the 19th century had to answer.

1. THE PATTERN OF REFORM, 1815-1914

Before 1832 Parliament made no large-scale attempt to tackle social problems. The property-owning classes could not forget the French Revolution, and many of them thought that reform was a dangerous incitement to revolution. There was little prospect of Parliament carrying out reforms until Parliament itself was reformed: and until 1832 it was firmly under the control of the landowners. Moreover, this was the age of *laissez-faire*. It was widely held, especially among merchants and businessmen, that government intervention in economic matters was certain to be disastrous: there were economic laws just as there were scientific ones, and

[1] A. J. Taylor: *The Standard of Living in Britain in the Industrial Revolution* (1975), pp. l. and xlvi.

it was as foolish to meddle with one as to defy the other. Any government that interfered with the 'iron laws' of economics, for example by limiting hours of work, would bring ruin on the community, factory-owner and worker alike.

Nevertheless, in the 1820's, when times were a little better than they had been immediately after Waterloo, the Tory governments did in fact introduce some modest but important reforms. Robert Peel began to reform the penal code and the prisons, and created the Metropolitan Police:[1] the repeal of the Combination Acts abolished the ban on the existence of trade unions:[2] and the repeal of the Test and Corporation Acts (1828) and the passage of Catholic Emancipation (1829) removed civil and political disabilities from Nonconformists and Roman Catholics.[3] These beginnings heralded greater things and stimulated the movement for parliamentary reform, which triumphed in the Reform Act of 1832, a major turning-point in British history. Its terms meant that the landowners had to share their monopoly of political power with the middle-class, who now for the first time were given the right to vote. Its long-term result was to open the way to further extensions of the franchise: what had been done once could be done again, to benefit other classes. Its immediate result was to stimulate a series of major reforms within the next twenty years.

Between 1832 and 1855 the Whig governments, under Grey and Melbourne, introduced the first effective Factory Act,[4] made the first grant of public money to education,[5] abolished slavery in the British Empire,[6] transformed the system of the Poor Law,[7] and created a new plan of local government;[8] and in 1840 they set up the Penny Post.[9] Then the Tories took up the task. Peel's great ministry (1841–6) passed important measures affecting mines,[10] factories,[11] banks,[12] and railways[13]—in addition to his work as a Free trade reformer, culminating in the Repeal of the Corn Laws. Finally the Whigs under Lord John Russell passed in 1847 yet another Factory Act[14] and in 1848 the first Public Health Act.[15] The passage of these laws was, so to speak, the first burst of social reform in the 19th century. After them came a lull, a period of about twenty years (1848–67) in which no major reforming measure was passed.

A second spell of reform was initiated by the Second Reform Act of 1867, which gave the vote to the town workmen. Gladstone's Liberal government (1868–74) put through a great series of varied laws. They carried a group of radical reforms in education, affecting elementary and grammar schools and the universities;[16] reorganised the Army; passed two important trade union Acts;[17] regulated the methods of entry to the civil service;[18] created the Local Government Board;[19] introduced the secret ballot for voting at

[1] See below, p. 223. [2] See above, p. 153. [3] See below, p. 213.
[4] See below, pp. 179–80. [5] See below, p. 207. [6] See above, p. 132.
[7] See below, pp. 182–3. [8] See below, p. 184. [9] See above, p. 109.
[10] See below, p. 181. [11] See below, p. 180. [12] See above, p. 144.
[13] See above, pp. 78–79. [14] See below, p. 180. [15] See below, p. 194.
[16] See below, pp. 205, 208, 210. [17] See above, pp. 156–7.
[18] See below, pp. 178–9. [19] See below, p. 184.

parliamentary elections; attempted to create a satisfactory system of licensing laws for public houses; and reformed the principal law-courts.[1] It was a considerable programme, and it is little wonder that in 1873 Benjamin Disraeli, the leader of the Conservative opposition, could describe the Liberals as 'a range of exhausted volcanoes'. Yet when in the next year the swing of the pendulum brought him to power as Prime Minister (1874–80), Disraeli's own Conservative government proceeded to pass its own great group of reforms. Thirty years earlier Disraeli as a young man had spoken and written in favour of using the powers of state to protect the poverty-stricken industrial workers. That had been radical doctrine in the 1840's: now, in the 1870's, times had changed. *Laissez-faire*, though far from dead, was no longer the ruling belief, as Conservative Acts demonstrated. Another Factory Act,[2] another Education Act,[3] more trade union legislation;[4] a great Public Health Act, creating the modern code of public health;[5] the Artisans' Dwellings Act, an attack on the problems of working class housing;[6] an Act to safeguard what was left of common land near towns, another to prevent the overloading of merchant shipping[7]—here was lawmaking quite comparable with that of the Liberals. After this, Gladstone's second Liberal Ministry (1880–5) did relatively little, except pass the Third Reform Act (1884) giving the vote to the agricultural labourer.[8]

Once again there came a lull, a halt in the series of major reforms—caused partly by the attention of the public being diverted to imperialism, its problems and its glamour.[9] Yet this time it was a lull in which there were several highly important isolated measures, like the creation of County Councils in 1888,[10] or the introduction of Death Duties in 1894,[11] as well as a good deal of minor reforming: indeed half-a-century earlier this lull would itself have been looked on as a time of vigorous reforming. It lasted about twenty years, and was abruptly ended by the record success of the Liberals at the polls in 1906. There followed a third spell of reform at least as far-reaching as the previous two, which was only broken by the outbreak of a World War in 1914. The Liberals, inspired by Lloyd George, the Welsh Radical who became Chancellor of the Exchequer in 1908, were not only willing to use the power of the state to carry out policies far removed from *laissez-faire*: they were ready to go a long way in order to outbid the new Labour party on their left. So parliament poured forth a flood of laws on many social problems—including trade unions[12] and Labour Exchanges,[13] the Army, merchant shipping and the Port of London Authority, education and the general well-being of children,[14] the hours of coal-miners[15] and shop assistants,[16] Old Age Pensions[17] and National Insurance.[18] And there came in 1909, as we have seen, the most revolutionary Budget of

[1] See below, pp. 225–6.   [2] See below, p. 181.   [3] See below, p. 208.
[4] See above, p. 157.   [5] See below, p. 195.   [6] See below, p. 195.
[7] See below, p. 187.   [8] See above, p. 168.   [9] See above, pp. 135–6.
[10] See below, pp. 184–5.   [11] See above, pp. 150–1.   [12] See above, pp. 158–9.
[13] See below, p. 188.   [14] See below, p. 187.   [15] See below, p. 188.
[16] See below, p. 188.   [17] See below, pp. 188–9.   [18] See below, pp. 188–9.

modern times, whose aim was to divert money from the pockets of the rich to those of the poor.[1]

These spells of reform were the work of Parliaments nearly all of whose members were men of substantial wealth. They were carried through by both the established political parties; after the Reform Act of 1867 Conservatives and Liberals were competing against one another for working-class votes. Much of the impetus for reform came from religion, through philanthropists like William Wilberforce and Lord Shaftesbury.[2] Some of the earlier reforms are often known as 'Benthamite' reforms because they reflect the teachings of Jeremy Bentham (1743-1832), an advocate of parliamentary reform and the improvement of the law. He and his followers (such as Edwin Chadwick)[3] became known as 'Utilitarians' because the test they applied to every law and institution was 'What use is it?' His influence was strong in the 1820's and 1830's, and contributed much to the reform of the penal code and of the Poor Law. In like manner in the early 20th century Sidney and Beatrice Webb (1859-1947 and 1858-1943), two leading members of the Fabian Society, did much by their writings and by their careful investigations of social problems to promote reforms. They wrote notable books on Trade Unionism and Local Government; they were prominent members of Royal Commissions on such subjects as the Poor Law and Unemployment; and their influence appeared in such reforms as the Education Act of 1902.[4] They were socialists, and their work did much to spread belief in state intervention on behalf of the weaker and poorer members of the community.

Two other important features of this process of reform may be noted here. One is the development of a regular system of enquiry into social problems, first extensively used in the 1830's and 1840's. When a problem forced itself on public notice—as, for example, the rise in the poor rates compelled people to think about the Poor Law in the years after Waterloo— a Royal or Parliamentary Commission of enquiry was set up. Its members investigated the problem, visiting any areas specially concerned (this was most illuminating to the Children's Employment Commission which reported on child labour in coal-mines in 1842), and they called witnesses before them, whose evidence—as for example that given to the Factory Commissioners in 1833—might be dramatic and revealing. When the enquiries were completed, the Commission published a report, in the form of an official 'Blue Book', and any Act of Parliament which followed was normally based on this. Secondly, the growth of laws meant the creation of civil servants to carry them out: thus when in 1833 public money was for the first time spent on education, inspectors—the first of the familiar 'H.M.I.s' of later years—were soon appointed to see that it was properly spent. The gradual growth of the Civil Service, especially in the second half

[1] Above, pp. 151-2.
[2] Above, p. 61, and below, pp. 216-7.
[3] Below, pp. 182, 193-4.
[4] Below, p. 209.

of the 19th century, is a highly important piece of 'backroom' history. Some important regulations were made about them, particularly about methods of appointment. In the early years this was done largely by favouritism or 'influence'. But a system of limited competition based on merit was begun in 1855, with the appointment of the Civil Service Commission to organise entrance examinations; and in 1870 Gladstone's Liberal government ruled that all posts in the civil service, except those in the foreign office, should be filled by competitive examination.

2. REFORM IN THE FACTORIES AND MINES

Some lines of reform illustrate particularly well the social problems of the 19th century, and the kind of answers that were given to them: one of these is the long process of reform in factories and mines.

Child labour was the evil on which the early reformers fastened; and their first success came in 1802, when Parliament passed the Health and Morals of Apprentices Act, which was promoted by Sir Robert Peel, father of the statesman. It limited the hours of pauper children, apprenticed in cotton mills, to twelve a day. It was not a very encouraging start to a reform campaign, for no effective provision was made for inspection to see that it was carried out. And it came too late. It was meant to give a little protection to the parish children who had been sent from London workhouses to be 'apprenticed', in effect, virtually sold as slaves. But by 1802 this traffic was diminishing, for the supplies of parish children were inadequate to the demand. Their places were being filled by those whom the law rather oddly called 'free' children—that is, children whose parents felt compelled to send them to work in order to earn a few extra shillings for the family; and it was these children who now needed protection. They did not get it from the Act of 1802. A second Factory Act came in 1819, again backed by the elder Peel and vigorously fought for by Robert Owen. This one forbade the employment in cotton mills of any children under nine, pauper or 'free', and limited the hours of those between nine and sixteen to twelve per day. But it too achieved little, because it too made no effective provision for inspection of mills: this was left to J.P.s, and usually they neglected their duty.

In the 1820's a strong movement for factory reform grew up, especially in the industrial areas of the north. Richard Oastler, a land agent from Huddersfield, who in 1830 published a series of letters denouncing what he called the 'Yorkshire Slavery' endured by the children in the woollen factories, led it in Yorkshire: John Fielden, himself a mill-owner from Todmorden, was its leading champion in the cotton area of Lancashire. It won widespread working class backing: in Parliament the cause was taken up by a Tory M.P., Michael Sadler, who got an official commission of enquiry into factory conditions appointed, and who laid before Parliament a Bill demanding what became the watchword of the movement, a ten hours working day. It was unsuccessful: yet the evidence laid before the commission shocked public opinion and made some reform inevitable.

Children were starting work at four or five o'clock in the morning and living in the ceaseless rush of the factory until six or seven at night, when they went home too tired to eat: often beaten at work to keep them awake, sometimes maimed by falling into moving machinery, many were deformed or stunted for life.

At the election of 1833 Sadler lost his seat in the Commons, and the leadership of the factory cause in Parliament passed to Lord Ashley (who succeeded his father as Earl of Shaftesbury in 1851). Ashley was a man of high intelligence deeply influenced by the Evangelical Movement; he dedicated his life to a series of good causes of which Factory Reform was only the chief. His leadership was fully needed, for opposition was strong. Most manufacturers, stout champions of *laissez-faire*, prophesied ruin if Parliament imposed any restrictions on the hours for which they worked their 'hands': even men as humane as the Quaker, John Bright, who was a mill-owner at Rochdale, sincerely held this view. Children in mills, it was said, were not overworked, and the discipline of the factory, though no doubt severe, was good for them. But the evidence on the other side was too strong: and in 1833 Althorp's Factory Act (taking its name from the Home Secretary at the time) was passed. It applied to all textile factories except lace and silk mills; it forbade the employment of children under nine; it fixed a maximum of nine hours for those from nine to thirteen, and of twelve for those from thirteen to eighteen; and it prohibited night-work for all under eighteen. Most important of all, it decreed that government inspectors, responsible to the Home Office, were to be appointed to see that the law was kept.

This Act was a landmark, making possible for the first time successful control of factory conditions, and it led to the Act of 1836 making the Registration of Births and Deaths compulsory, without which regulations against child labour could not have been enforced. But it satisfied neither Ashley nor his working-class supporters, who wanted a shorter working day for adults, and the Ten Hours Movement continued. It met with opposition from the Anti-Corn Law League, whose leading figures were Lancashire manufacturers. Yet further Factory Acts followed. In 1844 came Graham's Act which fixed a maximum six-and-a-half hour day for children from eight to thirteen and a twelve-hour day for women; it also laid down rules for fencing machinery. In 1847 Fielden's (Ten Hours) Act limited the hours of women and young persons (13–18) to fifty-eight per week, with a maximum of ten on any one day. The millowners got round this by organising the work in relays (shifts), and keeping men on the job for up to thirteen hours. Not until Grey's Act (1850) did male operatives in effect secure a 10½ hour day. One result Factory Acts certainly did not have, despite the gloomy forebodings of their opponents—they did not ruin the British textile industry. They were in fact followed by half-a-century of remarkable industrial prosperity. Their benefit to workers and their families in health and happiness is immeasurable.

So far Factory Acts extended only to textile mills, and not to all of them: for example, lace factories remained unregulated until 1861. In 1864 another Act extended the regulations to various other trades, including some which were dangerous because of industrial diseases, like the pottery industry. Finally in 1878 Disraeli's government carried a great consolidating Factory Act, on which the modern code of regulations for conditions in factories and workshops is based. There still remained many trades which needed regulation, and which gradually obtained it during the next few decades: most of these were not properly factory industries but something very like large-scale domestic industry, such as the 'sweatshops' of the East End of London, where tailors and seamstresses worked for long hours in insanitary attics and basements. Yet the establishment of a Factory Code by 1878 meant that the community had clearly accepted the responsibility for controlling working conditions.

The coal-mines provide a parallel story, leading first to the Mines Act of 1842. Conditions in the pits had been bad from the earliest days. In Scotland miners were virtually slaves, bound for life to the collieries where they worked and sold with them, until Parliament gave them legal freedom towards the end of the 18th century. In the greatest of British coalfields, that of Northumberland and Durham, women were not employed underground: but elsewhere this was common, and in some coalfields it was increasing in the early 19th century. Women were cheaper than men: they were not employed for the skilled work of hewing, but for pushing the loaded wagons about underground and, notably in Scotland, for carrying baskets of coal up ladders or steep ramps to the surface. Children were commonly employed in the pits on a variety of jobs. Often at seven or eight years of age they were set to open and shut the ventilating doors leading from the main shaft to the galleries, spending long hours alone in the darkness of the pit; older boys and girls, strapped to the loaded wagons, hauled these along the tramways underground. On the surface small children were left in charge of the pithead winding gear, responsible for the lives of colliers being hauled up and down the shaft: and there is more than one story of terrible accidents occurring because the child's attention wandered for the moment from the machinery, perhaps to chase a mouse across the floor.

Such were the conditions revealed by the commission of enquiry which Ashley and others managed to get appointed, and which published its report—with illustrations—in 1842. The revelations roused the public conscience, and Peel's government got a Mines Act passed in that same year, despite the opposition of landowners who drew much wealth from mining royalties. This forbade the employment of all women and children underground in mines: and prohibited mine-owners from employing any children under ten, and from putting those under fifteen in charge of machinery. A further Act of 1850 ensured success by appointing government inspectors of mines. Here was another notable turning-point in the story of effective regulation of working conditions.

3. THE POOR LAW

In the early 19th century the relief of the poor over much of southern England was carried out under the Speenhamland system.[1] This was costly to the ratepayer and it encouraged farmers to pay low wages, and labourers to be idle: both had come to look on parish relief as normal, and the labourer regarded his allowance from the rates as his right. In the north there was no effective system of poor relief to cope with industrial unemployment on a great scale. In 1832 a commission was appointed to investigate; some of its members, especially its secretary, Edwin Chadwick (1800–90), were much influenced by Benthamite ideas which condemned Speenhamland as wasteful and inefficient. Their report was the basis of the Poor Law Amendment Act of 1834. Its main terms were few but radical. Henceforward there was to be no outdoor relief, except for the old and sick. Instead relief for the poor was to be provided in workhouses, and conditions in the workhouses were to be 'less eligible'—that is, less desirable—than those of the lowest-paid worker outside. Parishes were to be grouped in unions, each of which was to maintain a workhouse. The workhouses were to be managed locally by Boards of Guardians, elected by the ratepayers. Finally, to supervise the whole scheme, a central body of three Commissioners, with a paid secretary and with headquarters at Somerset House, was to be set up by the government.

This 'New Poor Law' was a drastic remedy. It reduced the rates; whereas in 1831 nearly £7,000,000 was spent on poor relief, by 1851 the expenditure was below £5,000,000—and this despite a 29 per cent increase in the population during those twenty years. It undoubtedly did much to restore self-respect to working men by compelling them to work hard in order to avoid for themselves and their families the shame and hardships of the workhouse. Thus it achieved its main purposes. But it achieved them at a high price, a price paid in the misery of thousands of poor folk in the generation immediately after the Act was passed at a time when perhaps one in five of the population were paupers. For many workhouses—the 'Bastilles' as the poor bitterly nicknamed them—were harsh places harshly administered. Families were separated, meals were taken in silence and a multitude of petty rules prevented any suspicion of comfort entering them. This régime fell with special severity on the old and on the children. Charles Dickens' *Oliver Twist*, published in 1837, drew attention to the evils which the system could breed. The three Commissioners who administered the law—the 'three Bashaws of Somerset House'—became highly unpopular, as did Chadwick, their secretary, whose autocratic and energetic spirit was the power behind the entire scheme.

It is scarcely surprising that the New Poor Law was one of the principal causes of Chartism, especially in the industrial areas where depressions brought periodic large-scale unemployment. Here the 1834 Act was irrelevant, and opposition to the new system was violent; in some places Poor

[1] See above, pp. 65–67.

Law officials were stoned out of the district. On the other hand in many areas local Guardians, hating centralisation, kept outdoor relief going. Various developments—notably the building of railways—in the 1840's did much to provide employment and so to absorb the poor who previously had been unable to find jobs. The 'three Bashaws' were replaced in 1847 by a Poor Law Board, responsible to Parliament: and this in turn was abolished and its work put under the Local Government Board, created in 1871. But the essentials of the system created in 1834 lasted well into the 20th century. The workhouses, long, severe and high barrack-like buildings, often locally called 'unions', became familiar features of the landscape.

One major attempt to reform the Poor Law was made early in the 20th century. In 1905 the government appointed a Royal Commission to investigate the Poor Law, and in 1909 it issued two Reports, Majority and Minority, the latter being largely inspired by the Fabian, Beatrice Webb. Although they differed in detail, and the Minority Report would have gone further than the Majority one, they had much in common. Both wanted the guardians abolished and their powers transferred to the County and County Borough Councils, and both wanted expert officials to handle the various branches of Poor Law work. But no action was taken, largely because of the attitude of John Burns, the former dockers' leader who was now President of the Local Government Board: and reform had to wait another twenty years. In 1929 the specially-elected Boards of Guardians were at last abolished. By that time the development of Old Age Pensions, National Insurance and similar features of the 'Welfare State' had undermined the old-established Poor Law System.

4. LOCAL GOVERNMENT

No social reform could have been effective in the 19th century if a working system of local government—for carrying out the day-to-day rule of town and countryside—had not been developed. Until 1835 there was nothing that could really be called a 'system'. The older towns, some greatly enlarged by the growth of industry, others much diminished by the passage of years, were chartered boroughs, with a mayor and corporation. Officially these governed the town in the name of its inhabitants. In practice they had long ceased to be elected by anyone but themselves, and were often very corrupt. Their powers were limited; thus, although they customarily enjoyed old-established rights like those of holding a market and collecting tolls and local rates like 'scot and lot', they usually had no legal power to undertake any large-scale developments or town planning. They often tended to spend their revenues either on building handsome civic buildings —guildhalls, corn exchanges and the like—or on banquets, presents to local M.P.s and similar items. In contrast to these older towns were some of the new industrial areas, factory towns where not long before there had been nothing but small villages. Here many of the ancient rights of the Lord of the

Manor might still persist: and great numbers of inhabitants, factory owner and millhands alike, found themselves dependent on the whims of a single landowner. Over the countryside as a whole the Justices of the Peace still reigned supreme, as they had done since Tudor times—arresting vagabonds and trying thieves, organising the repair of roads and bridges (except where Turnpike Trusts had taken over), controlling the relief of the poor, licensing ale-houses, and so on.

Such methods could not cope with the immense social problems created by the industrial changes—least of all with the problems of order and health, transport and finance, which sprang up as the new towns swelled in size. In some more enterprising areas, as for example in Liverpool and Manchester, go-ahead and conscientious citizens got private Acts of Parliament passed setting up bodies of Improvement Commissioners with powers to tackle some particular problem, like lighting or water supply: but this was an expensive and limited process. Social reform in the new towns could not make real headway until town government was reformed. Many people wanted such a reform—like merchants and manufacturers whose livelihood would benefit, and Benthamite reformers who hated inefficiency; and it followed naturally upon the reform of Parliament itself. In 1835 the Municipal Reform Act was passed. As a result of it 178 chartered boroughs obtained town councils elected by all ratepaying householders who had lived in them for three years. Unchartered towns might adopt the same type of government. The accounts of town councils were to be audited. They were to take over the property of the old corporations; they could if they wished take over the duties of the Improvement Commissioners, and they were given greatly extended powers within the town boundaries. The Act came slowly into full operation in the unchartered towns: and as late as 1870 a wide variety of bodies was still responsible for services like scavenging, lighting and paving. Yet the 1835 Act, with its elected councillors responsible to the ratepayers, set a new pattern for English local government. It made possible real municipal self-government: henceforward the citizens of English towns could provide the social services—police and health, lighting and housing and education and many others—which were so urgently needed then, and which have since become accepted features of town life.

Further developments of the structure of local government took place in the second half of the 19th century. In 1871 the Local Government Board was created as an office of the central government (in 1919 it became the Ministry of Health). In 1888 came another major reform—the Local Government Act (often known as the County Councils Act). This carried out a considerable reorganisation. First, it dealt with the countryside by creating elected County Councils which took over most of the administrative work previously undertaken by J.P.s; henceforward the counties, like the towns, were governed by the elected representatives of their ratepayers. Secondly, the larger boroughs—generally those with over 50,000 inhabitants—were, so to speak, removed from their county areas and given full control of their own affairs under County Borough Councils. Thirdly, the great area of London (excluding the City) was made a distinct local government district, under an elected London County Council. Six years later, in 1894, yet another Local Government Act completed the broad structure of local government by setting up nearly 7,000 parish councils, and also the further system of elected Urban and Rural District Councils, in general subordinate to the County Councils but with certain powers of their own. Thus before the end of the 19th century the whole of English local government rested upon a foundation of popular election.

How did this system work in the period before 1914? Clearly some parts of it worked better than others. The Local Government Board was not very successful. It was too much concerned with restraining local councils, too little with encouraging them; and this did much to slow down progress in matters like housing. At one extreme the Parish Councils were from the beginning very ineffective. They aroused great hopes of village democracy, but in practice they were hamstrung because they were not allowed to spend more than, at most, the proceeds of a 6*d.* rate, which gave nearly all parishes a tiny budget. By contrast, the London County Council, at the other end of the scale, worked well from the start. Its ranks included men of wide and varied abilities, Liberals, Conservatives and Socialists (Sidney Webb among these) alike being in the 'Progressive' party which governed London for most of the first twenty years after the creation of the Council: and it provided an enlightened and effective municipal government for the millions who lived in London.

During the second half of the 19th century Parliament gradually extended the range of local government activity by passing Acts which gave local councils greater powers and responsibilities. Occasionally Parliament set up specially elected bodies for particular purposes: two examples of these *ad hoc* bodies, as they are called, were the Poor Law Guardians created by the Act of 1834, and the elected School Boards set up to run elementary schools by Forster's Education Act of 1870.[1] But usually it was the local councils who were given the work to do, or given the power to undertake particular tasks if they wanted to do so. After the Second Reform Act of 1867 town councils became appreciably more vigorous in their activities. Thus, for example, the Torrens Act of 1868 gave them the right to compel the owners of insanitary properties to put them in order, and the Artisans' Dwellings Act of 1875 empowered them to pull down and rebuild whole areas of slums. The Public Health Act of 1875 compelled them to appoint Medical Officers of Health. After the County Councils Act of 1888 those bodies were responsible for roads and bridges: after the Education Act of 1902 elementary and secondary education, with some exceptions, were dealt with by committees of the County and County Borough Councils. These are merely examples of the kind of duties that increasingly fell upon local government. The list could be greatly extended.

Some of the great cities, where the social problems were most serious,

[1] See below, p. 208.

took the lead in using their powers. Liverpool, for example, appointed a Medical Officer of Health in 1847; and in the middle years of the century began a series of great improvements to its docks. The progress of Birmingham in the years 1873–6, when Joseph Chamberlain was its mayor, captured public interest throughout the country. The most notable single achievement was an extensive piece of slum clearance, opening the way for the building of the modern Corporation Street: yet the work of the council covered a wide range. Birmingham, in Chamberlain's own words, was 'parked, paved, assized, marketed, Gas-and-Watered, and *improved*—all as a result of three years' active work'. Furthermore, in the later years of the century the great provincial cities—Glasgow and Manchester as well as Liverpool and Birmingham—led the way in what came to be called 'municipal socialism'—the provision of services which they sold to the public— water, gas, electricity, transport. Their citizens regarded with pride their newly-built Town Halls, like that of Manchester, finished in 1877: they took a similar pride in the development of municipal activities. By 1914 the pay-roll of county boroughs and counties covered a range of occupations unimagined in 1835. They were employing dustmen and doctors, road engineers and sanitary inspectors, teachers and tram-drivers, architects and accountants, plumbers and firemen.

5. OTHER SOCIAL REFORMS

An important group of the social reforms of the 19th and early 20th centuries were specially concerned with *children*. The children of the poor were only too often the victims of exploitation, and were in frequent need of protection. We have already noted the early movements to regulate child labour in factories. A notable—though belated—development of the 19th century was that of the public provision of education: the first government grant to education was made in 1833, a national system of elementary schools was created in 1870, a national system of secondary schools in 1902.[1]

Slow yet ultimately successful attempts were made to rescue particular groups of children from victimisation. Perhaps the most famous of these was the long campaign fought on behalf of *climbing boys,* the assistants of sweeps. These wretched children spent their working lives—often cut short by the hardships of their horrible trade—clambering through the long winding chimneys of the houses of the well-to-do in order to clean them. In the 18th century the philanthropist Jonas Hanway had awakened public feelings on the subject: but little effective was done until the 19th century, when other champions took up their cause, particularly Shaftesbury and the novelist Charles Kingsley. Legislation was slow, in great part because of the opposition of the House of Lords. Acts of 1834 and 1842 were of very limited effect, although the second was useful in London. In 1863 Kingsley

[1] See below, Chap. 20, for a fuller account of Education. The statements in the sentence do not apply to Scotland.

published *The Water Babies* in an attempt to expose the evil, and an Act of Parliament of 1864 forbade sweeps to employ children under ten, and to have any assistance from children under sixteen in the actual cleaning of a chimney. Control became finally effective with a fourth Act, of 1875, which made sweeps take out an annual licence and gave the police the task of enforcing the regulations. About the same time, also, laws were passed preventing the employment of children in agricultural 'gangs'.

Concern for the treatment of children increased during the latter part of the 19th century, and the Liberal governments after 1905 passed several laws which protected children and promoted their well-being. Those which empowered local councils to provide school meals (1906) and the beginnings of school medical inspection (1907) were important strides, indicating a new and broader outlook upon education. The Children's Act of 1908, sometimes called the 'Children's Charter', tried to safeguard children by a series of regulations, for example by prohibiting them from entering public-houses or buying cigarettes under the age of eighteen; and by prohibiting the imprisonment of children under fourteen. Laws of this kind were appropriate to a period of British history which also saw, for example, the foundation by Sir Robert (later Lord) Baden-Powell of the Boy Scout Movement in 1907 and the development about the same time of Infants' Welfare Centres.

A quite different group of laws arose to protect many adults from exploitation by their employers. For example, in the middle years of the 19th century there was a long campaign, powerfully backed by the working class, for the abolition of *truck*—i.e. payment of wages in kind rather than in cash. In one form truck meant that the workman was paid in the articles which he made, in another it involved payments in goods at a store owned by the employer, or in coupons only exchangeable at such a store. Invariably its effect was to lower the value of the workman's wages: that was why the employer used it. In many areas in the north the rise of the Co-operative stores helped to destroy truck. Yet it was necessary to pass a succession of laws against it, of which the first came in 1831; others, more detailed and more effective, followed in 1854 and 1871. A second, very different, form of exploitation was that connected with *merchant seamen* and denounced for years by Samuel Plimsoll, the 'sailor's friend'. Ships were sent to sea overloaded and in poor condition yet heavily insured: the owners' pockets were secure, but sailors' lives were needlessly risked and often lost. After many useless protests, Plimsoll lost his temper and made a violent scene on the floor of the House of Commons. He was suspended for his behaviour, but in the following year (1876) Parliament passed the Merchant Shipping Act, which made a load-line, the familiar 'Plimsoll Line', compulsory on all British merchant ships. Thirdly, towards the end of the 19th century, the view that the employer must accept responsibility for accidents occurring to his employees in the course of their work, and that he must compensate them for injury and loss, came to be widely accepted. A succession of Acts of Parliament put it into practice. The most important of these was the

Workmen's Compensation Act of 1897, the work of Joseph Chamberlain: this made employers in many occupations liable to pay compensation to their employees for injury suffered in the course of work. Certain occupations—e.g. those of seamen, domestic servants and agricultural labourers—which at first were not covered were included in similar later acts.

6. PENSIONS AND NATIONAL INSURANCE

By 1900 social reform was in full swing; state interference on behalf of the weaker members of the community was becoming accepted as normal. The early years of the 20th century accelerated the pace. In 1905 a Liberal government took office and proceeded to carry through a remarkable series of social reforms, which dealt with a wide range of problems. Some—like the two great measures affecting trade unions, the Trade Disputes Act of 1906 and the Trade Union Act of 1913, and the various laws affecting children—have already been mentioned. There were many others. The Merchant Shipping Act (1906) laid down regulations about food and living-quarters on British ships. The Port of London Authority Act (1908) established a single governing body to control the docks of the capital. The Coal Mines Act (1908) fixed a maximum working day for coal-miners. The Trade Boards Act (1909), in part a result of Charles Booth's investigation of poverty in London, fixed minimum wages in some of the worst-paid 'sweated' industries like ready-made tailoring. The creation (1909) of Labour Exchanges—proposed by William Beveridge, who was appointed to organise them—provided official machinery to enable workmen to get and exchange jobs. The Shops Act (1911) secured a weekly half-holiday for shop assistants.

Yet two measures of the Liberals in this period were of quite special importance—Old Age Pensions and National Insurance. Old Age Pensions were introduced in 1908: they were at first non-contributory, and they provided 5s. a week for old people over seventy whose income was under 10s. per week. A sliding scale, the pension falling by 1s. a week, provided for those whose income went up to 12s. National Insurance began in 1911, and was modelled on the scheme introduced in Germany some twenty-five years previously. A state-run insurance fund was created; to it employers contributed 3d. a week and employees 4d. by means of stamps placed on cards, and the state added 2d. From the fund workmen could, through their 'approved' Friendly Societies, draw benefit in times of sickness and unemployment. This scheme was a limited one, for at first the insurance against unemployment applied only to wage-earners in building, engineering, shipbuilding, iron-founding, and a small number of other occupations.[1] There was much opposition to this National Health and Unemployment Insurance, both from doctors who disliked the scheme of 'panels' of

---

[1] By 1920 it had been extended to cover practically all wage-earners except domestic servants and agricultural labourers. For fuller details of the health clauses of the Act, see below, p. 201.

patients, and from well-to-do people who disapproved of the whole idea of these new 'social services'. Lloyd George, the minister responsible for the 1911 Act, wanted to go much further, by including pensions for widows and orphans, but he could not overcome the opposition of the commercial insurance companies, whose 80,000 door-to-door collectors might have turned innumerable voters against the Liberals. The nation thus had to be content with what came to be known as 'Lloyd George's ambulance wagon'.

This reform programme, and Old Age Pensions and National Insurance in particular, were in part a response by the Liberals to the challenge offered by the rise of the Labour party. Lloyd George, the outstanding reformer in the Cabinet, was shrewd enough to see that the Liberals must try to steal the Socialist thunder. But they also reflected a deep change in public opinion. A new attitude towards social problems was arising. In Victorian times widespread poverty and distress were accepted as inevitable. Now it was coming to be believed that the nation ought to take steps to guard its members at any rate against the extremes of hardship in sickness, old age, or unemployment. There was much discussion of a 'national minimum' standard of life below which individuals ought not to be allowed to fall. It would be provided by various measures of 'social security', including such devices as pensions, a state medical service, and a national system of education. Here in fact were the opening moves in the development in Britain of what later came to be called the 'Welfare State'—the state in which the community, acting through the government, provides for its citizens a great range of social services whose purpose is to guarantee to all the opportunity of a reasonable life. The social security which began with Old Age Pensions and National Insurance before 1914 was to reach a high level in the years after 1945.

19 Public Health Since 1700

In 1845 Friedrich Engels wrote an account of *The Condition of the Labouring Classes in England*. Engels was an unusual man. The son of a well-to-do mill owner of Manchester, he was an advanced socialist, sharing the political views of Karl Marx. His book exposed appalling conditions of life in the new industrial towns in the 'Hungry Forties'. It was a picture of slums and squalor, of low wages and long hours and the grim discipline of the factories; its force was strengthened by reference to contemporary statistics and by detailed examples. The most impressive feature of all was his emphasis on the terrible waste of human lives in the new towns, a waste brought about by unnecessary disease and death. Engels' book, written after only a short time in England, was prejudiced by his own political doctrines. He used statistics in a misleading way; for example, he quoted figures of the increase in the number of crimes without setting against them the rise in the population over the same period, which would have shown that proportionately crime actually decreased. He took little account of the other side of the picture, the real gains brought by the industrial changes. Yet his book was founded upon the facts behind such episodes as the terrible cholera epidemic of 1831, which killed thousands of the poor. In Engels' eyes English society stood condemned because it created the conditions in which such diseases flourished. Engels was by no means unique in his own day. For example, in the very same year (1845), the Report of a Parliamentary Commission of Enquiry into the State of Large Towns underlined most of what he had said, by its revelations of the conditions of housing and sanitation in the great cities. In fact, as we shall see, important changes bearing on the health of the poor had begun to take place well before 1845. Nevertheless, Engels was very much to the point in stressing the connection between public health and living conditions.

The story of this chapter is one of gradual yet striking progress—of remarkable improvements in the conquest of disease and in the general health of people in Britain. In that progress there were three distinct elements: they are interrelated, but it is important to see them apart before we begin. First, there was a great advance in the skill and knowledge of doctors and surgeons—in their ability to diagnose diseases and in their power to conquer them. This is *medical reform*. Secondly, over this period vast changes took place in men's environment—in food, clothing, buildings, and so on—which in fact did much to make them healthier. These are changes in *social environment*. Thirdly, and perhaps most revolutionary of all, this period saw a transformation of the attitude of the community towards health, and of the laws and regulations about it. This is the growth of *public health*. It was the combination of these three elements that brought progress in the health of the people of Britain.

I. HEALTH FROM 1700 TO ABOUT 1830

By the standards of a later age, the health of the people of Britain in the early 18th century was appallingly bad. The death-rate, especially in London, was very high: it has been estimated at 35·8 per 1,000 in the years 1731–40, a time when the growth of gin-drinking among the London poor made the situation worse than ever. It was devastatingly high among small children: in these same years it was reckoned that about three-quarters of all the children born in the capital died before reaching the age of five. Although the plague itself had almost died out after its last visitation in 1665, other epidemic diseases took regular and terrible toll. Among these were typhus or 'gaol fever', which extended its range far beyond the prisons (at the Old Bailey trials of 1754 it carried off most of the judges, jury and court officers as well as the prisoners); and small-pox, from which a doctor of the time calculated that one person in every nine above the age of two years would eventually die. Little was known about many non-epidemic diseases. Surgery was inevitably primitive, for there were no anaesthetics except rum and other strong drinks: complicated operations were therefore impossible. There was no scientific knowledge of the nature of germs, or of effective antiseptics. Hospitals were comparatively rare; indeed, where they existed they were usually insanitary and were looked upon as dangerous and probably fatal to their patients.

In such circumstances the medical profession itself had no very high reputation. Few doctors existed who could be regarded as 'qualified': there was no satisfactory register of doctors until as late as 1858. There were the apothecaries—part chemists, part doctors—many of whom were quacks or rogues, with patent remedies for any complaint. Surgeons were widely distrusted: this is scarcely surprising, for many were 'barber-surgeons', brutal and ignorant. It was difficult for surgeons and doctors to be efficiently trained. There was general public opposition to the dissection of human bodies (which led in later years to the growth of the practice of body-snatching from cemeteries), and this greatly handicapped surgeons. The lack of hospitals meant that it was not easy to build up careful records of the observation of diseases: and without such 'clinical' records doctors could not readily learn how to distinguish one illness from another. Only as towns grew larger with the industrial changes and as hospitals were built did it become easier to accumulate the clinical material and so to train doctors. Also the growth of towns meant that disease became more obvious: this encouraged the growth of humanitarian feelings which in turn stimulated the foundation of hospitals.

During the 18th century itself there were few notable developments in medicine or in matters of health: yet there were important social changes which laid the foundation of later growth. In the field of medicine itself, a group of doctors emerged who were more scientific in their attitude than their predecessors. Scotsmen were prominent among them. The surgeon John Hunter (1728–93) was one, with his pioneer anatomical collection of 13,000 specimens; he did much to transform surgery into an experimental science. His methods were based on careful observation—the same sort of observation which enabled Captain Cook to eliminate scurvy among the crews on his Pacific voyages (1768–79) by cleanliness and by the use of lemon-juice. The most striking single medical advance came at the end of the century, when in 1796 the Gloucestershire doctor Edward Jenner discovered vaccination as a means of preventing smallpox. For many years previously inoculation, brought by travellers from Turkey, had been used. But this method, which involved giving the patient a mild dose of smallpox as a means of preventing a serious attack, was risky; whereas vaccination—based on Jenner's observation that milkmaids were generally immune from smallpox—safeguarded the patient against smallpox by giving him the harmless cowpox. It spread fast and sharply reduced the impact of smallpox as a killing disease by 1850.[1]

[1] Inoculation had been made illegal in 1840; vaccination was made compulsory in 1853.

Many changes brought about by the Industrial Revolution pointed the way towards better health. The manufacture of cheap cotton clothes in the new mills meant that the poor could have more clothes, and therefore cleaner clothes; the rise of a chemical industry meant the manufacture of more and cheaper soap; the large-scale production of bricks and the making of cast-iron pipes brought better houses and drains. The enclosure movement and the other agricultural changes made it possible to produce far more food. Indirectly, too, the steam-engine and the other technical developments were to make possible great progress in health, for example by the improvement of transport and by the invention of more effective heating devices. Ultimately such changes in environment were to be of incalculable benefit to health. But they were slow to come, in many areas taking a generation or more to become effective: and it is doubtful whether many people benefited much from them before 1800.

Meanwhile, unfortunately, the disadvantages to health of the industrial changes were immediate and only too clear. Sometimes technical improvements which were devised to benefit health themselves had an unfortunate effect. The improved water closet which Joseph Bramah first patented in 1778 was one of these: for it led to the rapid contamination of the Thames, from which London drew its water supply. More obviously and generally, the new developments brought about the unhealthy factories and over-crowding of the large industrial towns. These arrived quickly, and were visible to all. Their precise effects upon health are a little difficult to assess: for the coming of power-driven industry did, as we have noticed, broadly coincide in time with a great rise in the population. But there is no doubt at all that the people of the industrial areas in the early 19th century suffered greatly from frequent epidemics of fevers, especially of typhus and typhoid. It is interesting to note that the downward movement of the death-rate was reversed and that it began to rise again for a number of years after about 1820, when conditions in the industrial areas were probably at their worst. Moreover, this happened at a time when one major killing disease, smallpox, was being reduced. It seems not unlikely that the new towns were breeding a notable increase in tuberculosis, less obvious than the epidemics but equally destructive, and peculiarly the result of bad housing conditions. In fact, the Industrial Revolution created a great health problem at once, and only slowly offered assistance in its solution.

In the third element of health, that of public health, the activity of the community to improve health conditions, the 18th century had little to show. The idea of *laissez-faire*, 'let it alone', applied only too well here. There were certain exceptions to this. For example, the quarantine laws, against disease-bearing ships from foreign ports, were usually stringent. Again, Parliament was prepared eventually to take action when some menace to health became extremely serious: in the middle of the century it passed laws about the sale of gin. More important, numerous hospitals were founded—usually by private charitable enterprise. Between 1700 and 1825, 154 hospitals and dispensaries were founded in Britain. The hospitals included four of the five greatest London ones, notably that of Thomas Guy begun in 1722, and a number of provincial cities to-day have hospitals which began in the 18th century. Among them were some specially built as children's hospitals, and others as lying-in hospitals. Yet this great spell of hospital building, important though it was, reflects not so much any deep public concern about health as that 'individual benevolence of soul' which became so strong in the 18th century. A handful of cities set up more or less efficient local boards of health around 1800. But there was no kind of national plan—nothing remotely comparable with the proposals put forward as early as 1714 by John Bellers, who wrote a pamphlet advocating a kind of national health service. Something like a national crisis was needed to arouse a public health movement in the early nineteenth century.

2. HEALTH IN THE MIDDLE YEARS OF THE 19TH CENTURY

The crisis came in 1831, when for the first time an epidemic of cholera struck Great Britain. This disease came from Asia, where it had been rife for centuries, and spread across eastern Europe in 1830. It was mysterious in its origin; it struck its victims with appalling suddenness, and frequently killed them within a few hours; the doctors understood little about it, and certainly not how to cure it. But one thing was clear. Cholera hit hardest in the slums. It was the poorest who suffered most: in Britain the most severely affected areas were the poorest quarters of the towns of Scotland and Ireland, where overcrowding was worst. The immediate result of its coming was to awaken a widespread interest in the whole problem of public hygiene. Previously only a comparatively small number of enthusiasts, backed by reformers like Robert Owen, had been concerned about public health. Now the terror inspired by Asiatic cholera came to reinforce their work. The next forty years saw a great extension of local and national effort to lay down and put into practice rules about public health—an effort stimulated by periodic outbreaks of cholera and other fevers. The very fact that these diseases were difficult or impossible to cure meant that the emphasis must be on prevention; and prevention here involved a whole campaign for social reform—for purer water, for effective drainage, for the destruction of slums and their replacement by well-built and well-ventilated houses. In short, a great social revolution was needed, comparable in scale with the industrial changes of the late 18th century.

This revolution has continued right on to the present day, taking innumerable forms. On the one hand, for example, it has brought about the elaborate code of sanitary regulations about drainpipes, cesspits, and water supplies which has been built up by local health authorities: on the other, the growth of town planning and the creation of housing estates, especially in the large cities. Its beginnings came in the 1830's, with a direct concentration on health. The first necessary step was investigation on a grand scale; and these years saw a series of public enquiries into health and living conditions, promoted by pioneers like the Poor Law reformer Edwin

Chadwick, or by energetic doctors like Southwood Smith. Three were especially notable. In 1838 a bad outbreak of fever in Whitechapel prompted a Poor Law enquiry into London: its reports, especially one by Southwood Smith on disease and water supply, had thousands of readers and shocked the public. Next in 1842 Chadwick himself on behalf of the Poor Law Board drew up a *Report on the Sanitary Condition of the Labouring Population of Great Britain*: this contained information supplied by all the Poor Law physicians in the country on health conditions in their 'unions', and was really the first attempt at a comprehensive survey of national health. Finally Peel's government (1841–6) appointed a Royal Commission to investigate the state of *Large Towns and Populous Districts*, and this published two massive reports in 1844 and 1845.

These and other enquiries revealed a grim state of affairs. Cellar dwellings crammed with people: vast refuse heaps in the midst of towns: rivers foul with sewage: swamps draining into water supplies—such things were a commonplace in the industrial areas: and as Southwood Smith pointed out in a moving *Address to the Working Classes* in 1847, they were every year the direct causes of the deaths of many thousands who could have been saved. The reports led to action: not always immediate or very effective, but action which during the next generation got rid of the worst abuses, improved standards of health and laid down rules on which further advance was based. The most effective part of this action was local. In many areas permanent boards of health were set up, and a start was made in constructing sewerage and water systems, made practicable by improved earthenware pipes: in others, especially in London, voluntary organisations established housing schemes. Macclesfield in Cheshire, a textile town, provides an example of local progress. In 1847 its death-rate was 42 per 1,000 and the average age at death was 24. In 1848 its inhabitants began extensive improvements in water supply, drainage, scavenging and sewage disposal. Within ten years the death-rate was down to 26, and the expectation of life had risen accordingly.

The national effort, through Parliament, was at first disappointing. A Public Health Act was passed in 1848. It set up a national Board of Health whose first members included Southwood Smith, Shaftesbury and Chadwick. This was given power to create local boards of health where 10 per cent. of the inhabitants asked for them, or where the death-rate was above 23 per 1,000: once local boards were set up it could do little more than give advice. It was not very successful, because it came up against powerful opposition from owners of slum property and others whose financial interests were directly threatened by reform. Moreover, Chadwick's persistent attacks on this opposition aroused a wider hostility, with strong local feeling against interference by the central government: and the board itself was dissolved in 1858, although its work went on. In 1866 the Sanitary Act compelled local authorities to appoint sanitary inspectors and gave the government power to make these authorities take action about water, sewerage and nuisances.

A Royal Commission of 1869 investigated the problems of public health once again: it declared that among things 'necessary for civilised social life' were good water supplies and proper drainage, the removal of nuisances (including smoke), healthy houses, clean streets, the inspection of food, and the provision of adequate burial-grounds. This led in 1871 to the creation of the Local Government Board, with responsibility, among other matters, for public health. Then in 1874 Disraeli came to power as Prime Minister. He had earlier proclaimed as his social policy '*sanitas sanitatum, omnia sanitas*', and in 1875 his government passed another Public Health Act. This consolidated various laws and regulations on public health into a single code, on which sanitary law has been based ever since: all local councils had to attain the standard of this code, as well as to appoint medical officers of health. Its results were of course not magical. Many local authorities had to be goaded to take action; promotion of sewerage schemes and similar developments was costly, and the worse the problem, the greater the burden which fell on the local ratepayers. And the Local Government Board was not at all enterprising. Nevertheless the progress made since the 1830's was great, particularly in the bigger cities like Liverpool, which appointed in 1847 the first Medical Officer of Health in the country. In the City of London John Simon achieved remarkable improvements in his seven years (1848–55) as M.O.H., so that the cholera outbreak of 1854 killed only one-quarter as many as that of 1848 had done, and now Parliament had laid down standards at which to aim.

Rather behind developments in health regulation came others in housing. During the very years when the campaign for sanitation was getting under way, thousands of houses of shoddy quality were being built for the rapidly increasing population of the great cities. Many were 'jerry-built', with limited ground space and wretched ventilation: packed close round narrow streets and courts or back to back, they were designed to make as much profit as possible for their builders. A handful of pioneers tried to tackle the problem of working class housing. These included Octavia Hill (1838–1912), who set out in the 1860's to improve tenement housing in Marylebone and pressed for the introduction of compulsory minimum standards,[1] and James Wilson who built (1853) a self-contained housing estate for Price's Patent Candle Company at Bromborough in the Wirral. In the early 1860's progressive cities, such as Glasgow and Liverpool, got special powers to clear slum areas and rebuild. The Torrens Act of 1868 gave local authorities power to compel owners of houses to keep them in good repair. In 1875 the Artisans' Dwellings Act (known as Cross's Housing Act from the Home Secretary responsible for it, Richard Cross) provided wider powers, under which authorities could clear whole districts and build new houses for their inhabitants. These Acts led to vigorous action in some areas. But progress was very slow; only the very worst slums began to be tackled, and there was little attempt at planning. In this field of health activity the reform came unhappily late.

---

[1] She was later (1895) the leading figure in the foundation of the National Trust.

Advance in public health was aided in these middle years of the century by technical developments in industry: indeed in some ways technical advance alone made it possible at all. This was particularly true of drainage and water supplies. For populations of many thousands these set gigantic engineering problems, when the rivers which had formerly supplied water became polluted by sewage. Iron pipes began to replace wooden ones in the 18th century, and their use for water supplies became general in the first half of the 19th century. This foreshadowed later progress: so that when it became possible to draw large supplies of fresh water from a great distance, Liverpool and Birmingham were able to go to central Wales, and Manchester to the Lake District, for their supplies.[1]

During the 19th century there were also great strides in the field of medicine itself. Thus for example a great medical school at Guy's Hospital continued the work of doctors like Hunter—although it was also much stimulated by French ideas. In particular some of its doctors by thorough investigation succeeded in separating from one another a wide range of different illnesses which had overlapping symptoms, thus opening the way to the future possibility of effective treatment. Other advances were very closely connected with the work of contemporary scientists; and one of these was an outstanding medical development. The many-sided genius Sir Humphrey Davy, discoverer of sodium and potassium and inventor of the most famous of miners' safety lamps, had as early as 1800 experimented with the use of nitrous oxide ('laughing gas') as an anaesthetic: and in 1818 Michael Faraday had shown that ether produced insensibility to pain. These experiments foreshadowed the greatest medical development of the 1840's, the introduction of anaesthetics in surgical operations. In the early 1840's ether was successfully used to kill pain during an operation in America; in 1847 the Scottish surgeon James Simpson first used chloroform, having tried out its effects on himself. Chloroform was the easier of the two to use and rapidly came into widespread use. This was a great gift to human well-being, for it opened the way to surgical achievements hitherto impossible. Thus for example later in the nineteenth century it became practicable to remove an appendix, and so operations for appendicitis gradually became the normal form of treatment.

Yet this great advance created its own problems. The growth in the number of operations gravely increased the risks of infection in hospitals from blood-poisoning and gangrene: this was particularly serious because the hospitals in the cities were becoming terribly overcrowded. In 1869 Simpson himself found that two out of every five operations performed in the hospitals of London, Edinburgh and Glasgow were fatal, a death-rate far higher than that for operations performed in private houses. Anaesthetics had in fact come before any satisfactory development of antiseptics to conquer the poisons. Here the answer was supplied first by the work of Joseph (later Lord) Lister (1827–1912), Professor of Surgery in Glasgow.

[1] For the general effect of these and other developments on the death-rate, see above, p. 9, and Table III, p. 5.

He had studied the work of the great French doctor, Louis Pasteur (1822–1895), who in 1858 demonstrated that bacteria and small living organisms, carried in the air or on the hands, caused fermentation: and he put this idea to a careful test in the wards of the Glasgow Infirmary. He cleaned the hands of the surgeon and his instruments in dilute carbolic acid, and kept the air sprayed with this powerful antiseptic throughout the operations. It was at once clear that these methods prevented infection: the death-rate from sepsis (poisoning) of wounds fell immediately. There was at first some conservative opposition to the new technique, but it was not long before it was generally adopted. Anaesthetics had made operations pain-less: antiseptics made them safer. Between them they represented a revolution in surgery, and they have saved millions of human lives in the last century.

3. DEVELOPMENTS BETWEEN 1870 AND 1914

In many ways medical progress after the 1870's was very rapid. One aspect of this progress deserves special stress—namely, that it was made possible by the co-operation of doctors and scientists of many different countries. Medicine, like the illnesses with which it deals, is international. This has always been to some extent true: yet during the last century improved means of communication have made medical co-operation between different lands much more practicable and swifter. Doctors have been able to travel more readily and exchange ideas in international conferences. They have gained greatly from the growth of world-wide postal services; and also from advances in printing, which have made easier the widespread publication of books and articles on medical problems. As a result, British people have benefited inestimably from the research work of French, German, Austrian, American and Canadian doctors, to mention only the most obvious examples. Innumerable British lives have been saved by new forms of treatment devised by foreign doctors.

The later years of the 19th century witnessed astonishing advances in bacteriology—the study of *bacteria*, the tiny organisms responsible for fermentation and for the poisoning set up in open wounds. Broadly, three great steps were taken here. The first was to demonstrate that these minute creatures were responsible for a great range of contagious diseases: the second, to identify and isolate the particular bacteria responsible for each disease: the third—from the ordinary man's point of view the most impor-tant—to devise some means of controlling the creatures so as to cure, or, even better, to prevent the disease. The pioneers were the Frenchman Louis Pasteur and the German Robert Koch. Pasteur had blazed the trail; it was Koch who in 1876 showed beyond any doubt that one particular microbe or bacillus caused one particular disease. The disease was anthrax in sheep. Thenceforward numerous workers went ahead fast in various countries on the new lines, and before the end of the century the bacteria responsible for cholera, tuberculosis, diphtheria, typhoid fever and plague

—among others—had been found. None of these were British discoveries: yet the people of Britain, a thickly populated industrial country where such epidemic diseases caused much suffering and many deaths every year, were to benefit very greatly.

The application of these scientific discoveries to the saving of life involved various different processes. One of these was to extend the work of the sanitary reformers in public health—with the important difference that they were now no longer working mainly in the dark. It had, for example, been strongly suspected for many years that cholera was carried in water: Koch's investigations, conducted during a terrible cholera epidemic in Egypt, made this clear beyond doubt: and the same was shown to be true of typhoid fever. Thus the effective prevention of these two diseases depended almost entirely on securing pure water supplies. So from the latter years of the 19th century the great cities introduced effective methods of filtering their water. Other epidemic diseases, like diphtheria, were not water-borne. Isolation was vital here. and so public health authorities revised and tightened up their quarantine regulations. When more exact knowledge was gained about the length of time each disease took to develop, it became possible, for example, to fix the number of days during which a given ship carrying a suspected 'case' had to be held.

Yet it was to turn out that the most effective answer to diphtheria lay in a totally different direction. Nearly a century earlier Jenner's discovery of vaccination had given a hint of what that direction could be. Now that the particular bacteria responsible for particular diseases had been run to earth, the way might be open to use them for what came to be known as 'immunisation'—namely, to give people a mild dose of a disease in order to stop them having a severe one. The actual process was in fact far more complex than this, involving the use of substances derived ultimately from the diseases themselves and known as vaccines and antitoxins. Its first pioneer was Pasteur, who won European fame by his preparation of a vaccine against hydrophobia, the disease caused by the bite of a mad dog. By 1890 similar protection had been devised against tetanus. The 20th century was to see remarkable successes achieved by this sort of weapon, particularly in the fight against diphtheria, backed by educational campaigns by the public authorities.

Such developments—strengthened by other reforms like the higher standard of nursing promoted by the work of Florence Nightingale—had immense effects. As we have seen,[1] during the years after about 1870, when the sanitary reforms first began to take effect, the death-rate from the chief infectious diseases began to fall, and to fall with growing rapidity. In Great Britain smallpox, typhoid, typhus, cholera and diphtheria were either sharply checked or virtually extinguished during the next half-century. Cholera had almost entirely gone by 1895. The death-rate from typhoid fever, which had averaged 332 per 1,000,000

---

[1] Above, p. 9.

between 1871 and 1880, was down to 25 per 1,000,000 by 1925. Smallpox, that most terrible of 18th-century ailments, had of course been tackled much earlier by Jenner's discovery: it declined remarkably during the 19th century. There were still liable to be serious epidemics, as in 1872, when 23,000 people died from it in England, but by 1906 it had been almost eliminated.

In other directions too medical science made great advances, even though their results were not so dramatic as those of the work on bacteria. The German physicist Wilhelm Röntgen discovered in 1895 the X-rays which could be used for the observation of hidden parts of the body, and these have proved vitally important in the understanding of many diseases. There was prolonged study of the mysterious glands of the human body, one outcome of which was to be the discovery in 1922 by the Canadian doctor Banting of insulin as a remedy for the hitherto incurable disease of diabetes. Investigation of diet and its effects on man produced about 1911 the identification of various substances as 'vitamins', whose presence was essential to health. The uses of certain drugs in treatment of illness became much more fully understood: and important new drugs were invented. Such things were merely the peaks of medical achievement: below them lay a whole range of developments, in operating techniques, nursing standards and hospital conditions, whose total effect was to lengthen life, and greatly to diminish the ill-health which had hitherto been accepted as inevitable by millions of people.

Their value was much heightened by various contemporary changes in ways of life, which in countless ways helped to improve the health of many people in Britain. Greater quantities of the basic foods, like meat, butter and sugar, became available: better transport facilities meant that a wider range of foodstuffs, like fruit from overseas, could be obtained. The amount of milk being consumed was going up, as it became easier to transport it to the great cities. Better transport also meant more fresh air for city-dwellers. The railways took an increasing number of people to the seaside for annual holidays, and into the countryside at week-ends. The bicycle, which came into widespread use in the last years of the 19th century, also enabled great numbers of young people to get away from the towns: and it made clothes, particularly those of women, simpler and healthier. The coming of organised games, spreading from the public schools in the years after 1870, was another very important influence in the direction of better health among younger people. Working hours were gradually being reduced in a wide range of occupations, giving much more leisure: the eight-hour day became normal in many jobs even before 1900, as did the custom of a Saturday half-day. All these things made life more comfortable and enjoyable for millions: they also did a very great deal to promote better health for the community, especially for its younger members.

Child welfare became a matter of special public concern at this time. Clearly children benefited more than others from some of the medical measures just described—for example from vaccination, from the diphtheria immunisation, and from the safeguards against diseases carried in water and milk. Milk dispensaries for poor mothers were started just before 1900; infant welfare centres began a few years later. Both these ideas came from abroad, yet were very successfully copied in Britain. The results were great: the death-rate among infants, which had been practically stationary during most of the 19th century, fell very sharply in the 20th. For older children, a revolutionary step was taken in 1907, when local educational authorities were first compelled to undertake the medical inspection of all children in their schools. It took several years for the system to become comprehensive: once fairly launched, it became the most important single measure of preventive medicine ever undertaken in this country. For henceforward doctors were able to check and control the ailments and physical defects of the great majority of the population in their early years. Its effective founder and for many years its principal supervisor was Sir George Newman, Chief Medical Officer of the Board of Education from 1907 to 1935: and it has been suggested that historians may find in him 'a public servant who by his work saved more lives than were ever lost in our national wars'.[1] Starting about the same time as this medical inspection service but growing much more slowly came the provision of meals by school authorities. This was to be a boon to many of the poorest members of the community during bad times.

So far as public health as a whole was concerned general progress continued along the lines laid down by the earlier sanitary reformers. Gradually the great majority of the community obtained pure water supplies and adequate and safe drainage systems: gradually the code of sanitary law laid down in the Public Health Acts was universally applied. Progress was slowest in the rural areas. Public opinion now accepted without any doubt the standards at which earlier reformers had aimed. Dirt and disease were enemies to be banished or destroyed; no longer were they taken for granted as inevitable features of human life. This was a revolution in people's ways of thinking: in practice it was immensely important, for it meant that most people would generally support active measures taken for public health, instead of opposing them or ignoring them. A notable single advance of the 20th century has been a considerable increase in the number of hospitals and an expansion in the services they provide. The earlier hospitals had been voluntary foundations, the product of private charity: more recent ones have been founded by local authorities.

But the campaign for improved working class housing, which had opened promisingly in the 1870's, did not go ahead as fast as many of its supporters had hoped. This was partly because local authorities, although ready to pull down slums, were not so willing to commit themselves to the costly business of house-building, especially as the rents which the former slum-dwellers could afford to pay were insufficient to meet the costs. The Housing of the Working Classes Act (1890) gave local councils more powers to demolish property, and laid down firmer sanitary regulations. There were several examples of model housing estates put up by private

[1] G. A. N. Lowndes: *The Silent Social Revolution*, p. 231.

enterprise, such as those built by Cadburys at Bournville (from 1879) and by the soap magnate William Lever at Port Sunlight (from 1888). But comparatively little was done under the Act. Not until 1909 was back-to-back house building finally forbidden. The census of 1911, the last before the First World War, revealed some alarming facts about housing. One-tenth of the entire population was still living in overcrowded conditions: and 'overcrowded' meant more than two persons to a room, with two children counting as equal to one adult. In certain areas, notably the East End of London, the north-eastern coalfield cities, and Scotland, many more than one-tenth were over-crowded. In Scotland, where conditions both in city and countryside were bad, nearly half the entire population lived in houses with one or two rooms only. In fact the housing situation was bad in 1914; and then the First World War put a stop to building.

The most famous contribution of the early 20th century to public health was the development of a system of national health insurance. Germany and New Zealand were the pioneers here, in the late 19th century: and Great Britain, as we have seen, took its first step in 1911 with a National Insurance Act. Its health clauses provided that health insurance should be compulsory for all manual workers between 16 and 70 years of age, and for all non-manual workers whose pay was less than £160 per annum. Doctors who were willing to enter the scheme formed 'panels' or lists of patients to whom they could give treatment: chemists came in to the scheme to make up the prescriptions, and there was provision for hospital and sanatorium treatment. At first there was much hostility to the proposals, including opposition organised through the doctors' professional association, the British Medical Association; yet it was not long before they came to be accepted as a normal element of English social life. In later years the upper age limit came down from 70 to 65, and the non-manual workers' income limit was raised first to £240 and then to £420. The scheme had some serious defects in detail, especially in the limits imposed upon types of treatment and of medicines. Nevertheless, taken as a whole, it was of inestimable benefit to the majority of the population: it safeguarded health and made the nation fitter, and it did much to accustom wage-earners to medical attention. As for the doctors themselves, it gave most of them a higher and more reliable income; and it led indirectly to an increase in their numbers. It was the forerunner of the more comprehensive and nation-wide health service introduced by the Labour government of 1945–50.

20 Education

I. EDUCATION IN THE 18TH CENTURY

It is safe to say that most English children in the 18th century either did not go to school at all, or, at best, went for a very short time. There was no national system of education in England. Scottish children were better off, for parish schools had been in existence over most of Scotland since the middle of the 17th century. So far as the children of the poor got any teaching in England, they received it through private charity. In the early 18th century many Charity Schools came into existence financed by local collections and run by local trustees, most of them under the supervision of the Society for the Promotion of Christian Knowledge (founded in 1699). By the end of George I's reign in 1727, such schools existed in all but two of the English and Welsh counties, and had over 20,000 pupils on their rolls.[1] They gave elementary teaching in the 'three R's' (Reading, Writing and Arithmetic), and also in useful trades; a fair number of their pupils were paupers or orphans. But they did not flourish for very long; and in the second half of the century they fell into decline.

For education which was more than merely elementary, most towns of any size had Grammar Schools, many of which had been founded under the Tudors. For much of the 18th century they flourished. They catered mainly for the sons of the middle classes, the wealthier merchants of the towns; although they had originally been founded for able boys of every class, it was increasingly difficult for poor children to gain entry to them. Their curriculum was usually limited to a study of the classics, and by the later years of the century this was becoming too narrow. In this they differed from the schools run by the nonconformists, the Dissenting Academies, which were undoubtedly the best of the time. These had been founded in the 17th century in many of the larger towns, where dissenters were numerous. Their approach to teaching (in which Unitarians were prominent) and their textbooks was fresh and lively, and their curriculum more suited to the business world into which most of their pupils went. Moreover, they seem to have been well endowed and to have been able to provide for poorer children. Many of their pupils, excluded by their religion from Oxford and Cambridge, went instead to the more progressive Scottish or Dutch universities.

Many of the sons of the landowning nobility and gentry, the ruling class of the age, were taught by private tutors at home. Others went to a very small group of boarding schools, those 'Public Schools' which already existed: these included Eton, Winchester, Charterhouse, Shrewsbury and Westminster, the last possibly the most eminent of that day. Here as in the Grammar Schools the curriculum was overwhelmingly classical. Most of the masters were Anglican clergymen; customs like 'fagging' had already developed and the evidence suggests that conditions in these schools were tough and violent, with much bullying and tyrannical discipline. The age of organised games had scarely begun; the cricket match between Eton and Westminster in 1796 was so unofficial that all the Eton XI were flogged afterwards by the Headmaster (they had lost anyway). One other feature of upper class education in the 18th century deserves special mention. This was the 'grand tour' of Europe undertaken by young men of wealth, accompanied

[1] The population of England and Wales at that time was probably about 5½ million.

often by learned scholars as their tutors. It was a long and leisurely enterprise of many months or years; it took them especially to France, the most civilised country in the world, and to Italy with its Roman remains, its Renaissance traditions and its opera; and it made the rulers of 18th century England citizens of Europe in a way that few Englishmen have been since.

Certainly it gave them a better education than that provided at the time by the two English universities, Oxford and Cambridge. Oxford was at its lowest ebb. Its students paid little regard to learning: most of them seem to have spent their days in hunting, drinking and gambling. Its professors rarely lectured: its examinations both for entrance and for degrees were farcical. Scholarships and fellowships at colleges were largely restricted either to certain schools or to relatives of the founders. Its students in this century included the greatest of English historians, Edward Gibbon, and the political philosopher Jeremy Bentham, both of whom have left bitter accounts of the 'education' Oxford offered. Cambridge was a little less bad: its examinations were genuine, and the study of mathematics in particular —under the impulse from Sir Isaac Newton, who had been a Cambridge professor—was carried on with some diligence. Yet even at Cambridge the majority of undergraduates seem to have been unbelievably idle. Neither Oxford nor Cambridge made the contribution to learning or to training men for public affairs which might have been expected of them.

By contrast the Scottish universities, especially Edinburgh and Glasgow, were notably progressive.[1] Scottish education was much more democratic than English. The parish schools gave an opening to the 'lad of parts' from a humble home, and most university students in Scotland came from poor homes. They had no money to waste on riotous living; instead the majority of them were determined to make the most of their education. Scotland had hitherto been a poor and backward country; in the 18th century its people made great efforts to catch up with England. The universities reflected a national movement for greater prosperity and higher standards. Hence they became thriving centres of intellectual progress. Edinburgh, for example, started a vigorous medical school in 1720; this and the similar school at Glasgow became the leading centres of medical education in Britain. Both universities also made much progress in the study of science, especially of chemistry: we have already noticed the influence of Glasgow University upon its scientific instrument maker, James Watt: and the growth of industry in Scotland owed much to this scientific work. Adam Smith, the great prophet of free trade, was a Glasgow professor. It is not surprising that the Scottish universities attracted many able students from England and elsewhere at this time.

[1] There were five—Edinburgh, Glasgow, St. Andrews and the two colleges, Marischal and King's, at Aberdeen.

2. GRAMMAR SCHOOLS AND PUBLIC SCHOOLS IN THE 19TH
CENTURY

Towards the end of the 18th century the old-established English Grammar Schools, with rare exceptions, fell into rapid decay. The local corporations which were responsible for them had also fallen into decline, and
usually showed as little interest in education as in other matters connected
with the welfare of their towns. Moreover, the Grammar Schools did not
meet the needs of the new industrial age. Their classical curriculum, to
which they were tied by the charters of foundation, was out of date; and
very often the masters (i.e. headmasters) and ushers (i.e. assistant masters)
were incompetent, having obtained their posts not by reason of their
qualifications but because they had friends on the corporation. Some of
them tried to transform their schools to their own profit, by charging high
fees for teaching extra subjects like English and Mathematics, but few were
successful in doing so for any length of time. Many were content to be idle.
Legally they could not be removed from their posts so long as they continued to teach Latin and Greek in accordance with their charter, and if
few pupils, or even no pupils at all, came to be taught, life was so much the
easier for the masters. Some actively discouraged scholars from attending;
drew their stipends; combined their 'work' as teachers with a local church
living; and enjoyed leisurely and comfortable lives. There were schools
where for forty years a master drew his stipend and never had a pupil to
teach, or where at one time there were two masters and one boy. By the
early 19th century these ancient schools seemed utterly decayed.

Meanwhile sons of the middle class, who might have attended them,
went to the many private schools which grew up after about 1800. Some of
these were appalling places: Charles Dickens' terrible picture (in *Nicholas
Nickleby*) of Dotheboys Hall, with the brutal Whackford Squeers as its
master, is no doubt a caricature, yet a caricature founded upon reality. A
few were progressive and well ahead of their time: among these was the
school at Birmingham run by Rowland Hill and his family. Here the
subjects taught included mathematics, French, history and geography, as
well as swimming and gymnastics; and even self-government, with discipline organised by an elected committee of boys. But this was not at all
typical. Most private schools were narrow and limited in their curriculum,
and their teaching consisted largely of mechanical drilling.

The Municipal Reform Act (1835) rescued the Grammar Schools, by
getting rid of the old type of corporation and thus opening the way to
progress. Reform was in the air; and the Evangelical Movement was
awakening a strong sense of public duty among the prosperous middle class.
Gradually during the next thirty years the Grammar Schools revived,
with groups of public-spirited citizens as trustees or governors. The larger
cities, with more money as well as greater need for education, led the way.
In 1864 a government commission under Lord Taunton investigated great
numbers of schools providing secondary education, and as a result of its

work the Endowed Schools Act of 1869 was passed. This encouraged the revival of the Grammar Schools by making available to them numerous charitable funds which, originally started for various purposes, were now lying idle. The main subjects of study in the reformed grammar schools were classics and mathematics; yet in the later years of the century they widened their range to include modern languages and science. This process was stimulated by the growth of a system of external examinations conducted by the universities: the Oxford and the Cambridge Local Examinations, the pioneers in the movement which was later to develop into the School Certificate and the General Certificate of Education, began in 1858. Thus the Grammar Schools made much progress in the 19th century. Nevertheless two major defects remained. First, there were not enough of them: the Taunton Commission had suggested the establishment of new schools paid for by local rates, but this proposal was not adopted. Secondly, they catered almost entirely for the middle class: they provided few places for the children of the poor.

The Public Schools underwent remarkable change in the 19th century. At first they continued to be notorious for brutality, with savage discipline maintained by flogging. Sometimes the boys rebelled: in 1808 there was a great mutiny at Harrow, and ten years later soldiers had to be called in at Winchester. The number of boys attending the Public Schools began to fall off, and they might have disappeared had it not been for two developments. The first of these was the Industrial Revolution. This created a class of wealthy merchants and manufacturers who wanted a boarding-school education for their sons and were prepared to spend money to get it. It also created the railways, which made it easier to transport large numbers of boys to boarding-schools. The second development was a movement of reform inside the schools themselves, led by a group of outstanding headmasters much influenced in their outlook by the Evangelical Movement. The results of these developments were great. They gave a new lease of life to the existing Public Schools. They led to the foundation of many new ones, like Marlborough (1841), Cheltenham (1842) and Clifton (1862). Above all, they radically altered the life and outlook of the schools, giving them the stamp they have retained ever since.

Three of the reforming headmasters deserve special notice. Samuel Butler (Headmaster of Shrewsbury 1798–1836) was not only a fine scholar and gifted teacher many of whose pupils won high fame at Oxford and Cambridge. His work at Shrewsbury led the way in developing one central feature of Public School life, that of promoting self-reliance: at Shrewsbury he organised a system of praepostors (i.e. prefects) and encouraged his pupils to plan their own leisure time. Thomas Arnold (Headmaster of Rugby 1828–42) set out to make his pupils Christian gentlemen with a strong sense of their responsibility as leaders in English life. The chapel became the heart of school life; the prefectorial system was further developed; the curriculum was widened to give greater scope to other subjects than the classics. Arnold, who had many disciples and imitators, made Rugby the most influential school in England: its achievements included the invention of a new game,[1] and it was the scene of the most famous of English School stories, *Tom Brown's Schooldays*, by Thomas Hughes (1857). Thirdly, Edward Thring (Headmaster of Uppingham 1853–87) was a pioneer in establishing many institutions which have become accepted features of Public Schools since his day. When he was appointed to Uppingham it was a country grammar school with twenty pupils. Thirty years later it was a great school with separate boarding houses, gymnasium and swimming bath, organised games, workshops and music-rooms, and an old boys' organisation—all of them novelties in Thring's day.

These men and their contemporaries set the pattern within which the Public Schools have grown since that time. Gradually their curriculum widened, to include modern studies like history and modern languages, and, rather later, science. Organised games rapidly came to play an important part in them. The Officers' Training Corps, first founded in 1909 (later developed into the Combined Cadet Force), became a normal feature of most of them. Their aim from the start was not so much to develop intellect as to train character. Until after the First World War they provided most of the entrants to Oxford and Cambridge, and they were aware that they were educating the vast majority of the boys who would one day occupy the leading positions in the nation. Their importance in the community was thus far greater than might be expected from the comparatively small number of boys who went to them. Nearly all were religious foundations, most of them Anglican. They provided the great majority of the clergy, of statesmen and members of both Houses of Parliament, of senior civil servants both at home and in the colonies: and this situation lasted almost unchanged until the middle years of the 20th century. Moreover, their influence upon secondary education in England was very great. Many Grammar Schools, especially in their 'out of school' activities, tended to model themselves upon the Public Schools. Foreign visitors and critics instinctively looked upon them as 'typical' of English education, even though these schools catered only for a small and on the whole a wealthy minority of the population.

3. THE GROWTH OF AN ORGANISED NATIONAL SYSTEM OF EDUCATION

The beginnings of an organised national system of education in England and Wales came in the early years of the 19th century. By this time the Charity Schools had fallen into decline, and a strange mixture of schools gave some sort of teaching to an uncertain number of the children of the poor. Among these were Sunday Schools, first started by Robert Raikes in

---

[1] Rugby Football is traditionally supposed to date from 1823, when William Webb Ellis, a boy at Rugby School, 'picked up the ball and ran with it' in a game of football.

Gloucester in 1780: they spread fairly rapidly in the larger towns, where they were provided and run by the clergy and other charitable persons. Many other schools were run for private profit. Among these were numerous Dames' Schools, often little more than small classes in a single room, sometimes in a cellar or a garret, taught by an old lady as a means of earning a few coppers; they seem to have been of little value beyond teaching a few children to learn their letters. Some cities had Common Day Schools: these too were of small worth. The most effective of the schools for the poor in the early 19th century were those run by two religious societies, the National Society (for Anglicans) and the British and Foreign Society (for Nonconformists). They used a new development in methods of teaching, called the monitorial system, whose invention was claimed both by Joseph Lancaster, a Quaker, and by Andrew Bell, an Anglican clergyman. Under this system one master taught a select group of older pupils, the monitors, and these in turn taught, parrot-fashion, the rest. This teaching consisted merely in mechanical drilling, for example in spelling, and in learning information by rote. It was very narrow and limited, in some ways not unlike the early factory system which was arising at the same time.

The proportion of the children of the poor who went to these schools was quite small, and certainly a great many children grew up unable either to read or write. The need for education became more obvious as the industrial changes went on.[1] In 1833 public money was for the first time provided for education, when a government grant, of £20,000, was made for schools. It was divided between the two religious societies mentioned above. During the next forty years the grant rose appreciably: before 1860 it was over £500,000 per annum. Inspectors of schools were appointed by the government to see that it was not wasted, and in 1839 a special committee of the Privy Council was created to deal with education. Yet progress was very slow. Such schools as were built were cramped, ill-lit and ill-ventilated. The teachers were badly paid and often wholly unqualified for their work: the historian Macaulay, living at this time, described them as 'the sweepings of other callings'. Religious disputes hindered progress. It was soon argued that the 'voluntary' schools, as those run by the two societies were called, could not by themselves cope with the educational needs of the community, and there were many proposals for building and maintaining schools out of the local rates. But these for long came to naught because Anglican ratepayers were opposed to spending the rates on schools which did not teach the Anglican catechism, while Nonconformists objected to giving financial help to Church schools; Anglican opposition nearly prevented the establishment of the committee of 1839, while in 1843 the Nonconformists wrecked a bill which would have sent all children employed in factories to school for three hours daily, on the ground that the schools would be managed by Anglicans. In the 1850's and 1860's a series of officially-appointed commissions investigated universities and schools of every kind: and the one responsible for elementary education, the Newcastle

[1] It was indicated by the foundation (1823) by Dr. George Birkbeck of Mechanics' Institutes for working-men, which by 1850 had 600,000 members.

Commission of 1858, recommended the setting up of local boards of education with powers to levy rates. This proposal was turned down.

In the schools themselves little was taught beyond the 'Three R's'. In the early 1860's another suggestion of the Newcastle Commission was adopted. This was the system of 'payment by results', under which the salaries of teachers in schools which received government grants were made to depend in part upon the number of their pupils who passed the annual examination in the Three R's conducted by Her Majesty's Inspectors. This device saved money and appealed to the middle-class business men who had the right to vote: and it did something to promote efficient teaching. But, besides its unfairness to the teachers, it led to a neglect of anything beyond the elementary work which was necessary to get children through the examinations: thus it penalised the more intelligent children of the poor. Robert Lowe, who as minister responsible for education from 1859 to 1864 was mainly responsible for its introduction, once said that 'the lower classes ought to be educated to discharge the duties cast upon them': and payment by results seemed admirably adapted to fulfil that view of education.

The English system of education was at this time in many ways behind those of Scotland, France and Prussia, all of which had some kind of national system; and eventually growing criticism led to the most important reform in its history, Forster's Education Act of 1870. This followed naturally upon the Second Reform Act of 1867. As Robert Lowe himself said, 'I believe it will be absolutely necessary to compel our new masters to learn their letters'; the new voters had to be educated in order that they might have the chance to exercise their votes intelligently. For the first time Parliament took upon itself the responsibility of seeing that every child in the land had the chance of going to school. Elementary schools were to be built in all districts where efficient schools were not already provided by religious bodies. These new schools were to be controlled by locally-elected School Boards, given the power to levy rates to pay for them. The Act itself did not make education compulsory everywhere, although local School Boards could do so in their own areas. The religious difficulty was to some extent met by the Cowper-Temple clause of the Act, which provided that the religious teaching in the new schools was to be undenominational, based on simple Bible teaching: parents could withdraw their children from the scripture lessons if they wished. The Act was a landmark because it created a nation-wide network of elementary schools, the Board Schools, described by Sherlock Holmes to Watson as 'Capsules, with hundreds of bright seeds in each, out of which will spring the wiser, better England for the future.'[1] Sandon's Act of 1876 and Mundella's Act of 1880 together made education compulsory to the age of 10, and in 1891 this elementary education was made free. In 1889 a Technical Instruction Act started Evening Institutes, and in the 1890's some School Boards established Higher Grade Schools (strong in industrial Lancashire) going beyond elementary education.

A generation after Forster's Act came a second great measure which

[1] In *The Naval Treaty*.

further extended the national system. This was the Balfour Act of 1902, put into operation by a great civil servant, Sir Robert Morant, Permanent Secretary at the Board of Education 1902–11, who shared with many contemporaries the belief that England must undertake further educational reform in order to keep pace with Germany and other countries which in their view were outstripping her in industry and science because their people were better educated. The Balfour Act carried out two major reforms. First, it abolished the School Boards and set in their place education committees of the County and County Borough Councils: these were to be known as Local Education Authorities (L.E.A.s) and were to have wide powers for the control of education in their own areas; the voluntary schools, those provided by the churches, could in future be helped from the rates. The central Board of Education, which had in 1899 replaced the old committee of the Privy Council as the government department responsible for education, exercised a general supervision over the L.E.A.s: most of its duties consisted of giving advice, rather than of issuing orders, for local feeling was strong on the subject of education. Secondly, the Balfour Act did much to strengthen secondary education. Henceforward it was possible for the old endowed Grammar Schools to be aided from the rates, and many of them received a new lease of life. More important still, the Local Education Authorities themselves could now build and maintain secondary schools: and during the years after the Act many new secondary schools were opened. These schools charged fees, and continued to do so for nearly half-a-century: but soon after 1902 they began to admit a proportion of 'scholarship' or 'free place' pupils from the local elementary schools. This was a stage in the building of 'the educational ladder', by which a clever child could win his way from a poor home to the university. The ladder was far from complete in the years after 1902; many children were unable to go further than the secondary schools on account of the poverty of their parents—and many others who had won free places at the secondary schools could not accept them because their families needed their earnings. Nevertheless, the Balfour Act was a step in the right direction, and in the years after 1902 England made appreciable progress in extending its national system of education. The school-leaving age, which had been raised to 12 in 1899, went up to 14 by 1918. Many more schools were built, and more and better-qualified teachers were recruited and trained. Medical inspection and school meals services began. The Inspectors appointed by the Board of Education did much to spread higher standards inside the schools. All this meant that the English people as a whole were much better educated than they had been, for example, a century earlier. Nevertheless, the progress was uneven. There were drawbacks as well as advantages in local control. Some Local Education Authorities were progressive, yet others were very backward. Children in areas which were prepared to spend money from the rates upon education had a far better chance than those in areas—especially some of the predominantly agricultural counties—where less money was available.

4. UNIVERSITIES IN THE 19TH AND EARLY 20TH CENTURIES

The reform movement of the 19th century had notable influence on the universities of Oxford and Cambridge, making them far more effective both as centres of research work and as teaching institutions. Oxford began to put its house in order by establishing a genuine system of examinations. Both of them greatly widened their fields of study, establishing new professorships and courses of lectures, Cambridge leading the way in the natural sciences. The barriers which had prevented the admission of dissenters and other non-Anglicans were gradually removed: the final stage in this process was the Universities Tests Act of 1871, which opened all posts and places, and all degrees except those in Divinity, at Oxford and Cambridge to any candidates irrespective of their religious beliefs. Thus the older universities ceased to be special preserves of the Church of England. Several commissions, notably in the 1850's, investigated the methods of government of Oxford and Cambridge and the uses to which the various colleges put their endowments. The result was a succession of reforms—strongly opposed by the conservative elements in the universities—which reorganised their constitutions and enabled them to make better use of their funds. One of the most important single changes was the abolition of the system whereby relatives of the founders of colleges had held fellowships for life without the obligation to do any work.

By 1900 the two older English universities were on the whole healthy and efficient, in contrast with their state a century before. Their graduates were contributing to national life in ways far more varied and numerous—particularly perhaps as scientists and doctors, as teachers, and in the fast-growing civil service. The most serious social criticism that could be levelled at them was that they still drew their students from a narrow section of the community. The majority of their entrants came from the Public Schools and were children of the wealthier upper and upper-middle classes[1]; and this situation remained true of the first part of the 20th century. Even by 1930, two generations after Forster's Act had set up a national system of elementary education, less than one-quarter of all the students at Oxford and Cambridge were former pupils of the state elementary schools.

Reform in the older English universities was one great change of this period: a second was the establishment of a number of new ones. The earliest of these were at London and Durham. University College, London, was opened in 1828 as a place of learning free from religious tests. In reply a group of Anglicans quickly started King's College: and in 1836 the two colleges were incorporated as the University of London. At Durham the establishment of a university had been suggested as early as Oliver Cromwell's time. It was actually set up in 1832, and twenty years later the college of medicine at Newcastle-upon-Tyne was united with it. This college was

---

[1] It is, however, worth noting that an important proportion were the sons of country clergymen, who were often by no means well-to-do: and many of these achieved high distinction both at the university and in their future careers.

one of a number, in medicine and technology, which grew up in the big northern cities in the first half of the 19th century, encouraged by industrialists who needed skilled men for their expanding factories; and in them lay the roots of later universities.

In 1851 a benefaction of £97,000 left by a nonconformist radical named John Owens was used to found a technical college at Manchester; and in 1884 this Owens College joined with similar ones at Liverpool and Leeds to form the Victoria University. In 1893 three Welsh colleges (Aberystwyth, Bangor and Cardiff) combined to form the University of Wales. In 1903–4 the Victoria University was re-divided to form the three distinct Universities of Manchester, Liverpool and Leeds: meanwhile, in 1900, Birmingham University had already been established, and the University of London was reorganised to include various separate bodies (e.g. the London School of Economics, 1895, and Imperial College, 1907) and to become a more efficient teaching centre. Sheffield University was given its charter in 1905, and Bristol in 1909. Besides these, university colleges grew up at other provincial centres in the early years of the 20th century. Thus the country was covered comparatively rapidly with a series of institutions of university type, most of them in or near great industrial cities, either offering their own degrees or enabling students to take the external degrees established by the University of London.

These newer universities differed in many ways from Oxford and Cambridge. They were strongly local. The initiative in developing them came from local citizens; local industrialists, like George Cadbury at Birmingham and the Wills and Fry families at Bristol, contributed heavily to their endowments; and most of their students came from the localities around the universities. They were mainly non-resident: despite a number of successful attempts to set up hostels, most of their undergraduates lived either at home or in lodgings. They laid a new emphasis upon scientific studies or upon courses allied to science, like medicine and various branches of engineering; this reflected their close relationship with the industrial activities of their own regions. Nearly all their pupils came not from the Public Schools but from day schools—either the old-established city Grammar Schools or the newer secondary schools which sprang up after the Balfour Act. Finally, in contrast to Oxford and Cambridge, they admitted women students on equal terms with men, and admitted them in large numbers. This was possibly their most revolutionary and important achievement of all.[1]

---

[1] This chapter has said practically nothing about the education of girls. This is because that subject is so closely bound up with the whole question of the emancipation of women: and details will be found in Chapter 23.

21 Religion and Social Life

Throughout the years since 1700 organised religion has been a force of great influence in British social life: and at certain times its power has been very profound indeed. The purpose of this chapter is not to give an account of the history of the Church of England or other religious bodies, still less to trace any alterations in their doctrines or forms of government. Its object is rather to describe some of the principal religious movements of the period and to suggest their effects upon social development.

I. THE REMOVAL OF RELIGIOUS PRIVILEGE

In 1689 the Toleration Act was passed. It permitted Protestant Dissenters to worship freely in their own way in their own chapels and meeting houses, thus granting religious toleration to the majority of non-Anglicans. The Act did not apply to Unitarians or to Roman Catholics; in practice, however, they were allowed to worship with little interference. The year 1689 was therefore a milestone in the growth of religious liberty. The persecutions—the fines for non-attendance at Anglican worship, the imprisonments, the executions and burnings—now became memories of a harsher age. But the liberty granted was in important ways incomplete. In particular, members of the Church of England retained almost a monopoly of political power. The Corporation Act of 1661 remained law, excluding from membership of town corporations all those who were not prepared to take the sacrament according to the rites of the Church of England: so did the Test Act of 1673, which imposed the same test upon holders of civil or military office under the Crown. Roman Catholics and Protestant Dissenters were to remain politically unprivileged, excluded from government both national and local. Moreover, the Universities of Oxford and Cambridge excluded all but Anglicans from their degrees.

These restrictions did much to drive Dissenters—or Nonconformists, as they came to be called—into trade and industry during the 18th century: such names as Benjamin Huntsman and the Darbys of Coalbrookdale provide examples. For one short period ardent Anglicans made an attempt to make the laws more intolerant still; the Schism Act of 1714 forbade any Dissenter to keep a school. Had it ever been seriously enforced it would have done grave harm to the Protestant sects, by destroying their schools, the Dissenting Academies. But it was repealed in 1719. In practice, the plight of the Protestant Nonconformists was not as bad as the law suggests. Many of them, in order to take local office, indulged in 'occasional conformity', receiving the Anglican Communion once a year. Moreover, from 1728 onwards an annual Indemnity Act was passed, granting a formal pardon to those who had held office without subscribing to the Anglican 'test'. The 18th century was a tolerant age: and the Whigs, who were the dominant political party for much of its course, drew considerable support from Nonconformist elements in the towns. Roman Catholics, however, remained entirely excluded from a share in government, in fact as well as at law. Not until 1793 were they given the right to vote; and this benefited very few in Great Britain (as distinct from Ireland).

The 1820's, that period of modest reforms now that the worst stresses resulting from the French wars were over, brought two important changes in the law here. In 1828 the Test and Corporation Acts were repealed; and in 1829 the Catholic Emancipation Act became law, allowing Roman Catholics to sit in Parliament and to hold all offices under the Crown except those of Lord Chancellor and Viceroy of Ireland.[1] Other changes, of different kinds but all in the same general direction of removing inequalities followed gradually during the next half-century. Thus in 1836 civil marriage was permitted, and Nonconformists no longer had to publish their banns in an Anglican church. In 1858 those holding the Jewish faith, hitherto excluded, were permitted to become members of Parliament. In 1871 the last major stronghold of Anglican privilege, the Universities of Oxford and Cambridge, fell after a prolonged attack: the Universities Tests Act of that year finally opened them on equal terms to Anglicans and non-Anglicans alike.

2. THE 18TH CENTURY AND THE METHODIST MOVEMENT

The 17th century had been a time of remarkable religious enthusiasm and activity in Britain. A great Civil War had been fought in which religious freedom had been a major issue—indeed, for many of the contestants, the supreme issue. A group of Puritan sects had broken away from the Church of England and established themselves as separate 'dissenting' churches in the teeth of severe persecution: men and women had been fined, imprisoned, deprived of livelihood, denied political freedom, and put to death because their religious beliefs differed from those of the ruling authorities. It had been a period of storm. Towards its close the storm had died away: and the 18th century, or at any rate its first half, was a period of calm. Some historians would go further, and call it a period of torpor, or sleep. Certainly the most violent controversies and disputes of the previous age had died away. Dissenters ceased to be rebels and agitators; in the 18th century they became quiet and contented citizens, deliberately keeping out of disputes with their Anglican neighbours and concentrating their energies upon their daily work and business. Even Roman Catholics, so bitterly hated and feared in the previous century because of memories of the Spanish Inquisition and Gunpowder Plot, were now usually allowed to live peaceably. Legally they were still liable to persecution for worshipping publicly: in fact, so long as they did not thrust themselves forward to try to convert their neighbours, they were permitted to build and use their own

---

[1] The Bill of Rights (1689) prohibits the Sovereign from being a Roman Catholic and from marrying a Roman Catholic.

chapels, and apart from occasional mob-outbursts (as in the Gordon Riots of 1780)[1] nobody bothered very much about them. In Scotland, too, where religious passion had previously run high, the much-persecuted Presbyterian Church had in 1689 become the established church of the land.

In England the great majority of the people belonged to the established church, the Church of England. They accepted its beliefs without question, and they attended its services every Sunday. Its organised ritual played a central part in their lives. The great majority of its parsons were good and sincere men, teaching Christian doctrine to their parishioners, helping the poor, the sick and the troubled, and setting an example of Christian conduct by their own daily lives. Yet there were grave weaknesses in the Church of England in the 18th century. At its head, its bishops were chosen very largely for political and not religious reasons, and many of them, attending to give their votes to the government in the House of Lords, neglected their dioceses. Some of the parish clergy were more interested in farming, or hunting, or the bottle, than in their pastoral duties: very many were shockingly ill-paid: and nearly all seem to have failed to inspire their parishioners with any lively faith or enthusiasm. Perhaps the most serious social criticism of the Church was that great numbers of the very poor were almost entirely neglected by it; with these people the ordinary parish clergyman was wholly out of touch. They included many thousands dwelling in the slums of London; the colliers of the North East, the Black Country, and other areas, and the tinners of Cornwall, living half-barbaric lives, cut off from the rest of the community by the nature of their work; and growing numbers of working men in the rising industrial towns. Here was a great gap to be filled, a great spiritual task to be accomplished—but only by men who could offer something more than the charity and good works of the parish clergy.

It was out of this need that there sprang a religious movement which gave new meaning to the lives of thousands of the poorest and humblest of English people. This was the Methodist Movement, whose central figure was John Wesley (1703–91). The son of a Lincolnshire rector, John Wesley at Oxford had been a member of a group of serious-minded students whose regular prayer-meetings and Bible readings had won them the nickname of 'Methodists'. Ordained as a clergyman, he had served in his father's parish and then as a missionary in Georgia, lately founded as a colony by General Oglethorpe: there he had failed, offending many by his arrogance as well as by his efforts to impose stricter standards of conduct on the colonies. In 1738 he came back to England, doubting his own faith: yet then came the turning-point of his life, when in May, 1738, he underwent a conversion. As he wrote in his *Journal*, 'I felt I did trust in Christ, Christ alone, for Salvation, and an assurance was given me that He had taken away *my* sins.' To this sense of his own faith was added the conviction that it was his duty to go out and preach to others the gospel of personal salvation by faith.

[1] See below, pp. 221–2.

There were others whose beliefs at this time led them in the same direction, like George Whitefield, once the tapster of the Bell Inn at Gloucester, and Wesley's own brother Charles: and from henceforward such men began to make a series of missionary journeys through the British Isles.

Thus began the Methodist Movement. It had many features remarkable in 18th-century Britain. Wesley and his fellow-missionaries had little support from the parish clergy, many of whom strongly opposed them. They found the pulpits closed against them, and so they took to open-air preaching, to crowds of many thousands. Their work was above all directed to the neglected poor of the cities and the mining areas; for the 18th-century upper class, with its contempt for any form of enthusiasm, found in the preachers only an interesting and slightly alarming novelty. Wesley, who preached 40,000 sermons in fifty years, was a remarkable preacher: his sermons—like those of many of his fellows—moved great crowds to wild joy and to tears, in scenes of frenzy in which numbers of his hearers rent the air with shrieks and groans or fell senseless to the ground. He had no intention of founding a new church or sect, and himself remained an Anglican throughout his life. But he had earlier taken a decisive step by ordaining ministers to work in the American Colonies, and soon after his death in 1791 the separate Methodist Church was formed.

The Methodists encountered great hostility in their early years. Parsons organised mobs against them: their preachers were stoned, beaten up, flung into rivers: they were arrested as Jacobites and press-ganged for the Navy: employers dismissed Methodists and innkeepers refused to give them lodgings. Yet the movement was profoundly successful, winning converts by the thousand among the poor and establishing itself in the colonies in Wesley's own lifetime. By 1815 there were nearly a quarter of a million Wesleyan Methodists in Great Britain, and over 200,000 in the United States. It succeeded because its preachers offered a new hope, proclaiming a message of eternal salvation through faith: those who were outcasts of society learned that their souls too were of eternal worth. Its social effects were immense. It gave a new self-respect to many thousands, making them hard-working, thrifty and sober, so that in the later years of the 18th century employers, far from opposing the movement, preferred Methodist workmen to others. It was of quite peculiar influence in the growing industrial areas, and helped to soften the impact of the industrial changes. It did much to civilise those parts of England where civilisation seemed most remote at that time. Its permanent legacy is the largest of the English Nonconformist Churches.

3. THE EVANGELICAL MOVEMENT

Towards the end of the 18th century another religious movement began to win influence in England. It is known as the Evangelical Movement (or Evangelical Revival), and as its name rather suggests it had certain things in common with the Methodist Movement, which indeed did much to stimulate it. It stressed the importance of faith in personal salvation, as the essential basis of a religious life: it called upon the individual to be thrifty, sober, industrious and self-sacrificing. Yet, unlike Methodism, it spread among the upper and middle classes, and among the clergy of the Established Church: and it spread not by revivalist mass meetings but by a kind of gradual penetration. It came as a reaction against the slackness and indifference of the 18th-century Church: and its progress was accelerated by the French Revolution against which Britain was fighting and which in the eyes of many Englishmen appeared to stand for atheism and evil. It is difficult to trace its development, for it came in almost imperceptibly, like a slow-flowing tide. The first notable Evangelical in public life was William Wilberforce (1759–1833), the champion of the negro slaves, who underwent conversion in 1785: and perhaps the most notable of all Evangelicals was Lord Shaftesbury, the crusader for factory reform and many other causes, who died in 1885, by which time the influence of Evangelicalism was waning. Its coming brought a gradual and almost complete transformation of the tone of English upper and middle class life: and if one date had to be selected to mark its triumph, perhaps the best to choose would be 1837, the year in which Queen Victoria ascended the throne.

For in many ways Evangelicalism stood for the ideas which later ages have come to associate with Victorian England. The Queen herself embodied many of them. Thus she was 'Low Church', distrusting any form of ritual, which to her as to the Puritans of the 17th century smacked of Roman Catholicism; she held very strong views on what was right moral conduct; she believed in the strict observance of Sunday, detesting what came to be called 'the Continental Sunday' with its feasts and amusements; perhaps most important of all, she had an immensely powerful sense of duty. Her views were shared by a great number of her subjects, certainly by a majority among the ruling upper and middle classes. In some ways Evangelicalism seems to us a hard and narrow faith, with little mercy towards the sinners. Its virtues of hard work and thrift tended to make men wealthy, and encouraged them to believe that the poor were necessarily idle and feckless. Yet that should not lead us to ignore another vital element in it—namely, the force with which the Evangelical faith drove men to give their lives to campaigns for social reforms to help the poor and suffering. For its influence in this way was enormously wide: Wilberforce and Shaftesbury are merely the giants among the Evangelical social reformers.

The most important group of Evangelicals were those who came to be called the Clapham Sect because most of them lived at Clapham, then a country village on the outskirts of London. Their leading figure was William Wilberforce, who resided at Clapham from 1795 to 1808, when his campaign against the Slave Trade was at its height. They were well-to-do and influential laymen, with bankers and landowners among them: some, like Wilberforce, were in Parliament where with other like-minded M.P.s they formed the small group nicknamed 'the Saints'. To promote the spread of their views within the Church of England, they bought Church livings and installed in them Evangelical clergy.[1] The proposals in which they were actively interested, besides the abolition of the Slave Trade, included the establishment of foreign missions and Bible societies, the enforcement of Sunday observance, the prohibition of duelling, the banning of bull and bear baiting, and the reform of prisons. Closely associated with the Saints was Charles Simeon, who as Vicar of Holy Trinity at Cambridge for fifty-two years did much to fill later generations of clergy with Evangelical ideas.

Lord Shaftesbury (formerly Lord Ashley) was a Dorset landowner whose Evangelical faith inspired him to devote his long life (1801–85) and high abilities to a series of good causes. He became the leader of the Factory Reform Movement, a role no doubt not unwelcome to him as a landowner; he fought a long hard battle for the Climbing Boys; he got the employment of women and children in the mines prohibited; he founded the Ragged Schools for pauper children; and he did more than any other man to get the Lunacy Laws made at once safe and humane. By such achievements he lifted heavy burdens from millions of lives. His Evangelicalism was equally evident in his narrow sabbatarianism: he was chairman of the Lord's Day Observance Society, and in 1856 he got the playing of military bands in London parks on Sundays stopped.

Three further examples will illustrate the contribution of Evangelicalism to social reform in the 19th century; in each of them the reformers were inspired to action against a social evil by this religious faith. One was the development of the movement for stopping cruelty to animals, in which the leading figure was Richard 'Humanity' Martin. The first Act against ill-treatment of cattle and horses was passed in 1823, and the Royal Society for the Prevention of Cruelty to Animals was founded in 1824. Another was the foundation in 1867 of the first of Barnardo's Homes, in Stepney in the slums of London's East End. Thomas John Barnardo was a London doctor who gave up his intended missionary career to devote his life to the rescue of London's hundreds of homeless children. The third and most extraordinary example came in 1878 when William Booth, who had spent thirteen years as an Evangelical missionary in the East End, started his Salvation Army. No Englishman of his time was more remarkable and more noble than Booth, 'the General next to God', at once preacher and organiser, inspired idealist and practical opportunist, the man who said 'Why *should* the Devil have all the best tunes?' Originally a revivalist movement amongst the very poor, it soon extended its work to include relief and training centres to help outcast and broken men and women to make a new start in life. No movement in all English history has shown more single-minded devotion to the relief of the poor and suffering.

---

[1] One of the most remarkable Evangelical clergymen of his day was John Newton (1725–1807), best known to us as the author of 'Glorious things of thee are spoken' and other hymns. He was a former captain of a slave-ship who had undergone conversion.

4. THE OXFORD MOVEMENT, THE CATHOLIC REVIVAL, AND THE CHRISTIAN SOCIALISTS

Evangelicalism was the main foundation-stone of Victorian religion. But England saw other important religious movements in the middle 19th century. The most famous of these began in part as a reaction against certain features of Evangelicalism. It was called the Oxford Movement because its leaders were prominent Oxford dons of their day; the three outstanding among them, John Henry Newman, John Keble and Edward Pusey, were all Fellows of Oriel College, Oxford. Their aims, expressed in a series of *Tracts for the Times* (the first of which, written by Newman, appeared in 1833), were to arouse in the Anglican Church a sense of tradition; to stress the fact that the Church of England, though not owing allegiance to the Pope at Rome, remained part of a universal Catholic Church; and to emphasise the church's right and duty to be independent of the state. In the services of the church these Tractarians—as they were sometimes called—attached great importance to ritualism, to the value of the ceremonies handed down from the past. The fascinating and inspiring personality of Newman won many followers among Oxford students, and in its early years the movement spread fast. It secured followers among those of the clergy who felt dissatisfied with 'Low Church' Evangelicalism: and it led to the growth of 'Anglo-Catholicism' and of a 'High Church' party within the Church of England.

But it aroused violent opposition in Victorian England. To the average 19th-century Evangelical its ritualist practices savoured of Roman Catholicism. The Tractarians appeared to many people to be Roman Catholics in all but name, undermining the Anglican Church from within. The most famous and controversial of their writings, *Tract XC*, written by Newman in 1841, set out to prove that there was nothing in the Thirty Nine Articles (which every Anglican clergyman had to accept on ordination) which was contrary to traditional Catholic doctrine. Protestants were outraged by this; and their worst suspicions seemed to be confirmed when in the 1840's a number of members of the Oxford Movement went over to Rome. One of these was Newman, by far the most gifted of the Tractarians, who was received into the Roman Catholic Church in 1845 and who in later years (1879) became a Cardinal. He was one of the most brilliant men of his age, with a personality at once saintly and dominating: the book in which he justified his change of belief, his *Apologia pro Vita Sua*, is a masterpiece of English prose. His departure was a severe blow to the Oxford Movement. Nevertheless its effect continued to be great. It did much to strengthen the clergy, by calling upon them to aim at higher standards of learning and devotion; and in the later years of the 19th century many Anglo-Catholic priests were to be found doing fine work in the slum areas of great cities. On the other hand, the Movement caused deep division within the Anglican Church. Although a growing number of clergy were Anglo-Catholic, the majority of the laity remained firmly Evangelical; and many shared the views of Queen Victoria, who wanted legal action taken against the ritualists. Eventually in 1874 parliament passed a Public Worship Act, under which Anglican clergy who used in their services ritual not authorised by the Prayer Book could be summoned in the courts. A number were prosecuted, and one was actually imprisoned; but the Act was very difficult to enforce; besides, it made martyrs of its victims. The controversy between ritualists and extreme Protestants damaged the Anglican Church by revealing the disunity in its ranks: its embers have continued to smoulder on, bursting into flame from time to time in some local crisis.

The anger generated by the Oxford Movement was sharpened by a contemporary development of Roman Catholicism. The British Roman Catholic community in the 18th century, headed by a few noble families, was a tiny minority except in one or two areas like the Scottish Highlands and parts of Lancashire and Staffordshire. In the early 19th century its numbers were increased by the migration of Irish workmen to Glasgow, Liverpool, and other towns; and by 1840 there were in Great Britain (excluding Ireland) perhaps a quarter of a million Roman Catholics all told. The English Roman Catholics were a notably loyal and quiet community; yet as the Gordon Riots had shown in 1780, anti-Catholic feeling was not difficult to awaken, and there was another less violent outburst of it in 1850 when Pope Pius IX announced a plan to re-establish Roman Catholic archbishoprics and bishoprics in England. There had in fact long been Roman Catholic priests of high rank in England; what was proposed now was merely to create a diocesan system similar to that of the Anglican Church. But there was a considerable outcry in which the Whig Prime Minister (Lord John Russell) and most of the Anglican Bishops took part. An Ecclesiastical Titles Act was passed (1851) which decreed that no other clergy could hold titles already in use by Anglican clergy. Since the Roman Catholics had carefully chosen as their bishoprics places to which no Anglican bishops were attached, the Act was not very much to the point, and it was in fact repealed twenty years later with general approval.

Another development of these middle years of the 19th century was the rise of the group known as the Christian Socialists. Their aim, as the name implies, was to promote social reform by showing that Christianity was a way of life applicable to the industrial society of the 19th century: they had much sympathy with the Chartists, and their interests extended to slum clearance, co-operative experiments and adult schools. The leading Christian Socialists were Charles Kingsley (1819–75), the novelist and historian; Thomas Hughes (1822–96), the author of *Tom Brown's School-days*, who became Principal of the Working Men's College which the group started; and F. D. Maurice (1805–72), the leading spirit in the group. Kingsley and Maurice in particular wrote many pamphlets in the 1850's, and their ideas had much influence among the upper-middle class, although their immediate practical achievement was small.

5. THE DECLINE OF ORGANISED RELIGION

Victorian England, at any rate until its final years, was a deeply religious country. A great number of its people were habitual church or chapel-goers, at least once and probably twice every Sunday; there were large and growing areas in London and other great cities which were exceptions to this statement, yet it was true of the people as a whole, and particularly so in the smaller towns and country villages. Most Victorians, too, had no doubts about the truth of their version of the Christian gospel, whether it was High Church or, as was more likely, Low Church or chapel. The Bible was widely and frequently read by people of every class: so too were such books as John Bunyan's *Pilgrim's Progress*. It was the normal custom in upper and middle class households to begin the day with family prayers. Strict Sunday observance was the rule: for the great majority of Englishmen it was the day on which work was forbidden and pleasure condemned —a day set aside for church-going and Sunday Schools, improving reading (sermons perhaps: certainly not novels, even those of the great contemporary writers like Dickens and Thackeray) and serious thinking. In this the Queen and the Court set a notable example. Nor was this religion superficial, merely a matter of rules and outward observances. There was much about it which later ages have criticised or regarded as mistaken: yet it was real and profound in the daily lives of millions of the Queen's subjects. No doubt it made them self-satisfied and narrow: it also made them confident, energetic and hard-working, and it filled them with an immensely strong sense of duty. And as we have seen, it inspired some of them to outstanding achievements.

Yet towards the end of Queen Victoria's reign (1837–1901) the hold of organised religion upon the English people began to slacken. Many different forces in English life combined to produce this change. To take one element only, church and chapel alike began to find by the 1890's that they could no longer attract such able men as priests and ministers as had been the custom in the past; and the reasons for this were very varied. So far as ordination in the Established Church was concerned, the graduates of the universities were beginning to have a far wider range of careers to choose from, including the growing civil service, and many more opportunities in education, business and scientific work. At the same time the depression in agriculture, which brought wheat prices tumbling down, made a clerical career less attractive, for the stipends of the country clergy depended on tithes and so ultimately on wheat prices. Recruitment to the Nonconformist ministry was challenged in quite a different way: by the growth of the trade unions and the beginnings of the Labour party, which attracted into their ranks as officials or lecturers working class men of ability who earlier would have become Nonconformist preachers.

Yet the main factors in the challenge to religion were two—the growth of scientific doubt, and the pursuit of pleasure. In 1859 Charles Darwin published *The Origin of Species*, in which he maintained that man, far from being separately created, had evolved like other species of living things by a process of natural selection in response to his environment. The book provided a prolonged controversy (in which Darwin himself took no part), because it clearly destroyed the possibility of rational belief in the literal truth of the opening chapters of the Bible. Some scientists went further, maintaining that Darwin's theory proved that Christianity was false: among them was Thomas Henry Huxley (1825–95), who was a writer of great force and influence. A later age found it quite possible to reconcile Darwin's ideas with Christian doctrines. But most churchmen at first condemned the book despite his abundant evidence and their own ignorance. The details of the controversy do not matter here. What is important is that the rise of 'Darwinism' destroyed the certainty and the confidence of Victorian religion. In particular, a growing number of the ablest of the rising generation in the later years of the 19th century ceased to believe in the faith of their fathers.

At about the same time an increased devotion to pleasure led not to positive disbelief but to indifference to religion, which ceased to occupy a central position in men's minds. This took all sorts of forms, and particularly affected church-going and Sunday observance. The growth of Sunday railway excursions; the custom of going away for the 'week-end'; the opening of museums and art galleries on Sundays (from 1896 onwards); the example set by the Prince of Wales (later Edward VII), which was notably different from the severity of the Queen—all these things were signs of change, change which came earlier in the town than in the countryside. By 1900 the habit of church-going was beginning to lose its hold, as investigations made in London suggested. Yet the change was slow, even by 1914. Organised games remained taboo on Sundays; and the great majority of couples still got married in church, not in the registry office. Victorian Evangelicalism remained a powerful force right up to and after the outbreak of the First World War in 1914.

22 Law and Order

I. POLICE

In 1780 the Gordon Riots occurred in London. The government had just lightened the penal laws against Roman Catholics, and by doing so had reawakened in many Englishmen a deep-rooted anti-Catholic prejudice. Lord George Gordon, a half-crazy Scottish nobleman, stirred up London crowds to fury by violent speeches against the Pope; the authorities lost their nerve; and for four days much of the city was at the mercy of a mob. They destroyed Catholic chapels, they looted and burned the houses of Catholics; they threw open the prisons and then set fire to them; they

sacked breweries and distilleries and got drunk on their loot. Eventually
the politician John Wilkes and King George III himself between them
managed to collect sufficient troops to quell the rioters, although it was
nearly a fortnight before order was completely restored. All this, it is to be
observed, took place at a time when Britain was engaged in a desperate war
with her American colonies, with France and with Spain. It was altogether
a remarkable episode.[1] And it throws up in sharp relief one of the most
extraordinary features of British life in the 18th century—the absence of
any really effective means of keeping order.

The 18th century was a rough and disorderly age. Highwaymen terrorised
the roads, especially in lonely areas like Hampstead Heath on the outskirts
of London. Smugglers enjoyed a golden age, with the active approval of
most of the population of the coastal areas. Noblemen fought duels, lesser
mortals fought with bare fists. Crimes of violence were frequent. Local
riots, against food prices or turnpikes or Methodist preachers or election
candidates, were constantly taking place. The London mob, riff-raff from
the slums and dark alleys which occupied much of the city, was always
ready to overturn an unpopular minister's coach and pelt him with filth and
stones. The English had a European reputation as a pugnacious and rowdy
people.

To cope with all this disorder, the authorities had astonishingly few
resources. In the country parishes and smaller market towns there were the
constables and the local watch. The constables, who acted under the control
of the Justices of the Peace, were elected and unpaid; and the task usually
fell to unpopular and unsuitable men, who did their work without enthusiasm and with little success. The watchmen were often old and incompetent, in London as well as elsewhere. Smugglers were dealt with by a host
of revenue officers; small-scale battles between the two were by no means
infrequent, and it was not always the smugglers who lost. In London there
were the Bow Street Runners, started as a police force in 1742 by the blind
magistrate Sir John Fielding. With their scarlet waistcoats they were a
familiar sight to Londoners; but they were not very numerous, they were
poorly paid, and they were only spasmodically efficient; and certainly they
were quite incapable of dealing with any large-scale disturbance. Fielding
also started a mounted police force; and later in the 18th century a group of
merchants organised a marine police on the Thames to protect their
vessels from criminals. There remained the troops. But the British Army
was a small one throughout the 18th century (and throughout the 19th too).
Since Cromwell's Roundheads had governed the land in the 1650's, the
English people had been very hostile to soldiers. The series of wars against
France in the 18th century led to periodic increases in the army: but when
each war ended, Parliament at once cut down the number of troops. In
peace-time such soldiers as there were were scattered on garrison duty.
Moreover, they were very unreliable for the business of keeping order at

[1] There is a lively description of the Gordon Riots in Charles Dickens' novel,
Barnaby Rudge.

home. Pay and conditions in the army were so appallingly bad that few men of character willingly joined up. The ranks contained a high proportion of desperadoes, runaways, adventurers, pressed men, and criminals sent to serve as an alternative to gaol. Such forces could scarcely be relied on to quell rioters.

Upon a land so ill-equipped to check serious disorder there fell the Industrial Revolution and all the social problems that came with it. These provided new temptations to disorder. There were the new machines which it was so easy to break in order to put pressure on employers. There were the pheasants and hares so carefully preserved for their own shooting by the landlords who carried out the enclosures, yet so terribly attractive to the half-starved agricultural labourer. There were the growing industrial cities, with crowds of factory workers flung together in squalid conditions, unplanned, unlit and unpoliced. The French wars after 1793 brought high prices and increased misery: peace in 1815 brought, as we have seen, no improvement in conditions. In 1812 Luddites in the Midlands rose in riots and took hammers to the hated machines; in 1816 the Spa Fields disturbances in London revived memories of the Gordon Riots; in 1820 Arthur Thistlewood and his fellow conspirators of Cato Street plotted to murder the entire Cabinet at once. Somehow the government managed to avoid a serious upheaval, by using the middle class volunteer yeomanry, spies, and—sparingly—the troops. Yet it is scarcely surprising that Lord Sidmouth, who as Home Secretary (1812–22) was the minister directly responsible for maintaining order, was frequently in a state of serious alarm. There was clearly a very urgent need for some more effective method of preserving the peace within the country.

In 1829 that new method arrived. It took shape first in the Metropolitan Police Force, organised by Sir Robert Peel to keep order in London. Peel's step owed something both to his own earlier experience with a constabulary while he was Chief Secretary in Ireland, and to the advice of the Duke of Wellington. The new force, under a Commissioner of Police with headquarters at Scotland Yard, was essentially a civilian one: its members were armed only with wooden truncheons, and at first wore top-hats and blue frock-coats. Most Londoners greeted these 'Peelers' or 'Bobbies' with derision: and there were some who saw in them a new instrument to destroy the liberties of the subject. But they were quickly accepted. From the start it was clear that their primary purpose was to prevent crime. The criminals of London paid a high tribute to their efficiency by migrating in some numbers to the larger provincial towns, which in turn established their own police forces on the Metropolitan model: whereupon many criminals moved on to the smaller towns and to the countryside. These rural areas, ruled by the landowners as J.P.s, were slower to adopt the new system: by 1853 only twenty-two counties had set up police forces to cover the whole of their areas.

It was clearly desirable to cover the entire country with a network of police forces, and essential to secure co-operation between them. So in 1856

Parliament passed an act co-ordinating the work of the various forces, and giving the Home Secretary power to inspect them. It was laid down that grants of money from the Home Office were payable to efficient local police forces. This gave the central government the whip-hand, yet encouraged the local authorities to make their police forces good ones. The County Councils Act of 1888 led to further changes affecting the control of the police. In London—outside the comparatively small area of the old City, which had its own separate force—the Metropolitan Police at Scotland Yard remained under the Commissioner appointed by the Home Office. In the counties under the Police Act of 1890 the police now became the combined responsibility of the County Council and the Justices of the Peace, a joint committee of the two being set up to control them. All boroughs with more than 10,000 inhabitants kept separate police forces, run by the Watch Committees of their councils.

In the course of the 19th century Britain became an orderly country, where riots and disturbances involving any large number of people were rare occurrences, even in the tougher quarters of London and the other large cities. All sorts of causes contributed to this; among them were the Evangelical Movement, the gradual extension of education, and the general rise in the standard of living after 1850. Yet the role of the police was undoubtedly vital. There were occasions when their resources were stretched to the utmost, as for example during the days of the Chartists; or when the government believed it necessary to call in troops, as at Featherstone in Yorkshire during the miners' lock-out of 1893. But it was in these years that the British police force established a reputation for humane and kindly efficiency. Their mere existence did much to prevent crime: and they built up what was on the whole a highly effective system of investigation and arrest. Above all, in city and countryside alike they won the confidence of the community. Thus they came to be regarded not as the agents of a tyrannical government, but as symbols of law and order in a democratic community.

2. LAW COURTS

The English system of law courts was firmly established long before the 18th century.[1] The main central courts in London, King's Bench, Common Pleas, and the Court of Chancery; the Assizes held periodically in the county towns, when the King's judges from the central courts came down to try offenders in their own shires; the jury system used in these courts; the local sessions held by Justices of the Peace, both the Petty Sessions at which they dealt with minor offences and the Quarter Sessions for more serious crimes—these were the principal features of a system whose origins lay in

[1] It should be made clear at this point that this is one of the matters on which Scotland differs most sharply from England. Scottish law and Scottish law courts are quite separate from those of England, and in numerous important ways different. This section of this book does not attempt to deal with them.

the Middle Ages. The 18th century brought no major changes to it. Nevertheless the developments of that century made it quite clear that changes would soon have to be made.

The rise in population called for an increase in the number of courts. The Industrial and Agricultural Revolutions in many ways threw violent strain on the legal system. Crime increased in town and country. The repressive policy of Pitt's government during the French Wars and of Liverpool's government after 1815 brought much more work to the courts: and the use of the courts to stifle political discontent led naturally to much criticism of the whole legal system. The spread of manufacturing or mining towns into the countryside threw heavier burdens on the country justices; and in some places there was a shortage of J.P.s, in part because snobbery forbade the appointment of the new manufacturers to the bench. Moreover, some of the courts were antiquated and slow in their procedure, and had become clogged with work. The worst example of this was the Court of Chancery, where cases dragged on for twenty years or more. At a rather later date Charles Dickens was to pour violent scorn on the courts in several of his novels, especially *Pickwick Papers* and *Bleak House*. Among the abuses he satirised, as well as the monstrous delays, were the fees exacted by corrupt court officials, the unscrupulousness of lawyers, and the in-humanity of the entire system.

In fact, reform had begun even before Dickens wrote. It was based on the ideas of the utilitarian Jeremy Bentham; its practical beginnings owed much to a brilliant but eccentric Scottish lawyer, Henry Brougham (1778–1868), who became Lord Chancellor in 1830. As a Whig M.P. in the 1820's he had persuaded the Tory government to make some minor reforms: now as the official head of the legal system he carried out extensive changes. For his own Court of Chancery he introduced various new rules to accelerate its activity; he got rid of numerous minor officials; he made the procedure of the central courts as a whole simpler; and he created a special new court to deal with cases of bankruptcy. Brougham was Lord Chancellor for four years only, but this short career in office was an important turning-point in the history of the law-courts, beginning a steady improvement in their operation. Further developments in the 19th century included the setting up in 1846 of County Courts, whose chief purpose was to provide a cheap and quick means by which creditors could recover small debts: and an extension of the use of Stipendiary Magistrates to assist the unpaid J.P.s in the cities. The stipendiaries, as their name indicates, were paid magistrates: they had first appeared in London in 1792, and the growth of cities in the 19th century led to their appointment in the provinces, to deal with cases which had become far too numerous for the J.P.s.

A much-needed major reform of the law courts took place in 1873, when Parliament passed the Judicature Act. This reorganised the central courts. It grouped the seven major courts—Queen's Bench, Common Pleas, Exchequer (which dealt with appeals from the first two), Admiralty (for maritime cases), Probate (for disputes arising out of wills), Divorce and

Chancery—into one Supreme Court of Judicature, with headquarters at the newly-built Central Courts in London. At first this Act abolished the old custom of a final appeal to the House of Lords, but three years later this was restored: although as a Court of Appeal the House of Lords consists not of all the peers but of a group of 'law lords' especially created for the purpose. On these lines, with certain detailed changes, the Supreme Court continued to function for nearly a hundred years.

3. THE PENAL CODE AND PRISONS

Another feature of English life in the 18th century upon which foreigners commented critically was the penal code, the list of punishments imposed for breaches of the law. It was notably savage, and by the standards of a later age absurd as well as barbaric. The absence of an effective police force led the authorities to try to deter law-breakers by harsher penalties, even for relatively trivial offences. So by 1800 some two hundred crimes were punishable by death. They included (besides treason, murder, and attempted murder) forgery, horse-stealing, sheep-stealing, picking pockets, stealing five shillings from a shop, damaging Westminster Bridge, and impersonating a Chelsea Pensioner. To impose the capital penalty for trivial offences was simply to tempt the offenders to commit murder if they were caught in the act. In fact, in many cases juries refused to convict: and in many more the death-sentence was never carried out, but was commuted to transportation or other lesser punishment. The law was in practice more humane than it appeared to be. But this, as reformers pointed out, only showed how absurd the penal code was.

Transportation, the most usual alternative to the death penalty, had begun in the 17th century, when prisoners were sent in batches to Barbados and other American colonies to spend a term of years as 'indentured servants' of plantation owners. It provided cheap labour for the colonists, and it was less expensive than maintaining prisons at home. In the later years of the 18th century it became for various reasons more difficult to send convicts to America, and Australia, whose coasts had just been explored by Captain Cook, was used instead. In 1787 the first cargo of prisoners, 717 in all, of whom 183 were women, was sent to Botany Bay;[1] and convicts continued to be transported to New South Wales until 1840 and to Van Diemen's Land (Tasmania) until 1852. Although many of the convicts made good in Australia, transportation was a grim business. Conditions on the long voyage, much of it in the tropics, were so bad that it was not uncommon for one in five to die; in Australia their work was often to clear the bush, toiling in chains in the heat of the southern sun. For most there was little hope of return or of seeing friends and relations again, even when they were sent out only for a limited term of years. Those sentenced for life

---

[1] In fact, the penal settlement was not established in Botany Bay at all; it had been chosen as the site but proved unsuitable, and the settlement was established at Port Jackson, farther north. But the expression 'sent to Botany Bay' stuck.

were liable to the death penalty if they returned to Britain. Many of the victims of this system were poor men and women driven to theft or poaching because their families were starving; others were political reformers, like the young lawyer Thomas Muir and the Unitarian minister Thomas Palmer, two Scottish Radicals sentenced to seven years' transportation in 1793.

A movement for penal reform began early in the 19th century, under the leadership of Sir Samuel Romilly (1757–1818). In 1808 he won his first success, a modest one: in future pickpockets were not to be hanged, but transported for life instead. In 1810 he proposed the abolition of the death penalty for several petty offences, including stealing five shillings from a shop; he was defeated in the House of Lords by a majority which included the Archbishop of Canterbury and six other bishops. He tried again three times in later years, but without avail, even though he pointed out that the law was not in fact carried out. Romilly committed suicide in 1818. The cause of penal reform was taken up by Sir James Mackintosh; and in the 1820's conditions were more favourable. The utilitarian ideas of Jeremy Bentham were gaining acceptance, and it was quite obvious that much of the penal code could not stand up to the question, 'What use is it?' In 1823 Robert Peel, the Home Secretary, got Parliament to pass laws abolishing the death penalty for about one hundred offences. Further progress followed in the 1830's, when, among others, sheep-stealing and house-breaking ceased to be capital crimes. Since 1838 no person has been hanged in Britain except for treason, murder and (only up to 1861) attempted murder. The swing of public opinion, once it had begun, proceeded fast.

The later history of penal reform is closely connected with the development of prisons. In the 18th century these were bad almost beyond belief. They were verminous and insanitary, breeding grounds for the deadly 'gaol fever' (typhus); cramped and overcrowded, with prisoners of every degree of wickedness flung together; and managed by gaolers who made what profit they could out of the necessities of the prisoners. There was no trace of the idea that a prison should reform its inmates; and the great majority in such vile conditions rapidly became degraded and demoralised. It must also be added that people could be imprisoned even for small debts, and that thousands languished for years in notorious gaols like the Fleet in London merely because they could never free themselves from debt. In the later years of the century John Howard (1726–90), a philanthropic Bedfordshire magistrate, devoted his life to making a thorough investigation of Newgate and other English prisons, and to writing an account of what he had seen. This was published in 1777 as *The State of Prisons in England and Wales*, and its appalling revelations shocked public opinion. They were the first shots in a campaign for prison reform. But Howard died in 1790; the French Revolution halted the cause of prison reform as it halted every other progressive movement; and nothing more was done for twenty years.

Then Elizabeth Fry (1780–1845), a Quaker, continued Howard's work.

She began to visit Newgate in 1813, and for the next thirty years she worked tirelessly, aided by Romilly among others, to persuade public opinion of the urgent need to improve conditions in prisons and convict ships. Her energies did much to secure many minor reforms, carried through by Peel as Home Secretary. Prisons were to be regularly inspected and reported on to the Home Office; prisoners were to be graded for work, and visited by the prison chaplain and surgeon; gaolers were to be paid, instead of depending on fees from the prisoners; and women prisoners were in future to be in the care of women warders. Unfortunately these steps applied neither to debtors' prisons nor to the gaols in many small towns; nevertheless, they were a real beginning. It was equally important that Elizabeth Fry, as well as stimulating particular reforms, tried with success to introduce a new spirit of humanity into English prisons.

Yet improvement in the 19th century was slow. One real advance was the gradual abolition of imprisonment for debt, completed in 1869. In the 1830's rules were introduced requiring prisoners to have separate cells; some effort was made to give them useful work to do; they were encouraged to read, and permitted to talk while working together. Yet there was little real attempt to make prisons reformative. The final abolition of transportation in the 1850's increased the prison population in Britain; and in 1877 the Home Office at last accepted responsibility for the control of all the prisons in the country, setting up the Prison Commission for the purpose. Towards the end of the 19th century public opinion turned again to the question of prison reform, especially in connection with the treatment of young prisoners and first offenders; and the Liberal governments from 1906 passed several measures of first-rate importance. In 1907 the Probation of Offenders Act began the system of putting first offenders on probation, which stopped many young people from entering what might so easily have turned into a lifetime's career of crime. In 1908, the year in which the imprisonment of children was at last stopped, the Borstal System was introduced, as well as 'preventive detention' for older and more hardened criminals. Finally in 1914 the Criminal Justice Administration Act compelled magistrates to grant sufficient time for the payment of fines; this was economical as well as merciful, for it reduced the prison population.

23 The Emancipation of Women

In the middle of the 20th century we take it for granted that women are citizens and members of the community on equal terms with men. In general they enjoy the same rights as men. They vote in elections, they become members of Parliament; they own property; they occupy important posts in the civil service and in business. Millions of women earn their own living in a wide range of jobs—as barristers, secretaries and engineers, doctors and film stars, bus drivers and nuclear scientists; in the armed forces, on the land, at factory benches; as nurses, typists, authors, police-women, teachers, shop assistants—the list is endless, demonstrating that a woman's place is no longer merely the home, whatever it may have been in the past. Some women are aviators and others swim the Channel, great numbers play tennis and hockey and cricket, others run in cross-country races or play bowls: this merely brings in pleasure to strengthen the argument from business. It is no doubt true that there are certain pursuits into which for obvious reasons women have not followed men: women Rugby footballers and women stokers are fortunately rare. It is also true that for other reasons there are certain occupations into which women have not been admitted: they may not, for example, take Holy Orders in the Church of England. There is a wide range of employments in which it is not yet possible for women to earn as much as men, even where they may be doing work of the same standard. This has led to the growth of a campaign by women for 'equal pay for equal work'. Nevertheless it remains broadly true that women as members of the community are in most respects on equal terms with men.

Now this state of affairs is a comparatively new one in English history. The name given to the process by which it has come about is the phrase 'the emancipation of women'; and this emancipation, this setting free of women from masculine control, has for practical purposes taken place only within the last hundred years or so. Its main features up to 1914, together with some consideration of the situation before it began, are the subject-matter of this chapter.

1. WOMEN IN THE 18TH AND EARLY 19TH CENTURIES

The 18th and the early 19th centuries were a period of almost unchallenged masculine supremacy, during which women were in many ways treated as inferior creatures. Their rights were limited. They had no vote and they took no part in government, except of course when a woman was the monarch: and it is interesting to note that Queen Victoria, who reigned from 1837 to 1901, believed firmly, though rather illogically, that a woman's place was the home, and opposed the grant of political rights to her own sex. Their right to own property was limited. When a woman married all her possessions became legally the property of her husband, as did anything she inherited after marriage, and any money which she earned. The husband was master of the home: his word was law. The functions of women were to bear children, to bring them up, and to manage the household. They had little real independence, and were normally the more or less willing slaves of their husbands. It was the duty of women to be dependent and submissive. There were of course notable exceptions, women of ability and determination who asserted their independence in various ways: most of these were unmarried women of the well-to-do classes. There were travellers like

Celia Fiennes who recorded her impressions of English life about 1700; or like Lady Mary Wortley Montagu, who travelled in the Near East during the 18th century and among other things took the courageous step of getting herself inoculated in Turkey against smallpox. There were writers like Jane Austen (1775–1817), whose novels (including *Pride and Prejudice*, *Sense and Sensibility*, and *Emma*) describe the lives of the upper middle class at the time of the Napoleonic War, and Fanny Burney (1752–1845), the author of *Evelina*. There were pious women like the Evangelical Hannah More (1745–1833), 'the old Bishop in petticoats', as William Cobbett called her, who founded village schools in Somerset and wrote popular tracts and improving novels to encourage the poor to behave themselves in that station in life in which providence had placed them. Then too there were women who won rare distinction in some particular occupation, like Mrs. Sarah Siddons, the brilliant 18th-century actress. But such women were exceptions to the general rule of the age. Man was dominant in English life.

Upper class women of the 18th century lived lives of considerable luxury and idleness; for domestic servants were cheap and plentiful. They enjoyed the fine new Georgian houses which were being built in great numbers in town and country alike. They visited Bath, Cheltenham, Tunbridge Wells and other fashionable spas: they drank coffee and tea, they danced, they played cards, they gossiped. Their successors, the wives and daughters of the wealthy Victorian merchants and manufacturers, enjoyed at least as much solid material comfort, for the industrial changes had brought many improvements in everyday life, and domestic servants were even more plentiful. Yet the Evangelical Revival had changed standards, and so there was less gambling and less frivolous idleness. In their place had come regular churchgoing and good works, and time rather consciously spent in 'useful' activities like embroidery and needlework. Neither in the 18th century nor in the early 19th was there much serious attempt to give the girls of the well-to-do any very deep education, apart of course from exceptional households. Generally they were brought up at home, often in the charge of governesses. They learned to read, so that they might be able to read aloud to their fathers in later years; to sew, to knit, to embroider; and often additional 'accomplishments' like playing the piano, painting in water-colours, or perhaps a little elementary French. Serious intellectual study was rare, as was anything which might fit them for employment. For their first duty was to get married, and their education was designed only to enable them to win a husband. If they failed in this, they remained utterly dependent on their fathers or other male relatives. If, as not infrequently happened, poverty compelled them to try to earn a living for themselves, the conventions of the time drove them to become governesses; in this overcrowded occupation they starved in genteel poverty, the victims of unending humiliation and with little security against illness and old age.

But the majority of women belonged to the working class, and for them there was no life of comfort and ease, nor any conventional ban on going out to earn a living. They had to carry a double burden: they bore and brought up children, and contributed to the family income as well. In the days of domestic industry women and girls worked at the spinning wheel in the cottage while the men wove on the hand-loom. When the factories came, a high proportion of their workers were women. They worked on the land, digging, reaping and milking. Until 1842 many worked in coal-mines in some areas, hauling coaltrucks and carrying heavy sacks of coal to the surface. Around Birmingham much of the work in the various metal industries, the manufacture of pins, nails, buttons and the like was done by women and girls. In the trades that catered especially for the fashionable classes—millinery, laundry-work, lace-making, hairdressing, glove-making and above all dress-making—women did much of the work: and in many of these trades, carried on not in factories but in attics and cellars, hours were notoriously long and conditions deplorably bad. And then there were the hordes of domestic servants—in 1841 over 700,000 of them, six times as many as in any other single form of women's employment. Here indeed was a startling contrast to the lot of well-to-do women. Here among the working class, women were certainly employed outside their homes; but it was undoubtedly not employment of a kind that indicated emancipation.

2. THE CHALLENGE TO MALE SUPREMACY: THE EDUCATION OF WOMEN

Until the middle years of the 19th century there was little protest about the plight in which women found themselves, and little attempt to alter the situation. In 1792 Mary Wollstonecraft wrote a *Vindication of the Rights of Women*, in an attempt to 'restore to them their lost dignity'. She demanded that women of the middle class should be permitted to earn their living and thus win their independence, and that women should be educated in a way that would give their abilities a chance equal to that customarily enjoyed by men. But she was far in advance of her time, and she preached to ears made deaf to reform by the thunder of the French Revolution. Not for another fifty years was any real step taken towards general emancipation, although there continued to be numerous individual examples of feminine achievement. The work of Elizabeth Fry in prison reform has already been noted.[1] A little later came Mary Carpenter (1807–77), a pioneer in the Ragged School Movement and the founder of the first reformatory school for girls. The 1840's and 1850's saw a group of distinguished women novelists at work: Emily Brontë published *Wuthering Heights* and her sister Charlotte published *Jane Eyre* in the same year, 1847, and George Eliot[2] wrote *Adam Bede* in 1859. At this time, too, Florence Nightingale (1820–1910), the daughter of a prosperous middle-class family, rebelled against the conventions which would have condemned her immense abilities and formidable

[1] See above, pp. 227–8.
[2] The pen name of a woman: Mary Ann Evans.

energy to waste in an empty routine of visits and gossip. She insisted upon taking up as a career nursing, then the occupation of unskilled and disreputable women: and in 1854 led her famous band of nurses to the Crimea. Her work and example did much to make nursing a great profession, and she gave much of her long life to the reorganisation of hospital conditions and to the reform of public health. Yet she was an individualist, not particularly interested in women's emancipation in general. A later little came Octavia Hill (1838–1912), pioneer in creating housing estates for the poor, member of the Poor Law Commission of 1905–9, and vigorous champion of the movement to preserve the countryside which led in 1895 to the foundation of the National Trust.

But emancipation in fact came not so much through the work of outstanding women in varied fields of activity, as by the development of education which enabled a large number of ordinary women to emancipate themselves. The pioneering work in secondary and higher education for girls took place after 1840. In 1848 two of the Christian Socialists, F. D. Maurice and Charles Kingsley, took the lead in the foundation of Queen's College, London, as a training college for women teachers: and two of its students, Frances Mary Buss (Headmistress in 1850 of what later became the North London Collegiate School) and Dorothea Beale (Principal of Cheltenham Ladies' College in 1858), set standards for a notable improvement in girls' schools. There arose a demand for the admission of women as students at universities, and in 1846 Bedford College for Women began its career as the first centre of higher education for women in England. In the north of England during the 1860's university extension lectures for women were started in large cities. In 1869 Emily Davies, who had fought to get the older universities to open their doors to women, opened a small hall of residence at Hitchin, twenty-six miles from Cambridge: in 1873 it was transferred to Girton, a village two miles from Cambridge, and became Girton College. The second of the Cambridge women's colleges, Newnham, was opened in 1876: and within the next twenty years a group of women's colleges were opened at Oxford. The colleges were successful from the start, even though they worked under considerable restrictions of various kinds. The numbers of students were limited; although they were allowed to attend lectures and to sit for examinations, they were not admitted as full members of either university until after the First World War. Moreover, in their early years the students were carefully guarded from the perils of life in university towns, with chaperones accompanying them on shopping expeditions and even to lectures. Nevertheless, it was a major achievement to have entered the citadels of higher education in the older universities. London and the newer provincial universities were from the first much more liberal in their attitude towards women students.

So far as girls' schools were concerned, improvement was a slow process, in which university-trained teachers played an important part. The Taunton Commission was very critical indeed both of the number of girls' secondary schools and of what was taught in them. In 1871 the Girls'

Public Day Schools Trust was formed and began to found good-quality day schools for girls throughout the country, modelled on that of Miss Buss in North London: and schools of this type set the standard for those established in the 20th century after the Balfour Act. Schools built under this Act did much to overcome the shortage of places for girls in secondary education: and from about 1910 onwards grammar school education was over the country as a whole as readily available to girls as to boys, although there were often serious variations between one area and another. In general the curriculum in these schools tended to follow rather slavishly that in use in boys' grammar schools, with the addition in later years of such subjects as domestic science.

3. THE RIGHT TO VOTE AND OTHER FEATURES OF EMANCIPATION

The agitation for 'votes for women' may be said to have started in 1851, when Harriet Taylor, the wife of the Radical philosopher John Stuart Mill, wrote an article in the *Westminster Review* demanding that the right to vote should be given to women. Mill himself, who was elected as M.P. for Westminster in 1865, was a whole-hearted champion of the cause, and in 1867, during the debates on the Second Reform Act, he introduced a motion for female suffrage. It was defeated by 196 votes to 73: and later proposals by others were no more successful. A long struggle lay ahead. The proposal cut across normal party lines, and it had to overcome a firm Victorian belief that politics were not women's business. Meanwhile women did in fact win various minor political rights during the half-century after Mill's first proposal. For example, the Education Act of 1870 permitted women ratepayers to vote for and be members of School Boards; from 1888 they had the right to vote in County and County Borough Council elections, and from 1907 to be elected to those bodies.

In 1897 the National Union of Women's Suffrage Societies united various organisations trying to get 'votes for women'. Its members, called 'Suffragists', were peaceful in their methods. But the foundation in Manchester in 1903 of the Women's Social and Political Union began a new phase, starting what became known as the 'Suffragette' movement. Its most famous leaders were Mrs. Emmeline Pankhurst and her daughter Christabel, who got a good deal of support from the Independent Labour party. They began with a policy of nuisance tactics, directed principally after 1906 against the Liberal government. They heckled the speeches of Cabinet Ministers; they broke windows and set fire to pillar-boxes in order to be imprisoned and so draw attention to their cause; they chained themselves to railings in Downing Street. This was very embarrassing to the government; so, too, was the behaviour of those imprisoned suffragettes who, from 1909 onwards, went on hunger strike in prison and had to be forcibly fed, which brought much sympathy for the women. These tactics led ultimately to the passing, in 1913, of the 'Cat and Mouse' Act, which empowered the government to release hunger-strikers from goal and then to re-arrest them when it wished. Meanwhile the movement had become even more militant under the inspiration of Christabel Pankhurst, who withdrew to Paris and organised from there a new campaign of violence. This included the deliberate burning down of railway stations, schools and country houses, the slashing of priceless pictures in art galleries and the cutting of telephone wires. This did more harm than good to their cause; it shocked public opinion, and at the same time split the Suffragette Movement itself, causing the more moderate elements to break away from the Pankhursts. The Suffragette Movement was an exciting feature of Edwardian life, especially in London; it led to several extraordinary episodes, including the tragic one of the young woman who was killed when she threw herself under the King's horse while it was racing in the Derby at Epsom; and it called for great courage from its members, many of whom gave up easy and comfortable lives in pursuit of the cause. But it did not achieve votes for women. What did in fact bring them about was the part played by women in the First World War. In 1918 the Representation of the People Act gave the right to vote to all women over thirty. Another act of the same year enabled women to become members of the House of Commons.[1] Ten years later a further parliamentary reform act gave the right to vote to all women over twenty-one (the 'flapper vote'), thus giving women the same electoral rights as men.

Parallel with this process of winning political rights went the development of other forms of emancipation. These were very various and numerous in the course of a century, and it is only possible here to suggest some of the more interesting of them. One which in late Victorian England marked almost a social revolution on its own was the process whereby women came to own property on the same terms as men. After a good deal of agitation this was carried out in three Married Women's Property Acts of 1870, 1882 (the most important) and 1893. The total effect of these was to give married women full legal control of all the property of every kind which they owned at marriage or which they acquired after marriage either by inheritance or by their own earnings. It put an end to those abductions and forcible marriages of heiresses by scoundrels which were by no means unknown in early Victorian England and were a favourite theme of romantic fiction: it also gave women a legal status and a sense of security as well as of equality which they had hitherto not possessed. This particular change benefited upper and middle class women. Others were shared in by women of every class.

The most notable of them concerned the employment of women, and the range of occupations which opened to them. They gained, for example, admission to the medical and legal professions, and an increasing number came to take high place in the universities. The governesses declined in

---

[1] The first woman to take her seat at Westminster was the American, Lady Astor, elected for Plymouth in 1919.

number, but were more than replaced by the many thousands who went to teach in the new elementary schools. Nursing, now made respectable by the example of Florence Nightingale, and looked upon as far more important in an age which was increasingly conscious of public health, attracted many more recruits. Domestic servants were still very plentiful until the First World War: there were almost a million and a half of them in 1911, although later years were to bring a sharp decline. In the metal industries where they had been numerous, women workers either disappeared or the nature of their work was transformed by the coming of new types of machinery. Increasing numbers of women were employed from the beginning of the 20th century in two quite new forms of manufacture—the electrical industries, and cycle and motor works. Yet the most marked development of all was in commerce and in office work. A great increase in the number of retail shops in the later years of the 19th century brought a swift expansion of the number of women employed as shop assistants. Contemporary with this, and largely dependent on the invention of the typewriter (which began to come into general use in England in the 1880's), was a similar rise in the number of girls employed as clerks, typists, book-keepers and secretaries.

Such changes were in themselves a gigantic emancipation for many millions of women, giving them a new sense of independence and taking them out into the world in ways which their mothers and grandmothers had never known. Inevitably they transformed social life and customs, freeing women from Victorian restrictions. Other forces worked in the same direction. Thus the gradual spread in the 20th century of labour-saving devices in the home, especially those made possible by the use of electricity, freed many married women from some of the drudgery of domestic chores: the decline in the size of families, which began in the 1870's, also eased this burden. The whole process is symbolised by the contrast between the clothes worn by Victorian women and the fashions of the 20th century. The crinolines, the bustles, the steel and whalebone corsets, the trailing skirts, the 'leg of mutton' sleeves, the thick petticoats—all these Victorian items fell out of favour. Lawn tennis, which came in the 1870's, and cycling, which first became fashionable in the 1890's, did much to alter women's dress, making it simpler and healthier. Other factors continued the process after 1900—among them the annual seaside holiday, the coming of motor-ing, the increased concern for health, the belief in fresh air and, perhaps most influential of all, the growth of mass production in clothes and the habit of buying ready-made goods. The result has been the frocks and simple costumes, the slacks and jeans, of present-day women, outward signs of a century of emancipation[1].

[1] See also below, pp. 240, 263, 267, 305.

24 The First World War 1914-18

On 4 August 1914, Great Britain declared war on Germany. So began for the British people the First World War. What started as a conflict between two rival groups of European great powers spread swiftly until it involved most countries upon earth. Millions of men fought and killed one another in Flanders and East Prussia and the Italian Alps, Gallipoli and Mesopotamia and East Africa, on and beneath the surface of the seas and in the air. The conflict lasted for four terrible years until the armistice of 11 November, 1918; and for all that time it absorbed and concentrated the energies of the British nation, in a way that no previous war, not even the long struggle against Revolutionary and Napoleonic France, had ever come near to doing. Over six million men served in the British armed forces; nearly one million of these—three-quarters of them from the United Kingdom—sacrificed their lives. Military conscription, direction of labour into war factories, government management of industries and control of prices, food rationing, censorship of the press—all these things came to be accepted in order to win the war. To those who lived through the war, it seemed that the whole community had for four years turned away from the normal pattern of its life.

This book is not concerned with the battles or with the diplomacy. Nor of course can anyone attempt to measure the real cost of the war to the generation that endured it; for there were few families in the land that did not lose one of their members in the holocaust. The purposes of this chapter are more limited. They are to describe the main changes which the course of the war brought to British economic life, in trade, industry, agriculture, and finance; to show how it altered the social life of the British people between 1914 and 1918; and to suggest a few of the principal ways in which it affected the future of Great Britain, especially in economic affairs.

I. THE WAR AND BRITISH ECONOMIC AFFAIRS

In 1914 the economic life of Britain was more vulnerable to a world-wide war than that of any other country. Her survival as well as her prosperity depended on overseas trade; among the nations she was the international trader *par excellence*. She was by 1914 a predominantly industrial country: and the biggest of her industries were those whose products were exported all over the globe—coal-mining, textiles (especially cotton), iron and steel, heavy engineering, shipbuilding, the great staple industries on which her Victorian prosperity had been built. These and other British industries relied very heavily on raw materials from overseas; all the cotton, most of the wool, much of the metals and the timber, was imported. Moreover, some two-thirds of all her food—most of the wheat, the butter, the meat, the sugar, all the tea, an increasing proportion of the fruit—had to be bought and shipped from abroad. She had for many years imported more goods than she had exported. The balance of trade had been tilted in her favour by the 'invisible exports'; mainly by the earnings of her merchant navy, which in 1913 amounted to 39 per cent of the world's total, and by the interest on her overseas investment, which in that year yielded £200,000,000. Both these huge assets, shipping and overseas investment, were immediately imperilled by the outbreak of a world war.

Shipping was directly attacked by the Germans from the start, first by surface-raiders and then by a ruthless submarine campaign. The U-boats (submarines) represented an up-to-date version of the Continental System of a century before; their aim, unlike that of Napoleon, was to starve Britain out, and at one time in 1917 they were within six weeks of success. Losses of merchantmen were appallingly severe, totalling during the war over 8,000,000 tons. The prior demands of the navy and the shortages of man-power and of steel made it desperately difficult to build replacements; and the tonnage of the British merchant fleet in 1919 was 14 per cent less than it had been at the outbreak of war. Great Britain for her part used her naval supremacy to drive German merchantmen off the seas, and to impose a blockade upon Germany and her allies. The Orders-in-Council had been a retaliation to Napoleon's Continental System; but the British blockade in the First World War preceded the German use of the submarine, and grew tighter as the war went on. The term 'contraband' at first included only goods directly helpful to the German war effort; by 1917 it had come to cover food, in a calculated attempt to starve the enemy out; and undoubtedly the blockade contributed considerably to the Allied victory.

Such interference with shipping indicates only the most brutal way in which the war was bound to disrupt overseas trade and thus affect British industries. There were many others, besides the obvious fact that trade with Germany, one of Britain's biggest customers before the war, was now at an end. So, virtually, was Britain's export trade in coal to Europe, which had grown rapidly since about 1870; and most of Britain's trade with Russia. When the toll taken by the U-boats was mounting, the government established a rigid system of priorities and controls (including import duties) in order to make the best use of shipping space; and this struck severely, for example, at the timber trade. Among the major industries cotton was hardest hit; it depended wholly on an imported raw material, and cotton goods were not in such demand for military needs as woollen ones. The newly-established motor-car industry which had just started a flourishing export trade was checked; its factories were turned over to the manufacture of shells and aero-engines, while the government imported vehicles from the United States.

By contrast, some British industries flourished greatly. Iron and steel was one of these, and Britain's capacity for steel production in particular rose by over 50 per cent. Nearly all the metal industries prospered; while engineering, the key to the mass output of munitions in the twentieth century, expanded vastly. Shipbuilding and coal-mining were kept at full stretch, despite shortages of skilled man-power. Yet coal production fell below the level reached in 1913; and even in 1918, after prodigious efforts, the output of British shipyards was 600,000 tons lower than that of 1913. The oldest of all industries, agriculture, enjoyed a brief period of prosperity. The government slashed imports of foodstuffs and encouraged home production; farmers were given guaranteed prices for crops, and exhorted (and paid) to grow more wheat, potatoes, and sugar-beet; and farm labourers at last obtained a fixed minimum wage.

Finance was necessarily a major problem. The cost of the war was immense. In the year 1913–14 the government had spent £197,000,000; in 1917–18 it spent £2,696,000,000—well over thirteen times as much. Even though prices rose considerably during the war, and the pound therefore fell in value, the real increase in government expenditure was gigantic. Taxes rose steeply; income tax, for example, went up from 1s. 8d. in the £ in 1914 to 6s. by 1918. Under a greatly-stimulated National Savings movement huge 'War Loans' were raised. On the other hand, some of Britain's overseas investment was liquidated in order to pay for munitions and other imports from overseas, especially from the United States. And Britain borrowed heavily from American sources: this was to lead to post-war trouble over War Debts. In fact, Britain lent more—by some £485 millions —to her allies than she borrowed. The sum was covered by the sale of securities: that is, Britain paid her way in the First World War, fighting it out of her own financial resources.

All these things involved radical changes in the pattern of British economic life. Perhaps the most important change of all, with the greatest future consequences, was one which necessarily came to embrace all the others— namely an extraordinary increase of government control of economic affairs. Ten new ministries and 160 new boards and commissions of various kinds were set up. This development proved essential in order to make the most effective use both of materials and of man-power. It did not come about suddenly in 1914; control was gradually extended as it became evident that the war was not going to be a short one. In 1915 the Defence of the Realm Act gave the government authority to take over factories, as well as wide powers to interfere with the daily life of everybody in the land; a desperate shortage of shells led to the creation of a Ministry of Munitions with special powers; and the government took over railways and coal-mines. Yet the event which caused a swift and thorough-going extension of government action was a grave shipping crisis in 1917, resulting from intensified U-boat activity. This brought direct Admiralty control of the shipbuilding industry, and led also to virtual control of many other industries. Such control was exercised in various ways; one example was the Cotton Control Board, which included representatives of the employers, the trade unions, and the government, and which fixed a maximum percentage of machinery to be worked in each mill, thus rationing the limited amount of cotton available.

2. LIFE AND LABOUR DURING THE WAR

Great Britain was in one way far more fortunate than most of the other major powers involved in the First World War. Her people saw no fighting on their own soil. Several east coast towns, like Whitby and Scarborough, were bombarded by German naval units. Air raids were an unpleasant novelty, first by great airships, the Zeppelins, and later by aeroplanes; most of the damage was done in London, and 1,400 persons were killed. But Britain endured none of the havoc which the war brought to the towns of northern France or Russia; the homeless refugees her people saw were not English folk but exiles from occupied Belgium. None the less, war brought many changes to the pattern of English life, some lasting only 'for the duration', others to be permanent.

The most revolutionary single change was the temporary introduction of military conscription. When the war began volunteers poured into the recruiting offices for many months. As the struggle stretched on and became more destructive, however, so man-power became the scarcest of all commodities. This point was cruelly emphasised by the ghastly slaughter of the Battle of the Somme in 1916, when British losses on the first day alone were 60,000: and in that year conscription was introduced, first for single and later for married men. By the end of the fighting the age-limit for compulsory military service had risen to fifty. Special tribunals were set up to deal with cases of hardship, and with those who objected to military service on grounds of conscience. There were some 16,000 conscientious objectors, an appreciable number of them members of the Society of Friends (Quakers), and many of them went to prison for their beliefs, although most accepted some kind of alternative service, for example on the land or on ambulance or relief work.

In the mines and munition factories there was something very like industrial conscription. A good many workers were directed to particular sorts of employment, and many others, notably of course skilled men, were 'reserved' from military call-up on condition that they remained in their jobs. Besides direction of labour, there was also a good deal of 'dilution' of labour—the employment in factories of large numbers of unskilled people, especially women. Neither 'direction' nor 'dilution' was liked by trade unionists; and dilution, which lowered wages, caused unrest in industry. In 1915 there were strikes on Clydeside and in South Wales (though far fewer working hours were lost than in the immediate pre-war or post-war years). Discontent came also from the failure to take effective action against profiteers, manufacturers and merchants who made fat profits out of shortages of goods; and from the fact that wages, despite their growth, did not keep pace with prices. Trade Unions expanded greatly; membership rose from some 4,000,000 in 1913 to some 8,000,000 in 1919. Shop stewards, hitherto not particularly important union officials, became prominent as mouthpieces of the workers' grievances. In the later stages of the war a considerable anti-war movement developed in some industrial areas; it was particularly strong on Clydeside.

Women took the places of men in a vast range of jobs. Factory work—often dangerous work, like the filling of shells—was only one example. They were to be found in increasing numbers as tram-conductors, railway porters, shop assistants, sweeps, bakers, postal officials; for the farms a special Land Army was formed which enrolled 18,000 members; and 150,000 women joined the armed forces. In face of these activities it was no longer possible to deny women the vote. The masculine prejudice against which the suffragettes had fought in vain only a few years earlier had to yield now. In 1918 Parliament (the same Parliament which had rejected 'votes for women' before the war) passed the Representation of the People Act which, besides giving the right to vote to all men over twenty-one,[1] enfranchised women for the first time in British history. Not all women got the vote; women voters had to be over thirty, and either the woman voter or her husband had to own or occupy property of an annual value of at least £5.

Food supplies remained on the whole adequate in amount. Even after two years of war the government was saying 'we want to avoid any rationing of our people in food'; and not until 1917, when the effects of the submarine campaign compelled action, was anything done to ensure fair distribution throughout the community. Then sugar was rationed; meat, fats, and other foods followed in 1918. Nor were the government's efforts to control prices successful, and by the end of the war these were 133 per cent greater than in 1914. So poorer people suffered real hardships. The quality of foodstuffs declined appreciably. 'Standard' bread was introduced in 1916; it contained soya and potato flour as well as wheat, and became dirty grey in colour. Margarine, not always very tasty, took the place of butter for most people on most occasions; jams of dubious content sold much better than in normal times; the consumption of potatoes rose sharply. Nobody went hungry. But there was probably an increase in rickets, caused by a deficiency of vitamin D.

Finally, one wartime change of a peculiar kind deserves special mention. This was the introduction in 1916 of Summer Time, with its 'extra hour' of daylight, a reform long advocated by William Willett. Its adoption was a sign that time, like manpower and materials, was a scarce commodity in those desperate days.

3. THE ECONOMIC LEGACY OF THE WAR

The First World War left Britain with many serious economic problems to face. Some of these were obvious and immediate. The men in the forces had to be demobilised and returned to civilian employment; the munition factories closed down and their workers transferred to peace-time jobs. These were big tasks. Others were more complicated. The coal industry was in dire need of reorganisation; during the war it had little new equipment,

---

[1] Except peers of the realm, lunatics, convicts serving a term of imprisonment, and—for five years after 1918 only—conscientious objectors.

and coal had been hewn from the most accessible seams without thought for future development. Railways too had been starved of new equipment. The building of houses had virtually stopped during the war, and it was reckoned that some 800,000 new ones were needed. Here was a second series of problems, stretching farther ahead into the future than the first.

And beyond these lay a third set, more serious and more difficult to assess than the other two. The war had done no direct damage to British industry; the factories and the pits, unlike those of Belgium or of the Ukraine, were unscathed by shells and bombs. What it had destroyed or cut off were many of the markets to which Britain had formerly sold her goods. In 1919 British exports were 35 per cent (in volume) less than they had been in 1913. How were the old markets to be recaptured? Would India and Japan, for example, want to buy cottons from Lancashire in the quantities they had done before 1914, now that Indians were building their own mills and the Japanese selling their own cotton products throughout the Far East? Would South American countries, now buying goods from the United States, come back to the British firms they dealt with in pre-war days? Would European countries ever again want to import millions of tons of British coal? Would they not prefer to go on developing alternative sources of power at home, as they had been driven to do during the war? Would British shipping lines recover that appreciable proportion of the world's carrying trade which they had lost? On the answers to such questions would depend the livelihood of millions of people in the British Isles. Another important source of livelihood had gone, at least temporarily. A substantial proportion of British overseas investment had been swallowed up in paying for armaments. It was an open question whether she would ever be able to regain her position as a great supplier of capital to newly-developing lands.

Debt indeed was a most important element in the economic legacy of the war. At its end the interest on the National Debt was running at some £326,000,000 per annum; this internal debt would have to be paid out of taxation, and so was a continuing burden on trade and industry (even if the fall in the value of the pound made it a less real burden than it seemed). Overseas, Britain had lent about £1,825 million to her allies, and had borrowed about £1,340 million. To the United States Britain owed War Debts of some £850,000,000. For most Englishmen, this question was tied up with that of Reparations—the great sums, originally fixed at £6,600,000,000, which the victorious Allies insisted that the Germans should pay them in compensation for the damage caused by the war. The British view was that their payment of War Debts was conditional on the German settlement of Reparations; the American, that the two matters were entirely separate, and that War Debts must be paid in full whatever the Germans did. This problem hung like a shadow over international trade after 1919, threatening the flooding of the British market by German goods sent in settlement of Reparations, and hindering the efforts of British manufacturers to sell their wares in the United States.

This legacy of economic difficulty might not have been so formidable had it come at a different time. The First World War occurred at an unfortunate stage in Britain's economic development. As we have seen,[1] British economic supremacy had, from about 1870 onwards, been challenged by Germany and the United States. British supremacy in iron and steel had been lost. In many new industries as, for example, the electrical and the motor-car industries, other countries had made a better start than Britain. The British export trade had been changing to face a new situation; coal, machinery and shipping were becoming more important items. Although in 1914 Britain as a whole was still rich and prosperous, and in certain spheres, like shipbuilding and the mercantile marine, well ahead of her competitors, she was entering a period when she would in any event have had to readjust her economic affairs. The war made the readjustment infinitely more difficult. It greatly accelerated the process—which had already started before 1914—by which other countries began to manufacture for themselves goods which they had previously bought from Britain. The situation was scarcely improved by the fact that not infrequently the machines which made the goods, and the coal which drove them, themselves came from Britain.

4. RECONSTRUCTION

During the war there was much talk of building 'a fit country for heroes to live in', as Lloyd George put it. In fact little was done in the war years to lay foundations for a better society. Men were too preoccupied with the overwhelming task of winning the war, and in its later stages too weary; and Britain's mood at the armistice was one of exhaustion rather than of hope. Such idealism as there was after victory was dedicated not to home affairs but to international relations, to the creation of the League of Nations.

Since 1916 David Lloyd George had been Prime Minister at the head of a coalition government—a coalition most of whose members were Conservatives; and this government had in 1917 created a Ministry of Reconstruction with Dr. Christopher Addison at its head. This Ministry had set up committees and issued reports on innumerable subjects such as health, housing, education, and local government. But nothing much came of them. There was no blueprint for a new Britain; instead, there were a few isolated pieces of legislation. One was the Representation of the People Act (1918), already mentioned[2]. Another was an Education Act (1918), called the Fisher Act after the then President of the Board of Education, the Oxford historian H. A. L. Fisher. This increased the powers of the Board of Education (and the money it could give to Local Education Authorities), raised the school-leaving age to 14, and started a system of day-continuation schools which youths between the ages of 14 and 16 could be compelled to attend for at least one day a week. Finally, there were two

[1] Above, chapter 14, especially pp. 113–15.
[2] Above, p. 234.

attempts to improve relations in industry. In 1917 the Whitley Committee recommended the creation of Joint Industrial Councils representing both employers and workers; most industries rejected these Whitley Councils, and the most successful ones were those which negotiated agreements about wages and hours for the employees of the government and local councils. The Trade Boards Act of 1918 was on lines similar to those of the earlier act of 1909.[1] It authorised the establishment of Trade Boards, representing employers and employed and containing independent members, to fix wages in industries which had no satisfactory negotiating machinery; and by 1912 such boards had been set up in some forty trades employing 1,500,000 workers.

Three days after the armistice Lloyd George announced his intention of holding a general election, the first since 1910, one month later. This frank use of victory to secure political power at home was highly successful for him and for his supporters. He and Bonar Law, the Conservative leader, commended Coalition candidates in a letter to the electors; those who got this 'coupon', as the Liberal leader Asquith nicknamed the letter, thus shared in Lloyd George's prestige as the architect of victory, and they won a handsome victory at the polls, capturing 484 seats. Stanley Baldwin, in a famous phrase quoted by the economist John Maynard Keynes, described many of these members as 'hard-faced men who looked as if they had done well out of the war'. This may have been less than fair to them. Yet they were certainly not idealists dreaming visions of a brave new world. They looked back rather than forward, and preferred security to visions. 338 of the 484 were Conservatives, and for all but three of the years between 1918 and 1939 Britain had governments in which the Conservatives were supreme.

This 'Coupon Election' of 1918 was a turning-point in one other respect. Apart from the Irish Sinn Feiners, who did not take their seats anyway, the biggest single opposition group was the Labour party, with 59 M.P.s—which thus became the official Opposition for the first time. Its popular vote increased from 400,000 to 2,374,000 (not very far short of half as many as the coalition candidates, who nevertheless got eight times as many seats in the Commons). This was a portent for the future. For the Labour party proclaimed itself to be both a working class and a socialist party. On social issues it was the party of the poor, demanding radical reforms in matters of housing, unemployment relief, and the like; on economic ones it called for public ownership of major industries, like the mines and the railways. The practice of the Labour party would differ a good deal from its theory, especially when it was in office rather than in opposition; and its political fortunes were to fluctuate violently in the next thirty years. Nevertheless its gains in the election of 1918 were one of the signs that post-war Britain was going to be a very different land from pre-war Britain.

---

[1] See above, p. 188.

25 Economic Change in Britain between the Two World Wars

I. THE PATTERN OF CHANGE

The coming of peace brought at first a spell of prosperity, a boom in which wages and prices rose sharply as people bought many goods they had been unable to get during the war. But this was short-lived, and a slump followed, with the number of unemployed rising to over 2,000,000 in the summer of 1921. Henceforward unemployment, which reflected the health or sickness of British industry, was to be by far the gravest domestic problem until the outbreak of the Second World War in 1939. At no time between 1921 and 1939 did the number out of work fall below 1,000,000, and this figure by itself is a clear sign that even in the best of times in these inter-war years much was wrong with Britain's industry.

European trade and industry as a whole only picked up slowly during the early 1920's; after 1925 recovery was much more rapid. To some extent this statement applies to Britain too; by 1929, it has been estimated, the average real income per head of her population was about 10 per cent higher than it had been in 1924—even though well over a million people were unemployed and were therefore living on very low incomes. But in certain industries there was chronic depression—above all in some of the great 'staple' industries like cotton, coal-mining, and parts of the engineering and shipbuilding industries upon which Britain's economic strength had been built in the 19th century. The reasons for this were very complicated and varied from one industry to another. The main one was undoubtedly Britain's failure to recapture her pre-war export trade. In 1929 the volume of British exports was still below that of 1913. It was this that caused the unemployment which was to be found throughout the 1920's in areas like the North-East coast, South Wales, Clydeside and South Lancashire. On the other hand, many industries flourished, especially relatively new ones like the motor-car and electrical industries. Most of these grew up not on the coalfields (for they tended to use electricity as their source of power) but in the south Midlands and near London; here they were closer to the great market of London, with plenty of space available for new factories and far more attractive living conditions for their workers. Thus places like Coventry and Oxford, Reading and Slough, and parts of Outer London like Dagenham, Wembley, and Hayes, grew and prospered in the 1920's.

In 1929 the major industrial nations, the United States and Germany as well as Britain, were hit by an economic blizzard. In what has come to be known as 'the Great Depression of the 1930's' prices collapsed, there was a sharp drop in the output of industry and a steep rise in the number of unemployed, and the amount of international trade fell heavily. Financial crises and, over the world as a whole, the ruin of many banks, added to the disaster. The causes of the catastrophe were international; they were centred partly in the United States and reflected the extent to which that country—now the world's greatest industrial producer, agricultural producer, consumer market and financial power—had cut herself off from world trade by a policy of high tariffs. When in the autumn of 1929 prices on the New York stock market suddenly crashed and a prolonged banking and industrial crisis followed in the United States, the consequences were felt rapidly in the rest of the world—and above all in countries like Britain which were heavily dependent upon international trade. Between 1929 and 1931 industrial production in Britain fell by 16 per cent. Unemployment reached 2,500,000 by the end of 1930. Exports fell; imports rose as other countries 'dumped' goods at low prices in Britain, the one great country unprotected by tariffs. Foreign investors began to withdraw their gold from London, and this process, threatening the entire structure of British money and trade, continued until eventually in the autumn of 1931 the government went off the traditional gold standard. At the depth of the depression in 1933 there were some 3,000,000 unemployed in Britain.

There seemed to be little that one government alone could do to give effective help to industry. The fate of British pits and mills and the livelihood of those who worked in them seemed to hang on decisions made by bankers in New York or Vienna or on the inability of farmers in the Argentine and peasants in India to buy British goods. Nevertheless British governments did take steps whose aim was to strengthen the resistance of British industry to depression. 'Going off gold' in 1931 was itself one of these; this devaluation lowered the prices of British goods on the world market and thus gave British manufacturers an advantage over countries which were still on the gold standard. But the advantage was short-lived, for other countries soon followed Britain's example. Secondly, Britain at last abandoned the policy of Free Trade. During the war the McKenna Duties (1915 onwards) had been levied on some goods as one means of restricting imports and saving shipping space; and under the Safeguarding of Industries Act (1921) the government had taxed some imports in order to 'safeguard' certain British industries. But the decisive change came with the Import Duties Act of 1932, which imposed a customs duty of 10 per cent on most imports. The only goods exempt were most foodstuffs and some important industrial raw materials like cotton, wool, and rubber. Later in the same year most duties were raised to 20 per cent and those on a few commodities went up higher still, while a number of raw materials were taken off the free list. Thirdly, agreements whose object was to encourage trade in certain goods hard hit by the depression, like coal, were made with foreign countries, e.g., with the Scandinavian countries in 1933–4. More important, a series of agreements was made at Ottawa in 1932 with the British Dominions. Britain agreed to extend the preference already given to foodstuffs from the Dominions by imposing higher duties on similar foreign foodstuffs; the Dominions were to help British industry by raising their duties on manufactured goods from other countries. These

Ottawa Agreements promised more than they performed. It was difficult to encourage Empire farmers too much without damaging British farmers who grew the same crops; it was even more difficult for the Dominion governments, especially for Canada and Australia with their close trading links with the United States, to limit their trade with foreign countries; and as a whole the Ottawa Agreements offended non-Empire countries. In fact they were appreciably altered in detail before 1939.

It is doubtful whether any of these activities of the government contributed greatly to industrial recovery; yet recovery did come after 1933 as the unemployment figures showed. They fell, terribly slowly; not until the summer of 1935 did they drop below 2,000,000, nor until that of 1937 below 1,500,000. By that year—the most prosperous of the 1930's—Great Britain's industrial output was 25 per cent above that of 1929. The recovery was incomplete and very uneven.[1] Newer industries (e.g. motor vehicles, electrical industries, chemicals), little affected by the depression, did well; while the building and allied trades (e.g. timber, furniture, building materials) prospered. These two groups, moreover, brought growth in a range of other businesses (such as oil refining, rubber, glass, metal goods, leather, paint). House building in particular stimulated a swift rise in the output of consumer goods based on electric power, and also a great demand for shops, schools, cinemas and other services. But in sharp contrast, only iron and steel of the old staple exporting industries made a genuine recovery. In the others like cotton and shipbuilding the bad times went on. By 1937 the volume of British exports was only 83 per cent of what it had been in 1929 when the depression started. And in 1937 there were signs that another depression was on the way. Only the start of rearmament, with its stimulus to engineering and the metal industries, halted its development. The outbreak in 1939 of the Second World War put an end to large-scale unemployment. This last fact is a grim comment on Britain's industrial history between the wars. War seemed the only means of preventing widespread unemployment.

Britain's 19th-century supremacy could not have lasted; she was bound to be overtaken once countries with greater natural resources, like the United States and Germany, had developed their industries. The old staple industries were certain to suffer as a result. Moreover other countries which had in the 19th century been customers of Britain began during the 20th to develop their own technical skill and to launch their own industries. The swift expansion of the Japanese cotton industry (which captured British markets in India and elsewhere in Asia) was merely one example of this process. Here as in many other directions the First World War accelerated a change which would have come anyway. Further, the course of technical discovery worked to Britain's disadvantage. The widespread use of oil as a fuel and the rapid development of the internal combustion engine—both of them in their infancy before 1914—struck severe blows at certain sections of British industry; the market for British coal was sharply reduced, and so

---

[1] For regional variations, see below, p.261.

too was that for British locomotives and rolling stock as steam railway construction overseas slowed down. The development of electricity, and especially perhaps of hydro-electricity in some European countries, had similar effects. Again, governments all over the world adopted policies whose object was to promote the economic well-being of their own peoples at the expense of all foreigners. These included high tariffs on imports; limitation of imports to certain 'quotas' of specified goods; controlled currencies, checking the outflow of money from their frontiers; heavy subsidies to home industries; and, in the dictatorships like Soviet Russia and Nazi Germany, ruthless direction of capital and labour into certain occupations. Such policies hindered international trade, and hit British exports peculiarly hard.

It was difficult for the older industries to respond to the challenge. British manufacturers had much capital invested in factories and plant in areas like South Wales and the North-East coast; hundreds of thousands of workpeople were settled there; to shift factories, to re-equip with new machines, above all to persuade vast numbers of workers to move, was a massive task which could only be carried out slowly in a democratic community. But time was not on Britain's side; the pace of industrial change in the world was too fast. There was indeed a brighter side to the British economic picture. The new industries in the Midlands and the south flourished in the later 1930's; the radio and motor-car industries in particular grew very rapidly. By 1937 industrial production, as a whole, was 80 per cent higher than in 1907; the output per worker—thanks to greater mechanisation—had risen considerably, as had the total income of the community. It would be quite incorrect to suggest that British industry stagnated between the two World Wars. But there was one disturbing fact about the prosperous industries. A great deal of their production was for the home markets; where it was for export, Britain had failed to capture a sufficient share of the world markets in goods like motor-cars, radio sets, electrical equipment, rayon and the like to offset the losses in the older industries. In the newer industries, other countries held the lead in international trade.

2. INDUSTRIES OLD AND NEW, 1919–39

In 1913 Great Britain produced 287,000,000 tons of *coal*, and exported 98,000,000 of them; the industry employed 1,230,000 persons.[1] But already there were clouds on the horizon; for costs of production were rising as less accessible seams were worked. The war prevented the installation of new equipment and wrecked the export trade. After it, world consumption of coal fell; industry was turning to electric power, and shipping to oil.[2]

[1] The figures for 1938 were: total production 227,000,000 tons, exports 46,000,000, workers employed 782,000.

[2] Whereas in 1914 only 3·4 per cent. of the world's merchantmen burned oil, by 1939 54 per cent of them did; and nearly all naval vessels had gone over to oil.

Yet the world's capacity for producing coal had increased, and Europe in particular was producing far more than before the war. Thus even before 1929 the British coal industry was struggling. The great depression brought output tumbling down and by the summer of 1932 41 per cent of coal workers were unemployed. Recovery was slow and limited. Exports in 1937, the industry's least depressed year, were only 68 per cent of what they had been in 1929 and not much more than half the 1913 figure. At home the amount of coal used was actually less on the eve of the Second World War than it had been in 1913: factories and homes were burning gas and electricity instead, and although coal was consumed in the manufacture of both, technical progress had brought great economies in its use. Moreover British pits were old; in their narrow and winding passages underground haulage was difficult and the introduction of mechanisation expensive. Innumerable remedies for the ills of the industry were proposed. Nationalisation was recommended by a majority of the Sankey Commission of 1919. There were various amalgamations of mines, and joint selling agencies were established, but these were of small value. Labour relations in the industry were bad, and strikes were frequent, the most notable being that of 1926, which in some areas lasted six months and which precipitated the General Strike;[1] and these grim years left behind them a bitter legacy of class hostility in mining areas like County Durham and South Wales.

The *iron and steel* industry had prospered mightily under the stimulus of war. It fluctuated greatly in the years which followed. Costs of manufacture in Britain were high; much British plant was old-fashioned, and Europe was far better off than Britain in the sort of iron ore suitable for the 'basic' steel which was in increasingly greater demand than the 'acid' steel in which many British firms had specialised.[2] The great depression halved British production of pig-iron and nearly halved that of steel; yet the industry recovered surprisingly rapidly, and by 1937 British steel production was more than one-third greater than it had been in 1929 (although pig-iron did not recover to the same extent). The recovery reflected a revival in large-scale engineering and shipbuilding, the growth of the motor-car industry, the replacement of timber by steel in the coal-mines, and the beginnings of rearmament. It was aided by the high tariffs ($33\frac{1}{3}$ per cent) imposed on many imported iron and steel goods in 1932; and by the quota agreements from 1935 onwards between British and European manufacturers, which further limited imports. But the vital test of full return to health lay in the export trade—and the figures were unsatisfactory; even by 1937 British iron and steel exports were only 59 per cent of what they had been in 1929. These inter-war years saw important changes

---

[1] See below, pp. 258–9.

[2] 'Basic' steel was produced from phosphoric ores by the Gilchrist-Thomas process of 1878 (see p. 107, above): in these post-war years it was fast replacing wrought iron, especially for cheap goods. 'Acid' steel, made by the earlier processes, needed non-phosphoric ores; it continued to be used where finer and more reliable steel was required.

in the industry. The iron fields of the Midlands, which had developed in the early years of the century, were producing three-fifths of British iron ore by 1939; great new steel works were built, notably at the new town of Corby and, in an attempt to relieve the distress which depression had brought, at Ebbw Vale. There was very extensive amalgamation of plants in an effort to cut production costs. In 1932 the employers, after much governmental pressure, formed the British Iron and Steel Federation, becoming in some ways a great monopoly controlling the planning and output of the entire industry. Nevertheless until the beginning of rearmament in 1937–8 the condition of the industry as a whole could hardly be regarded as good.

Shipbuilding had been an industry in which British supremacy remained clear until the outbreak of the First World War. Over the years 1910–14 Great Britain built 61 per cent of all the merchant shipping launched in the world. The war was a tremendous blow to British shipbuilding; moreover it brought an immense increase in American launchings. Immediately after the war there was a furious outburst of activity in the shipyards; 2,000,000 tons were launched from British yards alone in 1920, and by the end of 1921 the world's merchant fleet was over 25 per cent bigger than it had been before the war. Since international trade was far smaller than it had been, a slump followed, and by 1922 one-sixth of all the world's merchant ships were laid up. This in turn brought a steep decline in shipbuilding, and recovery did not begin until about 1927. Other factors added to the impact of these wild fluctuations. These were years of disarmament, with the demand for naval building much reduced. New types of ships were coming into general use, among them oil-burning ships, oil-tankers and motor ships;[1] for the building of these British yards and marine-engine shops were not adequately equipped. So Britain's export of ships declined, even though from 1927 to 1930 she launched over half the world's tonnage of new vessels. Then came the great depression. In 1933 only 131,000 tons were launched, and 63 per cent of shipbuilding workers were unemployed. From this plight British shipbuilding never fully recovered. Even by 1938 the output of British yards was well below that on the eve of the depression, and amounted to only just over one-third of the total world launchings. The export trade in ships had dwindled away. German exports of ships were far bigger than those of Britain in the later 1930's; and many British shipowners were having their vessels built in foreign yards. Government assistance to British shipowners did not help the export trade in ships much; under the British Shipping (Assistance) Act of 1935 subsidies were granted to tramp shipping, and by the 'scrap and build' scheme of 1936 owners who scrapped three times the amount of tonnage they built were given loans. The shipbuilding industry itself from 1930 onwards carried out 'rationalisation' schemes, forming a company whose aim was to buy up and scrap redundant shipyards. This policy reduced competition and raised

[1] In 1924 less than one quarter of all ships launched were motor ships; only six years later they outnumbered the steamship launchings.

prices, and so was of little advantage in the overseas market. Its human consequences could be appalling, as was shown by the effects of the closing down of Palmer's Shipyard at Jarrow; in 1935 72 per cent of the workers of the town were unemployed, and Jarrow became known as 'the town that was murdered'.

In 1913 over one-third of all British exports were *textiles*, cottons alone providing almost one-quarter of them. During the years between the wars British exports of textiles fell. Some parts of the trade, such as carpets, hosiery, and rayon, grew appreciably;[1] by contrast, the major textile trades, and above all *cotton*—the great glory of Britain's export business in the 19th century—declined steeply. The great depression, with the accompanying shrinkage in international trade, was a shattering blow to the Lancashire cotton industry. Yet the central cause of trouble was the undermining of Britain's trade in cotton piece goods with Asia and the Far East. Japanese manufacturers made astonishing progress, and by 1933 had surpassed Britain in the quantity of their cotton exports; meanwhile India, the largest single importer of British cottons before 1914, had doubled her own production, and Britain's exports to her fell by 1,000 million yards (914 million metres) by 1930. Such changes brought chronic unemployment—as well as much short-time working—to many Lancashire towns, especially those which produced the cheaper cottons. *Wool* did not fare nearly as badly, even though the European market, already shrinking before 1914, continued to do so after the war. A higher proportion of the output of woollen goods than of cotton was sold at home, and thus the industry was not so hard hit by the closing of overseas markets.

This was the darker side of British industry between 1919 and 1939. What of the brighter side, the newer industries which grew up in the Midlands and the south? These were numerous, most of them light industries and on a small scale; they included the electrical industry and plastics, stainless steel and aircraft, scientific instruments and a wide range of food-stuffs. Two must serve here as examples, the motor-car industry and the development of rayon. The *motor-car* industry was much the most important of the newer ones. Its beginning in England had been in 1896, with the foundation in that year of the English Daimler Motor Company, and it arose in the bicycle-manufacturing area of the west Midlands around Coventry and Birmingham. Before 1914 it made little progress compared with the pace and scale of the automobile industry in the United States; and the war halted development. But after initial post-war difficulties the industry began to forge ahead, mainly because of the partial adoption of the American system of mass production based on standardised parts; a few firms applied this to the making of light cars. Output rose from 32,000 in 1920 to 182,000 in 1929, by which date the manufacture of motor-cars was a major British industry. Its main centre was still in the west Midlands, but there had been big developments elsewhere, notably those started at Cowley near Oxford by William Morris (later Lord Nuffield). The great

[1] For details about rayon, see below, pp. 251–2.

depression made little difference; in one way it provided an opportunity, for it did much damage to the American automobile industry and thus enabled British motor firms to capture a bigger share of the world export market, hitherto dominated by the Americans. By 1938 the British output had risen to 342,000 private cars and 105,000 commercial vehicles.[1] British exports had doubled since 1929—a considerable achievement, although not enough to offset the loss of ground by other engineering exports. Overseas buyers preferred a car with a large powerful engine, whereas the British system of taxation by horse-power encouraged British firms to concentrate on the small high-speed engine, and this checked the rise of exports. The efficiency of the industry developed in various ways. The number of firms engaged in it fell from 90 in 1920 to 33 in 1939,[2] in which year about nine-tenths of the total output was made by six large groups; most firms concentrated on a few popular models, like the Austin Seven or the Morris Eight of the later 1930's; and components like starters and dynamos became increasingly standardised. 'Mass production' was developed into 'flow production', whereby the finished cars were built up piece by piece as they moved across the factory floor on a conveyor belt system. The fortunes of many other trades were encouraged by the growth of this great new industry; these included machine tools, leather, rubber, and non-ferrous metals.

The growth of the *rayon* industry is important for various reasons. It shows the part played in economic progress by the chemical industry; a part also illustrated in these years by the greatly increased manufacture of such varied products as dyestuffs, aspirins, saccharin, insulin, vitamins, cosmetics, disinfectants, artificial fertilisers, and high explosives, and by the formation in 1926 of Imperial Chemical Industries, Limited, a combine of four great firms with a total capital of £56,000,000 which became the largest industrial organisation in the British Empire. Rayon was one of a series of synthetic products,[3] substitutes for natural products, most of which came to be known as plastics; celluloid, the earliest of these, first produced in Great Britain in 1855, and bakelite were probably the best-known in 1939. The development of rayon was established in several countries before 1914. Its pioneers in Britain were Courtaulds, a silk firm established in Essex since the 18th century. Before the First World War they had become interested in artificial fibres and set up a factory for this purpose at Coventry; and they continued to dominate the British industry, producing four-fifths of the output, playing a leading role in the development of plastics, and manufacturing cellophane in the 1930's. Aided by a protective tariff (1925) on imports, Great Britain developed a rayon industry between the wars.

[1] The figures for 1955 were 898,000 private cars and 341,000 commercial vehicles.
[2] How many readers of this book have seen a Rhode car, or a Bean, an Amilcar or a Buckingham? These were among the makes that disappeared.
[3] Strictly, rayon is a semi-synthetic fibre made out of cellulose (obtained from wood pulp) and cotton. The later-developed nylon, first commercially produced in 1939, is a truly synthetic fibre.

Nevertheless she was far behind other nations, especially the United States, Japan, and Germany, in the international trade. Her exports of rayon in 1939 were only one-tenth of the value of her exports of cottons—re-emphasising the point that Britain was failing to offset her losses in the old industries by gains in the new ones.

3. AGRICULTURE

British agriculture had done well during the war, when it was vital to grow more food at home. When the urgency of crisis had gone, it fell upon lean times again. During the war the Corn Production Act (1917) guaranteed farmers minimum prices for their corn, and farm labourers minimum wages; in 1920 the Agriculture Act, to encourage home production, again guaranteed minimum prices for wheat and oats and maintained the machinery set up to fix fair agricultural wages. Then came the post-war slump, with a steep drop in world prices of foodstuffs, and in 1921 Parliament repealed the Act, left farmers unprotected against cheaper foreign produce, and scrapped the minimum wage. Farmers and labourers alike complained that they had been let down. So the pre-war decline in the amount of land under crops started again; in 1931 the acreage under wheat was the lowest ever recorded. With it went a fall in the number of labourers on the land, as men left to find better-paid jobs in the towns. In southern England this process was encouraged by the rapid development of better living conditions in the towns; the new council houses with their electricity and water supplies, the shopping centres and the cinemas, encouraged the flight from the land.

Few farmers would admit that times were good in these years. Yet there was another side to the picture. This was a period of swift technical advance in British farming, in some ways a kind of second Agrarian Revolution. Its most obvious symbol was the tractor. Before 1914 there were hardly any motor tractors on British farms; by 1939 there were 50,000. The difficulties of making a profit encouraged the spread of mechanisation, with the development of milking machinery, improved threshing machines, and the coming of the combine harvester. Sir George Stapledon, Director of the Welsh Plant-Breeding Station at Aberystwyth, was a pioneer in the reclamation and improvement of hill pastures. There were notable advances in animal feeding-stuffs, with greater reliance on hay and concentrates and less dependence on root crops. The milk yield of cows was greatly increased: so was the egg yield of hens. The development of the canning industry stimulated the production of vegetables and fruit. The improved transport provided by motor lorries put the farmer in closer touch with his markets in the cities. The general advance in communications—motor-car, telephone, and radio alike—spread new ideas and methods far faster than ever before in the countryside. Despite all the problems the number of owner-occupiers of farms increased considerably; war taxation and death duties drove many landlords to sell property, often to sitting tenants, while farmers who had

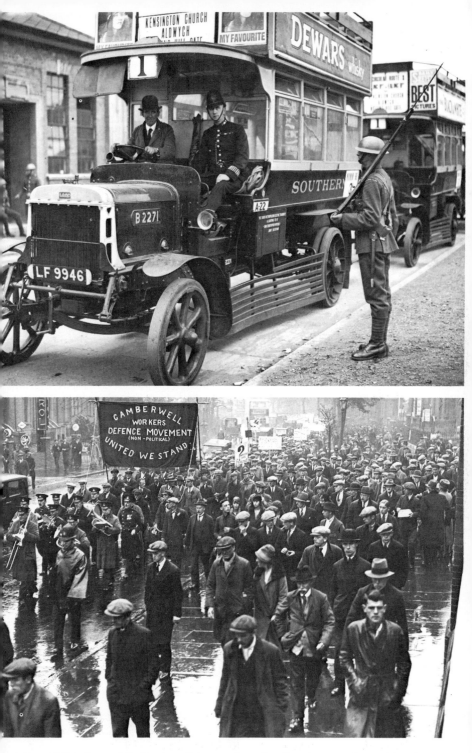

(*Above*) The General Strike (1926) (pp. 258–259): a London omnibus with volunteer driver leaves its garage under escort. (*Below*) The depression of the 1930's: unemployed workers demonstrate at Camberwell (1931) (pp. 261–262).

ENTERTAINMENT IN THE 1930's. (*Above*) A cinema of the 1930's (the Granada at Tooting): note the elaborate decorations and the organ. (*Right*) The last word in radio: the Fullotone 4-valve radio gramophone (price 16 guineas) (p. 262).

(*Above*) The new industry of the 1930's: the 'Morris Eight' assembly line at Cowley in 1939 (p. 251). (*Left*) Rationing in the Second World War set its problems (pp. 276–277).

Plymouth: (*above*) the blitz of 1941 (p. 275), and (*below*) rebuilt after the war.

NO, NO, **NO**! WRONG ADDRESS, I TELL YOU!

THE OLD HORSE DOESN'T LIKE BEING FENCED IN

(*Above*) The British Medical Association did not show much enthusiasm for Aneurin Bevan's National Health Service (cartoon by David Low, 1948) (p. 291). (*Below*) Low's cartoon (1946) suggests that the Trade Union Congress did not always agree with the socialism and controls of the Labour government.

BRITISH CIVIL AIRCRAFT AFTER THE SECOND WORLD WAR: (*Above*) B.O.A.C. Comet, and (*below*) British Airways' Concorde (p. 296).

The mechanisation of British farming after the Second World War: tractors and combine harvester at work (p. 296).

Energy: an oil rig in position in the North Sea (p. 295).

(*Above*) Scientific advance: the radio telescopes at Jodrell Bank in the 1960's. (*Left*) A symbol of transport progress: the Severn Bridge, opened in 1967 (p. 298).

built up capital in the war years and ex-servicemen with gratuities were ready to buy.

The policy of the government towards farming changed for the better. The Agricultural Wages Act (1924) set up agricultural wages boards in each county to fix rates of pay; this brought higher wages to labourers—but it also led many farmers to dismiss men and thus actually encouraged the decline in arable farming and the flight to the towns. Agricultural land and buildings were de-rated, i.e. required to pay lower rates (1923–5). One arable crop which had been subsidised during the war was again heavily subsidised from 1924 onwards; this was sugar beet, and by 1934 Britain was producing nearly a quarter of her total consumption of sugar. From about 1930 onwards state aid to the farming community was considerably increased. For the first time since the Repeal of the Corn Laws British governments set out deliberately to help those who lived in the country-side (now a small minority of the nation) even if this meant that town-dwellers had to pay more for their food. Tariffs and import quotas limited the quantity of foreign produce allowed into Britain; for example, the Ottawa Agreements of 1932 reduced the imports of foreign meat by over one-third. Subsidies paid by the government stimulated British producers and enabled them to lower their prices. In 1932 wheat was subsidised so that the farmer got a guaranteed price; as a result the acreage under wheat increased by nearly 50 per cent by 1939; barley and oats also were subsi-dised. Livestock producers got a subsidy in 1934, bacon producers in 1938. Another feature of state aid was the creation, under the Agricultural Marketing Acts of 1931 and 1933, of marketing boards whose ultimate aim was to keep up prices. Elected by the producers (provided two-thirds wanted them), these boards had considerable control over processing as well as over prices, buying and selling; they were set up for bacon, pigs, hops, potatoes, and milk. The Milk Marketing Board, created in 1933, controlled the sale of all liquid milk by farmers to the milk companies and fixed the price they got; its activities were assisted by government subsidies on 'manufactured milk' (i.e. milk to be turned into a wide range of goods from butter to umbrella handles) and on the distribution of cheap milk to mothers in the depressed areas and to school children. Many a farmer found financial security in his regular 'milk cheque'. Such varied help from government did not make farming immensely prosperous. But it saved many farmers from ruin and much of the countryside from decay.

4. TRANSPORT

During the war the government had temporarily taken over the railways; and the Ministry of Transport set up in 1919 wished to nationalise them. This was not acceptable to Parliament, and instead the Railways Act (1921) combined the 123 separate companies into four large groups—the London, Midland, and Scottish (L.M.S.), the London and North-Eastern (L.N.E.R.), the Southern (S.R.), and the Great Western (G.W.R.). So on January 1,

1923, the multitude of old-established companies, ranging from the Caledonian to the London, Tilbury, and Southend, from the Furness to the Taff Vale, from the North Staffordshire to the Hull, Barnsley, and West Riding, disappeared. With the amalgamations came greater state control; the act of 1921 also established the Railways Rates Tribunal, with powers to fix the rates and fares charged by the railways so that the companies might earn revenues equal to those of 1913. In some ways the post-war recovery of the railways was slow: track and rolling stock had deteriorated, and much new equipment was needed. Not until about 1931 was the average speed of express trains, for example, back to its pre-war level; after that there was much improvement, and by 1939 116 trains were booked to run at 60 m.p.h. (96 km/h) or over, compared with 4 in 1914. New types of locomotive were introduced, notably the Great Northern *Pacifics* (1922) and the G.W.R. *Castles* (1923). Signalling systems were improved, with power-worked signal boxes and the beginnings of colour-light signalling. There was considerable development of electrification on the Southern Railway (e.g. the Brighton line was electrified by 1933) and on the London Underground, which built well out into the suburbs, reaching Upminster in 1932 and Cockfosters in 1933; but little outside the area dominated by London.

Yet the main fact about the railways during these years was that they did not pay. They did not earn the expected revenue; and the control exercised by the Rates Tribunal prevented them from adjusting charges to meet the competition of road services. For the basic reason for the railways' difficulties was the extraordinary development of road transport. The motorcar, the lorry and the bus were coming into their own. By 1937 there were nearly six times as many cars on the roads as in 1922, and over three times as many goods vehicles. Lorries, able to go where the railways could not, ate into the goods traffic—including such specialised parts of it as milk and oil: buses captured short-distance passenger traffic in the swiftly-growing suburbs, and built up a network of cross-country services;[1] and charabancs competed successfully for outings and excursions. The railways retaliated by closing down unprofitable branches, by faster trains and cheap fares, even by buying up bus companies and road haulage businesses. But on the eve of the Second World War the great national asset of the railways was in a very unhealthy financial condition.

The arrival of the internal combustion engine had innumerable social results. For the roads themselves it demanded vast changes to cope with traffic on a scale never before experienced. The new Ministry of Transport took over the duties of the Road Board set up in 1910, and in 1920 it began classifying the principal roads as 'A' and 'B'. But the actual work of construction was left to local authorities. Since 1888 main roads had been in

---

[1] In the late 1920's and in the 1930's the motor bus, or the trolley bus, replaced the tram in many towns; the great cities kept their trams (in which they had much capital locked up) but developed bus services as well, especially for the outer suburbs in which new housing estates had grown up.

the charge of the County and County Borough Councils; in 1929 these bodies were given responsibility for all except unclassified (i.e., minor) roads. Among the important developments in these years were various roads in the London area (e.g. the Great West Road and the Kingston and Watford by-passes), the Mersey Road Tunnel and the new bridge carrying the Great North Road across the Tyne at Newcastle. Traffic lights came into general use in the 1930's. In 1930 the Road Traffic Act reorganised the system of licences, imposing a new series of rules (including compulsory insurance against third party risks) which particularly affected public service vehicles; a principal reason for this Act was the fierce competition between rival bus companies, often involving reckless races through busy streets. The regulations and the new roads alike were of immense and immediate value: and to some extent the new road construction changed the face of parts of Britain just as the railways had done in the days of Queen Victoria. Yet it should be noted that just as with the railways, so with the roads there was no effective attempt at planning their development on a national scale.

London presented special problems of transport. The population of Greater London rose from about 7,250,000 in 1911 to nearly 8,250,000 in 1931; the second figure amounted to over one-fifth of the entire population of England and Wales. The growth was in the outer suburbs, for the population of the central area was declining. Trams and buses (the first covered double-decker in London appeared in 1923), the extended Underground, the newly-electrified services of the main line railways—all were strained to the utmost in rush hours. To organise these services as a whole, Parliament in 1933 created the London Passenger Transport Board. This was given the monopoly of nearly all passenger services in London, and the power to extend its services in competition with others over a wide area around the capital. Only the suburban services of the main line railways were outside its control, and even these had to pool their receipts with those of the L.P.T.B.

This was a gloomy period in the history of British shipping. In 1939 the British merchant fleet was 1,800 ships fewer and a million tons less than it had been before the First World War; and whereas in 1913 Britain had 39 per cent of the world's tonnage, in 1939 she had only 26 per cent. Such figures speak for themselves—although even in 1939 the British merchant navy was still twice as big as that of its nearest rival, now (since the First World War) the United States. Britain's contribution to technical progress in these years was very limited; there was nothing worthy to compare with Parsons' invention of the steam turbine, and the most important single development, the motor marine engine, was only constructed in Britain under licence from foreign owners of its patents. The biggest achievement in British mercantile shipping in this period was the launching of the two Atlantic liners, the *Queen Mary* (81,000 tons) and the *Queen Elizabeth* (85,000 tons). 'Cunarder 534' had been lying half-built on the stocks at Clydebank for months, her completion halted by the depression, until the government, by the North Atlantic Shipping Act (1934), granted loans up to £9,500,000 to encourage the construction of vessels for the North Atlantic service; work re-started, and in 1936 she was launched as the *Queen Mary*. Another result of the act was the amalgamation of the Cunard and White Star companies, which saved the latter from American control. The *Queen Elizabeth* was still under construction on the Clyde when war broke out in 1939, and her maiden voyage was made in secret to New York in 1940.

These inter-war years were the time when the air began to replace the sea as a highway for man. There were many exciting pioneer flights. In 1919 two Royal Air Force men, John Alcock and Arthur Whitten-Brown, made the first transatlantic flight, from Newfoundland to Ireland, and two Australians, Keith and Ross Smith, flew from England to Australia in twenty-eight days; in 1926 the Australian Charles Kingsford Smith, with three companions, made the first trans-Pacific flight, from California to Queensland, and in 1927 the American, Charles Lindbergh, the first solo transatlantic flight, from New York to Paris. In 1919 daily commercial air services from London to Paris had started, shortly followed by services to other continental cities; they did not pay, and not until a single company, Imperial Airways, was created in 1924 to absorb the others and was given a government subsidy, did regular air travel from England to Europe establish itself. Further afield, Imperial Airways developed services over great distances, gradually extending its range to Egypt, Iraq, India, Capetown, Singapore, and—by 1934—Australia. In 1935 a rival company, British Airways, was formed to fly on various routes; it was granted a monopoly of the services to Berlin and to Scandinavia. By an Act of Parliament of 1939 the two companies were combined into a single concern, British Overseas Airways Corporation, which was heavily subsidised by the Treasury, and whose directors were appointed by the government; B.O.A.C. actually came into existence in April 1940. Before the outbreak of war in 1939, the first commercial transatlantic services had been started by Pan-American Airways and by Imperial Airways.

The beginning of air transport meant the start of the aircraft industry. The Bristol Aircraft Company, for example, had been founded as early as 1910; its eighty employees had built sixteen biplanes by the end of that year. By the end of 1935 it had 8,000 employees; and this development was paralleled in other areas and factories. Nevertheless it is easy to exaggerate the importance of the aeroplane before the Second World War. Air transport was on a very small scale indeed, when compared with the immense progress since 1939. The inter-war years were a pioneering period, with many false starts and dead ends. The most sensational of these was the use of airships, giant torpedo-shaped envelopes filled with gas and powered by engines, first developed in Germany by Count Zeppelin before 1914 and notorious in the air raids of the First World War; a series of disasters, revealing their extreme liability to fire and explosions, virtually put an end to their use in the 1930's. The future lay with the aeroplane; yet even the aeroplane in 1939 was only in its childhood stage.

26 The Working Class Movement and Social Change

The story of the working class movement between the wars is over-whelmingly the story of the trade unions and of the Labour party. Other elements of the movement continued and some prospered. The Co-opera-tive Movement, for example, had 8,600,000 members by 1940 (five times as many as in 1900); it had added to its activities, among other things, the production of a Sunday newspaper (*Reynolds' News*); and the C.W.S. was one of the biggest businesses in the country. Friendly Societies dwindled in importance, with the growth of National Insurance; the Workers' Educa-tional Association tended in many of its branches to become a middle class body, not one which attracted manual workers. Yet the two greatest areas of working class action were in the trade unions and the Labour party. For each these were years of mixed fortunes, marked by great successes and by great failures.

Trade unions emerged from the war with their membership almost doubled and their funds much increased. And the immediate post-war years brought developments which seemed to reveal vast strength. In 1920 the refusal of London dockers—backed by the trade union movement—to load the vessel *Jolly George* with munitions believed to be intended for use against the Soviet government, followed by the threat by the trade unions of a general strike, effectively stopped British help to Poland against Communist Russia. The creation, in the same year, of the General Council of the Trades Union Congress gave that body a 'general staff' to handle its affairs. Unions at this time were amalgamating into bigger units, like the Amalgamated Engineering Union (1920) and the Transport and General Workers' Union (1921). This last was largely the achievement of Ernest Bevin, the most remarkable trade union leader of the 20th century.[1] The formidable feature of their power seemed to be the rise of the so-called 'Triple Alliance' of the miners, the railwaymen, and the transport workers. Foreshadowed before the war, this was renewed in 1919. It was not an amalgamation, but an agreement for common action against the employers; and the combined strength of the three unions seemed to enable them to dictate terms to the employers, and perhaps also to the government.

---

[1] Bevin, a man of outstanding character and mind, was born of labouring stock in Somerset, left school at eleven, began work as a farm-boy and later became a carter in Bristol. After his career with the T.G.W.U., whose General Secretary he was from 1921 to 1940, be became Minister of Labour during the Second World War and Secretary of State for Foreign Affairs in the Labour government of 1945–50. See below, pp. 268, 278.

In reality the trade unions were nothing like as powerful as they appeared. Partly this was because their leaders were inexperienced men facing new problems; partly because the big unions did not in fact stand together in crises; the 'Triple Alliance' proved mostly a sham in practice. But the main reason was the existence after 1921 of widespread and continuous unemployment. With men far more numerous than jobs, employers had the whip hand, the ability to force wages down and hours up; the unions, instead of being able to press for better conditions, had to struggle very hard to keep conditions as they were—or, much more usually, even to limit the cuts in pay and the increases in hours. It is not surprising that this period saw deep industrial bitterness.

The worst troubles were in the coal industry. In 1919 the threat of a national stoppage in the mines was averted by the government's appointment of the Sankey Commission to investigate the situation. When the government did not act on its recommendations, the miners felt they had been deceived and the owners, for their part, were encouraged to resist change. In 1921 the miners, faced with proposed large-scale reductions in wages, came out again. There was talk of a 'general strike', with the 'Triple Alliance' in support; but at the eleventh hour, on what came to be known in the labour movement as 'Black Friday', the railwaymen and transport workers backed out, leaving the miners to fight on alone until eventually they had to accept the reductions. In 1926 the crisis came, when a second report (that of the Samuel Commission) recommended wage cuts for the miners, which they rejected. Their slogan, in the phrase of their secretary A. J. Cook, was 'not a penny off the pay, not a minute on the day'. Discontent among the working class was general; for in 1925 Britain had returned to the gold standard, action which damaged her export trade by putting up the prices of her goods, and thus led to a fall in employment. The miners came out on strike; the T.U.C. gave full support, and at midnight on May 3rd 1926 there began what came to be called the General Strike.

For nine days the overwhelming majority of workers in a group of vital industries (docks, railways and road transport; iron and steel and chemicals; printing; building; electricity and gas) were on strike in support of the miners' demands. The government, a Conservative one under Stanley Baldwin, resisted firmly. Many of its members wanted a 'showdown' with the unions; it had made preparations beforehand (unlike the T.U.C., which was quite unready with any sort of organisation) by creating a 'Secret Organisation for the Maintenance of Supplies'; it set up its own newspaper, the *British Gazette* (with Winston Churchill as editor), and used its control of the broadcasting service. Many middle class citizens volunteered, as special constables and transport workers; their efforts on the roads kept supplies moving, although on the railways they never operated more than one-fifth of the normal services.[1] For their part the rank and file of the

[1] Quite a few middle-aged men achieved a childhood ambition by becoming engine drivers; trains sped past signals, stopped mysteriously in tunnels, took the

workers stood firm, and many were angry and resentful when the T.U.C. leaders decided to call off the strike on May 12th. The miners stayed out another six months, until poverty and hunger compelled them to accept longer hours and lower wages. The government and the employers won a complete victory. Many workmen were victimised for having gone on strike: they were given worse jobs or lower wages, had their pension rights reduced or had to leave their unions. The strike cost the unions some £4,000,000. The number of union members declined sharply by over half a million to under 5,000,000 in 1927 (the lowest since 1916), and did not recover until the middle thirties. Baldwin's government drove its victory home with the Trade Disputes and Trade Union Act of 1927. This declared general strikes illegal; forbade civil service trade unions to belong to the T.U.C.; and struck a deliberate blow at working class political action by reversing the Trade Union Act of 1913[1] and requiring that in future all members who wished to contribute to the political fund of their union (in effect, the union's subscription to the Labour party) must give written notice of wishing to do so. The whole episode left memories of defeat and betrayal in the minds of many working class men.

At the time of the General Strike the Labour party was in opposition in Parliament. Its strength had grown rapidly since the war. In the general election held at the end of 1923 it won 191 seats, polling 4,300,000 votes; and in January 1924 took office for the first time, under Ramsay MacDonald as Prime Minister. From the start it was a minority government, dependent on Liberal support, for the Conservatives were still the largest single party; it achieved little, and fell in October 1924. After five more years of Conservative rule, the general election of 1929 made Labour the biggest single party, with 287 seats; and once again Ramsay MacDonald became Prime Minister. This second Labour government was in trouble from the start. Some of its difficulties stemmed from the circumstances of its election, for it was again a minority government. Not only was it still dependent on Liberal votes in the Commons; it was also notable that rather more people had voted Conservative than had voted Labour, even though the latter party had won 26 more seats.

But disaster came with the economic depression, whose arrival coincided almost exactly with the government's entry to office. At that time there were over a million unemployed; by the end of 1930 there were over 2,500,000. The ordinary National Insurance scheme was wholly inadequate

wrong lines and occasionally crashed, but there were no serious accidents. Many undergraduates enjoyed themselves driving trams or buses. Trams were driven hard and often proved difficult to stop. In London bus driving and conducting had its perils; few buses had any glass left in their windows, and the driver was often encased in a wire net to stop missiles. Some of them carried placards saying such things as 'A stone in the hand is worth two in the bus', 'Try our Fresh Air Cure', 'The driver of this bus is a student of Guy's Hospital. The conductor is a student of Guy's. Anybody who interferes with either is liable to be a patient of Guy's.'

[1] See p. 159, above.

and the government used what came to be known as the 'dole'—extra payments to the unemployed to cover the period when their benefit rights were exhausted. The 'dole' was barely enough to keep alive on, yet it aroused the fury of the well-to-do, who accused the government of wasteful expenditure. The depression grew worse as exports fell off; factories and businesses closed by the score and added their employees to the long ranks of the workless. During 1931 a severe financial crisis developed, as foreign investors withdrew their gold from Britain. Business men, orthodox financiers and the Conservative opposition demanded higher taxes and the slashing of unemployment benefit in order to 'save the pound'. Philip Snowden, the Chancellor of the Exchequer, appointed the May Committee (so-called from its chairman, Sir George May) to investigate the national finances. Its report, so alarming that it stimulated even greater foreign withdrawals of gold, recommended drastic economies, including a 20 per cent cut in unemployment benefit; and its effect was to break up the government. MacDonald, Snowden, and a handful of other leaders were ready to accept the report; the rest of the leaders and nearly all the party's rank and file declined to sacrifice the unemployed. Thereupon MacDonald resigned—only to form a new 'National' cabinet, containing four Labour men, four Conservatives and two Liberals, whose sole purpose, it was stated, was to deal with the financial crisis and save the pound.

Most of the Labour party, feeling that they had been betrayed, went into opposition. The new government introduced a severe budget, with cuts in the pay of all civil servants, servicemen, ministers and M.P.s, policemen and schoolteachers—and 10 per cent reduction in unemployment benefits. Within a month of the formation of the National government to save the pound, Britain, in September 1931, abandoned the gold standard. Finally, in October, MacDonald appealed to the country in a general election. The Labour party suffered an immense defeat. The National candidates got 14,500,000 votes and 558 seats; the Labour party 6,500,000 votes and 49 seats. This was as great a blow to the working class movement as the General Strike had been. Yet it needs, like the strike, to be seen in the perspective of years. By the later 1930's the trade unions were recovering their membership, rising from 4,300,000 in 1933 to 5,800,000 in 1937; and in the election of 1935 the Labour Party got a million and a half more votes than in 1931, and won 154 seats. Neither recovery was sensational; yet they indicated that the working class movement had not been shattered by the crises of 1926 and 1931.

2. THE CONDITION OF THE PEOPLE, 1918–39

It is difficult to talk about the condition of the people of Britain as a whole during the inter-war years. We have far more detailed information about how people lived than for any previous age. We have enormous quantities of statistics about prices, wages, what people ate, how they spent their money and their leisure; reports of numerous commissions of enquiry into social problems; books by novelists and journalists and, as never before, we have films and we have recordings of broadcasts. But what all this material reveals to us is not one country but two. The more we look at it, the sharper becomes the contrast between the older industrial areas which were on the decline, and where most of the heavy unemployment was to be found, and the rest of the country which was on the whole prosperous and comfortable.

Unemployment was the dominant social problem. Clydeside and industrial Scotland, Tyneside and Teeside, west Cumberland, Lancashire and Merseyside, South Wales and much of North Wales, such pockets of dying industry as the small tin-mining area of south-west Cornwall—these were the places where things were worst. Here, when the depression was blackest, were men out of work for long years, families living permanently on relief, shops boarded up, houses tumbling down. Towns seemed almost to be rotting away, while their people grew weary and bitter because they had no work nor hope of work. In 1934—when recovery from the depression had already begun—67 per cent of the insured workers in Jarrow were still out of a job; so were 61 per cent in Merthyr Tydfil, 57 per cent in Maryport, 49 per cent in Abertillery, 37 per cent in Motherwell. (By contrast the figure for Birmingham in the same year was 6 per cent, for Coventry and Oxford 5 per cent, for High Wycombe 3 per cent). The only real answer to this problem was to provide work, which neither government nor private enterprise succeeded in doing before the coming of a Second World War. Meanwhile, relief was provided—a vast problem, for early in 1933 there were over 3,000,000 unemployed, quite apart from those dependent on them. There was much private charitable effort to help; this included work by the Salvation Army and the Y.M.C.A., clubs and community centres started by the National Council of Social Service or by local enterprise, educational settlements (notably in South Wales), considerable construction schemes (like the parks at Brynmawr and Jarrow), allotments and farms. Yet the central need, that of money to keep people alive, was met through public funds—the new National Insurance scheme and the old Poor Law.

National Insurance against unemployment, started in 1911,[1] had been extended by a series of Acts, of which the most important was that of 1920. This had brought insurance to everybody earning less than £250 per annum except domestic servants, farm labourers and civil servants; and laid down scales of contributions, and of benefits for a limited number of weeks in a year. Almost at once, with the coming of large-scale and lasting unemployment in 1921, this scheme proved inadequate. Many families turned to the old-established Boards of Guardians for help under the Poor Law. Some gave none at all; others, for example those in Poplar, West Ham and Chester-le-Street, were so generous that Parliament empowered the Minister of Health to dismiss them; and in 1928 the whole system of Boards of Guardians was abolished, and the Poor Law was handed over to the County and County Borough Councils. Much more important, a

[1] See above, pp. 188–9.

national Unemployment Fund was created, out of which additional payments could be made to the chronically unemployed. This was the 'dole'—so humiliating to those who had to receive it, so infuriating to the well-to-do who regarded it as 'subsidising idleness'. In 1931 not only were unemployment benefits cut by 10 per cent; Parliament also introduced the 'Means Test', which involved an inquisition into the lives of those who claimed benefits and which was deeply resented. The Unemployment Act of 1934 set up the Unemployment Assistance Board to administer relief; it got off to a bad start, with great demonstrations in South Wales and other areas against its new scales of benefit, which were temporarily postponed. In the later thirties industrial conditions improved and the burden of unemployment diminished—although it never came near to vanishing. Some modest improvement came to the 'distressed areas', as the worst-hit regions were called, by the Special Areas Act of 1934 and similar measures. These encouraged public works (e.g., hospitals, swimming baths and housing schemes) in those areas; and created trading estates (e.g., at Treforest in South Wales and at North Hillington near Glasgow) where firms were persuaded to open factories and thus employ some of the workless.

Unemployment and its black shadow cover one side of the picture of Britain during these years. What of the brighter side? What of life in the areas where the motor industry was flourishing, in the outer suburbs of London and in the growing towns of the Thames Valley? These years were a period of real material progress for great numbers of British people, and especially for those who lived in the south. The standard of living of the average employed worker was about 30 per cent higher in 1937 than in 1914. Some 4,500,000 houses were built in Britain between the wars; over 2,500,000 of them in the thirties, most financed by building societies. Great strides were made in the provision of public services; there were 9,000,000 consumers of electricity, for example, in 1937, by contrast with 2,000,000 in 1923, and they used nearly a million electric cookers. The number of private cars licensed practically doubled during the thirties. There was a great increase in the numbers employed in what economists call the 'service industries'—such occupations as laundry-work, hotels and cafés, professional entertainment and sport, whose growth is a sign of more leisure and higher standards of living. The cinema, almost non-existent in Britain at the end of the war, became a normal feature of every town and a considerable minor industry; the first talking film in England was shown in 1928, and in the late thirties it was estimated that one in four of the population went to the films twice a week or more. The radio (then customarily known as the 'wireless') also took root; the British Broadcasting Company was founded in 1922 and transformed by a royal charter into the British Broadcasting Corporation, with a monopoly of sound radio, in 1926; and by 1939 there were 9,000,000 licence holders. These changes affected the country as a whole; yet most of the benefits, in comfort and leisure, went to the better-off areas and not to those hit by depression. Perhaps the best way to summarise the contrast is to say that the period brought possibilities of greater well-being to everyone—but that whether the wage-earner and his family enjoyed them or not depended mainly on where he lived. It was far better to be in Reading than in Sunderland, in St. Albans than in Llanelly.

Many aspects of the social changes of these years do not fit into this contrast. To take a single set of examples: the coming of the internal combustion engine did much in countless ways to alter the pattern of social life as a whole. It enabled workers to live further away from their jobs, and made practicable the building of housing estates on the edges of the big cities. It gave immense stimulus to the habit of going to the seaside, either for an annual holiday or at the weekend. It brought the farmer into town— and often helped the farm labourer to take a new job in the town; it brought the town-dweller into the country—with petrol pumps and teashops to cater for him. It enabled hospitals to give their life-saving benefits much more rapidly and over far wider areas; it also provided them with a growing burden of accident cases (250,000 in 1939).

There were also particular events of note—events of many kinds from which a bare selection will suggest very varied social change. In 1924, for example, many Englishmen would have said that the most important event of the year was the British Empire Exhibition held at the newly-constructed Wembley, the biggest show of its kind in this country since Prince Albert's Great Exhibition (1851); in the previous year the F.A. Cup Final had been played at Wembley for the first time.[1] In 1924 the first crossword puzzle is said to have appeared. Certainly in 1926 British greyhounds chased a mechanical hare for the first time. That same year saw the formation by the Electricity (Supply) Act of the Central Electricity Board, which gradually created the 'grid' with its now-familiar pylons and high-voltage transmission lines. In 1927 a proposed revision of the Church of England Prayer Book was rejected by the House of Commons after an unusually emotional debate. In 1928, the same house passed without much demur the Representation of the People (Equal Franchise) Act, giving the vote to 'flappers', that is, women between the age of 21 and 30. The events of the thirties—a decade overshadowed by depression and by the growing threat of war with Germany—were perhaps less varied in their interest. The Youth Hostels Association was formed in 1930 with the great historian G. M. Trevelyan as president, and it opened its first hostels in 1931. The *Daily Express*, owned by the Canadian Lord Beaverbrook, became in 1933 the first daily newspaper to attain a circulation of over 2,000,000. Sir Allen Lane began to publish Penguin Books in 1935; Mr. Billy Butlin opened his first holiday camp, at Skegness, in 1937.

---

[1] After part of the huge crowd—perhaps 200,000—had been cleared off the pitch, Bolton Wanderers beat West Ham United 2–0.

3. THE GROWTH OF GOVERNMENT ACTIVITY

It is probable that the most striking single line of social and economic development in Britain after 1918 was the extension of the power and activities of the central government. In part this reflected the fact that one of the leading political parties preached socialism, the doctrine of state ownership. But the Labour party was in office for only three years of the twenty-one; its two governments were minority ones, and put no full-scale socialist measures into practice. The expansion of government activity came under ministries which were predominantly Conservative and in theory committed to championing private enterprise. It continued the tradition started in the later 19th century, notably by Disraeli, and extended by the Liberals between 1906 and 1914. This tradition had gained greatly in force during the First World War when the needs of the community were paramount. Government power was increased simply because it seemed the only way to preserve order and efficiency and fairness in the highly complicated circumstances of the 20th century. There were an increasing number of tasks, it appeared, which only the government could fufil. Perhaps the most impressive symptom of the growth of government authority is the way in which most people came to take it for granted in these years that the government could and must tackle the problems created by the depression of the 1930's.

In economic affairs there was, it is true, little direct socialism in this period—nothing comparable with the great measures of nationalisation undertaken by the third Labour government after 1945. But in countless ways the state extended its power over economic activity. Such measures as the establishment of the London Passenger Transport Board and the Central Electricity Board set up semi-public authorities over important businesses. In agriculture state interference was on an elaborate scale. The efforts to promote efficiency in coal-mining, iron and steel, and shipbuilding are illustrations of the extent to which it had now come to be accepted that it was the task of the state to interfere to help industry—and if necessary to help it by steps which hurt. Tariffs, quotas, and subsidies were yet more signs of this. The Conservative governments of this period no doubt believed in private enterprise much more fully than their Labour opponents did; yet they showed little hesitation in using the powers of the state to direct industry when this seemed to be in the nation's interest. The days of *laissez-faire* were long past.

Advances in the 'social services' during this period were real, in certain directions; but they were not as considerable as might have been expected in view of the start made by the Liberals before 1914—and of the serious problems presented by chronic unemployment. Certainly they were not as great as the Labour party wanted, or as the war-time Prime Minister Lloyd George demanded in the Liberal 'yellow book', *Britain's Industrial Future*, issued in 1928. One reason why no more was done lay in financial policy. The governments of the period, backed by orthodox economists, believed that the national budget must be balanced by keeping government expenditure to a minimum. The opposite point of view was put forward with great clarity and force by the most distinguished English economist since Adam Smith, John Maynard Keynes (1883–1946), who in his book *The General Theory of Employment, Interest and Money* (1936) advocated controlled public investment and carefully-timed government expenditure on public works like roads, housing and schools in order to cure unemployment: spending, not economy, was the way to beat depression. Keynes' arguments would have encouraged much greater development of the social services; but his orthodox opponents held the field in the 1930's, and economy was the order of the day.

Several measures extended the scope of the National Insurance scheme, or at least of that part of it which dealt with unemployment.[1] But there was no great comprehensive policy, and in 1931 expenditure was cut. National Health insurance remained basically as it had been under the Liberals from 1911 onwards. In housing, important strides were made. The Addison Act of 1919 (named after Dr. Christopher Addison, the first Minister of Health) took the central government into housing for the first time. It required all local authorities to state what houses they needed to make up the leeway caused by the war, and offered government subsidies to help build them. Rather over 200,000 new houses were built by councils under the Addison Plan before it was destroyed in the economy drive of 1921–2 (the 'Geddes Axe', so named after Sir Eric Geddes, chairman of the committee which recommended the cuts). A second Housing Act (Neville Chamberlain's, 1923), also using government subsidies, brought some 400,000 houses, most of them by private builders; a third (Wheatley's, 1924), offering half as much subsidy again as Chamberlain's, produced over 500,000 built by local councils; a fourth (Greenwood's, 1930) started an extensive programme of slum clearance, which was temporarily halted by the economy measures after 1931. Under these schemes several great cities, notably Bristol and Manchester, built extensive housing estates on their outskirts, while London and Leeds, for example, erected blocks of flats on the sites of former slums. Many areas of bad housing remained in 1939, especially on Tyneside and in the East End of London; yet the progress had been considerable.

In education, Fisher's Act of 1918 (which fixed the school-leaving age at 14, provided increased money from the Exchequer for education, and began a scheme for part-time education at continuation schools between 16 and 18) was a principal victim of the Geddes Axe; and all the continuation schools expired (except one at Rugby). Thereafter there were no major education acts during these years, and a proposal to raise the leaving-age to 15 was thrown out by the Lords in 1931—the year in which teachers' salaries were cut by 10 per cent as part of the National government's economies to overcome the financial crisis. Yet there was one substantial change with great future results; under the Hadow Report of 1926 a

[1] Above, pp. 188–9, 259–60.

reorganisation of education began, whose principal aim was the provision of secondary schooling for all children.[1] In 1936 Parliament eventually passed an act providing for the raising of the school-leaving age to 15 on 3rd September 1939—the day on which the Second World War began.

Such policies appear modest compared with the rapid growth of the social services after the Second World War of 1939–45—with free secondary education for all, the increase in state and local scholarships to universities and other places of advanced education, the comprehensive insurance and pensions scheme covering the entire community, and the vastly-expanded Health Service. Governments of the inter-war years would not commit themselves to responsibility of this kind. Yet in fact, the total expenditure on the social services (including not only education, housing subsidies and old age pensions, but also unemployment benefits) multiplied eight-fold between 1910 and 1935. Here indeed was a tremendous increase of government activity, even allowing for the growth of population and the fall in the value of money which occurred over these years. The Welfare State did not exist in 1939. But Great Britain had moved on the road towards it.

27   The Second World War 1939-45

I. ECONOMIC STRAIN AND ACHIEVEMENT

The Second World War lasted almost exactly six years and Great Britain, with the Dominions and other parts of the Commonwealth, was involved throughout. From September 1939 until June 1940 she was in alliance with France against Nazi Germany. The collapse of France in that month and the German conquest of the Low Countries, Norway, and Denmark, left Britain fighting alone in Europe against Germany, now joined by Fascist Italy. After twelve months during which the British Isles were under siege, the pattern of war in 1941 was transformed by two events. In June the Germans invaded Soviet Russia; in December the Japanese attacked the United States naval base at Pearl Harbor. Henceforward Britain was a partner in a grand alliance, whose combined resources were ultimately too strong for the German–Italian–Japanese forces. But the road to victory was long. Its main milestones for the British people were the victory of the Eighth Army under General Montgomery at El Alamein in Egypt (October 1942), which turned the tide of battle in North Africa; the over-running of Southern Italy by allied forces in 1943; and, above all, the invasion of Normandy in the summer of 1944. In the autumn and winter of 1944–5 Allied armies—Russians from the East, British and Americans from the

---

[1] In education outside the state system, the University of Reading was chartered in 1926, and new university colleges were opened at Hull, Leicester, and Swansea. Three new 'public schools' were founded—Bryanston, Canford, and Stowe.

west—drove their way into Germany. The German Führer Adolf Hitler committed suicide in the ruins of Berlin in April, 1945, and German forces surrendered a week later. The war against Japan went on until August, when the destruction by atomic bombs of the cities of Hiroshima and Nagasaki—the first terrible evidence to men that they had now harnessed power far beyond anything they had previously known—brought surrender.

In this vast global conflict, fought on land and sea and in the air by nations with elaborate technological resources, Great Britain played a central role. Her contribution to the total war effort of the alliance was immense. In economic terms, it involved above all a colossal and intricate redistribution of the nation's greatest asset—its inhabitants. 'In September 1943 the British reached the peak of their wartime mobilisation. At that point over twenty-two million men and women out of a population of thirty-three million between the ages of fourteen and sixty-four were serving in the Armed Forces and Civil Defence or were employed in industry, an expansion of three and three-quarter millions in four years. ... The Armed Forces, less than half a million strong four years before, now numbered over four and a quarter millions. The munitions industries had grown by close on two million workers, the less essential industries had been reduced by more than three and a quarter millions.'[1] The British people were mobilised for war more thoroughly than those of any other nation. Every man between the ages of $18\frac{1}{2}$ and 51 was—eventually—made liable for military service; women up to the age of 30 could be directed into industrial work. There was compulsory liability for some civil defence (Air Raid Precautions) services, such as fire-watching. While comparatively few were specifically ordered into particular civilian jobs, the government—by various devices ranging from the Essential Work Order of 1941, which forbade workers to leave certain types of occupation, to the development of canteens and welfare services in factories—guided, persuaded and attracted the British people into a vastly complicated war effort.

This remarkable deployment of man-power was not achieved at once or quickly. In the first few months, the period of the 'phoney war' (September 1939–April 1940) when little seemed to be happening, things moved slowly on the economic front under Neville Chamberlain as Prime Minister. There had been some pre-war planning and the Emergency Powers (Defence) Act (August 1939) gave the government far-ranging powers over people and property. Some new Ministries were set up, among them Economic Warfare, Food, Information and (in 1940) Aircraft Production. One and a half million children, and many mothers, were evacuated from danger areas to safer rural ones. Conscription was extended to cover all men up to the age of 41. Some foodstuffs were rationed, and so was petrol; food subsidies— payments to producers out of taxation, in order to keep retail prices down— were introduced, originally as a short-term device to check the rising cost of living. Income Tax went up in 1939 to 7s. 6d. in the pound. Yet there

[1] Alan Bullock; *The Life and Times of Ernest Bevin*, Volume II (1967) pp. 291–2.

was astonishingly little sense of urgency. It was believed that the blockade, applied as it had been in the First World War, would inevitably strangle Germany. Meanwhile the production of weapons, for example, increased at a very leisurely pace; the manpower in munitions factories had gone up by only 11 per cent by May, 1940. At a time when Great Britain had to pay cash for everything she bought from the United States, and carry it away in her own ships (which were already being sunk in scores by German submarines), control of foreign exchange dealings was very slack, and there was little effective planning of the use of shipping space. Perhaps the most astounding fact of all was that in April 1940 there were still over one million unemployed workers in the country.

The tempo of war changed with appalling abruptness when German armies conquered most of Western Europe within two months (April–June 1940). The economic consequences were formidable. Great Britain herself was now under threat of blockade. German command of the European coastline from the North Cape to the Spanish frontier laid British ports, railways and cities open to air bombing; and exposed all shipping round the British Isles to continuous and concentrated attack by U-boats. Sources of supply, of foodstuffs and of such vital raw materials as iron ore, were lost. Under these siege conditions the 330,000 men rescued by 'the miracle of Dunkirk' (May 27–June 3 1940) had to be re-formed into an army; and almost all their weapons (destroyed or fallen into German hands) replaced —as well as the nearly 500 aircraft lost in covering the retreat. The tasks facing the British people were stupendous—even if they were given time in which to accomplish them; the daily threat of invasion hung over the British Isles through the long summer of 1940.

Yet there was gain in the disaster, and gain which led to swift results in economic matters. For one thing, peril sharpened and toughened national unity, and drove men to long hours of work as well as to great bravery. For another, the defeats swept away Chamberlain's government and brought to the head of affairs a man far more dynamic and inspiring. Under the leadership of Winston Churchill the Cabinet included new men of tougher calibre. Two in particular of these imposed their strong wills on economic affairs. Ernest Bevin, the Bristol carter who had become general secretary of the Transport and General Workers Union, was appointed Minister of Labour and National Service. A formidable character, alive to the economic developments of his day yet also sensitive to the problems war brought to individual workers; this outstanding trade union leader commanded working-class confidence more than any man of his time. Thus he could carry through such radical proposals as the conscription of women; and persuade trade unionists and his party colleagues to accept with little protest widespread dilution of labour by unskilled men and women workers, and the direction of men and women into essential jobs. Perhaps more than any other man Ernest Bevin was responsible for the successful use of Britain's man-power during the war. Yet just as tough and important as Bevin (with whom he was constantly at loggerheads) was Lord Beaverbrook, the

Canadian-born newspaper magnate, proprietor of the *Daily Express*, whom Churchill appointed to the new post of Minister of Aircraft Production. Ruthless, outspoken, imaginative, Beaverbrook displayed in this key job an outstanding capacity for getting things done—a quality vital in the siege conditions of 1940. Above all he directed his energies to increasing the output of fighter aircraft, the machines whose pilots drove off the German air force in the 'Battle of Britain' that August and September; and despite the cruel losses the R.A.F. sustained in that decisive conflict, it had, thanks to Beaverbrook's drive, more fighter aircraft available at its end than at its beginning.

The battle for the seas was no less important than that for the skies; the problem of shipping no less severe than that of aircraft. As in the First World War, German submarines threatened to strangle Great Britain by sinking the merchant ships bringing food and raw materials; and in this second war conditions favoured them far more, with French ports like Brest and St. Nazaire now under Nazi control and, with Eire neutral, no bases available to the British Navy in south-western Ireland. Even before the German conquest of France the U-boats had done great damage, and this was intensified by the magnetic mine, a device which ships inevitably attracted to their own destruction. From September 1939 to June 1940, 800,000 tons of merchant shipping were sunk. Thereafter the fortunes of British shipping fluctuated. As in the First World War, the convoy system did much to safeguard merchantmen; and so, within range of the British Isles, did the aircraft of Coastal Command. De-gaussing, a technique whose basic element was a strip of wire round the ships' hulls, neutralised the magnetic mines. But heavy losses continued from time to time. This was mainly the result of the vast range of uses to which British shipping had to be put, including the bringing of food and raw materials to Britain, the transport of troops and their supplies, the carrying (after 1941) of supplies through the grim northern seas to Soviet Russia, and (after 1942) the invasions of Africa and Europe; yet many losses occurred because too many resources were devoted to the building of bombers, too few to defensive aircraft. In April 1941 alone almost 700,000 tons of shipping were lost, to U-boats, mines and aircraft; and in 1942 the shipping situation grew worse rather than better. Not until the later months of 1943, when the contribution of U.S. destroyers and aircraft carriers became effective, and when allied occupation of the Portuguese islands of the Azores provided aircraft bases, did the situation change. At last what Churchill called 'the Battle of the Atlantic' was won, with a steep drop in the shipping tonnage sunk and a steep increase in the number of submarines destroyed.

At home the railways were a source of grave concern, indeed in 1940–1 of crisis. They were an obvious target for enemy bombers and very vulnerable. They were carrying immensely increased traffic—coal and other goods which could no longer be safely carried in coastal waters; far more goods, often of new kinds and sizes; great numbers of troops; and far more civilian passengers, as private motoring was curtailed. Bombs caused dislocation and delays; so too, often more so, did the stoppages imposed by the warnings of air-raids. Somehow the railways survived, often enough mainly because of the dogged persistence of railwaymen from drivers to signalmen (whose boxes were liable to machine gunning) and platelayers. Ironically, the piecemeal, unplanned development of British railways had advantages in this situation: there was very often another indirect line to use which would not have existed in a well-planned system. Another major industry which, for wholly different reasons, went through a crisis during the war was coal-mining. There was an unhappy legacy here from pre-war days—of bitter relations between owners and miners (relations which led in 1926 to the General Strike)[1] and of below-average wages. By 1942 the number of miners was 10 per cent below the pre-war figures partly because too many were allowed to join the armed forces, mainly because the younger men did not want to go down the pits to earn their living. The average age of miners was rising, a serious matter in an industry which still depended so much on the physical strength of the man wielding the pick. Output had been 227 million tons in 1938; it was only 204 million in 1942. The best seams were being worked out, pithead and underground equipment was deteriorating, and there was great anger among the miners about their wages. A project for rationing coal to consumers was dropped, though supplies to householders were 'controlled', which meant 'reduced'. In 1942 miners were given a considerable increase in wages. But their complaints were not permanently stilled and there was much discontent in the mining areas throughout the war. It was impossible to recruit miners voluntarily and so some 22,000 'Bevin boys' were compulsorily directed to coal-mining, drawn from those conscripted for military service.

Agriculture once more, as in 1914-18, became a key industry; worth bothering about, as farmers rather bitterly observed, when the nation was in peril. In general the same sort of methods were used once more to encourage the maximum use of the land. Farmers were guaranteed prices for their produce and were paid subsidies, particularly to encourage them to plough up their land to grow crops—wheat, barley, oats, potatoes, and roots—thereby reducing the need to import food-stuffs for humans and animals alike and thus saving shipping space. The area under arable went up by about 50 per cent from almost 12 million to almost 18 million acres (48m to 72m ha). Sheep, pigs and poultry fell in numbers, although cattle increased, in order to produce more milk. Farm labourers' wages rose substantially; once more there was a women's Land Army and both conscientious objectors and prisoners of war were put to work on the land; once more townsfolk were exhorted to grow vegetables on allotments, ploughed-up sportsfields and parklands. The mechanisation of farming went ahead fast during the war; thus the number of tractors went up from 60,000 to 190,000 while the number of horses fell by about one-fifth. Output per man rose by between 10 per cent and 15 per cent. There was a

[1] Above, pp. 258-9.

good deal of government control, yet it was exercised through local County War Agricultural Committees; and the financial benefits which farmers obtained made it tolerable. British agriculture was more prosperous at the end of the Second World War than it had been at any time since the golden years of the nineteenth century; and it was the most mechanised in the world.

It was not by any means the only industry to do well out of the war—although this time government controls and steep taxation prevented the profiteering by many manufacturers which had marked the First World War. The virtual disappearance of unemployment in the years after 1940 reflected not only enlistment and conscription but also the remarkable development of those industries whose goods contributed more or less directly to the war effort—chemicals, electricity, iron and steel, aluminium, machine tools, radio, aircraft, shipbuilding. In general terms, it was above all the engineering industry, with its vast range of products, that prospered. The advance was not simply in quantity—in the huge increases, for example, in the numbers of aeroplanes and machine tools produced during the war. There were also giant strides in methods—in new designs and techniques, in ways of mass production and of organising industry. One circumstance which contributed powerfully to this was the alliance with the United States, which led directly, for example, to changes in the British machine tool industry. Another new element was the vastly increased use of science and of scientists. This was a war whose outcome depended very directly on the theoretical work of scientists and upon its rapid application. The manufacture in the United States by 1945 of the atomic bombs was only the supreme example of this. Others in Britain included the development of radar, for the detection of aircraft and shipping; of the jet engine, pioneered before the war by Frank Whittle and first used in an aeroplane in 1941; of D.D.T. and other pesticides; of such drugs as penicillin, and the sulphonamides and the new anti-malarial paludrin; and of a growing range of plastics and synthetic materials. In varying degrees these items were of economic importance. Many parts of British industry expanded fast during the war and provided solid foundations for post-war growth.

By contrast there were industries that lost heavily. This was inevitable, with the export trade violently interrupted (over the war as a whole British exports fell to less than one-third of their pre-1939 volume); with supplies of many raw materials sharply reduced, and labour diverted to war essentials and with many peacetime activities, ranging from private building to professional football and cricket, virtually coming to a halt. The pottery, textiles and clothing industries lost half their workers, as did the retail and building trades. The government itself organised 'concentration' schemes in some industries, e.g. cotton and hosiery, in an effort to economise in the use of resources. Moreover such non-essential industries all suffered from other difficulties which grew worse as the war went on and which would leave a serious legacy when it ended. They could not easily get more capital; their labour was unskilled and could not be properly trained;

maintenance of machinery and plant was neglected. Thus goods declined in quality and, more serious, craftsmanship and efficiency were lost and standards were lowered.

2. FINANCING THE WAR

The direct cost to Great Britain of the Second World War measured in financial terms was of course enormous. All nations fighting in major wars in modern times have paid for them by a mixture of taxation and borrowing; and perhaps the surprising thing about this war was the relatively big proportion of the cost which the British people met out of taxation—namely, 55 per cent, a greater share than in the First World War. In the grim summer of 1940 income tax went up to 8s. 6d. in the pound, and it rose to 10s. in 1941. Purchase Tax was introduced, for the first time in British history, on a wide range of goods. There were steep increases in the duties on tobacco, beer and spirits and such entertainments as the cinema. These duties served a dual purpose. Besides bringing money into the Treasury in what many people during the war regarded as a fairly painless fashion, they also mopped up a good deal of the money paid out in higher wages. Thus they helped to keep the prices of other goods down and so helped to prevent the inflation (leading to a fall in the value of money and demands for still higher wages) which might otherwise have come about. The government also helped to stop inflation by paying large subsidies and grants to farmers, amounting to £250 million per annum in 1945, in order to keep food prices down; other methods used to curb inflation included the control of rents, prices and railway fares. To offset income tax, post-war credits were devised: a proportion (not a large one) of the tax was credited to the tax-payer which it was promised would be repaid to him after the war. Another innovation of the war years was P.A.Y.E., the system of 'Pay-As-You-Earn' Income Tax, introduced in 1943. As for government borrowing, great sums were raised inside Britain as in the First World War by the promotion of a National Savings campaign and by the sale to the public of various types of War Bonds. Putting money in these was the more popular because of the lack during the war of alternative forms of investment. The government also took steps to borrow for its own needs the growing sums (they doubled during the war) which people deposited in the banks. But the vital problem, so far as borrowing was concerned, involved Britain's relations with foreign governments and citizens. The war could not have been conducted, at any rate for very long, without massive foreign assistance. For it was clear from the start that, while British exports would diminish substantially, her imports of essential raw materials were bound to rise sharply, quite apart from the continuing problem of paying for the large amounts of food which would still have to be bought from overseas. There was certain to be a huge 'balance of payments' problem, and this was the more severe because Britain had in 1939 fewer foreign investments than she had in 1914 to help pay for imports. Then came the events of 1940. These compelled the British government and people to abandon any kind of financial caution, and to devote all energies to war production whatever the costs.

The consequences were immense, and long-lasting. Besides the drastic fall in British exports, Britain's gold and dollar reserves were sacrificed for imports: two-thirds of the gold reserve held in 1939 was spent. British capital was turned into income: many of her overseas investments were sold off and the proceeds used to pay for war supplies, so cutting her income from this source by about half. These were by any yardstick sufficiently drastic financial measures for a country so greatly dependent on overseas trade, in normal times, as Great Britain. But they were over-shadowed by two others, the growth of the sterling balances and the creation of Lend-Lease.

The sterling balances were credits accumulated in blocked accounts in Britain by various countries, most of them in the Sterling Area, i.e. the group of countries which used sterling as their international currency. They were payments due by Britain for such items as supplies to her troops overseas and foodstuffs and raw materials shipped to this country; they were held by many countries, notably India (whose credit at the end of the war was well over £1,000 million even after heavy payments during the war), Egypt, the Sudan, the 'white dominions', the Argentine and Brazil; and they were in effect 'forced loans' from these countries to Britain, for the duration of the war. They were to have very serious financial consequences for Britain after the war.[1]

Lend-Lease was the name given to the most striking example of Anglo-American co-operation in the war. From the outbreak it had been plain that as in the First World War, Britain would depend greatly on foodstuffs, munitions and financial aid from North America. This 'dollar area' provided the British people during the war with rather over twice the amount which came from the rest of the world. Canada, most notably with a 'billion-dollar gift'[2] in 1943, supplied an immense amount in proportion to her strength. With the United States British financial relations were bound to be more difficult, thanks to the unhappy memories of 'War Debts' after the First World War, and to the American neutrality laws of the 1930's, which were designed to prevent the U.S.A. getting involved in European wars. In November 1939 the laws were modified to allow countries at war to buy arms and ammunition in the United States on 'cash and carry' terms. But after the summer of 1940 British orders, above all for military aircraft, were immensely increased, and before the end of the year it was clear that the supplies of cash were running out. Even if all British property and investments in the dollar area were sold, there would be nothing left to pay for the vital armaments for 1941. In this dire emergency the Lend-Lease programme, first proposed by the American president, Franklin Roosevelt, in December 1940 and passed by Congress in March 1941, provided a solution. It enabled the President to 'sell, transfer . . . exchange, lease, lend'

[1] Below, pp. 285-7. [2] i.e. One thousand million dollars.

war materials to any country whose defence he believed essential to the protection of the United States. Henceforward Britain had no fear of the collapse of her war effort through lack of financial resources; henceforward, until victory, she could draw upon the United States, which became, in Roosevelt's phrase, 'the arsenal of democracy'.

Under Lend-Lease agreements, Great Britain obtained $27,000 million worth of goods (other American allies during the war, including Soviet Russia, also obtained big Lend-Lease supplies) of every kind from tanks to canned meat. The early deliveries under the programme were predominantly machine tools, steel, food, tobacco and other supplies for civilian consumption; not until 1942 did aircraft arrive in large numbers under Lend-Lease or munitions come to be over half the goods delivered under the programme. Moreover, Lend-Lease made it possible for Britain to concentrate her own resources more effectively upon particular types of manufactured goods. At the end of the war the United States made no demand for repayment in cash; British repayment, in effect, lay in the essential value to the U.S.A. of her continued war effort. On the other hand Lend-Lease was by no means a gift without strings attached. Britain had to dispose of all her capital assets in the United States before the programme began; British exports containing any materials also supplied through Lend-Lease were severely restricted, with results disastrous for Britain's export trade, a good deal of which fell into American hands; and in the last two years of the war a number of commodities were removed from the Lend-Lease list, notably tobacco for civilian use. There was also 'reverse lend-lease', Britain supplying the U.S.A. with goods to the value of $6,000 million, with no strings attached, and also with free scientific information about jet aeroplanes, radar and nuclear fission. Lend-Lease made Britain a client, dependent upon the United States; and its sudden stopping after the defeat of Japan in 1945 was to create a grave economic crisis for Britain. Nevertheless the historical importance of the programme is clear. It was an absolute necessity of Britain's survival.

3. WARTIME BRITAIN

Twentieth century wars have become 'total wars', involving everybody. Conscription, higher taxes, food shortages and food rationing, air raids, innumerable government regulations—all these ensure that no individual can evade the effects of war or escape some hardship. The amount of hardship varies immensely. No one can attempt to assess the suffering and tragedy of those who are killed or maimed and the hardship of their dependents and relations. Some 400,000 British people were killed in the Second World War; 60,000 of them were civilians killed in air-raids on British soil and 30,000 were merchant seamen. This total loss was very much smaller than the 750,000, out of a United Kingdom population some 5 million fewer, who were killed in the First World War which lasted one year less. So far as Britain was concerned, there were no battle losses this time on the appalling scale of the Somme (1916) or Passchendaele (1917). But to the individuals involved the loss and the sadness were no less great.

When war broke out in September 1939 many people, probably most, anticipated an immediate aerial bombardment of London and other big cities, with hundreds of thousands of casualties and vast uncontrollable mobs fleeing in terror. Nothing of the kind happened, though there was indeed an exodus—partly a planned evacuation of one and a half million school children, teachers and mothers from danger areas in the great cities to the rural ones and partly an unplanned one of perhaps another two million people. For most, the first impact of war was a series of rules and regulations. Everybody was issued with an identity card and a gas mask; the former was to be useful in medical and welfare services, the latter—mercifully—was never needed.[1] A black-out was imposed on all lights after dark. This regulation was retained until the defeat of Germany; car head-lights, at first banned (with disastrous effects on the road casualty figures), were later masked. Church bells were no longer to be rung—except as a warning that German invaders had landed. Many normal activities stopped for the duration: thus the Football League programme just begun was abandoned, and continental holidays were no more. Petrol was rationed, not ungenerously, from the outbreak of war; food rationing started in January 1940. It was decreed that Summer Time should last the whole year.

The events of April–June 1940 brought sterner circumstances. They were revealed in such things as the internment of all 'enemy aliens',[2] the arrest of British Fascists and suspected pro-Germans, the sending of some thousands of children to safety in North America, and the formation of a 'Home Guard' one million strong. The sense of being besieged settled upon British people after the rescue of 300,000 troops from the beaches of Dunkirk (May 27—June 3) and during the Battle of Britain fought out in the skies over south-eastern England (July 10–September 15). Yet the events which gave millions of British civilians their most severe and bitter taste of war were the air-raids on the cities which went on from September 1940 to May 1941. First London (every night for two months), then Coventry, Birmingham, Manchester, Merseyside, Bristol, Southampton, Plymouth and other cities, suffered concentrated attack by high explosive and incendiary bombs. The raids in this 'Blitz', as it came to be known,[3] were in fact far less heavy than those which allied planes carried out upon German cities from 1943 onwards, but they did plenty of damage. 30,000 people were killed; 3,500,000 houses were ruined or damaged, and many notable buildings (the House of Commons, a number of Wren churches in London and Coventry Cathedral among them) destroyed. A great many people left London (including many who had returned after their first

---

[1] A good many people continued to carry gas masks around with them for some time. One housewife of the author's acquaintance found hers invaluable, she claimed, when she was peeling onions.

[2] Nearly all of whom were either Jews or political opponents of the Nazis, anyway.

[3] *Blitz*, shortened form of *Blitzkreig* = 'lightning war'.

departure in 1939); thousands of Londoners slept in the Underground stations; those who could get into the country each night from such provincial cities as Plymouth did so. But most people remained, many as wardens or ambulance drivers, firemen or special constables. Air Raid Precautions (A.R.P.) began as voluntary services; then their members were not permitted to resign; finally (after 1943) they became compulsory. The *blitz* did surprisingly little harm to factory production: this was partly at least because the government in the autumn of 1940 adopted a policy of factory dispersal, yet mainly because of a general determination among managers and men alike to get on with the job. The blitz petered out in the summer of 1941.

Small scale 'tip and run' or nuisance raids on small towns, harbours, isolated factories and railways, continued long after it was over. In 1942 the German air force carried out damaging 'Baedeker'[1] raids on some historic British towns, including Exeter and Bath, in retaliation for British attacks on Lubeck and other historic German towns. But the most serious resumption of enemy air-raids came in 1944, shortly after Allied armies had invaded Normandy. That June the Germans began to launch V1 flying bombs, pilotless planes which fell when their engines cut out; and in September V2 rockets, which gave no warning whatever. These two sinister weapons caused great damage in London and south east England, and killed almost 10,000 people. They also brought about a renewed evacuation of London. Only when their launching sites in France and Belgium were overrun by Allied forces in the spring of 1945 did they cease.

The crisis of 1940 brought other problems to civilians besides aerial bombardment. It led to more restrictions and greater austerity. Many beaches were mined and cordoned off with barbed wire and welcomed no holiday-makers until the war was over. Petrol for pleasure motoring was severely reduced and then (1942) eliminated. Sport suffered heavily: virtually all the major events disappeared (though horse-racing was treated more kindly than other sports). Houses grew shabby as paint became hard to get (and often enough draughty for lack of glass); books were printed in closer type on poor paper; newspapers became thinner; railings and iron gates were carried off by the authorities to be transformed into munitions. New clothes became scarcer and less elegant: for clothing and also for furniture the Board of Trade devised in 1941 schemes of 'utility' products, goods of tolerable standard to be sold at controlled prices. People's purchases of clothing fell to less than half the pre-war amount; and those of household goods—saucepans, cutlery, brooms and so forth—to less than 40 per cent. Indeed people spent a great deal less than in pre-war days on almost everything—except beer, tobacco and the cinema (sources of taxation as well as of pleasure), and public transport.

Food was undoubtedly the biggest source of grumbling about wartime restrictions. Rationing—readily accepted by public opinion—began in 1940 with meat (including bacon), sugar, tea and butter; it was extended in 1941

[1] Baedeker was the German author of a world-famous series of guide-books.

by the 'points' system under which the customer could choose which of various commodities like canned meat, breakfast cereals, rice, jam, biscuits, etc., he could get with his weekly issue of 'points' coupons; 'personal points' for sweets and chocolate followed in 1942. The weekly quantities allowed under the ration—specially of meat and cheese—looked very small[1], though they were adequate; and wartime recipes, with ingenious proposals for making a little go a long way or conjuring exciting meals out of potatoes and reconstituted dried eggs, show the difficulties of the wartime housewife. Yet on the whole the policy of the government supervised by Lord Woolton, the successful businessman from Lewis's whom Churchill made Minister of Food, was highly successful. The rations were never short. The schemes distributed vital foodstuffs equally and fairly, yet there were other reasons for success. One was the controlled prices which food subsidies made possible; another, the fact that food policy was closely based upon scientific principles of nutrition, thanks largely to Sir Jack Drummond, Scientific Adviser to the Ministry of Food 1940–6; a third, the deliberate development of canteens in schools and bigger factories and of 'British Restaurants' (especially in areas of small factories and numerous offices), all providing nutritious midday meals at cheap prices and thus adding substantially to the rations of many millions of the population. Yet it was at least as important— because of the measure of free choice this meant for the housewife—that quite a lot of foods remained unrationed and that people could spend almost half their weekly budget on these. They included bread—though not white bread, which disappeared in 1942, when the extraction rate of flour went up to 85 per cent—and flour, oatmeal, fish and fresh vegetables.

One measure of the quality of wartime food was the good health of the British people in the war years, at least after 1941. The government's handling of food was part of a broader welfare policy, whose aim was the well-being of the community as a whole, with special attention to certain groups, notably munition workers, children and expectant mothers. One notable feature of this policy was a great extension of school meals; the number served daily rose from 130,000 in 1940 to 1,650,000 in 1945. They had the double merit of giving clear help to the needy and of encouraging mothers to go into wartime jobs. Others included the establishment of nurseries where children could be left during the working day; cheap milk for expectant mothers and young children; the provision for children of cod-liver oil, vitamin tablets and orange juice; and a sharp increase in the numbers of welfare officers, factory doctors and industrial nurseries. Deliberately children—and thus later generations—were the greatest gainers from these policies; and the smallest of all gained most. The infant mortality rate fell substantially during the Second World War. There were, moreover, some highly important developments in medical science in the war years. Penicillin was developed in 1940 by Howard Florey; it had been identified by Alexander Fleming in 1928. Streptomycin, used in the treatment of tuberculosis, was extracted in 1943; quinine was synthesised in

[1] At the lowest, 56g of tea, 28g of cheese, 110g of bacon.

1944. The war brought the sulphonamide drugs, invaluable in the treatment of fevers, into mass production. There was notable progress in techniques, especially in plastic and orthopaedic surgery and in the use of blood transfusion. In one other way, too, there was a long-term gain. There was lively government propaganda for health, with hoardings carrying phrases like 'coughs and sneezes spread diseases'; thus people became far more aware of elementary rules about health than ever before and they remained so after the war.

The impact of the war upon individuals varied inevitably. But in many ways most people were better off than they had ever been. For the first year or so of the war, indeed, prices and wages both rose fast, bringing the dangers of inflation. But food subsidies, later followed by other means of price control (e.g. of rents, railway fares, coal, utility clothes and furniture) checked this. The budget of 1941 declared the government's intention to keep the cost of living stable, and on the whole this was successfully done for the remainder of the war. In fact wages rose more than prices, so real earnings were higher than they had been in 1938—for wage-earners. Salary earners, and those who lived on rents or dividends, were less well off than before the war; thus in effect, the total national income was considerably redistributed to the advantage of the mass of the population. The people who gained most were the skilled workers and those most ready to put in long hours. Moreover it was the luxuries of the well-to-do which were most savagely cut—private motoring, foreign travel, the more expensive imported goods. The workman still had his beer, tobacco and cinema; even if they were heavily taxed, rising wages—and the shortages of many other things—enabled him to enjoy them plentifully; a state of affairs which helped maintain civilian morale. Trade Unions prospered, their membership rising (largely through the employment of women) from 6,250,000 to almost 8,000,000. The number of working days lost through strikes rose: in 1945 it was twice what it had been in 1939. Yet basically working men and the Labour movement strongly supported the war. The leading trade unionist of the day, Ernest Bevin, was Minister of Labour; and there was remarkably little use of the government's power to compel individuals to go into particular jobs. By contrast, workers were much consulted in the factories, through the wartime Joint Production Committees which represented both sides of industry; while certain traditionally ill-paid jobs, e.g. farm work, road haulage and catering, had their wages raised and fixed by government intervention under laws passed before the war.

Everyday life, particularly in the cities, involved many tiresome hardships throughout the war. But there were things to be set against the queues, the overcrowded buses and trains, the shabbiness of houses and clothes, the shortages; even against the bombing. Thus the B.B.C. was not content with the role of dispenser of news, official information and propaganda. Especially in 1940–1 it became the chief source of entertainment for millions and it fulfilled this role with great success in diverse ways. It did much not merely to keep alive but to strengthen the place of music of every kind during the war years; it provided a remarkable variety of light entertainment for troops and factory workers; it put on one comic programme of outstanding brilliance, I.T.M.A. ('It's That Man Again') with Tommy Handley as its central figure, which curiously became one of the focal points of wartime unity for the ordinary man. In some ways the conditions of wartime positively helped music and some of the arts, by encouraging local societies and groups and by providing long hours of monotony during which people needed entertainment. In 1940 the Council for the Encouragement of Music and the Arts (C.E.M.A., in post-war years transformed into the Arts Council) was set up, an unofficial body but with a government grant. This enlightened step did much to secure the survival of orchestras like the London Philharmonic and the Hallé which might otherwise have collapsed. C.E.M.A. promoted plays and concerts throughout the country, thus positively developing taste and standards. The Sadlers Wells Opera Company was driven from London by the bombing of its own theatre in 1941 and the people of many provincial cities benefited from its tours as a result. Cinemas, after closing pessimistically for a fortnight at the start of the war, also flourished. Government assistance was used to ensure the survival of the British film industry, which was used for propaganda purposes, yet produced several films notable in originality including *Brief Encounter*. Laurence Olivier's version of Shakespeare's *Henry V*, with its patriotic appeal, was for many people perhaps the most memorable wartime film.

4. WARTIME POLITICS AND POSTWAR RECONSTRUCTION

The war evoked a remarkable unity among the British people. This was partly a result of the terrible emergency of 1940, which summoned up deep resources of patriotic feeling. Most felt quite simply that the only possible answer to the Nazi threat was to stand firmly together. Yet it also reflected the unusual circumstances of a new sort of war. Fighting men and civilians were in it together. Many naval and R.A.F. men spent the entire war in Britain; so, until the invasion of Normandy in 1944, did great numbers of soldiers. Air raids united people: bombs did not distinguish between soldier and civilian—or between rich and poor. Radio, too, linked troops overseas very closely with people at home: B.B.C. shortwave broadcasts overseas were in great part deliberately planned to do this. The unity was most clearly expressed in their readiness to accept wartime sacrifices under the leadership of Winston Churchill's coalition government, which contained Labour and Liberal leaders as well as Conservatives and several eminent men who had taken no part in politics at all. There were few pro-Germans in the country; about 1,700 Fascists and others believed to be sympathetic to the ideas for which the Nazis stood were gaoled, mostly for short periods. The small Communist party hitched its wagon to the Russian star; at the beginning of the war, when Nazi Germany and Soviet

Russia were at peace, it denounced the 'imperialist' war; after the Germans invaded Russia in 1941 it denounced Churchill's government for not doing enough to help the Soviet people. Before the war there had been a strong pacifist movement, and there were about 60,000 conscientious objectors.[1] They had to appear before special tribunals, and most were officially 'registered' as C.O.'s on various conditions (such as working on the land, or joining the A.R.P. service, or simply remaining in their existing jobs). Less than 4,000 were sent to gaol. Public opinion was far more tolerant of them than in the previous war. Young women did not go round offering white feathers to young men not in uniform. This deeper tolerance and understanding appeared also in a saner attitude towards the nation's enemies. There was astonishingly little of the savage and absurd 'Hun-hating' which had been a feature of the First World War. Prisoners of war set to work on the land were sympathetically treated; German music was played as freely as any other music; and dachshunds were not chased off the streets.

Yet neither the national unity nor the temporary disappearance of party politics meant that criticism of the government, in Parliament or outside, was absent. A good deal of this criticism was directed to the running of the war, and in particular to demands for opening a 'Second Front' to help the Russians in Europe: the *Daily Mirror* greatly extended its circulation by use of this theme. But the criticism was also, and increasingly as the war moved from near defeat to the approach of victory, concerned with preparations for the post-war period. From the start there had been widespread determination that out of the shock and furnace of war there must emerge a society better than that of the unemployment-haunted years of the 30's— one in which there should be more generous provision of social security and more equal opportunities for all. 'It was necessary to have something to fight for as well as *against*, and there were many who felt that to the Britain they were defending they owed little enough.'[2] Wartime circumstances compelled most British people to think of themselves as a community as never before. Some events in particular did so. One was the blitz. Another was the evacuation of city children to the countryside in 1939 and the later unplanned movement which followed the air-raids. For these episodes by practical experience taught many English people much that they did not know about English life. 'Country people, and to a certain extent even the wealthy, learnt for the first time how the city poor lived.'[3] A new spirit was abroad, especially among the younger men and women who carried much of the daily burden of fighting the war, and who did not intend to see promises of a better post-war world remain unfulfilled as they had been after 1914–18.

Churchill, who had appointed a minister to take charge of post-war planning as early as 1940, had no illusions about the need for change. In an address at his old school, Harrow, in 1941, he said 'When the war is won, it

---

[1] Compared with some 16,000 in the First World War.
[2] Maurice Bruce: *The Coming of the Welfare State* (1968 ed.) p. 297.
[3] A. J. P. Taylor; *English History 1914–1945*, (1965) p. 455.

must be one of our aims to work to establish a state of society where the advantages and privileges which hitherto have been enjoyed by the few shall be more widely shared by the men and youth of the nation'. But he had no wish to raise false hopes—or to go in for radical reforms; and he showed little enthusiasm for detailed schemes of reconstruction. In 1943 he was pushed into action by criticism in the Commons, and by the sudden rise of a new Common Wealth Party led by Sir Richard Acland: this demanded plans of reform for a more just and equal society, got much support from younger voters and won three by-elections. Churchill yielded so far as to appoint Lord Woolton as Minister of Reconstruction. Meanwhile one great pointer to the future had appeared—the Beveridge Plan for social reform published in 1942. This, the work of Sir William Beveridge, the organiser of Labour Exchanges,[1] contained detailed proposals for a new and comprehensive system of social security. This would cover old age, and widows' and orphans' pensions; sickness benefits; unemployment insurance; also funeral and maternity grants. In effect all would be guaranteed a minimum income to meet basic needs. The cost would be met out of contributions which everyone would pay. The plan assumed that it would be accompanied by a comprehensive National Health scheme, by a system of family allowances, and, perhaps most significant of all to those who had endured the depression of the Thirties, by government planning to avoid mass unemployment. It would be put into effect through a single national ministry, of Social Security. The plan captured public imagination, and boosted wartime morale; but the government was slow to show signs of approval, and was only prodded into doing so by widespread protests in the Commons and—notably—among serving soldiers. Nevertheless, the Beveridge Plan served in detail as the basis of measures passed by the Labour government after the war;[2] and one item discussed in the plan, Family Allowances (to be paid for each child after the first) became law in the summer of 1945, just before the end of the Japanese war. A further sign of the great wartime concern about the postwar growth of Britain was the establishment in 1943 of a Ministry of Town and Country Planning.

Another wartime signpost to the future was the Education Act of 1944. From the early months of war, education, especially in London and some of the great cities, had received severe blows. Evacuation, the commandeering of school buildings, bombing with its widespread destruction, the call-up of teachers to the forces—all these gravely interrupted the work of schools and left a legacy of difficulty for the post-war years. Yet the call of reconstruction in education was not just a recognition that there would be damage to repair and leeway to make up once the war was over. Like the enthusiasm for the Beveridge Plan, it was part of a national demand for a change, for a new start. In fact, the Butler Act of 1944—called after the minister who piloted it through the Commons, R. A. Butler—was largely based on proposals put forward in the Hadow Report of 1926.[3] Its main features

[1] p. 188 above.   [2] See below, pp. 290–1.   [3] Above, pp. 265–6.

included the establishment of secondary education for all children from the age of 11; the raising of the leaving-age to 15 and then 16 as soon as was practicable after the end of the war; the abolition of fees in all State-maintained and aided secondary schools; and the replacement of the Board of Education by a Ministry with stronger powers. The Butler Act was accepted with enthusiasm by men of all political parties. It would serve as the framework for much of the educational development of the next twenty years.

28   The Aftermath of War

1. POST-WAR TRENDS

The war of 1939–45 radically altered Britain's position in the world. She was no longer a Great Power, in a globe in which only the U.S.A. and the U.S.S.R. were Great Powers. She was dependent on American credit for survival, and the unfriendly relations between East and West, the so-called 'Cold War', tied her fast to the United States from 1945 onwards. Yet she had expensive defence commitments, both in Europe—especially after the formation of NATO in 1949—and east of Suez. Although she soon got rid of most of her overseas empire after 1945 (India and Pakistan became independent in 1947, Burma and Ceylon in 1948, great areas of Africa during the 1950's and 1960's) many former colonial territories continued to receive financial aid. In other ways too world politics affected economic development at home. The British attempt to maintain an independent nuclear deterrent involved costly experiments with a series of ineffective missiles such as Blue Streak, and eventually (1960) the purchase of nuclear submarines from the United States. Two world crises, the Korean War (1950–3) and the Suez Affair (1956), had serious economic consequences for Britain.

The post-war years brought numerous conferences and negotiations between nations, many of them about economic matters. They included attempts to restart international trade and to provide financial mechanisms for it; to prevent the regrowth of the system of tariff barriers which had throttled commerce between the wars; and to launch newly independent African and Asian states on an even financial keel. Britain was a leading member of the United Nations Organisation set up in 1945. She joined such international bodies as UNESCO (the United Nations Educational, Scientific, and Cultural Organisation, 1946) and WHO (the World Health Organisation, 1948), each of which made available to member states a range of technical knowledge and highly-qualified experts. In financial matters she had in the later stages of the war taken part in the Bretton Woods Agreement of 1944, which set up for purposes of post-war reconstruction the International Monetary Fund to give help

to nations in immediate need of foreign currencies and a Bank for Reconstruction and Development to provide for long-term international loans.
Out of Bretton Woods, too, there came (1948) the General Agreement on
Tariffs and Trade (GATT), whose signatories, including Britain, agreed
to eliminate discrimination in their trade with one another and to try to
reduce tariffs.

At home Churchill's wartime government had in economic matters
taken greater powers than any previous government had held; and in
1945 'Whitehall' controlled nearly twice as much of the national income
as in 1939. Post-war governments were unwilling to drop these powers,
even if occasionally they discarded some, as for example in the later 1940's,
when there was a 'bonfire of controls' which got rid of many restrictions
on prices and on the allocation of raw materials to industry. In fact the
war had brought a revolution in men's thinking about the role of government in economic affairs. Henceforward most British people, whatever
their political party, took it for granted that it was the government's duty
to take positive steps to attain certain economic ends—to promote and
maintain full employment, to expand British exports and make sure that
Britain had a good balance of foreign trade, to maintain the value of the
pound sterling, even to see that people were paid fair wages for what they
did in relation to what others were getting. As a result, after 1945 'Government economic policy assumed an importance such as it had never before
possessed in peacetime.'[1]

This was even more true of social policy. During the war the state, to
cope with urgent need, had developed a vast assortment of welfare
services—emergency hospitals, British Restaurants, orange juice and cod
liver oil and school meals, medical services in factories, disablement and
other pensions, allowances to families of men in the forces, relief payments
to those compelled to change their jobs. The Beveridge Report of 1942
had received a great popular welcome,[2] and all parties in the 1945 election
accepted its principles.[3] Thereafter the 'Welfare State', providing for all a
comprehensive system covering unemployment and ill-health, poverty
and old age, workmen's compensation, widows', orphans' and retirement
pensions, maternity benefit, family allowances, and funeral grants, was an
established foundation of British life.

A quite different kind of legacy was the technological progress which
the war had directly or indirectly stimulated, and to which the years of
peace gave full scope. It was visible and spectacular in such things as
computers, nuclear power stations, jet aircraft, television; quietly pervasive, as in the spread of automation and of unit design; seemingly small-
scale yet immensely widespread, as in man-made fibres, electric shavers,
blankets and typewriters, metal beer barrels, ballpoint pens, contact

---

[1] A. J. Youngson: *Britain's Economic Growth, 1920–1966* (2nd ed., 1968) p. 159.
[2] Above, p. 281.
[3] Although Sir William Beveridge himself, standing as a Liberal, was defeated
at Berwick-upon-Tweed.

lenses, washing machines, frozen and packaged foodstuffs—the list might be continued seemingly endlessly. These things, many of them originating from America, came into general or widespread use in Britain in the generation after the Second World War, and in many ways they created a new pattern of daily life for its people.

There remain two financial circumstances which have conditioned British history since 1945. One was inflation; the other was Britain's balance of payments position. Inflation, involving a sharp decline in the value of money and a rapid and steep rise in prices, had been a threat in the early stages of the war. Millions of men and women, drafted into the armed forces or employed in factories, began to get higher wages at a time when the number of things on which they could spend them was much reduced. The government successfully checked wartime inflation by various means—by rationing, by controlling food and other prices, by curbing rents, by campaigns for National Savings, and above all by high taxation, which mopped up surplus spending power.[1] But at the end of the war the problem recurred, sharpened by the fact that people were in the mood to spend after the years of denial. There was an enormous potential demand: to spend on clothes and household equipment, on cars and holidays, on building new houses, new factories, new shops and offices. The possibility of severe inflation affected, in varying measure, every country which had been involved in the war.

There was an unexpected element in the situation. In the light of the 1920's and 1930's, it had been assumed that sooner or later after the end of the war Britain would be faced once more with serious unemployment. Nothing of the kind happened for over twenty years. The war was followed by a continuous period of virtually full employment. Beveridge in his calculations about social insurance had assumed pessimistically that some $8\frac{1}{2}$ per cent of the working population might be unemployed; and in a further report, *Full Employment in a Free Society,* which he issued in 1944, he had taken a 3 per cent rate as the target to be aimed at. But in practice the rate over the twenty years after the war averaged around 1.6 per cent. There were areas, like Scotland and parts of Northern England, where the average was twice as high; and others, like the Midlands and South East, where it went down to around 1 per cent. Governments made it their business to keep the rate down; it might be said that maintaining full employment was the prime object of government economic policy after 1945. Yet, inevitably, this produced serious and continuing risk of inflation. For full employment, with jobs pursuing workers, meant high wages, with continuous pressure to push them up higher still; high wages meant ever-increasing pressure for goods and services, thus leading to higher prices; higher prices meant demands for still higher wages; and so the inflationary spiral mounted. In such circumstances governments were bound to follow a delicate course. Whereas pre-war governments had hoped to encourage demand in order to get industry going again after depression, post-war ones, ironically, found

[1] See above, p. 272.

themselves restraining demand in order to prevent the economy 'getting overheated'.

Inflation by itself was only half of the financial problem of the post-war years. Excessive demand, rising wages and prices, 'overheating the economy', all represented a dire peril because of Britain's balance of payments position. The war had drained Britain of many of her reserves of gold, dollars, and other foreign currencies; it had also seen other countries accumulating great 'sterling balances' in London.[1] This left Britain's financial position extremely vulnerable when inflation threatened. For high wages and high demand at home had two consequences which were unfortunate for Britain's trade. One was high prices of British goods, which discouraged foreign buyers and led to a fall in exports; the other was higher British demand for foreign goods, and hence an increase in imports. Thus the balance of payments (which was also tilted downwards by overseas military expenditure and grants to underdeveloped countries) became, in many of the years after 1945, unfavourable to Britain. This by itself was serious enough. What made it far worse was the effect of this state of affairs on those foreign governments and firms which held sterling balances in London, or large quantities of sterling for trading purposes. When the British trade deficit was unusually high, as it was on several occasions during the years after 1945, the holders of sterling became understandably nervous and set out to convert their balances into other currencies. There was a 'run on sterling', and British gold and dollar reserves fell steeply. Financial crises occurred, and Britain was rescued by great loans from overseas bankers. It was against this threatening financial background that all British governments had to conduct their economic and social policies after 1945.

2. THE LABOUR GOVERNMENT OF 1945–51 AND ITS PROBLEMS

The war with Germany ended in May 1945. At the General Election that July the Conservatives were overwhelmingly defeated and Labour under Clement Attlee took office. The result reflected the determination of the British people to put new policies into practice and to do so under new leaders, unconnected with the difficulties of the thirties. The new government was described by a later Conservative Prime Minister as 'one of the most able of modern times'.[2] Certainly its leading members had unusual and tough experience of governing, in Churchill's wartime coalition from 1940 to 1945. The remarkable range of their backgrounds— from Eton to the pits of the Rhondda, from the Bristol docks to the London School of Economics—seemed to fit them unusually well to rule the new post-war British society. They had fought the election on a wide-ranging programme of social reform, *Let us Face the Future*, saying Labour

[1] Above, p. 273.
[2] Harold Macmillan: *Tides of Fortune, 1945–55* (1969), p. 49.

would plan from the ground up, giving an appropriate place to constructive enterprise and private endeavour in the national plan.

The electorate in 1945 was 'in a strongly radical mood',[1] and the new government responded to this by carrying out over the next five years a notable group of social reforms. But from the outset of its term of office it faced formidable obstacles. Two major problems indeed were solved more easily than most Englishmen had dared to hope. The war with Japan ended abruptly in September, 1945, after the dropping of atomic bombs on the cities of Hiroshima and Nagasaki. Demobilisation was well planned; by the end of 1946 nearly 8 million men and women had been released from the armed forces and war industry with astonishing smoothness and very little even short-term unemployment.

The practical needs of the hour were symbolised by the ruins in London and the other bomb-damaged cities, with the massive rebuilding (and in some places, for example, Coventry and Plymouth, replanning of great central areas) that was urgently required. Housing presented the most difficult problems. It was estimated in 1945 that $1\frac{1}{4}$ million houses were needed at once to replace the $\frac{1}{2}$ million already needed in 1939, the further $\frac{1}{2}$ million lost by enemy action, the normal needs of six years' replacement, and the extra demand caused by the growth in the number of families. The shortage of schools and hospitals was scarcely less severe. But there was a far deeper economic problem, upon whose solution rested Britain's future standard of living, if not her very existence. From 1940 she had, for sheer survival, abandoned financial prudence. In the words of the great economist John Maynard Keynes, 'We threw good housekeeping to the winds. But we saved ourselves, and helped to save the world.' To pay for war supplies desperately needed she had sold over £1,000 million of capital assets and reduced her gold and dollar reserves by £150 millions. Her external debt, embodied mainly in the sterling balances held by other countries in London, increased by about £3,000 million. The British export trade by the end of the Japanese war was down to 40 per cent of the 1938 figure; and less than 2 per cent of British workers were employed on producing exports, by contrast with nearly 10 per cent before the war. Much of this export trade, notably in South America, had fallen into American hands. Important sectors of British industry were sadly run down, with their plant either grossly overworked or lamentably neglected. Railways, much electrical plant and important parts (though by no means all) of the iron and steel industry were in poor shape to serve as bases for any dramatic upsurge of British industry. As for the coalmines, the main source of power before the war, their output had fallen by almost a quarter and their workers by 70,000 between 1939 and 1945. Virtually every civilian industry had been starved of capital investment. Much irreplaceable skill and craft had been lost for ever as men moved

[1] R. B. McCallum and Alison Readman: *The British General Election of 1945* (1947), p. 269.

into wartime industries; and in many occupations apprenticeship had been shortened or dropped, thus imperilling the future. Not all was loss. Some industries had made such technical progress in the war that they could look forward to rapid peacetime growth: among these were electronics, synthetic fibres, and many branches of the engineering and chemical industries. Many men had learned new and valuable skills. Moreover, Germany and Japan, among Britain's strongest industrial rivals in the inter-war years, would be seriously weakened for some time. Nevertheless a calculation carried out by official economists in 1945 estimated that there would be a balance of payments deficit in 1946 alone of £750 millions. Even with the most vigorous 'export drive' and control of imports it would need exports 75 per cent greater than those of pre-war to eliminate the total balance of payments deficit within five years.

Then in September 1945 came a crisis. On the day the Japanese war ended, the U.S. government stopped Lend-Lease. Unless massive imports replaced Lend-Lease supplies, Britain would soon be desperately short of food, oil and other essentials; and those could only be had from America. So in December a British team headed by Lord Keynes went to Washington to negotiate a loan to pay for the imports. This Dollar Loan Agreement, signed in 1946, provided some £930 million which it was assumed would set the nation's economy on its feet in the immediate post-war period. But this turned out to be a serious miscalculation. Britain used up the dollars far more quickly than had been expected; a harsh winter and a grave coal shortage early in 1947 cut exports by £200 million and there was another financial crisis that summer. Again all Europe needed dollars and again the United States supplied them, this time through the plan known as Marshall Aid, which gave European countries $12 billion worth of help. Britain drew substantially on Marshall Aid from 1948 to 1950 and there was a brief improvement in her financial situation. Then again, in 1949, came a drop in exports. Her goods appeared to cost too much, especially in the American market; and so in 1949 the government took the drastic step of devaluing the pound (by the high proportion of about 30 per cent) in relation to the dollar. This brought a real measure of improvement in overseas trade, even though it sent up the cost of living at home. Money flowed into the gold and dollar reserves, and over the three years 1947–50 national output grew by nearly 4 per cent per annum. Recovery seemed to be proceeding fast. Then came a stroke of sheer bad luck—the outbreak in June 1950 of the Korean War, followed within two months by the seizure by the Persian government of the Anglo-Iranian Oil Company installations at Abadan, which produced a quarter of Britain's crude oil supplies. The Korean War pushed Britain into the red: imports cost much more, exports declined in value, defence costs were doubled. By 1951, when the Labour Party left office, the country was in the middle of another financial crisis.

This record of ups and downs indicates the kind of economic tightrope which the government had to walk. It is possible to exaggerate the difficulties and overlook the successes. The export target of a 75 per cent increase *was* achieved, full employment *was* maintained. There was a remarkable increase in output, especially of some parts of manufacturing industry: notably engineering, metals, chemical and electronics. The motor industry, increasingly concentrated into a few great firms (B.M.C. was formed in 1952 by the amalgamation of Austin and Morris) did well: even by 1950, when continental car firms were getting into their stride again, Britain was producing half the total European output. Aircraft manufacturing also did well. New plant, like the integrated plate mill opened at Margam, accelerated growth in the steel industry. The chemical industry benefited particularly from the temporary absence of German competition: plastics and pharmaceutical goods flourished and expanded very fast, yet the most notable developments were in oil refining. Britain had done practically none before 1939; but by 1951 imports of crude oil for refining were ten times what they had been in 1945, and the Esso plant at Fawley was the largest in Europe. Rapid growth was also registered in machine tools, in radio (now stimulated by the spread of television), and in paper and printing. Even the Lancashire cotton industry, which had been in poor shape before 1939 and had suffered heavy loss of labour during the war, enjoyed a brief boom in the late 1940's.

There was no lack of industrial progress or output. But inflation proceeded, and there was no improvement in the balance of payments position. The gold and dollar reserves declined by £1,000 million in the last quarter of 1951. Meanwhile, full employment, resulting from high home demand and the pressure to boost the export trade, cushioned the ordinary Englishman against crises. Government policy, indeed, imposed upon him measures of austerity which he did not expect or like. Food rationing grew more rather than less severe after the war. Bread was rationed in 1946. Next year came a crop of restrictions: the meat ration was reduced, the basic petrol ration was temporarily abolished, and so was the basic allowance of foreign currency. Clothes stayed subject to rationing until 1949. Taxation remained high throughout this time. Yet there were some big items on the other side of the citizen's balance sheet. The number of motor cars on the roads went up from 3 million to 5 million during the six years after 1945. Seaside holidays, with the beaches now cleared of the mines, were taken by far more people than ever before. In 1948 Britain staged the Olympic Games; in 1951 the centenary of the Great Exhibition was celebrated by a second Exhibition, on the South Bank in London, with its focus on the new Festival Hall. Even with the austerity, it was very different from the 1930's—and for most people far better.

3. NATIONALISATION

The new government, committed to a programme of nationalisation, set about it with zest. Its first reform, however was not one of nationalisation: yet it was a sign that a Labour government was in earnest about traditional Labour measures. The Trade Disputes and Trade Unions Act of 1946 remedied a grievance deeply felt in the Labour Movement, by repealing the Trade Disputes Act of 1927, passed in the reaction against the General Strike.[1] Henceforward a proportion of each union member's sub-scriptions, the 'political levy', would go automatically to the Labour Party, unless he deliberately stated his wish to 'contract out'.

The first measure of nationalisation also came in 1946, when the Bank of England was taken over by the state. This was perhaps not of great significance, for the Bank, though nominally a private company, had long been closely connected with the government. Stronger measures followed thick and fast. The Coal Mines Act (1946) took coal mines out of private hands and set up a public corporation, the National Coal Board, to run them. The Electricity Act (1947) nationalised the supply and distribution of electricity, replacing municipal undertakings and private companies by a group of regional boards. The Gas Act (1948) did the same for gas. The Transport Act (1947) put the railways—including the docks and canals, the hotels, certain bus services and other property they owned—under a national Railway Executive, and long-distance road haulage under a Road Executive. Finally the Iron and Steel Act (1949) established public control of the principal firms in what was probably the most important industry in the country. Other acts of the time, while not directly 'nationalising' measures, greatly extended the powers of the state or of local authorities. Thus the Town and Country Planning Act of 1947 gave the latter wide controls over building and development, together with rights of com-pulsory purchase of private property. The New Towns Act of 1946 created development corporations responsible for building new towns, e.g. at Harlow in Essex, Crawley in Sussex and Cumbernauld in Scotland.

Nationalisation became a central issue between the two main political parties, Conservative and Labour. The former condemned it as bureau-cratic, an attack on initiative and business enterprise; the latter praised it as the only fair and efficient means of using the basic resources of the community. In practice the changes nationalisation brought justified neither the fears of its opponents nor the hopes of its supporters. This was so for varying reasons in different industries. Electricity and gas, already to a great extent under public control locally, prospered because of the great demands from industry in the later 1940's: sales of electricity to industrial consumers rose by 46 per cent between 1946 and 1952. Coal and railways, by contrast, were far less successful. The four great railway companies which were amalgamated under nationalisation had for years paid few dividends to their shareholders and their lines and rolling stock had deteriorated sharply during the war. The coal industry was in poor shape. Both the number of miners and the output per man-shift had fallen during the war.[2] There was great discontent among the miners, who hoped for a miraculous transformation of the industry through

[1] See above, p. 259.   [2] Above, p. 270.

nationalisation. A bitter winter in 1947 used up stocks of coal and prevented replenishment for weeks. So the National Coal Board got off to a very bad start, although by 1950 output was slowly beginning to rise. In coal, as in railways, nationalisation was accepted in great part because it was only too clear that these industries could no longer pay their way under private ownership. By contrast, the nationalisation of iron and steel produced fierce dissension, precisely because this was a huge key industry with vast potential profits. So the Conservative opposition fought the Iron and Steel Bill hard; used their majority in the House of Lords to delay the state take-over of steel until 1951; and reversed the act when they came back to office, returning the industry to private enterprise in 1953. Probably the most important consequence of nationalisation was the wholesale reorganisation, during some ten years after 1945, of the industries concerned. This involved long-term plans and big investment of capital with the aim of putting the nationalised resources to the most effective use.

4. THE WELFARE STATE

The Liberal Governments between 1905 and 1914 had introduced social reforms, most notably Old Age Pensions (1908) and National Insurance (1911), whose aim was to provide protection against the hardships of life for those people in the community—like the old or the unemployed—who were least able to help themselves. Such measures meant in practice the beginning in Britain of what has come to be known as 'the Welfare State': the state which accepts a responsibility in certain ways for the basic well-being of all its members. The prolonged unemployment of millions in the depression years of the 1930's had focused attention on the problem of poverty. The Beveridge Report had captured the public imagination and convinced most people that the welfare state was not a dream but attainable practical politics.

The two main measures involved, the National Insurance Act and the National Health Service Act, were passed in 1946 and brought into operation in July 1948. The first covered the entire population and was compulsory. The weekly insurance stamp gave the right to unemployment, disablement, and sickness benefits; old age pensions; widows' and orphans' pensions. There were also maternity benefits; funeral grants; family allowances and industrial injuries benefits. Approximately 20 per cent of the cost was to be contributed by the insured person, 30 per cent by his employer, and 50 per cent by the state. In effect, this scheme meant that there was a national minimum income, enough to live on, below which nobody was to be allowed to fall. When prices rose and made the existing scales of benefits insufficient, the National Assistance Act (1948) was passed 'to assist persons . . . without resources or whose resources . . . must be supplemented.' Under this measure—which finally destroyed the old Poor Law system created in 1834—over a million people were drawing assistance by the end of 1948; the figure doubled by 1962. Thus a single system of social security for the entire community had developed from the original proposals of Lloyd George in 1911. The absence of any mass unemployment in the years after 1945 helped to make the scheme workable. Thus although the actual amount spent on social security rose steeply after the war, the percentage of government expenditure on it was lower in 1950 than in 1938.

The second great reform, the establishment of the National Health Service (which replaced the existing limited service based upon an insurance scheme), aroused far more controversy; partly because the doctors disliked the idea that they should become in some degree servants of the state, partly because of the vigorous and outspoken personality of the minister responsible for piloting the bill through the Commons, the Welshman Aneurin Bevan. The scheme provided that every kind of medical, optical and dental treatment should be available without charge to every member of the community. Costs were to be met out of taxation. Those who wished could pay for private doctors and private treatment. Within twelve months 95 per cent of the population had joined the scheme. Another important element was the reorganisation of hospitals under regional boards. The immediate impact of the reform was immense. Millions obtained attention and treatment—spectacles, dental services, drugs, minor operations—which they had needed but not been able to afford. Children and the old in particular benefited. On a long view it did much to improve the general health of the population. It cost far more than had been anticipated, largely because of the backlog of hidden demand; there was very little capital expenditure on building hospitals;[1] and Bevan himself resigned from the government in 1951 over a decision to impose charges for prescriptions and spectacles. Nevertheless, in terms of the amount of suffering alleviated and well-being created, the N.H.S. was unquestionably one of the major social reforms of the century.

The government was not idle in other areas of reform which indirectly widened the area of the Welfare State. In education it was the Labour government which put into practice the Butler Act of 1944, abolishing fees in state schools and establishing a system of secondary education for all up to the age of 15, which became the official leaving-age in 1947. One and a quarter million new houses were built between 1945 and 1951; rents were controlled (notably by the effects of the Rent Act of 1946, which created rent tribunals); the price of housing in Britain was thus kept relatively low, compared with that in other countries of western Europe. Fourteen 'New Towns' were started: planned, with new industries as well as housing estates, they were a deliberate attempt to halt the 'urban sprawl' which had spread like a rash before 1939. There were numerous

---

[1] 'Each year [to 1962] since 1945 less hospital construction had been undertaken than in each year in the decade before the Second World War; two thirds of the hospitals still in use had been built in the 19th century.' Arthur Marwick: *Britain in the Century of Total War*, (1968), p. 434.

lesser social reforms, some of great benefit to such groups, as for example, the blind and the mentally deficient, others more widely applicable, like the Employment and Training Act (1948) setting up an effective Youth Employment service, and the Legal Aid and Advice Act (1949) which made legal action possible for the poor. No doubt often real achievement was limited by the legacy of the war. This was obvious in education and in housing, where much effort had to go into the mere replacement of destroyed buildings. House-building in fact did not keep pace with the needs created by the growth in population and the increase in the number of married households, and the shortage of houses in 1951 was estimated at between one and two million. Nevertheless the Labour achievement in social development in the immediate post-war years was remarkable.

29   Since 1951

1. ECONOMIC CHANGE, 1951–82: FROM CONFIDENCE TO DOUBT

The thirty years after 1951 saw remarkable and contrasting changes in British economic affairs. On the one hand they brought economic advance at a pace never before known, and out of this most British people gained material comfort and well-being at a standard beyond that of all previous generations. Yet this period saw also an alarming relative decline in Britain's industrial output compared with that of other western nations; a spell of severe inflation; and, at its end, the rise of unemployment to a level unknown since the 1930s. To these problems neither Conservative nor Labour governments offered any effective answer; nor did City bankers or Trade Union leaders, captains of industry or economists.

An account of these years may be divided into three parts, each broadly corresponding to one decade of the period.

A.   The 1950's.   As we have seen, the immediate aftermath of war had brought its economic problems. Yet post-war Britain seemed to have healthy prospects, founded on a strong industrial tradition. Her people's morale was high after victory; their land had not been fought over, and their industrial plant was little damaged; British firms were well established in such key areas of mid-20th century growth as chemicals, aircraft and electronics. Certainly during the 1950's industrial production rose, wages by British standards were high, and there was virtually full employment. Financial crises occurred, caused by difficulties in maintaining the balance of payments, notably with the dollar area of North America; costly military commitments overseas were increased by the Korean War (1950–53); the Suez Crisis of 1956 cut off oil supplies to the west; prices, of houses and in the shops, were high and went on rising. Nevertheless these were the good times, noted by the Prime Minister who perhaps best symbolised the fifties, Harold Macmillan, in his phrase of 1957 'Most of our people have never had it so good.'

B. The 1960's. During the 1960's British industrial output grew by 30 per cent and at their end it was twice what it had been thirty years before, on the eve of the war. But it was now plain that British industry was growing much more slowly than that of other countries of western Europe. As Table IV shows, this relative decline, a serious symptom of economic ill-health, became more severe during the 1960's.

Table IV[1] *rates of growth of production*
(average per cent per annum, 1950–80)

	1950–5	1955–60	1960–4	1964–9	1969–73	1970–80
UK	2.9	2.5	3.4	2.5	2.8	1.9
France	4.4	4.8	6.0	5.9	6.1	3.6
Germany	9.1	6.4	5.1	4.6	4.5	2.8
Italy	6.3	5.4	5.5	5.6	4.1	3.0
Japan	7.1	9.0	11.7	10.9	9.3	4.9

Prosperity, indeed, continued for most British people; wages rose, shops and stores did well; what an American economist called 'the affluent society', with the majority of its people—for the first time in their history—living at a level clearly above poverty, had come into existence. But it was also clear that Britain was living beyond her means, buying more than she produced and dependent on foreign loans; and the later 1960's brought a prolonged 'credit squeeze', with governments trying by tax increases to check over-spending and the inflation of prices and wages that followed. In 1967, the year when the Six-Day War between Israel and Egypt closed the Suez Canal (not re-opened for ten years) and cut oil supplies to the west, the Labour government devalued the pound by one-seventh of its value. Most ominously of all, unemployment began to rise, reaching 600,000 in the later 1960's.

C. The 1970's. Into this new decade the gloomier trends of the 1960's continued, and accelerated. Industrial output went on rising, but at not much more than half the rate of the 1960's – and in the years of 1979–81 it actually fell catastrophically, by 15 per cent. Inflation increased sharply: in twelve months from mid-1974 to mid-75 average earnings rose by 28 per cent and retail prices by 25 per cent. This was exceptional, but the average level remained high throughout the decade. Foreign imports rose (taking, for example, almost 50 per cent of the British motorcar market by 1980—as against only 5 per cent in 1965). Worst of all, unemployment soared, reaching 1 million in 1975 and about 1.5 million in 1980 (going to about 3

[1] Sidney Pollard, *the Development of the British Economy* (3rd ed.), *1914–1980*, (1983), p. 346.

million by 1982). Changes of government and of policies did little to reverse these trends; one external event, a sudden rise in world oil prices (below, p. 298) certainly stimulated them. Despite many signs of continuing prosperity (e.g. increases in car sales, package holidays abroad, high consumer purchases in the stores), Britain by 1980 was moving into an economic future more uncertain than for half a century.

2. THE CAUSES OF THE BRITISH ECONOMIC PROBLEM

Why did this change of fortune occur? Why did Britain's share of world trade fall? In the sellers' market of 1950 she sold one-quarter of the world's manufactured exports; by 1981 her share was down to under 9 per cent. There would have been a fall anyway, as European, Japanese and American industry recovered from the war; but why was it so steep? Why did British industry fail to rise to the post-war challenge as effectively as her competitors? There can be no single or clear-cut answer. Economists as well as politicians differ widely. Some people of left-wing views put all the blame on the incompetence of management, others of right-wing opinions see trade unions as the villains of the piece. Such 'explanations' are by themselves wholly unacceptable. Nor is there much worth in general assertions such as that the English educational system is unsuited to produce either managers or industrious workmen; or that the British people are somehow less tough and energetic than they were before 1945; or that the creation of a national system of social security has stifled individual initiative.

Explanations which are more strictly economic, yet also wide-ranging, are more to the point. Certainly several of the circumstances which helped to put Britain in economic trouble were effectively outside British control, like the periodic pressure for repayment of loans from the USA and other creditors which produced balance of payments crises, leading, for example, to the devaluation of 1967; or the sudden rise in oil prices (below, p. 298) in the early 1970's and the world-wide recession in trade which followed, hitting exporting countries like Britain particularly hard. But these things affected Britain's competitors also: why was she more vulnerable?

The heart of the matter lay in the relative decline of overseas sales of British manufactured goods, sales which were falling at an ever-increasing rate. The evidence strongly indicates that in prices, in quality, and in punctuality of delivery most British firms were dropping behind their competitors—who were also, at the same time, invading Britain's home market with much success. Two elements undoubtedly contributed, in differing ways, to this state of affairs. One was a failure, over the years since the war, to undertake sufficient industrial investment to modernise plant and machinery, in order to compete successfully with factories in countries such as Germany and Japan where war damage had compelled total rebuilding. A second was the continuous pressure of trade unions, now far stronger than before the war (below, pp. 296–7), for wage increases, and their readiness to ask for more almost at once.

During these years government intervention in the economic affairs of the nation was on a scale never before (except in wartime) so great, so detailed or so continuous. Labour, supported by the trade unions, ruled for 12 of the years 1951–80; Conservatives, backed by the City, for the other 18. In theory their economic policies differed profoundly; in practice both parties in these years set out to guide and control the economy. Labour's policy from 1945 to 1950 had already nationalised some of the 'commanding heights' of the economy, such as the Bank of England, coal-mining, railways and other elements of transport, iron and steel, electricity and gas. The Conservatives accepted most of these changes but modified some in detail (most notably in iron and steel, denationalised by them in 1953, only to be renationalised by labour in 1967; and in road haulage, restored to private enterprise in 1953). Nationalisation was now extended as a means of rescuing certain firms from collapse; the most notable examples included British Leyland (the amalgamation of the British Motor Corporation, itself a combination of the two car firms of Austin and Morris, with Leyland Motors, makers of commerical vehicles), Rolls Royce[1], Upper Clyde Shipbuilders and Harland and Wolff. Such industries were run by boards operating within financial and other guidelines laid down annually by government policy, a method which gave Whitehall the decisive voice in important areas of the nation's economic life.

In economic affairs between 1951 and 1980 the governments of the day used an extraordinary range of short-term expedients to achieve various ends which at the time seemed essential or desirable – such as halting inflation, promoting investment, encouraging overseas buyers, checking the flight of capital abroad, and rescuing ailing industries. There were frequent fluctuations of policy, involving in practice variations in the levels and targets of taxation, with sharp rises to curb spending and reductions (customarily smaller, as inflation carried the cost of living mercilessly upwards) to promote consumption and investment. The old-established taxes—notably income tax, duties on beer and tobacco, taxes on inheritances—rose and fell; new ones were devised like purchase tax (1961), value-added tax (1973) and the selective employment tax (1966), some of which were sustained while others lasted only a short time. Governments imposed cuts—in imports, in tourist allowances of foreign exchange, in public spending. Bank loans were controlled by a 'credit squeeze', and there was a short (1966–7) 'wage freeze'. Such a series of measures produced a zigzag policy which came to be known as 'stop–go', alternating between checking the 'overheating' of the economy by various controls, and encouraging its expansion by reducing taxation. 'Stop–go' did not inspire great faith abroad. Foreign bankers, as well as overseas customers, lost confidence in Britain, and there were from time to time heavy withdrawals of sterling from London, which weakened Britain's reserves, increased her dependence on loans from sources like the International Monetary Fund, and threatened her entire economic position. The 1970's ended with the coming of a Conservative government led by Margaret

[1] Though here the celebrated prestige motor-car company remained under private ownership, as distinct from aero-engines and other elements.

Thatcher whose economic policy rested upon cuts in public expenditure (e.g. in the social services), with the primary aim of checking inflation; upon halting the rise of taxation, in order to encourage industry; and upon reducing state subsidies to the nationalized industries and 'privatizing' some of them (e.g. telecommunications). The rate of inflation was indeed lowered – but to the accompaniment of a sharp fall in industrial output and a steep rise in unemployment.

3. TRADE UNIONS, EEC AND OIL

Three very diverse developments of these years were so important, especially in their immediate impact upon government policy, that they deserve separate attention.

A. The growth of trade union power. Trade unions grasped and held a far stronger position in Britain's economic affairs than ever before. Their membership, rather over 9 million in 1950, reached 13.5 million (58 per cent of all employed labour) in 1979. They were closely connected with the Labour party, which was dependent on the political levy (pp. 158–9), and could in effect determine its policy and control its choice of leader. Many unions enjoyed the advantages of the closed shop, compelling employers to hire only union members.[1] The views of the Trades Union Congress on economic and social matters were sought and listened to by Conservative as well as Labour governments. These views were increasingly dominated by a few giant unions, like the Transport and General Workers' Union (TGWU) and the Amalgamated Engineering Union (AEU): in 1979 eleven big unions had between them 8.5 million members, nearly two-thirds of the total TUC membership. An important feature of these years was the growth of trade unionism among 'white collar' workers, like civil servants, local government employees, health workers and teachers.

Inevitably, in a period—like the 50's and early 60's—of full employment, the unions could exert continuous pressure for wages. High wages meant high prices, and the two together spelled inflation at home and balance of payments problems abroad. Moreover, the national leaders of huge unions were too often out of touch· with their members, and failed to control 'unofficial' or 'wildcat' strikes, which were common during these years. Such strikes, often by a few men over a local issue, could swiftly throw thousands out of work because of the lack of components in a complicated industry like car manufacture, the most notorious victim here—with serious effects upon Britain's export trade. 1979 and 1980 were years of particularly large-scale strikes. No government succeeded in solving the problem of industrial relations. In 1969 Labour dropped, because of union hostility, proposed laws based on a government document headed 'In Place of Strife', which suggested compulsory ballots of union members before strikes threatening

---

[1] In most European countries the closed shop is illegal.

the economy, and a conciliation pause of 28 days; the Conservatives under Edward Heath passed an Industrial Relations Act (1971) but could not successfully enforce it, and Labour repealed it in 1974 after Heath's government had fallen because of a crisis started by a national coal-miners' strike. Here lay perhaps the most intractable domestic problem of Britain's economic life.

B. Britain and the EEC In 1973 Britain joined the European Economic Community (EEC), which six west European countries (France, Germany, Italy, Belgium, Holland and Luxembourg) had formed 16 years before. There had been much controversy in Britain about joining. British trade with Europe had grown fast since the war, and supporters pointed to the immense potential advantages of belonging to the Common Market (as the EEC was generally called), a single free trade area containing almost 200 million people with high standards of living. Opponents preferred to stand by the established trade with the United States and the Commonwealth; they also had doubts about the effects upon certain British industries, notably agriculture, as well as about the loss of British independence of action. After failing in 1958 to become an 'associate' of the EEC rather than a full member, Britain took the lead in forming the European Free Trade Association (EFTA), consisting—in addition to herself—of Denmark, Norway, Sweden, Switzerland, Austria and Portugal. EFTA contained only about half as many people as the EEC, and was far less ambitious in aim, reducing tariffs only among its members. It brought a modest improvement to Britain's export trade—at a time when Britain's own tariffs against the rest of the world remained high.

British politicians—notably the Conservative Edward Heath – still hankered after the greater potential advantages of the EEC. After two failures (1961–3 and 1966–7), caused by the opposition of the French President, General de Gaulle, Britain was admitted to full membership in 1973 while Heath was Prime Minister. In 1975 Harold Wilson's Labour government, itself sharply divided on the issue, held a referendum (the first in British history) on the question whether to stay in the EEC or to leave it. A clear majority (67.2 per cent) of those who voted favoured staying in. The results of Britain's membership during the years 1975–80 are hard to measure. They certainly included a significant increase in British exports to Europe—but an even greater increase in European exports to Britain. Trade with the Commonwealth, compared with that with Europe, had already been on the decline before 1975; now joining the EEC checked the import of cheap foodstuffs from, e.g. New Zealand and Australia, in favour of dearer agricultural products from, e.g. France. Some of the benefits most hoped for—such as the stimulus that competition would give to the efficiency of British manufacturers and exporters—were long-term ones. Meanwhile much controversy began to arise within the Community because of the very high share (some three-quarters) of its expenditure which was given to continental farmers and from which Britain, with its small but very efficient agriculture, benefited little. This contrasted strongly with the 'unfair' amount which Britain had to pay in to the Community budget because of her large imports, which contributed to the income of the EEC. This dispute was reaching a climax in the early 1980's.

C. The problem of oil. Ships of the Royal Navy first used oil as fuel in 1903, and passenger liners began to convert from coal about the same time. Until the Second World War the oil was imported from the Middle East, from areas such as Persia (Iran) and Iraq where Britain was still politically dominant. The oil companies which developed the wells were multinational, mainly British and American; two, BP (British Petroleum) and Shell, had their headquarters in Britain. From 1951 onwards oil refining became a substantial industry in Britain, with several very large (over 10 million tons capacity) plants of which that built by Esso at Fawley on Southampton Water is the best known. After 1945 British consumption of oil grew steeply, though as late as 1962 almost three-quarters of the energy used in Britain was provided by coal.

With an ever-increasing world-wide demand for oil, particularly for petrol, the 1970's brought dramatic changes which put the problem of oil at the heart of Britain's economic situation – when for the first time (1972) British consumption of oil overhauled that of coal. For in 1973 OPEC (the Organisation of Petroleum Exporting Countries), now dominated by the oil-producing nations of Arabia and the Gulf States, put the price of crude oil up four-fold; six years later, in 1979–80, they doubled it again. Such huge increases led to serious recession in the oil-importing countries (including even the United States, itself a big oil producer but now unable to satisfy its own voracious appetite for petrol). This was accompanied by high prices, inflation and unemployment. Britain, already lagging in industrial growth, suffered the worst. Her imports of oil were reduced, and—somewhat ironically—by the 1980's coal returned to its long-established place as her principal source of energy.

But, on the other side of the balance, in this same decade Britain herself became a major oil producer, following the discovery of large reserves below the waters of the North Sea. These were confirmed as workable (as well worth working) in 1971; the first supply from the drills was brought ashore in Scotland in 1975; by 1978 North Sea oil was supplying over half of Britain's own needs; and by 1981 a surplus was available for export. North Sea oil had highly important effects, besides bringing wealth and jobs to Aberdeen, which quickly became a 'boom town'. It cushioned Britain's economic situation by solving the balance of payments problem for her governments, and restoring the value of the pound sterling. But it did little to reduce inflation because the government pegged its price to that fixed by OPEC. In 1980 its lasting economic consequences remained to be seen.

4. DEVELOPMENTS IN AGRICULTURE, INDUSTRY AND TRANSPORT
Two general developments, extremely relevant to the story of post-1945

manufacturing industry—though by no means to that of the United Kingdom alone—may serve to introduce this section. The first is that in the United Kingdom, as throughout the world, the 20th century brought a gradual shift of employment from manufacturing to service industries (including transport, banking and finance, the professions, government central and local, the armed forces, wholesale and retail trade). By 1980 well over half of British workers were employed in these industries—over twice as many as in manufacturing. Secondly, during the 1970's and especially after the United Kingdom joined the free trade market of the European Economic Community, her imports of manufactured goods rose very sharply indeed—certainly faster than her own manufactured exports; and not least in electrical and engineering equipment, and in goods requiring high technological skills.

Agriculture. After 1945 there was no post-war neglect of agriculture comparable with that of the 1920s. The Agriculture Act of 1947 offered farmers security by guaranteed markets for most important products and by an annual review of prices. Productivity was outstandingly high: between 1950 and 1980 output doubled while employment went down by a third. This progress was achieved by such methods as greatly increased mechanisation, with more tractors and many new types of machine; widespread use of scientifically devised pesticides; 'factory farming' and more intensive market gardening; and increased use of silage and new rotations. But it was challenged after Britain joined the EEC, whose Common Agricultural Policy offered little incentive to efficiency and produced surpluses of cheap foodstuffs.

The pesticides, fertilizers and diesel oil used by farmers were products of another industry which grew greatly in output with a relatively small labour force, the **Chemical Industry**. It increased its production of long-established goods like soap, dyes and cosmetics, as well as developing wartime inventions such as DDT and nylon. But its biggest advance was in a new field, the refining of crude oil, hitherto done almost entirely outside Britain: by the 1980's Britain was an exporter on a great scale. Chemicals as a whole had several giant firms, notably ICI, which employed one-third of the entire labour force. Although the industry grew faster than ever before in the United Kingdom, it was slower than in comparable countries, e.g. in the output of plastics.

Another fast-growing industry was **Aircraft Manufacture**, immensely stimulated by wartime demand, and the coming of the jet engine, first patented by Frank Whittle in 1930 and developed in Meteor aircraft during the war. Civil aviation was on an utterly new scale after 1945, and the Korean War (1950–53) furthered its expansion: for military reasons the government played an active part in the industry, and the taxpayer subsidised many new projects heavily. Among these were the first successful peacetime jet, the Vickers-Viscount turbo-prop (a gas turbine driving a propeller) of 1948; the Comet, a four-engined jet airliner built by De Haviland, which flourished in the 1950's until disasters caused by metal fatigue led to its withdrawal; and a giant Anglo-French airliner, the prestigious and hugely-expensive Concorde, whose maiden flight was in 1969 and first passenger-carrying flight in 1976. A feature of this industry, encouraged both by high costs and official policy, was its concentration into a small number of very big firms, such as the British Aircraft Corporation and Rolls-Royce.

The concentration also came to mark **Motor-car Manufacturing** after the war. The motor-car has been described as the 'symbol of the post-war prosperity: a product of advanced technology and mass production, a luxury which had become a necessity, international in its influence and markets.'[1] The industry grew remarkably in Britain after the war. In 1948 624,000 cars, commericial vehicles and tractors were built, over half the total of all Europe; by 1971 the British figure was 2,330,000. By the 60's over 90 per cent of the output was coming from a small group of giant firms, including Leyland, BMC (Morris and Austin), Ford, Rootes and Vauxhall; the last three were American-owned. Some areas, notably the West Midlands, Oxford, Luton and Dagenham became major centres of the industry and its subsidiaries, like car-body, electrical and tyre firms. Directly or indirectly it gave employment, at relatively high wages, to a great many people, and played a leading role in the post-war expansion of British exports. The annual total of vehicles exported (54,500 in 1938) rose from 299,000 in 1948 to over a million in 1969.

But the later 60's and the 70's brought harder days. By 1980 British firms were turning out only half the number of cars they had made ten years before—and exporting only about a quarter of them; worse, whereas in 1965 imported cars had taken only 5 per cent of Britain's home market, by the early 1980's they had over 50 per cent. The reasons alleged for this disastrous decline—in an industry central to modern economic progress—were numerous: they included insufficient investment, chronic labour troubles, the costly dispersal of plant into 'development areas' (e.g., Merseyside) where workers needed jobs, and changing tax and licence laws.

The **Electronics Industry**, generated by wartime needs, made considerable progress, which opened the way to the widespread manufacture of transistors (first invented in 1948) and television sets. It also made possible in the 1950's the extension of automation to many industries making standardised goods, and the first development of computers. The most celebrated early British computer, LEO, (Lyons Electronic Office), set up by the famous caterers and in operation 1951–65, when it was sent to the Science Museum as an historical monument, 'not only worked out the buying, pricing and weekly payroll of the firm, but also, in the course of time, calculated the ballistic problems of Blue Streak, the mortality tables used by insurance firms, 'flutter' phenomena for aircraft companies, the distance between some 7,000 railway stations, and the ways of making rain by seeding clouds.'[2]

[1] Sidney Pollard: *The Development of the British Economy* (Third Edition, 1914–80), 1983, p.288.
[2] W. H. G. Armytage: *A Social History of Engineering*, (1966 ed.), p. 312.

By contrast, the older staple industries were in trouble during these years. **Coal**, challenged by oil and also by the dawn of nuclear power (Calder Hall, opened in 1956, was the first of a series of nuclear-powered electricity stations), fell in importance, with the number of miners and output both declining. Less efficient pits were closed in large numbers, and far more machinery, e.g. for cutting and loading, was introduced. The British **Iron and Steel** industry's share of world output fell from 10 per cent in 1950 to 1.6 per cent in 1980. In the 1950's and 1960's a political football over the issue of nationalisation, it endured heavy financial losses and redundancies. Labour troubles, government interference, and a relatively low furnace capacity despite the building of new plants, all contributed to a failure to sustain rapid or large-scale progress, particularly in comparison with several EEC countries. In **Shipbuilding** Britain's overwhelming pre-1914 leadership of the world became a remote memory, partly at least because of a failure to get quickly enough into the oil tanker market; by 1980 she was in eighth place in the world order in volume of building, and her great yards on the Clyde and elsewhere faced a gloomy future. Among the **Textiles**, British cotton-manufacture declined sharply in the 50's, while that in Germany and Japan recovered and Indian competition grew very fast. The decline was only partially offset by the development of man-made fibres like nylon and terylene (the latter invented at Accrington in 1940).

The two main features of the history of **Transport** in Britain during these years were the vast multiplication of motor vehicles and the utter failure of successive governments to devise a satisfactory policy for public transport as a whole. **Railways** suffered harshly from both circumstances. Parliament by several Acts broke up British Rail's newly-won (1947) control of services ranging from road haulage to London Transport and from canals to Thomas Cook & Co. Between 1952 and 1980 the railways' share of passenger traffic tumbled from 21 per cent to 6.9 per cent, while that of private road vehicles soared from 34 per cent to 82.8 per cent; in goods carried they were left by 1980 with little more than mail and coal. The decline occurred despite the drastic surgery of the Beeching Plan (1963), under whose recommendations (not all acted upon) some 2,300 stations and 8,000 kilometres of track were to be closed to passenger traffic; and despite such notable technical improvements as the general introduction of diesel locomotives, the advent of high speed trains (125s) and the electrification of the west coast lines to Scotland (1966). These changes brought some gains in productivity, but were far from making the railways pay.

The advantages of **Road Transport** were too strong for the railways. The huge post-war increase in motor vehicles on Britain's roads speaks for itself: there were 7.5 times as many in 1981 as in 1945. By 1981 some 2,600 kilometres of motorway had been built, after a slow start (the first piece was the 13-kilometre Preston By-Pass of 1958, followed a year later by the first section, 120 kilometres, of the M1 from London). Road users gained substantially from new bridges across the Forth, Tay, Severn and Humber, and from new tunnels beneath the Tyne and Mersey. Motorways use a lot of money and land: even by 1970 they were costing £2 million per kilometre merely to build. From the 1950's onwards roads and road transport received far more capital investment than railways in Britain, a fact which by itself does much to account for the post-war difficulties of the latter. Other indicators of change on British roads during these years, reflecting continental influences, included the far greater use of container trucks, the arrival of the tachograph ('spy in the cab'), and the heavier EEC lorries.

In **water transport** three diverse developments are noteworthy. One was the growth of containerisation in the cargo trade, for ocean traffic and also, in the early 60's, for coastal shipping. A second was the decline of the ocean liner in face of competition from the long-distance aeroplane; the launching in 1969 of *Queen Elizabeth II* merely delayed this change. The third, a major British technical invention, was the hovercraft, based on Christopher Cockerell's experiments using coffee tins, which first crossed the Channel in 1959.

Air Transport, backed and encouraged by government during these years, did not prosper on domestic routes. But from the 1950's onwards overseas air travel flourished, stimulated by the development of jet aircraft, by the recovery and expansion of international trade, and by the increasing practice of taking holidays abroad, which indeed it did much to turn into a habit. British-owned scheduled aircraft services (i.e., excluding charter flights) carried 1,156,000 passengers abroad in 1950; by 1981 the figure had risen to 43,732,000. In 1972 the two state-supported enterprises BOAC and BEA (British European Airways) merged to form British Airways. The growth of world-wide, especially of transatlantic, flights made cut-throat competition in fares a feature of the 1970's.

5. SOCIAL CHANGE

These were years of rapid, and in many ways radical, social change, made possible by technological progress and material prosperity, and involving profound upheavals in attitudes and values. The spell of austerity which followed the war was replaced in the later 1950's by a period of rising wages and higher living standards. With these came sharp changes in patterns of life and thought, departing from those of pre-war days.

The most obvious symbols of prosperity were television sets and motor-cars. Television, started experimentally by the BBC in 1936, resumed ten years later. The Television Act of 1954 enabled the Independent Television Authority (ITA) to begin commercial showing. Colour first came in 1967: in that year the BBC put out the first European full colour programme, of the lawn tennis championships at Wimbledon. By 1981 over 18 million people had television licences, and a high proportion of the population were regular viewers. The statistics of the motor-car showed a similarly rapid rate of growth. Between 1945 and 1980 the number of private cars on British roads rose from about 1,500,000 to over 15 million, one car to every 3.6 inhabitants. The social effects of both television and the motor-car were immense, though hard to measure and much disputed. On one side of the balance were entertainment, holidays and relaxation available as never before to the majority of British people. On the other, television was accused of creating a 'mass mind', debasing standards, stopping children from reading, and encouraging violence; the car was condemned for its threats to the environment in town and country, particularly, but not solely, as a source of pollution. Such criticisms did nothing at all to halt the spread either of television or of the motor-car.

There were countless other indicators of British affluence during these years. They included the vast multiplication of washing machines, refrigerators and power-driven gadgets of every sort; the spread of central heating; the extraordinary growth of foreign travel; a remarkable expansion in the range and style of ready-made clothing; the rise of the 'supermarket'; packaged and processed 'convenience' foods of every kind; the widespread increase in the custom of 'eating out'; and the emergence of the 'two-car family', often owning a cottage in the country as well as a suburban house. As this last example suggests, not all the changes were open to the majority of the population. But most were, in varying measure, thanks to the great rise in personal incomes during these years. Even though the population had grown by about 12 per cent since 1951 (from 1973 onwards it was virtually stationary at around 56 million), and the cost of living had risen very substantially over those years, it was plain that by 1980 most British people were, in money and material well-being, far better off than their parents had ever been or dreamed of being. Other elements contributed to this state of affairs. One was the 'welfare state', a foundation of practical security to an extent that previous generations had not known, by way of pensions for the old, relief for the out-of-work, and a National Health Service. A second was the considerable increase (from 2.7 million in 1951 to around 6.7 million in 1976) in the number of married women in employment, adding considerably to the money coming in to many homes.

But not everybody gained from the 'affluent society'. There were corners of harsh poverty, notably in the central areas of big cities. Many critics maintained that progress in housing, even after 1951, had been lamentably slow. Others pointed to deficiencies in the social services; for example, to the limited capital invested in the building of hospitals, which by the early 1970's was causing serious problems in the Health Service. And there were, or seemed to be, darker and more dangerous features accompanying the new prosperity; most evidently, the growth of violence. Crime in general increased, and the greatest increase was in crimes of violence committed by those between 17 and 21. At the same time respect for the police was waning. Drug taking, venereal disease, and the illegitimacy rate all rose. These things, in part at least, marked the development of what came to be called a 'permissive society', where older traditions were in retreat. Organised Christianity, measured by churchgoing, declined (except among Roman Catholics—aided by Irish immigrants—and Quakers); and its sanctions had lost their force. The legalisation of abortion in 1967, the abolition of censorship in the Theatres Act of 1968, and the general and official approval of the contraceptive pill were each in different ways recognitions of a new attitude. People felt much more free than previous generations to live their lives in their own way and style (or in the style directed towards them by advertisers, television performers and 'pop stars'). Dress, language and behaviour, public as well as private, all reflected this freedom, notably among young people. Commercial interests, the purveyors of juke-boxes or of jeans, for example, cashed in on the 'youth cult'; yet a real change of heart in the community was revealed in the laws of 1969 which lowered the voting age and the age of majority from 21 to 18.

Public concern about violence and a widespread wish for more individual freedom inevitably produced important changes in the law of the land. The abolition of the death penalty (save for treason and piracy with violence) by the Murder Act of 1965 was the most controversial of them. The average citizen was more directly affected by measures of these years which revised the laws about theft, criminal damage and sexual offences, or which made 'suspended sentences' possible; or by the Divorce Reform Act (1969), which transformed English family law by providing that henceforward there would be only one ground for divorce, the irretrievable breakdown of a marriage (and opened the way to a steady increase in the divorce rate); or by the series of Acts which set up industrial tribunals to adjudicate claims by employees made redundant or allegedly unfairly dismissed. Significant alterations were made in legal procedure. The Administration of Justice Act (1970) reorganised the High Court (above, pp. 225–6) for the first time for almost a century. It dismantled the Probate, Divorce and Admiralty Division, instead creating the Family Division and transferring Admiralty work to the Queen's Bench Division. The Courts Act (1971) abolished the ancient courts of assizes and quarter sessions, and provided for the appointment of Circuit Judges. Two notable changes altered the traditional jury system: one (1967) introduced majority verdicts, the second (1972) extended liability for jury service to all those between the ages of 18 and 65 who were included in the electoral register, thus including on juries a higher proportion of women and young people.

Perhaps the most important single social force of these years was the widespread pressure for social equality, a direct legacy of wartime confirmed by the coming of general affluence. It found its strongest outlet in demands for the abolition of established privileges, whether these were based on race, sex, or class. The problem aroused by the arrival in Britain during the 50's and 60's of many thousands of coloured immigrants, especially from the West Indies and Pakistan, provides one illustration. Their coming created severe practical difficulties of housing, employment and education, as well as raising the spectre of racial strife like that in the contemporary United States. The number of British residents of 'New Commonwealth' origins rose from 218,000 in 1951 to 1,151,000 in 1971; by the latter date they formed one in fifty of the total population. The majority were concentrated in particular areas, such as Leicester, Birmingham, Bradford, and some London boroughs, e.g. Brixton, Notting Hill and Southall, and presented obvious targets for white prejudice. A series of Race Relations Acts (1965, 1968, and 1972), founded on an assertion of equal rights for British citizens of every colour, attempted, with real though limited success, to prevent discrimination against coloured people in employment and in everyday social life; but they did not prevent racial riots in London and several other cities. Another aspect of this pressure for racial equality was the anti-apartheid movement whose campaigns contributed to the ending of cricket test matches and other sporting fixtures with South Africa.

This same principle of equality led to a reawakening of the movement for the emancipation of women, dormant since the granting of equal voting rights in 1928. But 'Women's Lib' ('Lib' = 'Liberation') was in no sense an organised political force as the Suffragettes had been, and certainly did not copy them in violence (above, pp. 233–4). Nor was male society so resistant as it had been then. The targets for women's freedom after 1945 were economic and social rather than political. Even if 'equal pay for equal work' gained ground slowly in many jobs, far more women were now economically independent, including many married women, freed from the pressure of continued child-bearing much earlier than their mothers and grandmothers had been. The motor-car helped to put women on equal terms with men; so too did such changes in attitude as that which made it wholly respectable for women to drink in public houses. Under the Sex Discrimination Act (1975) it was unlawful to treat anyone, on grounds of sex, less favourably than a person of the opposite sex would be treated in the same circumstances. This was an attempt to make sure that jobs, education, and social amenities were open equally to men and women; it was also a clear recognition of a notable change in social attitudes.

A third example of the practical power of egalitarianism was provided by developments in education. Major reforms here came about in great part under the impulse towards social equality; yet also because of the obvious British need of fully-trained and well-educated manpower and woman-power. The reforms affected every stage of education in England and Wales[1], with a series of public commissions of enquiry into the working of the system, comparable with those a century before (above pp. 204–5 and 207–8). There were several detailed measures of great consequence to millions of children and young people, like the setting-up of a new pattern of public examinations, in the GCE (General Certificate of Education, from 1951) and the CSE (Certificate of Secondary Education, from 1965); the start of the Open University (1971), to make part-time degree courses available to all; and the raising of the school leaving-age to 16, a step foreshadowed in 1944 and put into effect in 1974. Other kinds of change, gradual and pervasive, transforming attitudes of parents and teachers alike and altering the style and tone of schools, brought a relaxation of discipline, an emphasis on more varied ways of learning and on the use of audio-visual and other

[1] Educational change in Scotland took on the whole a course parallel to that in England and Wales.

resources, and a broader spread and choice of subjects at secondary level.

Two areas of education above all felt the force of equality and of the need to make 'the career open to talent' a real possibility for children of every sort of financial background. One included the universities and other institutions of higher education. An important report by the Robbins Committee in 1963 recommended an increase in the total number of students in full-time higher education to about 560,000, and of university students to about 350,000, by 1980–81. The number of universities rose swiftly; by the promotion of university colleges like those at Nottingham, Hull, and Exeter to full university status, with power to grant their own degrees, by the creation of wholly new universities such as Sussex, Keele, Lancaster and East Anglia, and by the transformation of Colleges of Advanced Technology, as at Bath and Bradford, into universities. In fact the number of full-time students in universities grew at a rate faster than envisaged by the Robbins Committee. By 1973–4 there were almost half a million students in higher education as a whole, about 100,000 more than the Robbins estimate. These included students in Polytechnics, a new group of which was launched in the 1960's, and in colleges of education for teacher training. In 1938, on the eve of the Second World War, about 2.7 per cent of the appropriate age-group was entering some form of higher education; forty years later the figure was about 15 per cent. Such a development, available to students from every class in the community, was only made possible by an elaborate system of grants from public funds, to the institutions and to the students themselves.

The other area affected was secondary education, which saw the most controversial changes of this period. The Butler Act of 1944 (above, pp. 281–2), while providing for free secondary education for all and for the raising of the leaving-age to 15 (put into effect in 1947), made no ruling about the types of school in which the education was to be given. The established pattern of the 1940's and 1950's was the tripartite system, with about 20 per cent of children selected on academic ability by the 'eleven plus' examination to go to grammar schools, a rather smaller percentage going to technical schools (which did not exist in many areas), and the great majority to secondary modern schools. But a few areas (Coventry, Anglesey and, in part, London among them) had chosen instead to create comprehensive schools, embracing all children from 11 to 18, whatever their ability; and during the 1950's a powerful movement grew up urging the general establishment of such schools. At bottom this was a crusade for equality, applied to education. Its supporters fastened upon the weaknesses of selection at 11 +, which seemed to determine the whole future life of the majority of English children. Comprehensive education became a major political issue when the Labour Party adopted it as a policy; it did so hesitantly, for many Labour politicians had themselves found grammar schools gateways to success. Conservatives were also divided on the issue, for in some areas, such as Devon, councils under their control had set up comprehensive schools not at all for political reasons but as practical solutions to local education problems.

But in 1965 the Labour government under Harold Wilson issued Circular

10/65, requiring all Local Educational Authorities to draft plans for reorganizing their secondary education on comprehensive lines. This was a turning-point. Plans took time to draft and far longer to turn into schools; hostile LEAs stalled; the Conservative government elected in 1970 withdrew 10/65 and was plainly less sympathetic to the entire comprehensive pattern. But by that date the change was well launched in terms of children and teachers and buildings. In 1950 there had been 10 comprehensive schools in England and Wales, containing only 0.3 per cent of the country's secondary school children. By 1971 34 per cent of such children in England, and 58 per cent in Wales, were at such schools; by 1981 the English figure was 82.5 per cent, the Welsh 96.6 per cent. The Scottish percentages in both these years were virtually the same as the Welsh. Thus a trend had been set, involving the gradual transformation of secondary education on lines which its supporters acclaimed as a triumph for equality of opportunity, and it could not easily be reversed.

Yet the issue remained controversial, particularly in areas where the imposition of the comprehensive system meant the destruction of old-established and successful grammar schools. Some of the best English grammar schools, too, were 'Direct Grant' schools which were outside LEA control and which provided free places for between 25 and 50 per cent of their pupils, the cost being met by a direct grant from the central government to the schools. This system was scrapped by the Labour government in 1974 – and many such schools decided to become independent, joining the old-established Public Schools. A significant number of parents chose to send their children to the independent schools, and the evidence suggests continuing doubts about the quality of comprehensive schools, as well as the ability to pay relatively high fees. The debate over independent versus comprehensive education has continued into the 1980's.

It remains to mention what many British people would regard as the most blighting feature of recent social history, and the one that most plainly reflects Britain's economic crisis – the return of large-scale unemployment. The number of those registered as out of full-time work grew during the late 1960's, and reached 900,000 by 1972; after a fall, it rose again to 1 million by 1975, 1½ million through the later 1970's (and up to about 3 million by the end of 1982). Such lamentable figures inevitably suggested comparison with the 1930's (above, pp. 244–6). Some of the places and industries hit fifty years earlier were in trouble again, for example the cotton textile industry of the north-west; yet this time the range of severe unemployment was wider. Coventry and the West Midlands, which had survived well in the 1930's, were now blighted by the troubles of the motor-car industry. Moreover this time certain groups in the community were peculiarly the victims: these included the school-leavers of 16+, coloured immigrants, and the unskilled. A high proportion of the unemployed, too, remained unemployed for a long period of time. The provision of relief and benefits by the social services was no doubt a good deal more effective than it had been, thanks to the great reforms of the 1940's—though it was not as good as in some western

European countries (which also suffered from unemployment, rather less severely, in the late 1970's). But it was only too plain that the politicians, business men, and trade union leaders of the 'affluent society' had not exorcised this particular spectre.

Suggestions for Further Reading

Many students, of various levels of ability, may want to dig more deeply into topics dealt with in this book. The list that follows tries to help them to do so, both by the books it names and by the way in which it arranges them. Where the title of a book is not self-explanatory, a brief note is added about its contents. Books marked * are or have been available in paperback. The dates given are not necessarily those of the most recent edition; some, possibly many, have gone out of print and will have to be hunted for. Teachers will suggest further books; they will tell students about the value, for their special needs, of books listed here, and, in particular, point out which are too easy and which too difficult.

SHORTER BOOKS

* T. S. Ashton. *The Industrial Revolution, 1760–1830.* (1948)
* E. J. Hobsbawm. *Industry and Empire.* (1968) Not easy, but sparkles with ideas about Britain since the Industrial Revolution.
* R.A. Buchanan. *Technology and Social Progress.* (1965) The ways in which technology has promoted social change.
* V. J. K. Arkell. *Britain Transformed: British society since about 1750.* (1973)
* Anthony Armstrong. *The Church of England, the Methodists, and Society, 1700–1850.* (1973)
* John Burnett. *A History of the Cost of Living.* (1969)
* Henry Pelling. *A History of British Trade Unionism.* (1963)
* Malcolm Thomis. *The Luddites.* (1970)
* J. L. and B. Hammond. *The Village Labourer.* (1911). The rural poor, early 19th century.
* E. J. Hobsbawm and George Rudé. *Captain Swing.* (1969). The agricultural labourers' revolt of 1830.
* Marjorie Reeves. *Sheep Bell and Ploughshare: the Story of Two Village Families.* (1978). Late 19th century.
* Trevor May. *The Economy, 1815–1914.* (1972)
* Harold Perkin. *The Age of the Railway.* (1970)
* Terry Coleman. *The Railway Navvies.* (1965)
* J. D. Chambers. *The Workshop of the World.* (1961) British economic history, 1820–80.
* L. T. C. Rolt. *Victorian Engineering.* (1970)
* G. E. Mingay. *Rural Life in Victorian England.* (1977)
* J. J. Tobias. *Crime and Industrial Society in the 19th Century.* (1967)
* John Burnett. *Plenty and Want.* (1966). English diet since 1815.
* Henry Pelling. *Origins of the Labour Party.* (1965)
* Raphael Samuel, ed. *Village Life and Labour.* (1975). Late 19th century.
* J. Salt and B. J. Elliott. *British Society, 1870–1970.* (1975)
* R. S. Sayers. *Economic Change in England, 1880–1939.* (1967)
  L. T. C. Rolt. *Motoring History.* (1964)
* Donald Read. *Edwardian England.* (1972)
* Robert Roberts. *The Classic Slum.* (1971). Edwardian Salford.
* Arthur Marwick. *The Deluge (British Society and the First World War).* (1965)
* Robert Graves and Alan Hodge. *The Long Week-End.* (1940). British society between the two World Wars.
* Margaret Morris. *The General Strike.* (1976)
* George Orwell. *The Road to Wigan Pier.* (1937). Life during the depression of the 1930's.
  Ellen Wilkinson. *The Town that was Murdered.* (1939). Jarrow during the 1930's.
* John Stevenson. *Social Conditions between the Wars.* (1977)
* M. Sissons and P. French, eds. *The Age of Austerity, 1945–51.* (1963)
* John Stevenson. *British Society 1914–45*

LONGER BOOKS (mainly for reference or dipping into)

* G. M. Trevelyan. *English Social History* (Chs.XI–XVIII). (1942)
* R. A. Buchanan. *Industrial Archaeology in Britain.* (1972)
  G. E. Mingay, ed. *Arthur Young and his times.* (1975)
* Paul Mantoux. *The Industrial Revolution in the 18th Century.* (1961)
* Ivy Pinchbeck. *Women workers and the Industrial Revolution, 1750–1850.* (1930)
* P. S. Bagwell. *The Transport Revolution from 1770.* (1974)
* G. D. H. Cole. *The Common People, 1746–1946.* (5th ed., 1956)
* Eric Hopkins. *A Social History of the English Working Classes, 1815–1945.* (1979)
* T. C. Smout *A History of the Scottish People, 1560–1830.* (1969)

* J. D. Chambers and G. E. Mingay. *The Agricultural Revolution, 1750–1880.* (1966)
* Bruce Lenman. *An Economic History of Modern Scotland.* (1977)
* K. O. Morgan. *Rebirth of a Nation: Wales, 1880–1980.* (1981)
* C. L. Mowat. *Britain between the Wars, 1918–1940.* (1955)
* A. J. P. Taylor. *English History, 1914–1945.* (1965)
* Keith Robbins. *The Eclipse of a Great Power – Modern Britain, 1870–1975.* (1983)
* W. Hamish Fraser. *The Coming of the Mass Market, 1850–1914.* (1981)
* T. K. Derry and Trevor Williams. *A Short History of Technology.* (1960)
  C. Hadfield. *British Canals.* (1966)
* Jack Simmons. *The Railways of Britain.* (1961)
* Maurice Bruce. *The Coming of the Welfare State.* (4th ed., 1968)
* Derek Fraser. *The Evolution of the British Welfare State.* (1973)
* S. G. Checkland. *The Rise of Industrial Society in England, 1815–1885.* (1964)
* Sidney Pollard. *The Development of the British Economy, 1914–1980.* 3rd Edition, (1983)
* G. A. N. Lowndes. *The Silent Social Revolution—The Expansion of English Public Education, 1895–1965.* (2nd. 1965)
  Arthur Marwick. *Britain in the Century of Total War (War, Peace, and Social Change, 1900–1967).* (1968)
* John Stevenson and Chris Cook. *The Slump.* (1977)
* Angus Calder. *The People's War: Britain, 1939–45.* (1971)
* Norman Longmate. *How we lived then (A history of everyday life during the Second World War).* (1971)
* Arthur Marwick. *British Society since 1945.* (1982)
  J. C. Drummond and Anne Wilbraham. *The Englishman's Food.* (2nd ed., 1957)

BIOGRAPHIES (mainly, though not invariably, short)

  W. H. Chaloner. *People and Industries.* (1963). Includes, among others, Wilkinson, Macadam, and Bessemer.
* P. W. Kingsford. *Engineers, Inventors and Workers.* (1964). Assorted brief lives from Abraham Darby to Whittle.
  H. Malet. *The Canal Duke.* (1961)
  H. C. Pawson. *Robert Bakewell.* (1957)
  L. T. C. Rolt. *James Watt.* (1962)
* S.M. Archer. *Josiah Wedgwood and the Potteries.* (1973)
  L. T. C. Rolt. *Thomas Telford.* (1958)
  L. T. C. Rolt. *The Cornish Giant (Richard Trevithick).* (1960)
  Asa Briggs. *William Cobbett.* (1967)
* G. F. A. Best. *Shaftesbury.* (1964)
  J. C. Gill. *The Ten Hour Parson.* (1960). Factory reformers
  Michael Robbins. *George and Robert Stephenson.* (1966)
  L. T. C. Rolt. *George and Robert Stephenson.* (1960)
  N. W. Webster. *Joseph Locke, Railway Revolutionary.* (1970)
* L. T. C. Rolt. *Isambard Kingdom Brunel.* (1957)
  R. S. Lambert. *The Railway King, 1800–71 (George Hudson).* (1954)
  D. Read and E. Glasgow. *Feargus O'Connor.* (1961)
  David Williams. *John Frost, A Study in Chartism.* (1939)
  Donald Read. *Cobden and Bright.* (1967)
  Robert Olby. *Charles Darwin.* (1967)
  Josephine Kamm. *How Different from Us: A Biography of Miss Buss and Miss Beale.* (1958)
* Richard Collier. *The General Next to God.* (1965). Life of the founder of the Salvation Army.
* M. K. Ashby. *the Life of Joseph Ashby of Tysoe.* (1961). Late 19th Century agriculture.
  K. O. Morgan. *Keir Hardie.* (1967)
* Michael Foot. *Aneurin Bevan.* (Vol. I) (1962)

AUTOBIOGRAPHIES

  Samuel Bamford. *Passages in the Life of a Radical.* (1844)
  William Lovett. *Life and Struggles of William Lovett.* (1876)
  Joseph Arch. *Story of His Life, by Himself.* (1898)
* Flora Thompson. *Lark Rise to Candleford.* (1945). Story of life in an Oxfordshire village, late 19th century.
* Beatrice Webb. *My Apprenticeship.* (1926)
  Beatrice Webb. *Our Partnership.* (1948). The Life of Sidney and Beatrice Webb.
  B. L. Coombes. *These Poor Hands.* (1939). A South Wales miner's life, early 20th century.
  John Burnett, ed. *Useful Toil.* (1974). Autobiographies of working people from the 1820's to the 1920's.

DOCUMENTS AND CONTEMPORARY MATERIALS (often with valuable introductions by the editors whose names are given)

How They Lived, 1700–1815. (Asa Briggs, 1969)
* *Human Documents of the Industrial Revolution in Britain.* (E. Royston Pike, 1966)
* *British Working Class Movements: Selected Documents, 1789–1875.* (G. D. H. Cole & A. W. Filson, 1951)
  Readings in Economic and Social History. (M. W. Flinn, 1964)
* *They Saw It Happen, 1689–1897.* (T. Charles Edwards and Brian Richardson, 1958)
* *They Saw It Happen, 1897–1940.* (Asa Briggs, 1969)
* *British Economic History, 1870–1914: Commentary and Documents.* (W. H. B. Court, 1965).
* *British Economy and Society, 1870–1970.* (R. W. Breach and R. M. Hartwell, 1972).
* *The Poor Law Report of 1834.* (S. G. & E. O. A. Checkland, 1974)
* *Samuel Smiles' Self-Help (1859).* (Royden Harrison, 1968)
* *Charles Booth's London.* (A. Fried & R. M. Elman, 1969)
* *19th Century Crime: Prevention and Punishment.* (J. J. Tobias, 1972)
  How They Were Taught. (P. H. J. H. Gosden, 1969). Learning and Teaching in England, 1800 – 1950
* *Education (Examining the Evidence – 19th Century England).* (Evelyn E. Cowie, 1973)

The Archive Series (pub. Edward Arnold 1968–75) and the Seminar Studies in History (pub. Longmans since 1971) both offer relatively short collections of selected documents on a wide range of topics in British economic and social history since 1700.
Archives and documents, often in wallet form and for teaching purposes, and containing useful and stimulating material on many topics mentioned in this book, have been published by various public bodies, notably the National Museum of Wales; the County Councils of Staffordshire, Essex, Gloucestershire and Devon; the Department of Education of the University of Newcastle-upon-Tyne; and the Manchester Branch of the Historical Association; and also by Jonathan Cape in the Jackdaw Series.

FICTION

Many novels throw light on British social history. Writers whose books deserve special mention in this context include, in the 19th century, Mrs. Gaskell (*Mary Barton*), Charles Dickens (*Bleak House, Oliver Twist* and *Hard Times*), Charles Kingsley (*Alton Locke, The Water Babies*), Benjamin Disraeli (*Sybil*), Anthony Trollope (the several *Barchester* novels), Thomas Hughes (*Tom Brown's Schooldays*), and Thomas Hardy (*The Mayor of Casterbridge, The Woodlanders*); and, in the 20th, Howard Spring (*Fame is the Spur*), Walter Greenwood (*Love on the Dole*), Thomas Armstrong (*The Crowthers of Bankdam*), John Braine (*Room at the Top*) and Roger Armfelt (*County Affairs*). Teachers will have many other choices to recommend here.

MISCELLANEOUS

Celia Fiennes. *Journeys.* (ed. Christopher Morris, 1977). Travels round England, late 17th century.
Daniel Defoe. *Tour through England and Wales.* (1724–6)
* William Cobbett. *Rural Rides.* (1830)
F. Engels. *The Condition of the Working Class in England.* (1845)
J. B. Priestley. *English Journey.* (1934). During the 1930's depression.
Jeremy Warburg, ed. *The Industrial Muse (The Industrial Revolution in English poetry).* (1958)
* F. D. Klingender. *Art and the Industrial Revolution.* (Rev. ed., 1968).
Gordon Winter. *A Country Camera, 1844–1914.* English rural life.
Jack Simmons, ed. *The Visual History of Modern Britain.* A series of substantial books containing well-illustrated historical accounts, e.g. W.H. Chaloner and A.E. Musson, *Industry and Technology*, 1963; Malcolm Seaborne, *Education*, 1966.
S. D. Chapman and J. D. Chambers. *The Beginnings of Industrial Britain.* (1970). Amply-illustrated account of the Industrial Revolution.
Pamphlets from various sources, e.g. the Science Museum, the Historical Association, local museums.
Articles in such journals as *History To-Day, Transport History, Journal of Industrial Archaeology*.

Index